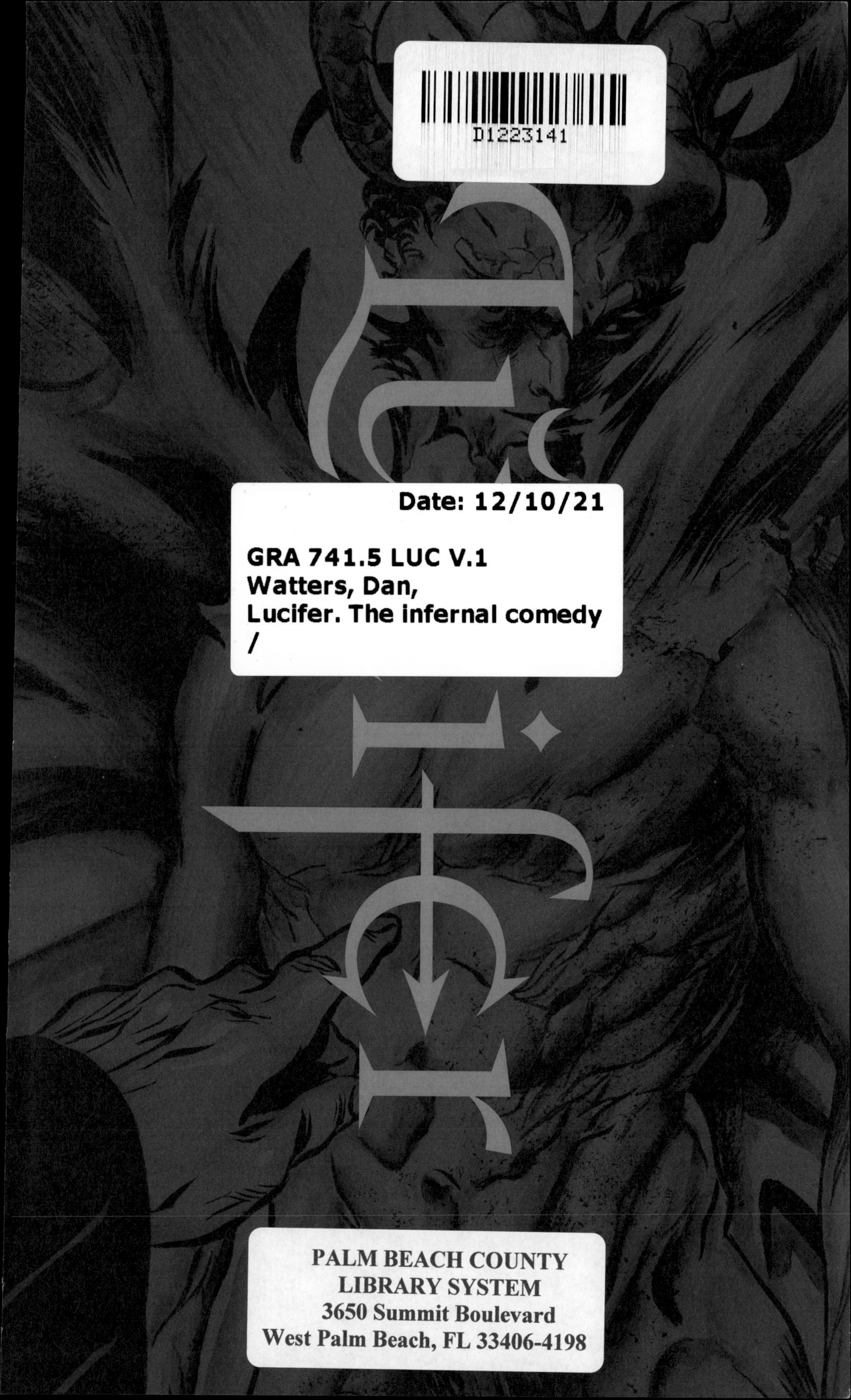
Lucifer

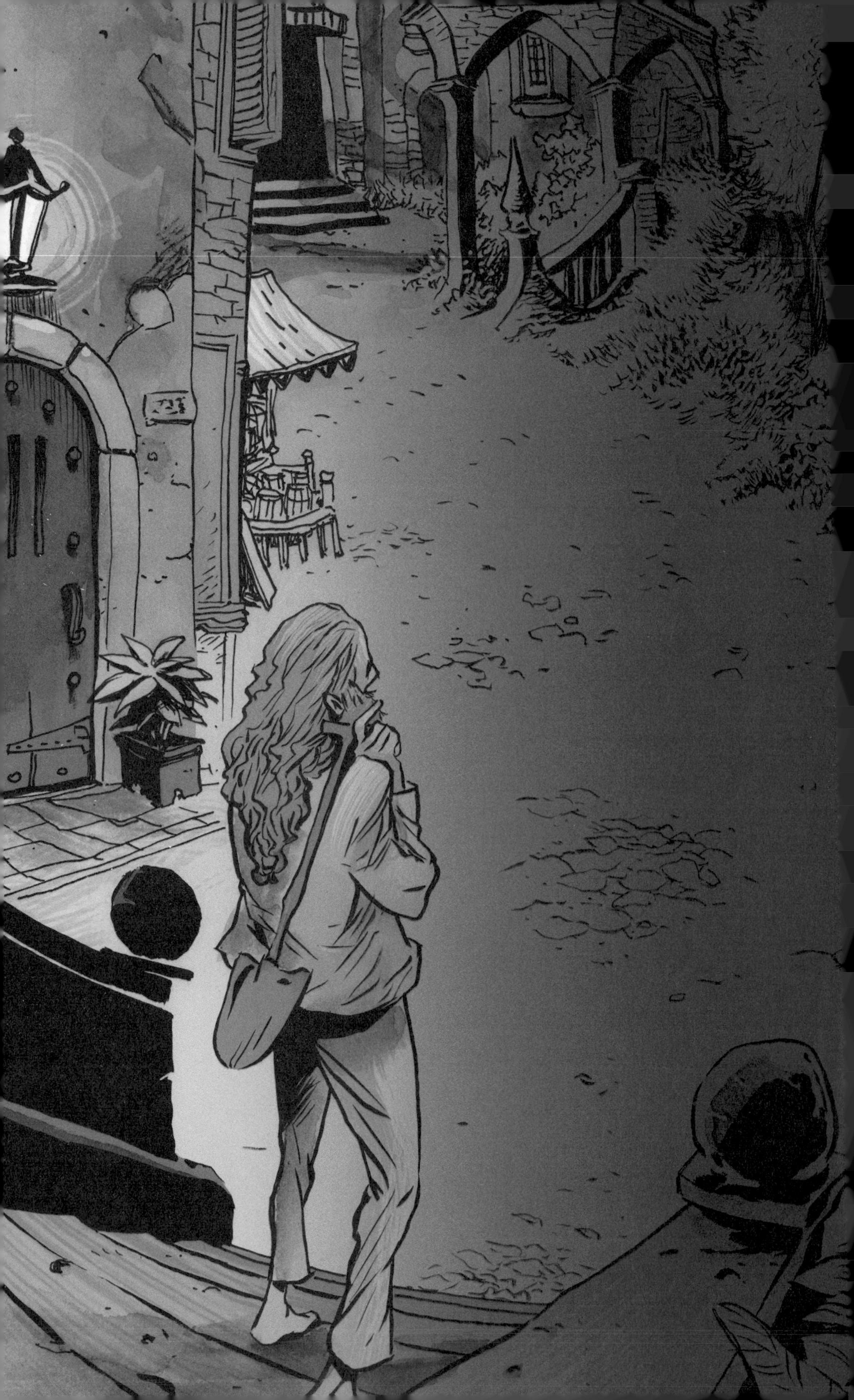

Lucifer

VOLUME ONE

The Infernal Comedy

WRITTEN BY
Dan Watters
Neil Gaiman
Simon Spurrier
Kat Howard
Nalo Hopkinson

ART BY
Max Fiumara
Sebastian Fiumara
Bilquis Evely
Tom Fowler
Dominike "DOMO" Stanton

COLORS BY
Dave McCaig
Mat Lopes

LETTERS BY
Steve Wands
Simon Bowland

COLLECTION COVER ART BY
Jock

ORIGINAL SERIES COVER ART BY
Jim Lee and Alex Sinclair
Jock
Tiffany Turrill
Kyle Hotz and Dean White
Sebastian Fiumara
and Dave Mccaig
Reiko Murakami

*Lucifer based on characters created by
Neil Gaiman, Sam Kieth, and Mike Dringenberg
The Sandman created by Neil Gaiman,
Sam Kieth, and Mike Dringenberg
The Sandman Universe curated by Neil Gaiman*

MOLLY MAHAN
AMEDEO TURTURRO   *Editors – Original Series*
MAGGIE HOWELL   *Assistant Editor – Original Series*
SCOTT NYBAKKEN   *Editor – Collected Edition*
STEVE COOK   *Design Director – Books
and Publication Design*

MARIE JAVINS   *Editor-in-Chief, DC Comics*

DANIEL CHERRY III   *Senior VP – General Manager*
JIM LEE   *Publisher & Chief Creative Officer*
DON FALLETTI   *VP – Manufacturing Operations & Workflow Management*
LAWRENCE GANEM   *VP – Talent Services*
ALISON GILL   *Senior VP – Manufacturing & Operations*
NICK J. NAPOLITANO   *VP – Manufacturing Administration & Design*
NANCY SPEARS   *VP – Revenue*
MICHELE R. WELLS   *VP & Executive Editor, Young Reader*

LUCIFER VOL. 1: THE INFERNAL COMEDY

Published by DC Comics. Compilation and all new material Copyright © 2019 DC Comics. All Rights Reserved.

Originally published in single magazine form as THE SANDMAN UNIVERSE 1 and LUCIFER 1-6. Copyright © 2018, 2019 DC Comics. All Rights Reserved. All characters, their distinctive likenesses and related elements featured in this publication are trademarks of DC Comics. The stories, characters and incidents featured in this publication are entirely fictional. DC Comics does not read or accept unsolicited submissions of ideas, stories or artwork. DC – a WarnerMedia Company.

DC Comics, 2900 West Alameda Ave., Burbank, CA 91505
Printed by LSC Communications, Owensville, MO, USA. 2/26/21. Third Printing.
ISBN: 978-1-4012-9133-4

Library of Congress Cataloging-in-Publication Data is available.

PEFC Certified

This product is from sustainably managed forests and controlled sources.

PEFC

PEFC/29-31-337   www.pefc.org

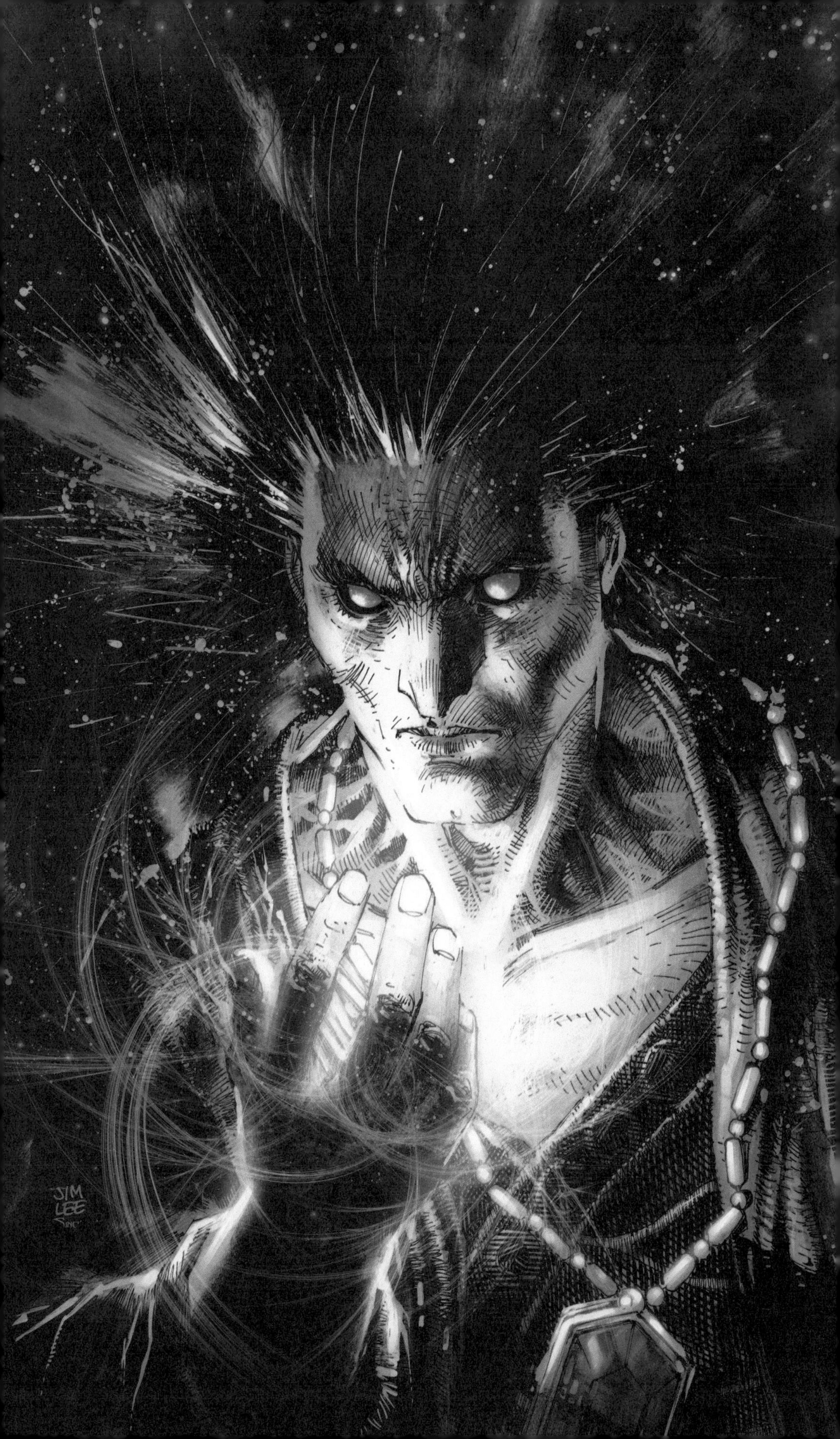
JIM LEE

The Sandman Universe

STORY BY

Neil Gaiman

WRITTEN BY

Simon Spurrier
Kat Howard
Nalo Hopkinson
Dan Watters

ILLUSTRATED BY

Bilquis Evely
Tom Fowler
Dominike "DOMO" Stanton
Max Fiumara
Sebastian Fiumara

COLORS BY

Mat Lopes

LETTERS BY

Simon Bowland

COVER ART BY

Jim Lee and Alex Sinclair

Special thanks to Cat Mihos

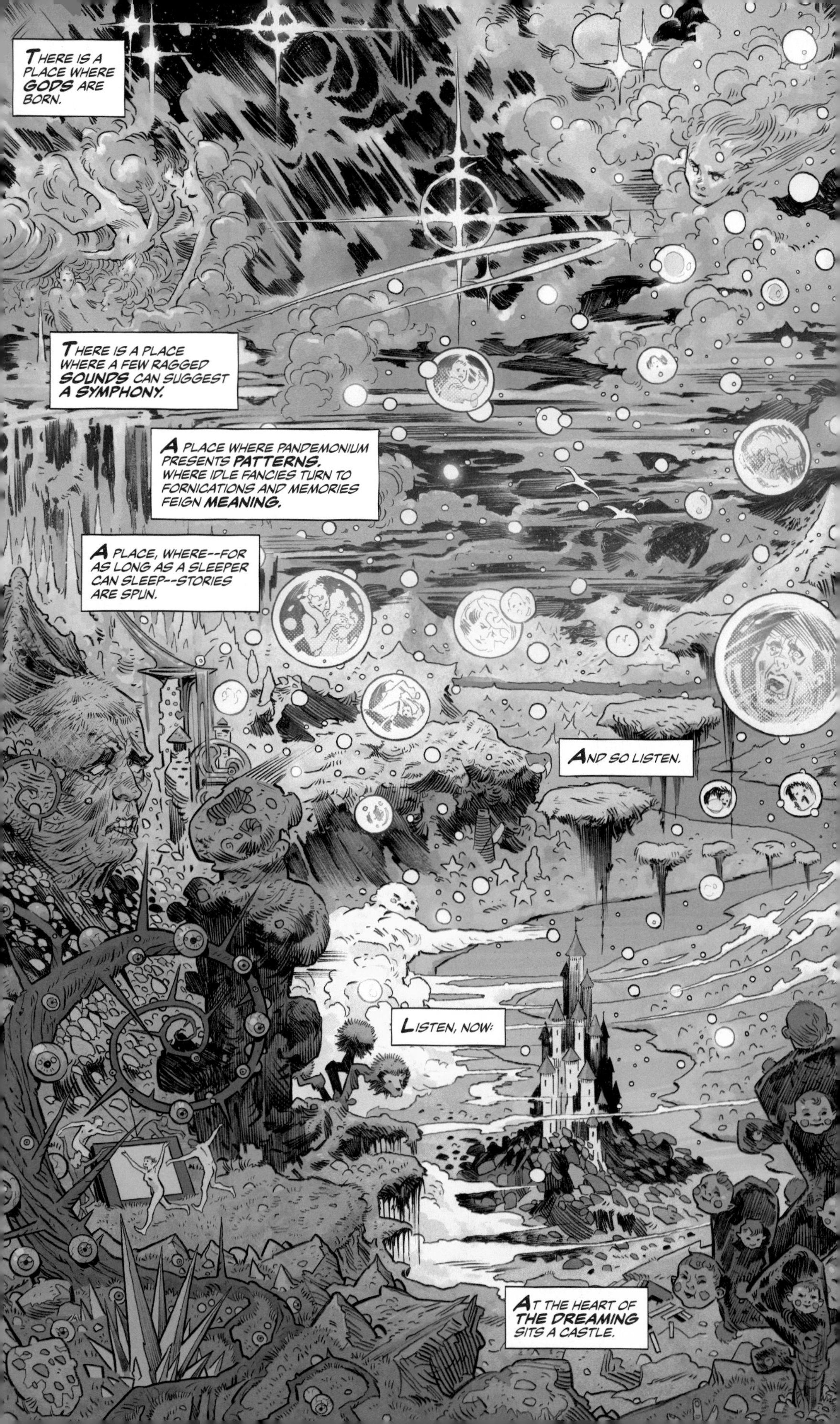
THERE IS A PLACE WHERE GODS ARE BORN.
THERE IS A PLACE WHERE A FEW RAGGED SOUNDS CAN SUGGEST A SYMPHONY.
A PLACE WHERE PANDEMONIUM PRESENTS PATTERNS. WHERE IDLE FANCIES TURN TO FORNICATIONS AND MEMORIES FEIGN MEANING.
A PLACE, WHERE--FOR AS LONG AS A SLEEPER CAN SLEEP--STORIES ARE SPUN.
AND SO LISTEN.
LISTEN, NOW:
AT THE HEART OF THE DREAMING SITS A CASTLE.

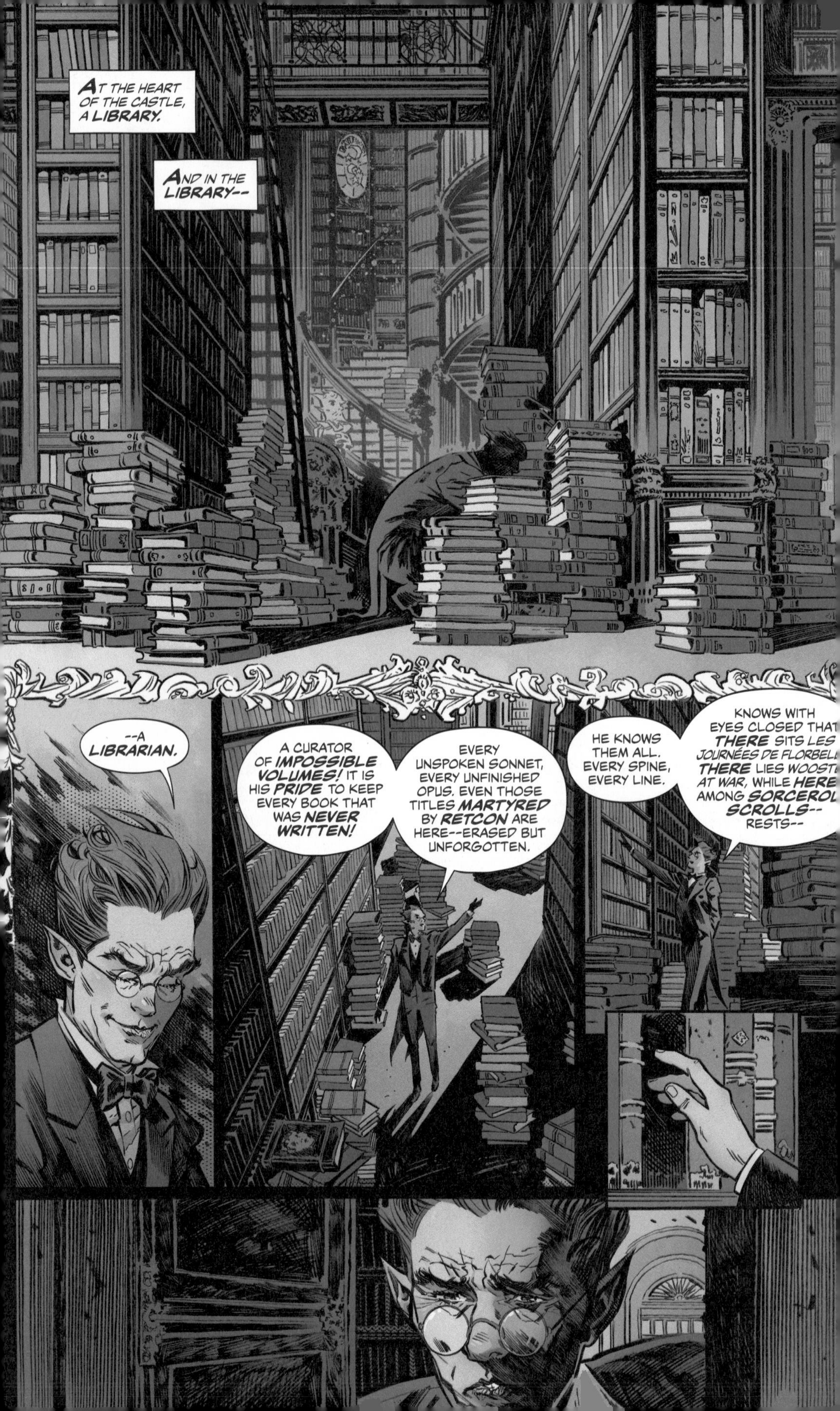
AT THE HEART OF THE CASTLE, A LIBRARY.
AND IN THE LIBRARY--
--A LIBRARIAN.
A CURATOR OF IMPOSSIBLE VOLUMES! IT IS HIS PRIDE TO KEEP EVERY BOOK THAT WAS NEVER WRITTEN!
EVERY UNSPOKEN SONNET, EVERY UNFINISHED OPUS. EVEN THOSE TITLES MARTYRED BY RETCON ARE HERE--ERASED BUT UNFORGOTTEN.
HE KNOWS THEM ALL. EVERY SPINE, EVERY LINE.
KNOWS WITH EYES CLOSED THAT THERE SITS LES JOURNÉES DE FLORBELL THERE LIES WOOST AT WAR, WHILE HERE AMONG SORCEROU SCROLLS-- RESTS--

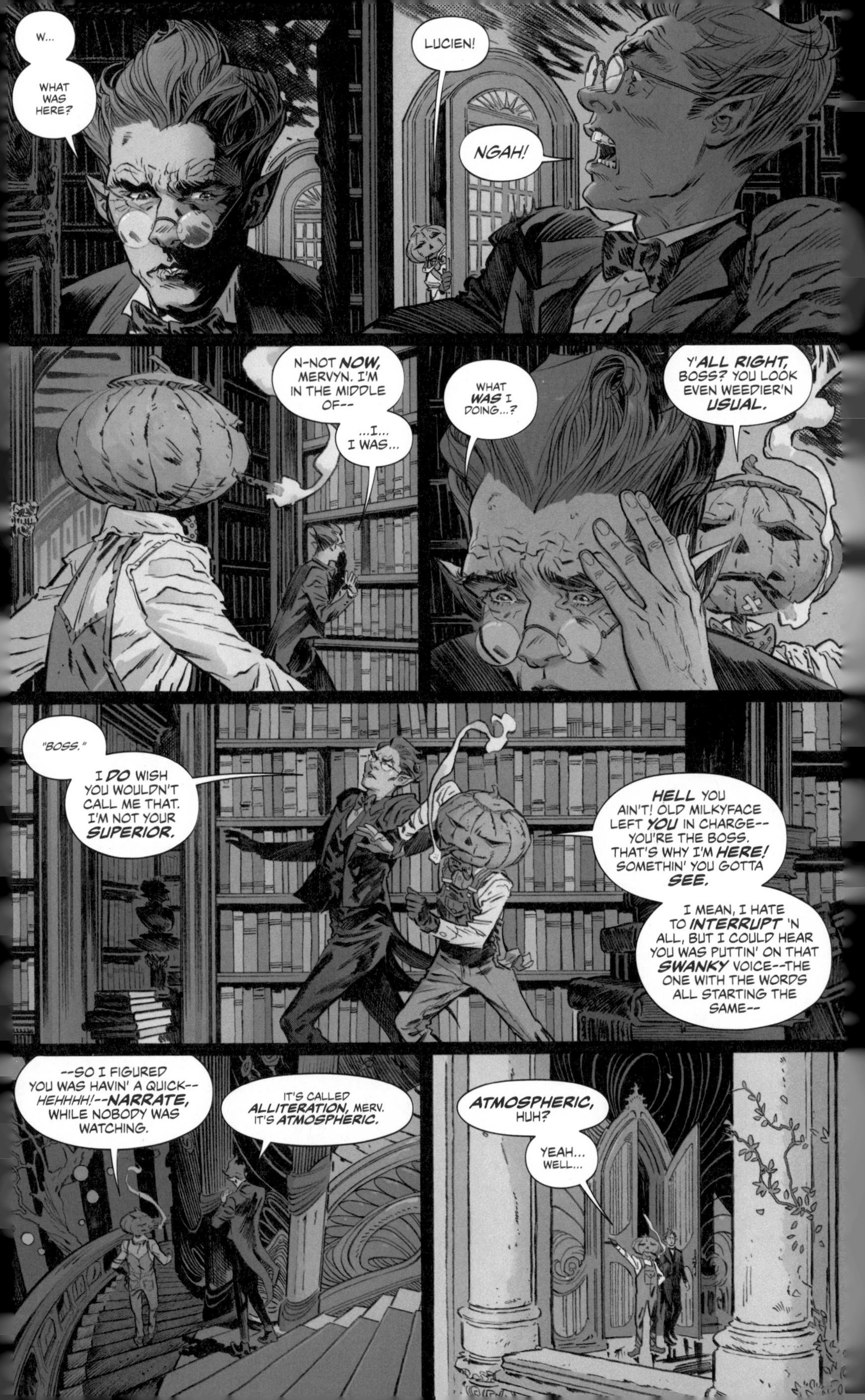
W...
WHAT WAS HERE?
LUCIEN!
NGAH!
N-NOT NOW, MERVYN. I'M IN THE MIDDLE OF--
...I... I WAS...
WHAT WAS I DOING...?
Y'ALL RIGHT, BOSS? YOU LOOK EVEN WEEDIER'N USUAL.
"BOSS."
I DO WISH YOU WOULDN'T CALL ME THAT. I'M NOT YOUR SUPERIOR.
HELL YOU AIN'T! OLD MILKYFACE LEFT YOU IN CHARGE--YOU'RE THE BOSS. THAT'S WHY I'M HERE! SOMETHIN' YOU GOTTA SEE.
I MEAN, I HATE TO INTERRUPT 'N ALL, BUT I COULD HEAR YOU WAS PUTTIN' ON THAT SWANKY VOICE--THE ONE WITH THE WORDS ALL STARTING THE SAME--
--SO I FIGURED YOU WAS HAVIN' A QUICK--HEHHHH!--NARRATE, WHILE NOBODY WAS WATCHING.
IT'S CALLED ALLITERATION, MERV. IT'S ATMOSPHERIC.
ATMOSPHERIC, HUH?
YEAH... WELL...

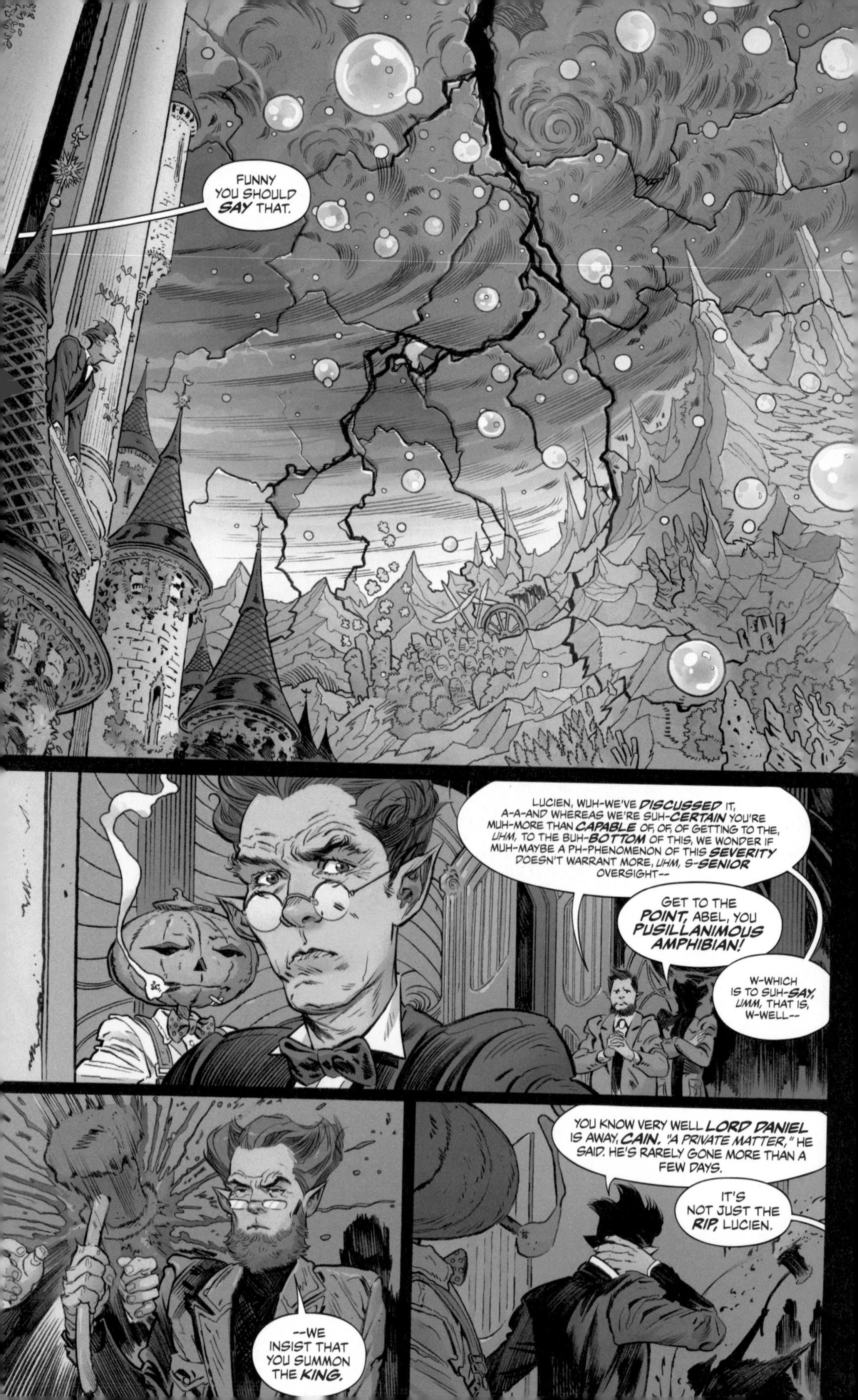
FUNNY YOU SHOULD SAY THAT.
LUCIEN, WUH-WE'VE DISCUSSED IT, A-A-AND WHEREAS WE'RE SUH-CERTAIN YOU'RE MUH-MORE THAN CAPABLE OF, OF, OF GETTING TO THE, UHM, TO THE BUH-BOTTOM OF THIS, WE WONDER IF MUH-MAYBE A PH-PHENOMENON OF THIS SEVERITY DOESN'T WARRANT MORE, UHM, S-SENIOR OVERSIGHT--
GET TO THE POINT, ABEL, YOU PUSILLANIMOUS AMPHIBIAN!
W-WHICH IS TO SUH-SAY, UMM, THAT IS, W-WELL--
--WE INSIST THAT YOU SUMMON THE KING.
YOU KNOW VERY WELL LORD DANIEL IS AWAY, CAIN. "A PRIVATE MATTER," HE SAID. HE'S RARELY GONE MORE THAN A FEW DAYS.
IT'S NOT JUST THE RIP, LUCIEN.

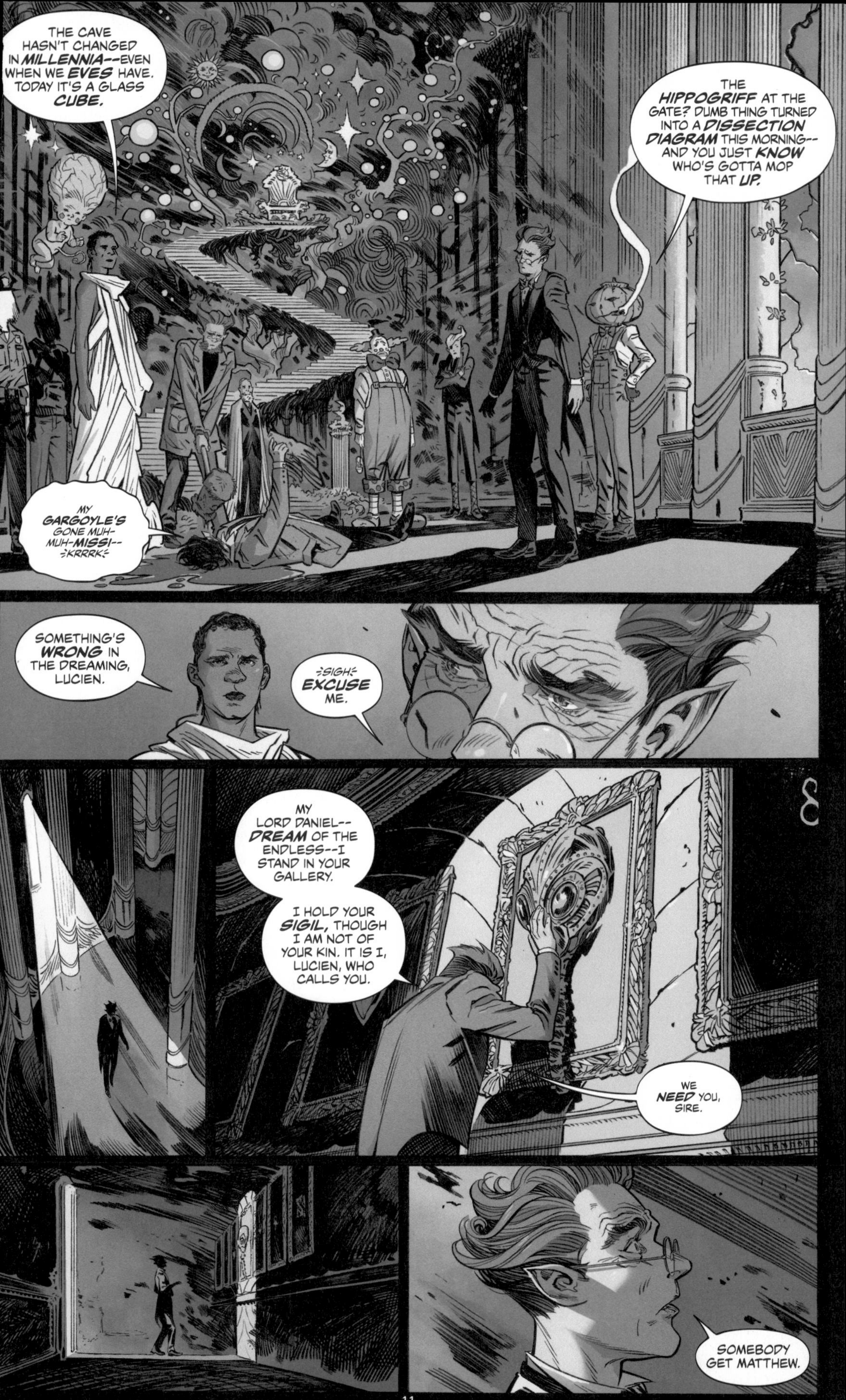
THE CAVE HASN'T CHANGED IN MILLENNIA--EVEN WHEN WE EVES HAVE. TODAY IT'S A GLASS CUBE.
THE HIPPOGRIFF AT THE GATE? DUMB THING TURNED INTO A DISSECTION DIAGRAM THIS MORNING--AND YOU JUST KNOW WHO'S GOTTA MOP THAT UP.
MY GARGOYLE'S GONE MUH-MUH-MISSI-- =KRRRK=
SOMETHING'S WRONG IN THE DREAMING, LUCIEN.
=SIGH= EXCUSE ME.
MY LORD DANIEL--DREAM OF THE ENDLESS--I STAND IN YOUR GALLERY.
I HOLD YOUR SIGIL, THOUGH I AM NOT OF YOUR KIN. IT IS I, LUCIEN, WHO CALLS YOU.
WE NEED YOU, SIRE.
SOMEBODY GET MATTHEW.

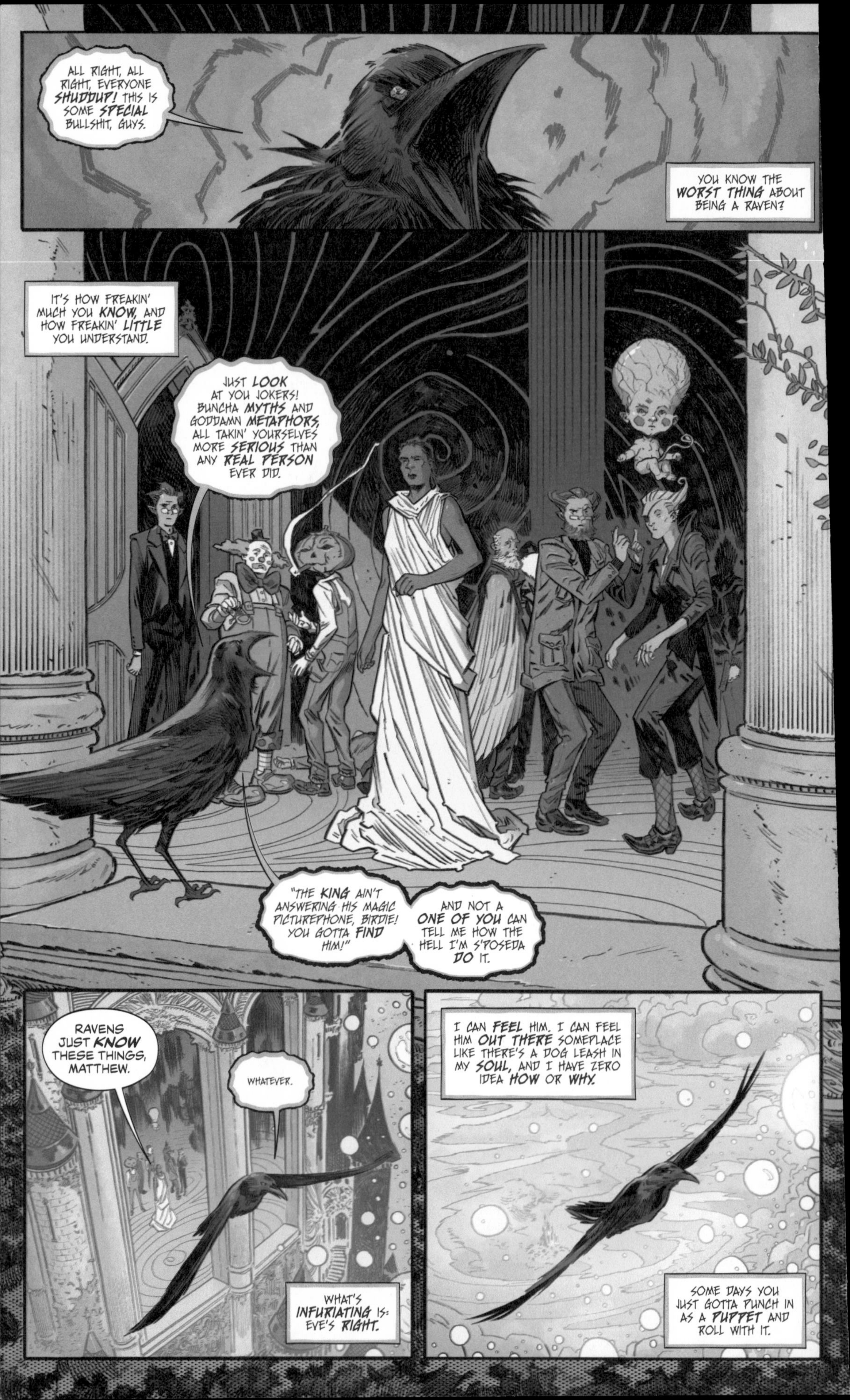
ALL RIGHT, ALL RIGHT, EVERYONE SHUDDUP! THIS IS SOME SPECIAL BULLSHIT, GUYS.
YOU KNOW THE WORST THING ABOUT BEING A RAVEN?
IT'S HOW FREAKIN' MUCH YOU KNOW, AND HOW FREAKIN' LITTLE YOU UNDERSTAND.
JUST LOOK AT YOU JOKERS! BUNCHA MYTHS AND GODDAMN METAPHORS, ALL TAKIN' YOURSELVES MORE SERIOUS THAN ANY REAL PERSON EVER DID.
"THE KING AIN'T ANSWERING HIS MAGIC PICTUREPHONE, BIRDIE! YOU GOTTA FIND HIM!"
AND NOT A ONE OF YOU CAN TELL ME HOW THE HELL I'M S'POSEDA DO IT.
RAVENS JUST KNOW THESE THINGS, MATTHEW.
WHATEVER.
WHAT'S INFURIATING IS: EVE'S RIGHT.
I CAN FEEL HIM. I CAN FEEL HIM OUT THERE SOMEPLACE LIKE THERE'S A DOG LEASH IN MY SOUL, AND I HAVE ZERO IDEA HOW OR WHY.
SOME DAYS YOU JUST GOTTA PUNCH IN AS A PUPPET AND ROLL WITH IT.

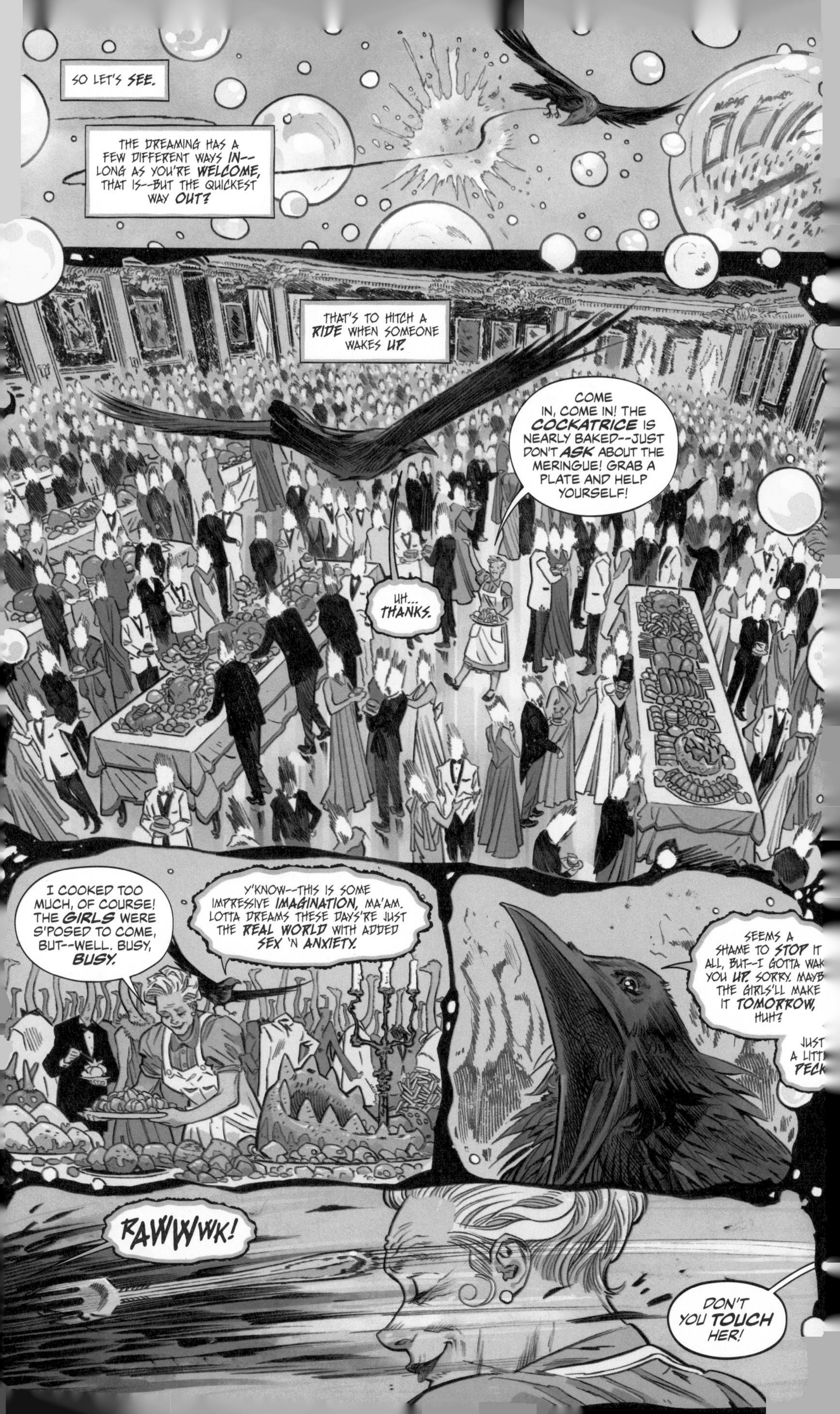
SO LET'S SEE.
THE DREAMING HAS A FEW DIFFERENT WAYS IN--LONG AS YOU'RE WELCOME, THAT IS--BUT THE QUICKEST WAY OUT?
THAT'S TO HITCH A RIDE WHEN SOMEONE WAKES UP.
COME IN, COME IN! THE COCKATRICE IS NEARLY BAKED--JUST DON'T ASK ABOUT THE MERINGUE! GRAB A PLATE AND HELP YOURSELF!
UH... THANKS.
I COOKED TOO MUCH, OF COURSE! THE GIRLS WERE S'POSED TO COME, BUT--WELL. BUSY, BUSY.
Y'KNOW--THIS IS SOME IMPRESSIVE IMAGINATION, MA'AM. LOTTA DREAMS THESE DAYS'RE JUST THE REAL WORLD WITH ADDED SEX 'N ANXIETY.
SEEMS A SHAME TO STOP IT ALL, BUT--I GOTTA WAK YOU UP. SORRY. MAYB THE GIRLS'LL MAKE IT TOMORROW, HUH?
JUST A LITT PECK
RAWWWK!
DON'T YOU TOUCH HER!

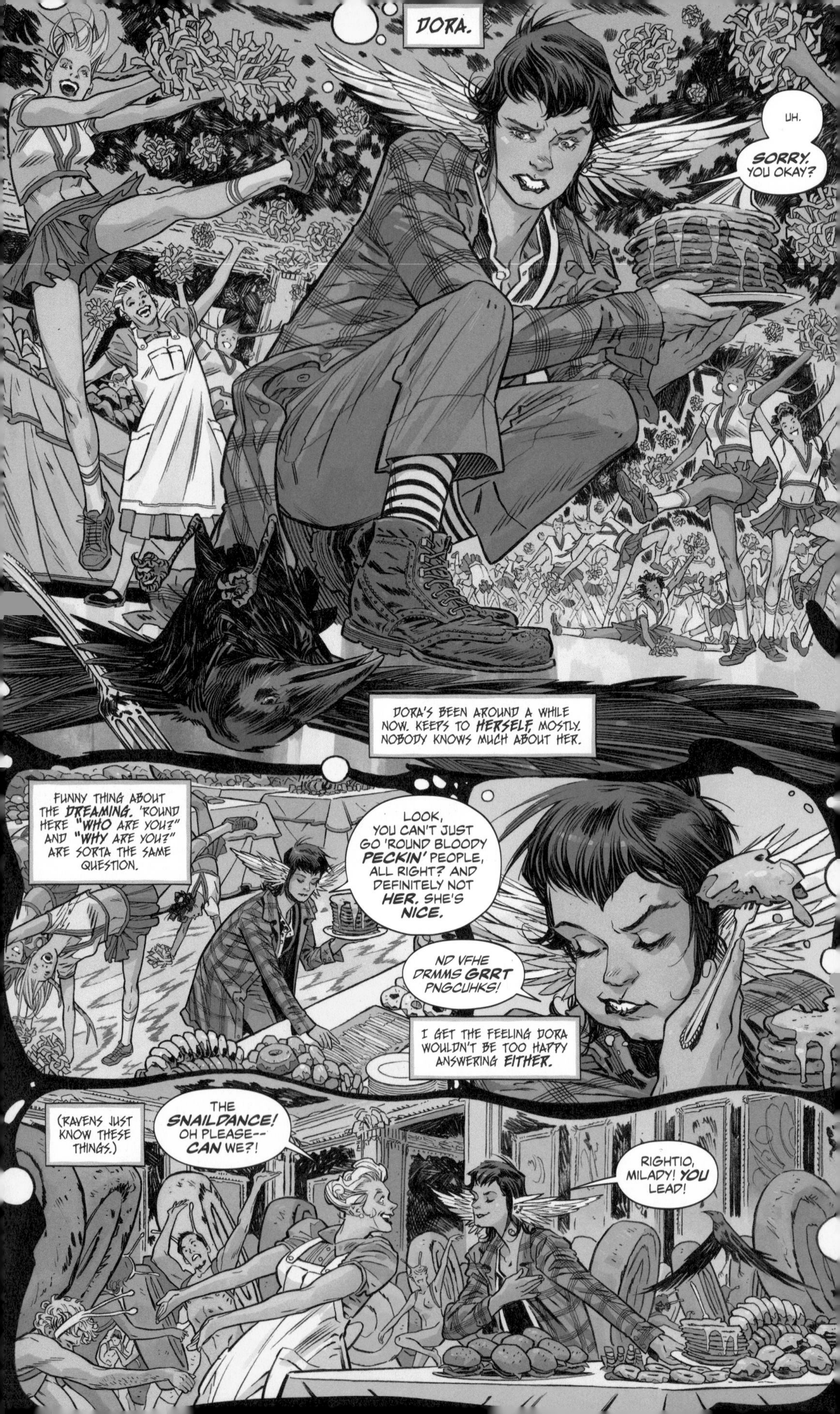
DORA.
UH.
SORRY. YOU OKAY?
DORA'S BEEN AROUND A WHILE NOW. KEEPS TO HERSELF, MOSTLY. NOBODY KNOWS MUCH ABOUT HER.
FUNNY THING ABOUT THE DREAMING. 'ROUND HERE "WHO ARE YOU?" AND "WHY ARE YOU?" ARE SORTA THE SAME QUESTION.
LOOK, YOU CAN'T JUST GO 'ROUND BLOODY PECKIN' PEOPLE, ALL RIGHT? AND DEFINITELY NOT HER. SHE'S NICE.
ND VFHE DRMMS GRRT PNGCUHKS!
I GET THE FEELING DORA WOULDN'T BE TOO HAPPY ANSWERING EITHER.
(RAVENS JUST KNOW THESE THINGS.)
THE SNAILDANCE! OH PLEASE-- CAN WE?!
RIGHTIO, MILADY! YOU LEAD!

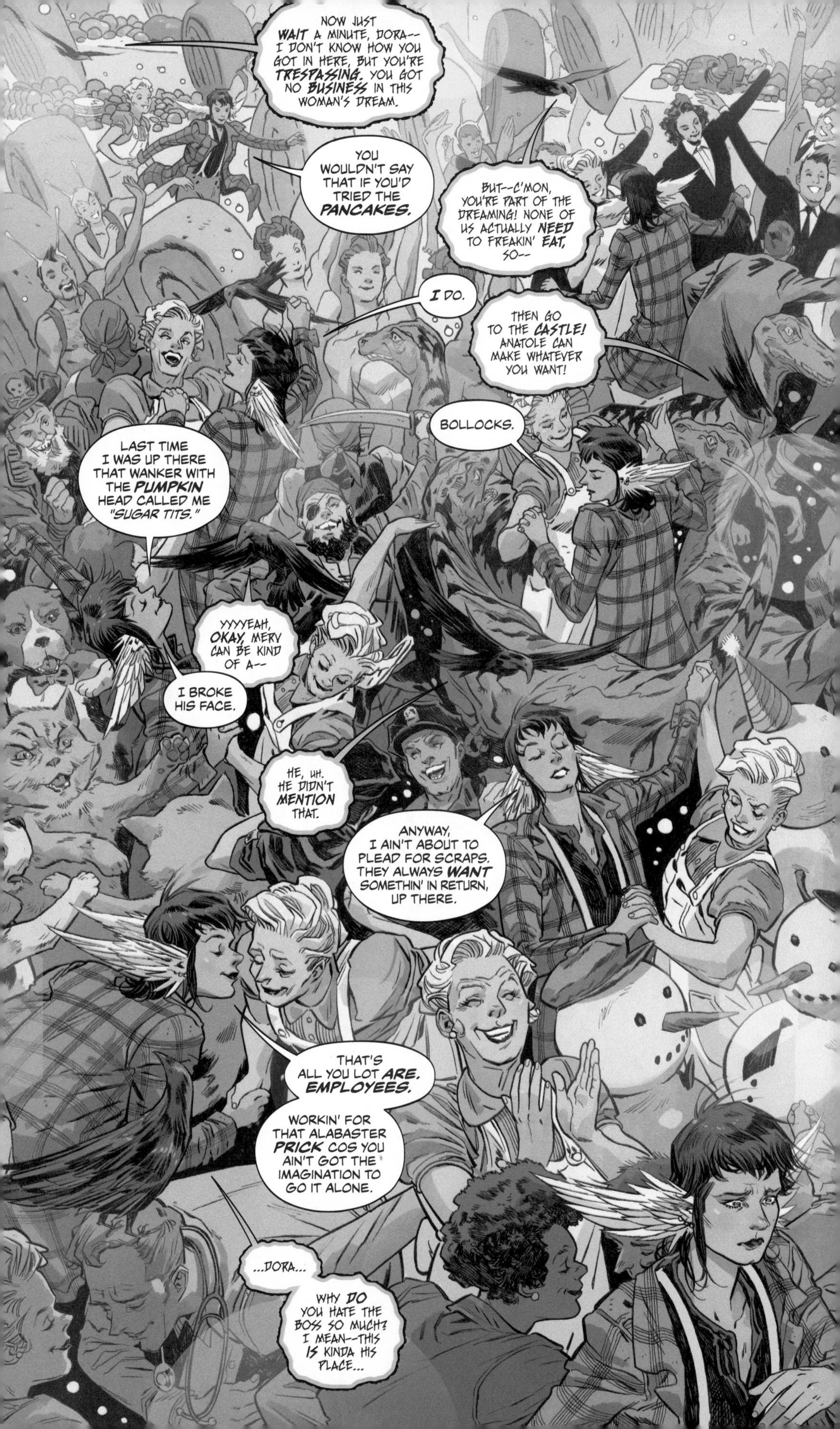
NOW JUST WAIT A MINUTE, DORA-- I DON'T KNOW HOW YOU GOT IN HERE, BUT YOU'RE TRESPASSING. YOU GOT NO BUSINESS IN THIS WOMAN'S DREAM.
YOU WOULDN'T SAY THAT IF YOU'D TRIED THE PANCAKES.
BUT--C'MON, YOU'RE PART OF THE DREAMING! NONE OF US ACTUALLY NEED TO FREAKIN' EAT, SO--
I DO.
THEN GO TO THE CASTLE! ANATOLE CAN MAKE WHATEVER YOU WANT!
BOLLOCKS.
LAST TIME I WAS UP THERE THAT WANKER WITH THE PUMPKIN HEAD CALLED ME "SUGAR TITS."
YYYYEAH, OKAY, MERV CAN BE KIND OF A--
I BROKE HIS FACE.
HE, UH. HE DIDN'T MENTION THAT.
ANYWAY, I AIN'T ABOUT TO PLEAD FOR SCRAPS. THEY ALWAYS WANT SOMETHIN' IN RETURN, UP THERE.
THAT'S ALL YOU LOT ARE. EMPLOYEES.
WORKIN' FOR THAT ALABASTER PRICK COS YOU AIN'T GOT THE IMAGINATION TO GO IT ALONE.
...DORA...
WHY DO YOU HATE THE BOSS SO MUCH? I MEAN--THIS IS KINDA HIS PLACE...

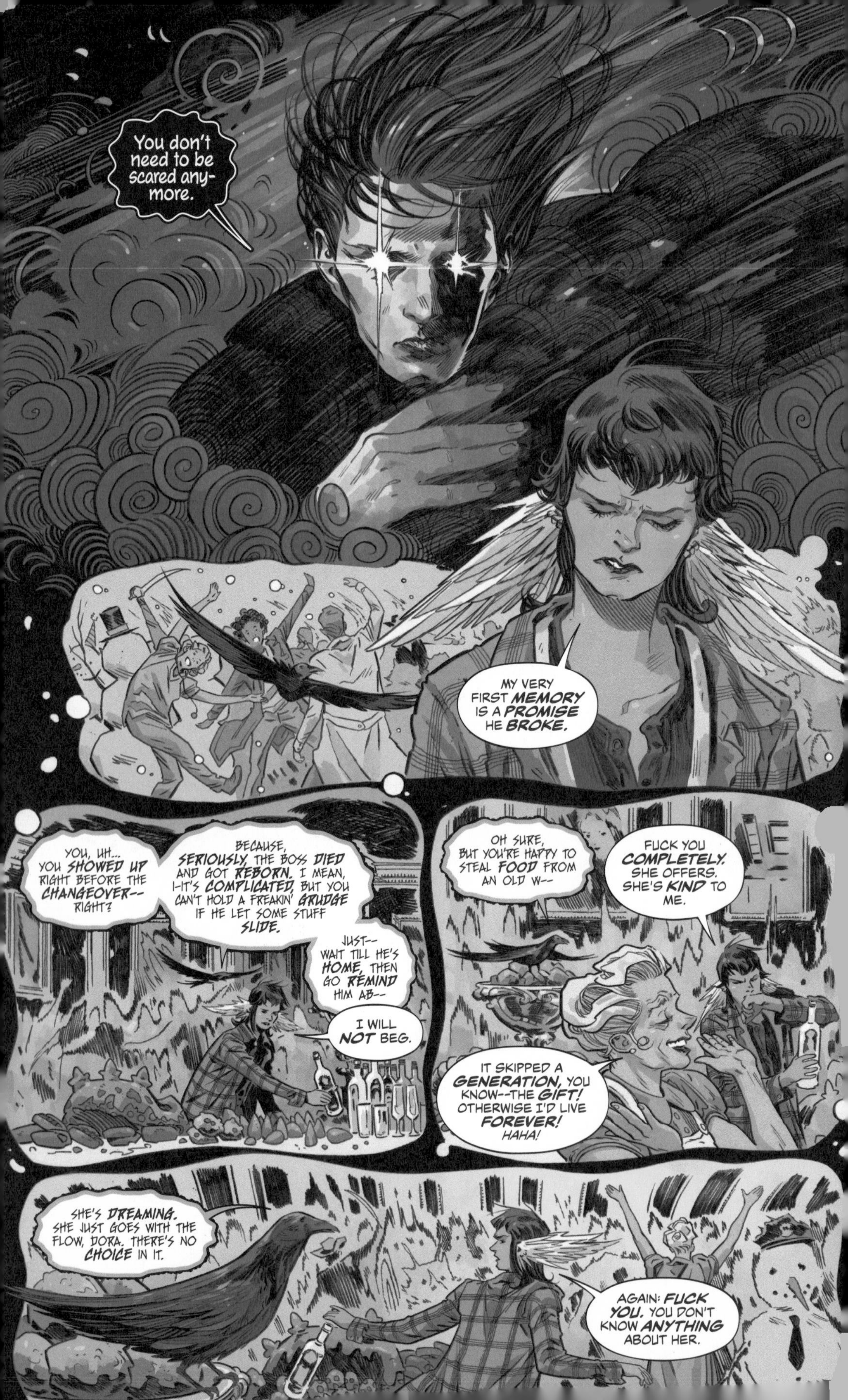

You don't need to be scared any-more.
MY VERY FIRST MEMORY IS A PROMISE HE BROKE.
YOU, UH... YOU SHOWED UP RIGHT BEFORE THE CHANGEOVER--RIGHT?
BECAUSE, SERIOUSLY, THE BOSS DIED AND GOT REBORN. I MEAN, I-IT'S COMPLICATED, BUT YOU CAN'T HOLD A FREAKIN' GRUDGE IF HE LET SOME STUFF SLIDE.
JUST--WAIT TILL HE'S HOME, THEN GO REMIND HIM AB--
I WILL NOT BEG.
OH SURE, BUT YOU'RE HAPPY TO STEAL FOOD FROM AN OLD W--
FUCK YOU COMPLETELY. SHE OFFERS. SHE'S KIND TO ME.
IT SKIPPED A GENERATION, YOU KNOW--THE GIFT! OTHERWISE I'D LIVE FOREVER! HAHA!
SHE'S DREAMING. SHE JUST GOES WITH THE FLOW, DORA. THERE'S NO CHOICE IN IT.
AGAIN: FUCK YOU. YOU DON'T KNOW ANYTHING ABOUT HER.

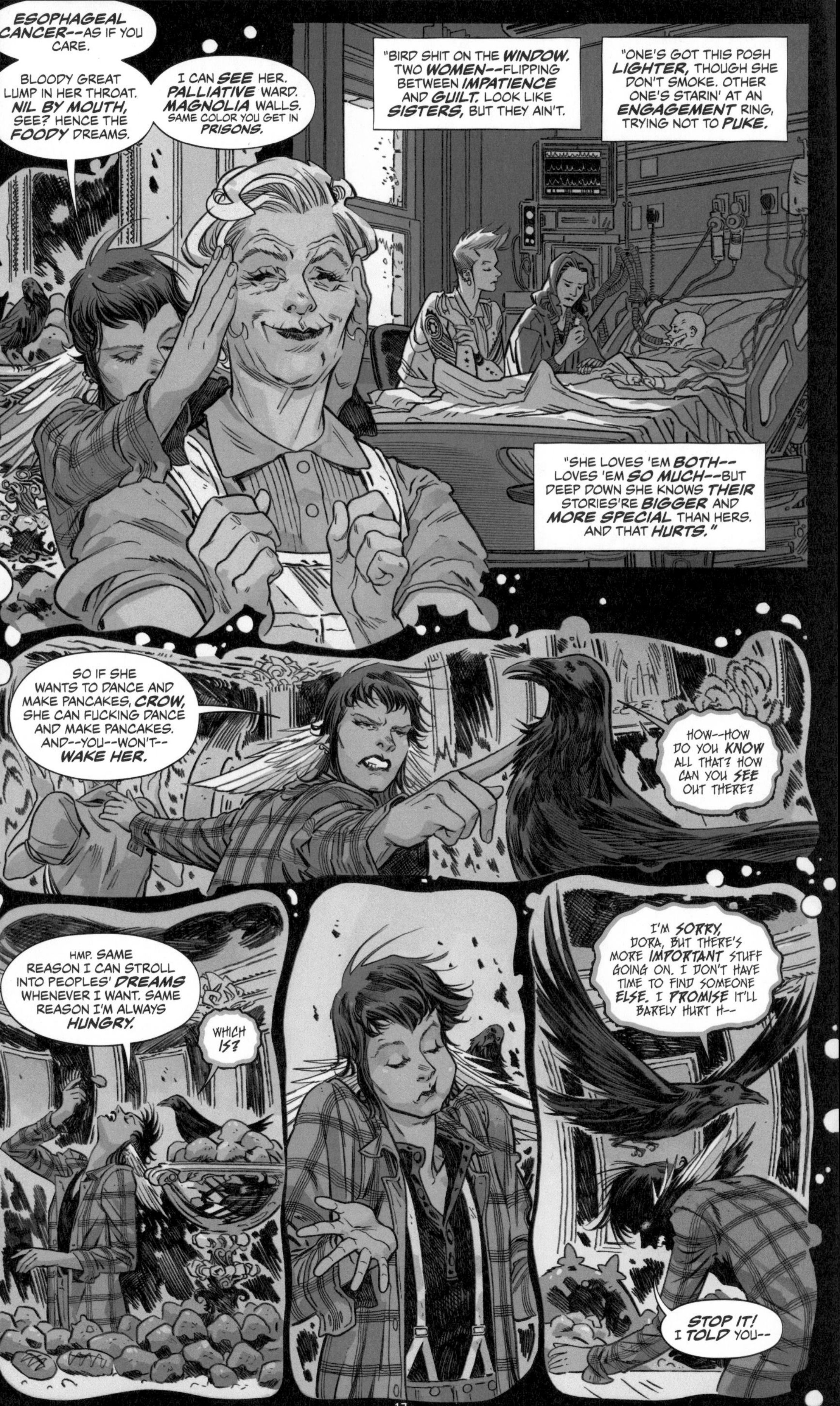
ESOPHAGEAL CANCER--AS IF YOU CARE.
BLOODY GREAT LUMP IN HER THROAT. NIL BY MOUTH, SEE? HENCE THE FOODY DREAMS.
I CAN SEE HER. PALLIATIVE WARD. MAGNOLIA WALLS. SAME COLOR YOU GET IN PRISONS.
"BIRD SHIT ON THE WINDOW. TWO WOMEN--FLIPPING BETWEEN IMPATIENCE AND GUILT. LOOK LIKE SISTERS, BUT THEY AIN'T.
"ONE'S GOT THIS POSH LIGHTER, THOUGH SHE DON'T SMOKE. OTHER ONE'S STARIN' AT AN ENGAGEMENT RING, TRYING NOT TO PUKE.
"SHE LOVES 'EM BOTH--LOVES 'EM SO MUCH--BUT DEEP DOWN SHE KNOWS THEIR STORIES'RE BIGGER AND MORE SPECIAL THAN HERS. AND THAT HURTS."
SO IF SHE WANTS TO DANCE AND MAKE PANCAKES, CROW, SHE CAN FUCKING DANCE AND MAKE PANCAKES. AND--YOU--WON'T--WAKE HER.
HOW--HOW DO YOU KNOW ALL THAT? HOW CAN YOU SEE OUT THERE?
HMP. SAME REASON I CAN STROLL INTO PEOPLES' DREAMS WHENEVER I WANT. SAME REASON I'M ALWAYS HUNGRY.
WHICH IS?
I'M SORRY, DORA, BUT THERE'S MORE IMPORTANT STUFF GOING ON. I DON'T HAVE TIME TO FIND SOMEONE ELSE. I PROMISE IT'LL BARELY HURT H--
STOP IT! I TOLD YOU--

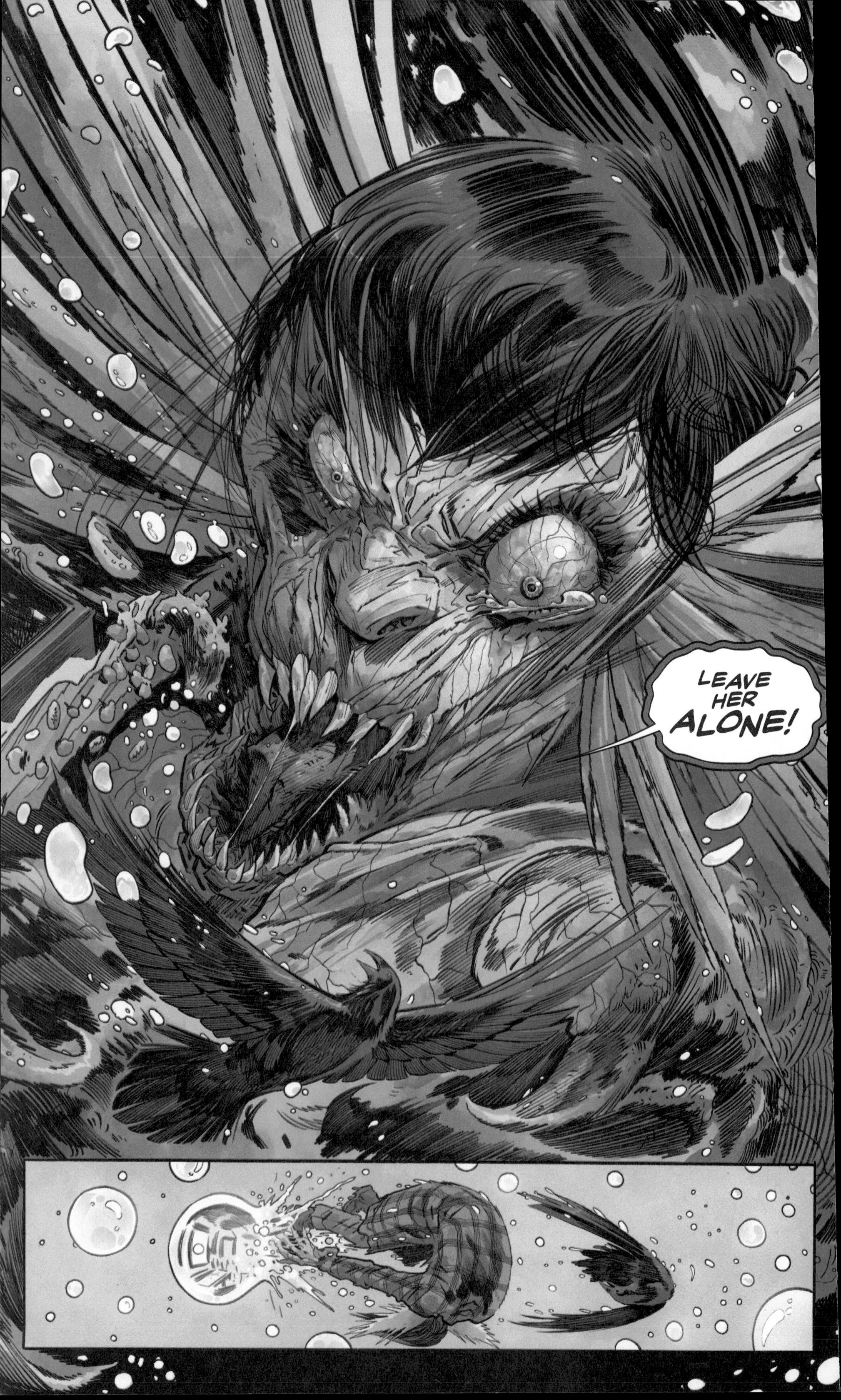
LEAVE HER ALONE!

YOU--YOU KICKED ME OUT OF HER *DREAM!* HOW DID YOU EVEN *DO* THAT?!

SORRY. *SORRY--* I JUST...

I GET *ANGRY.*

WHAT THE HELL *ARE* YOU?

MY FEATHERY FREAKIN' *ASS* THEY DO.

"RAVENS JUST *KNOW* THESE THINGS."

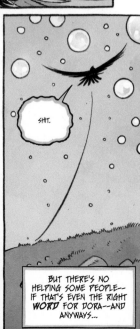

SHIT.

BUT THERE'S NO HELPING SOME PEOPLE-- IF THAT'S EVEN THE RIGHT *WORD* FOR DORA--AND ANYWAYS...

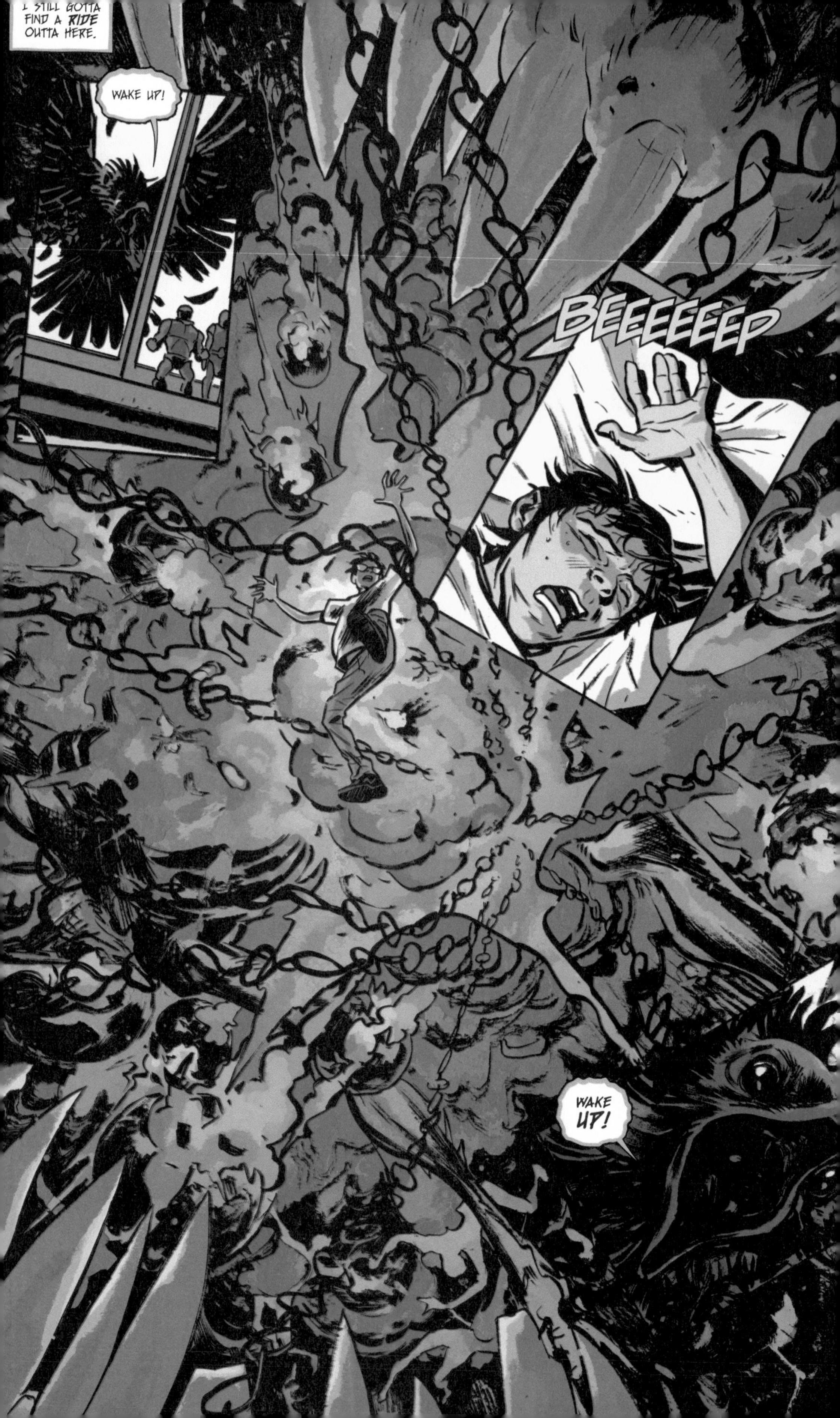
I STILL GOTTA FIND A RIDE OUTTA HERE.
WAKE UP!
BEEEEEEEP
WAKE UP!

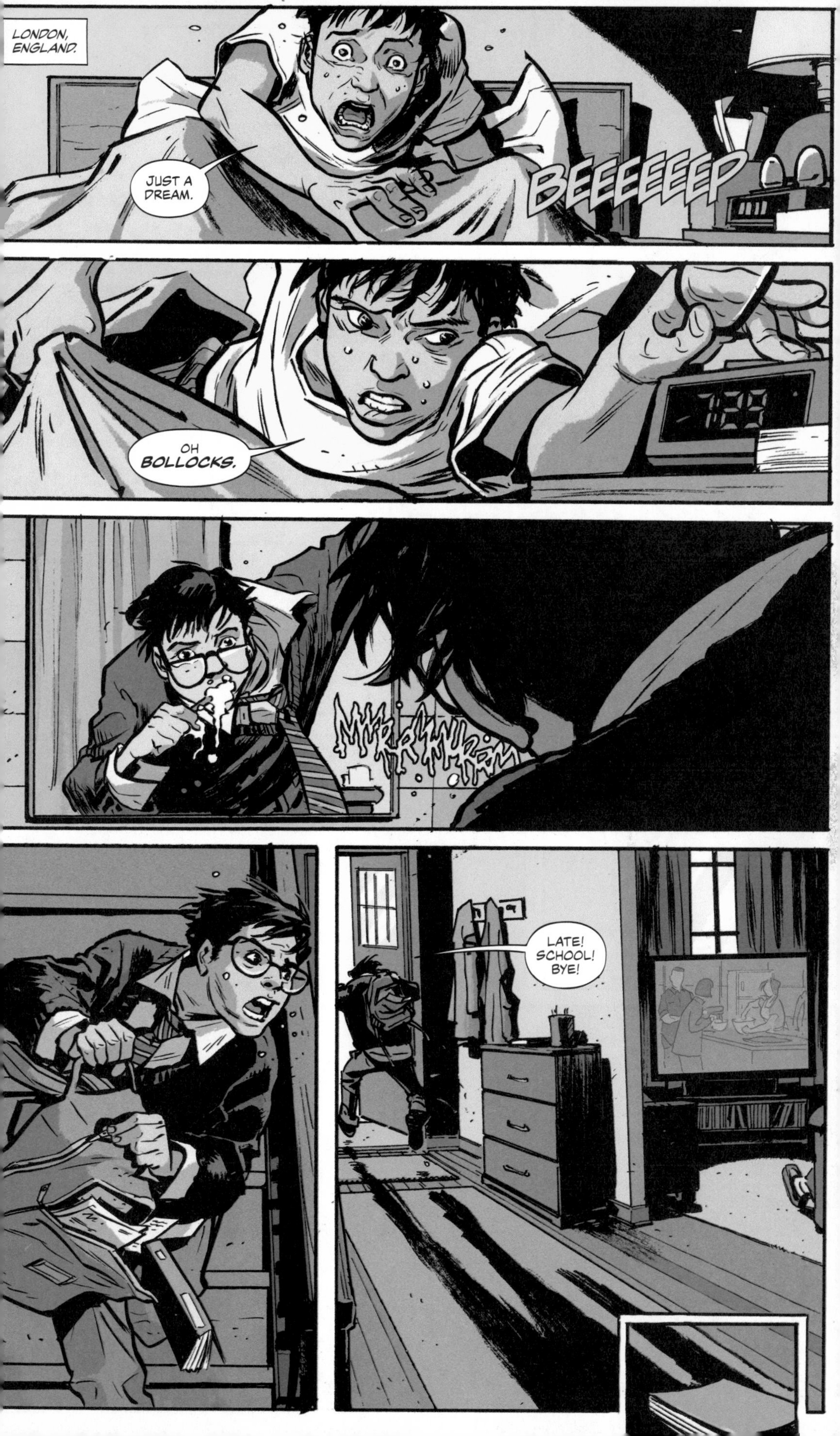
LONDON, ENGLAND.
JUST A DREAM.
BEEEEEEP
OH BOLLOCKS.
LATE! SCHOOL! BYE!

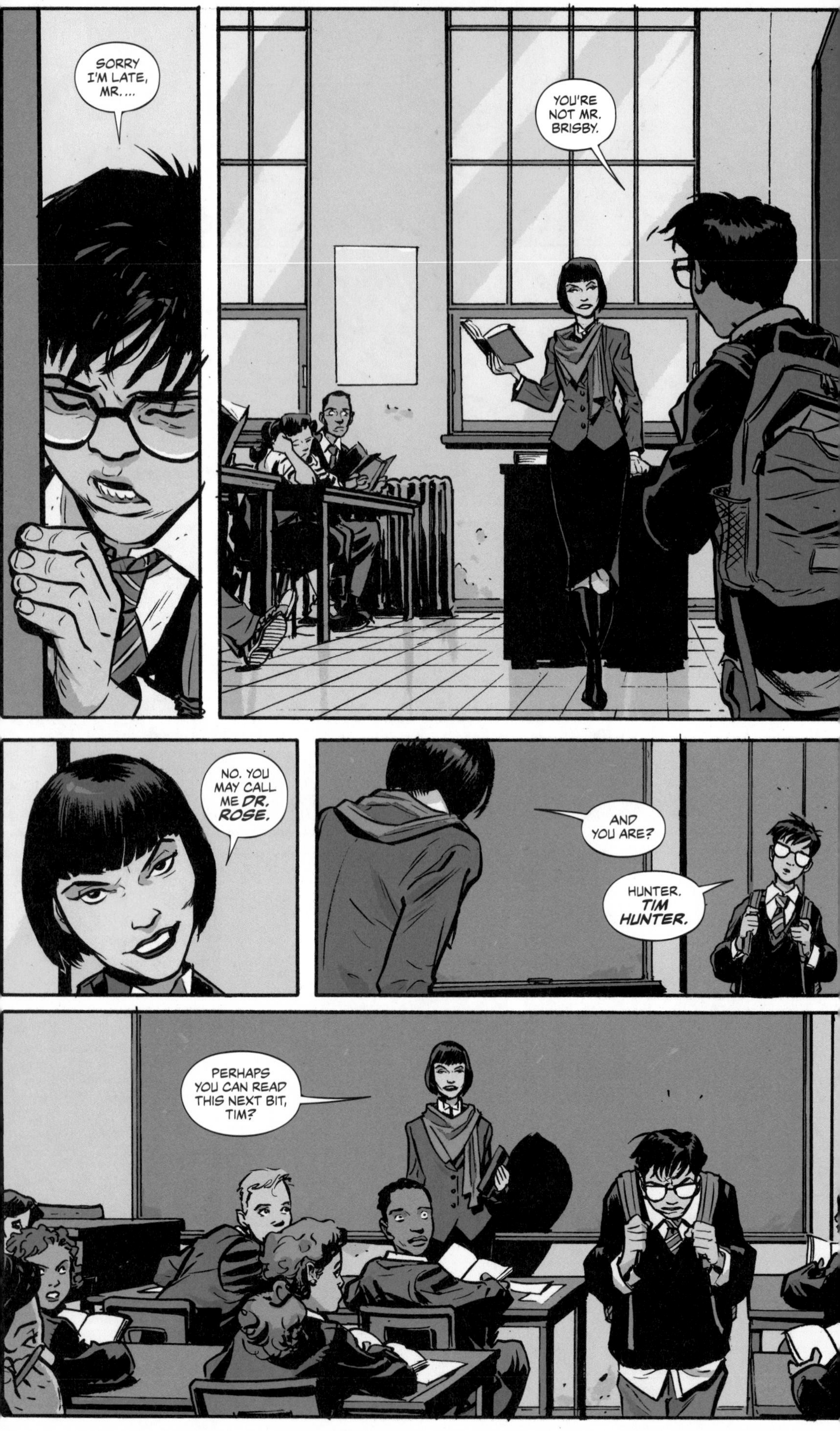
SORRY I'M LATE, MR....
YOU'RE NOT MR. BRISBY.
NO. YOU MAY CALL ME DR. ROSE.
AND YOU ARE?
HUNTER. TIM HUNTER.
PERHAPS YOU CAN READ THIS NEXT BIT, TIM?

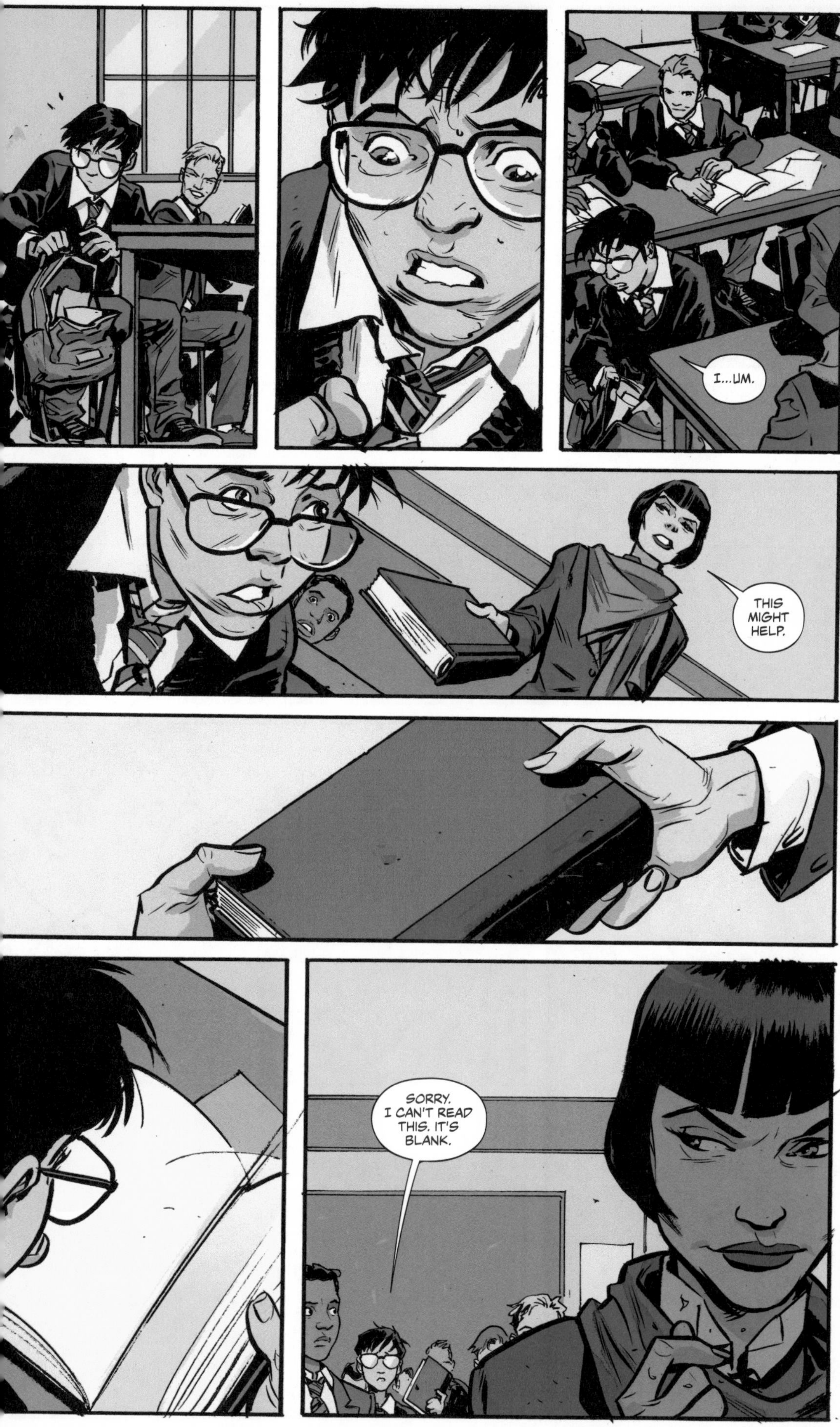
I...UM.
THIS MIGHT HELP.
SORRY. I CAN'T READ THIS. IT'S BLANK.

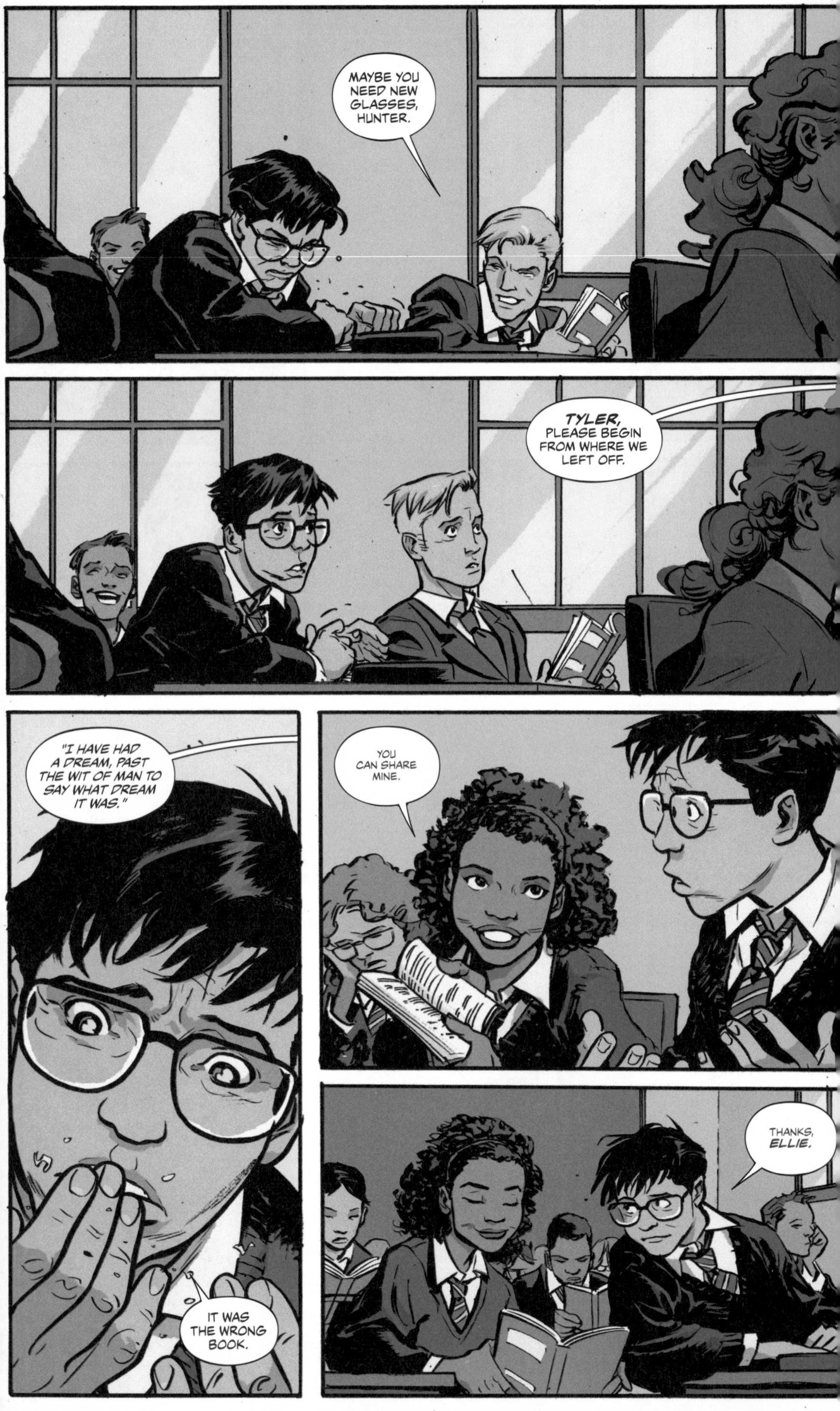
MAYBE YOU NEED NEW GLASSES, HUNTER.
TYLER, PLEASE BEGIN FROM WHERE WE LEFT OFF.
"I HAVE HAD A DREAM, PAST THE WIT OF MAN TO SAY WHAT DREAM IT WAS."
IT WAS THE WRONG BOOK.
YOU CAN SHARE MINE.
THANKS, ELLIE.

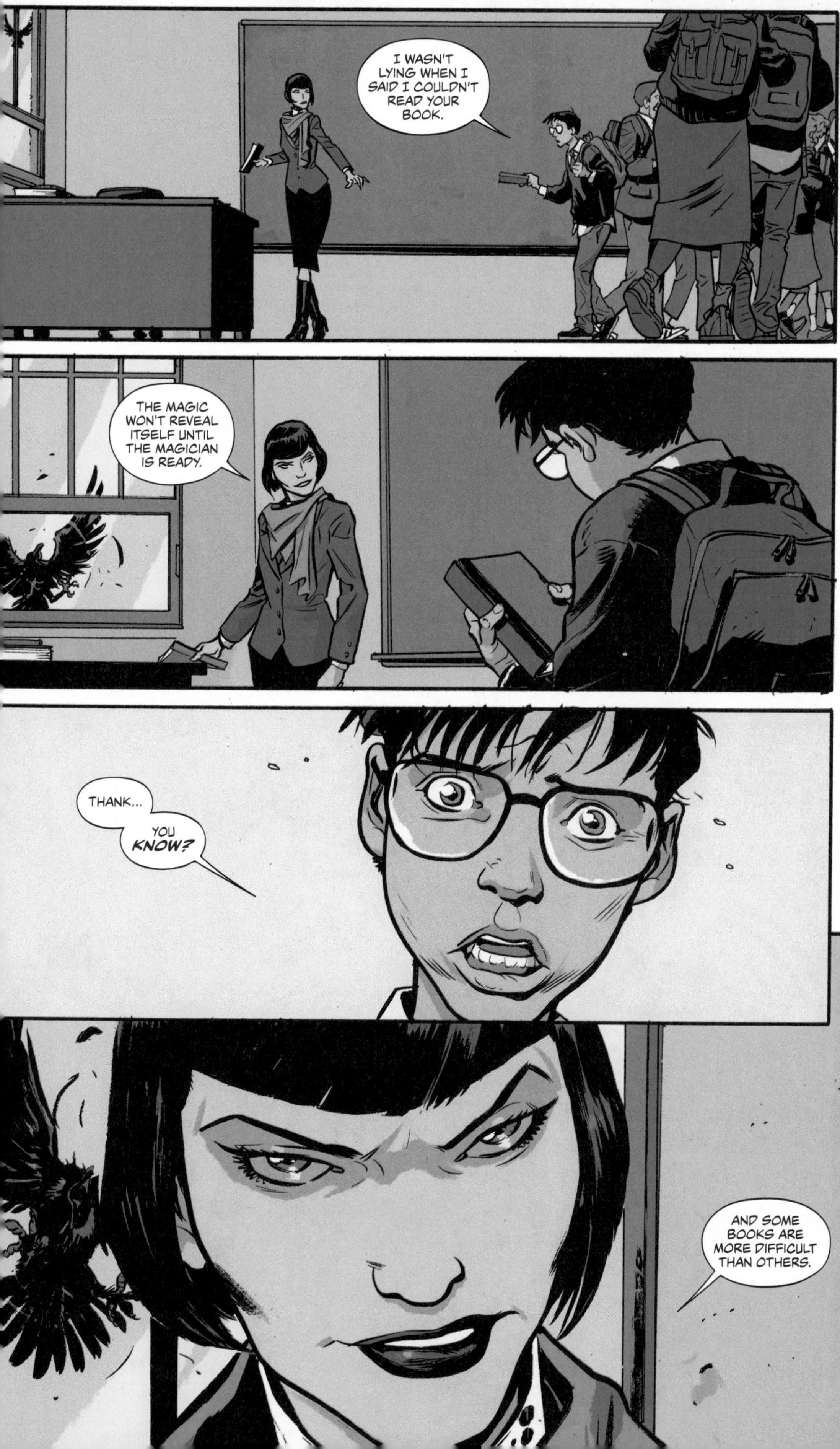
I WASN'T LYING WHEN I SAID I COULDN'T READ YOUR BOOK.
THE MAGIC WON'T REVEAL ITSELF UNTIL THE MAGICIAN IS READY.
THANK...
YOU *KNOW?*
AND SOME BOOKS ARE MORE DIFFICULT THAN OTHERS.

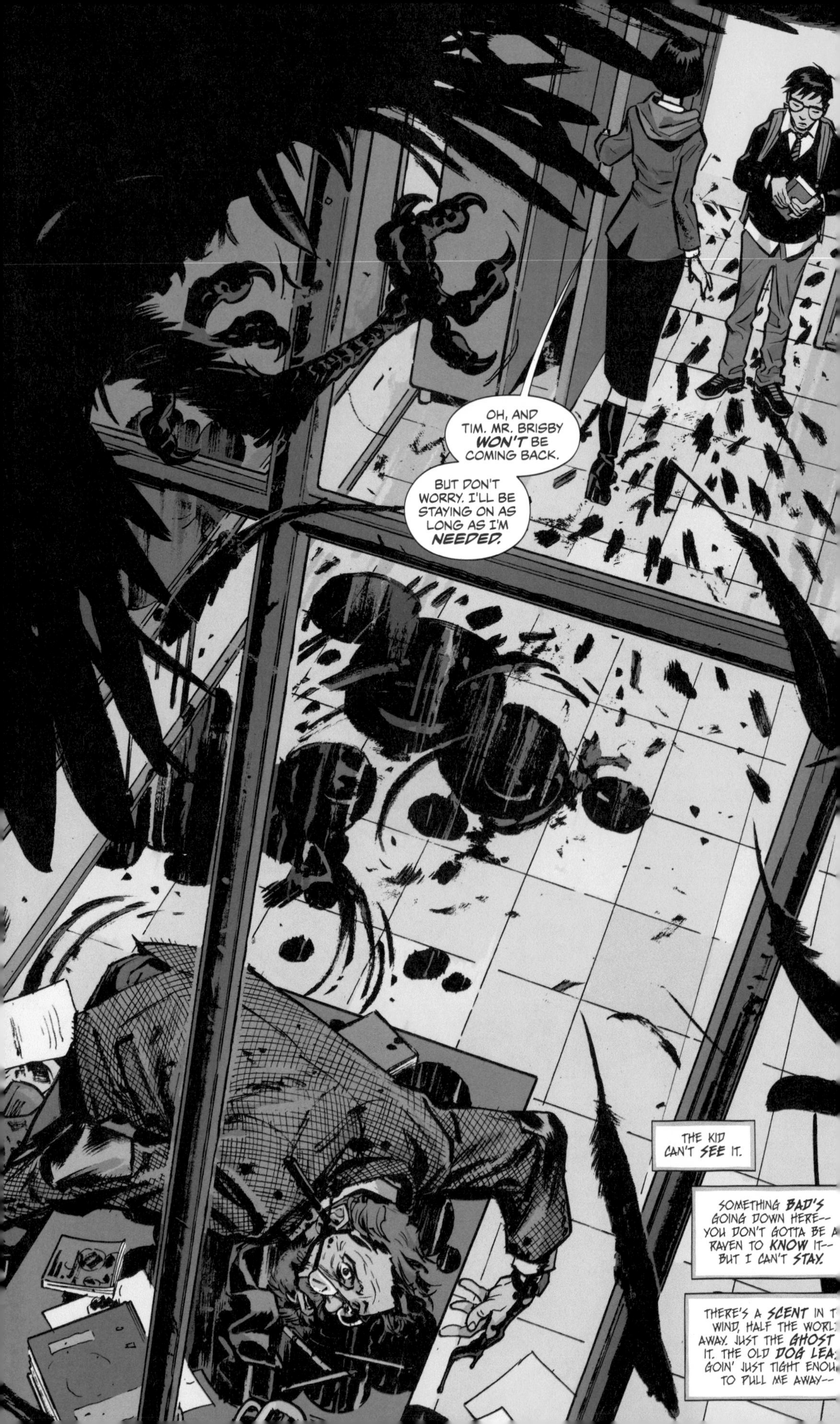

OH, AND TIM. MR. BRISBY **WON'T** BE COMING BACK.
BUT DON'T WORRY. I'LL BE STAYING ON AS LONG AS I'M **NEEDED**.
THE KID CAN'T **SEE** IT.
SOMETHING **BAD'S** GOING DOWN HERE-- YOU DON'T GOTTA BE A RAVEN TO **KNOW** IT-- BUT I CAN'T **STAY**.
THERE'S A **SCENT** IN T WIND, HALF THE WORL AWAY. JUST THE **GHOST** IT. THE OLD **DOG LEA** GOIN' JUST TIGHT ENOU TO PULL ME AWAY--

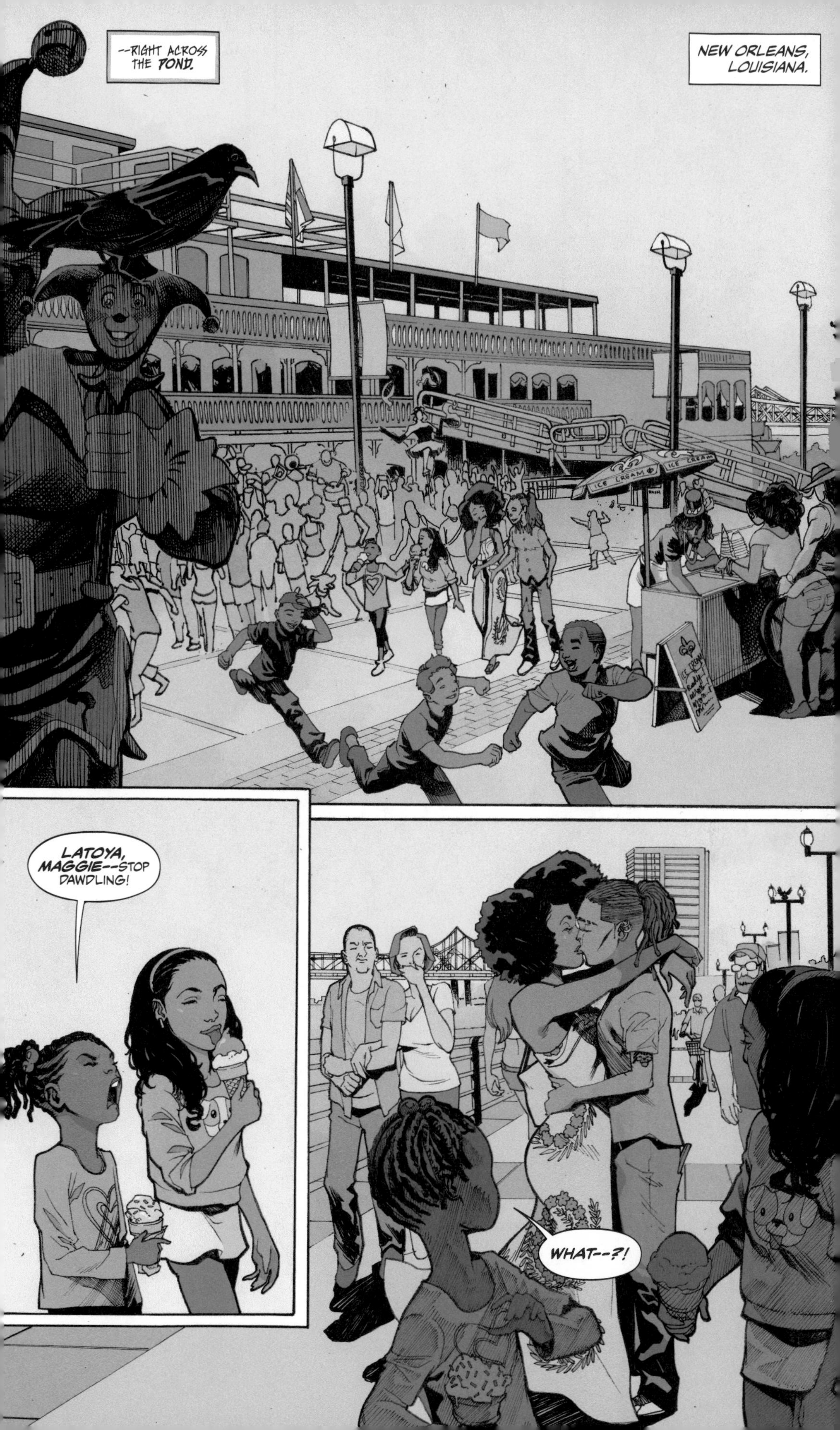
--RIGHT ACROSS THE POND.
NEW ORLEANS, LOUISIANA.
ICE CREAM
LATOYA, MAGGIE--STOP DAWDLING!
WHAT--?!

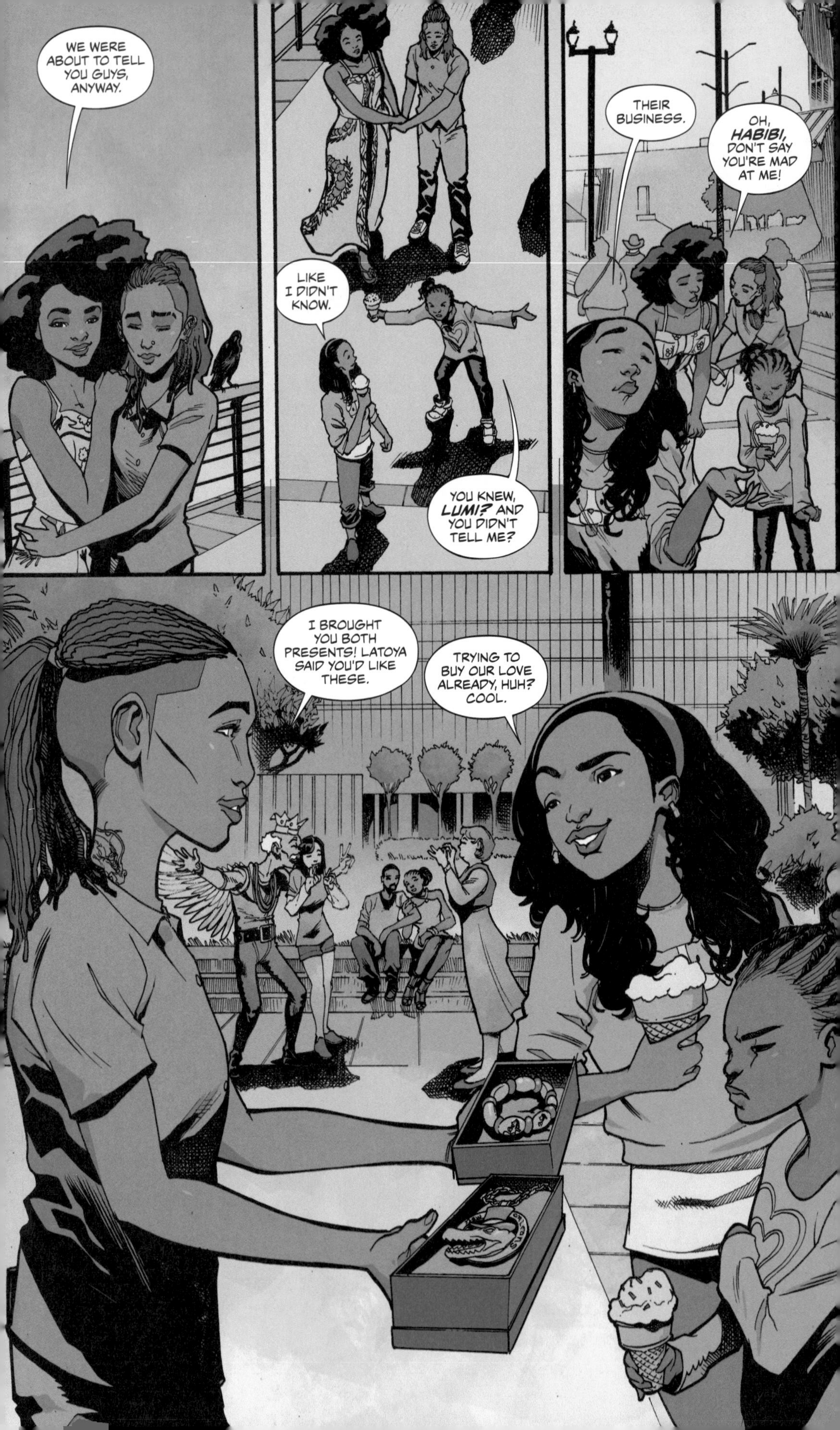
WE WERE ABOUT TO TELL YOU GUYS, ANYWAY.
LIKE I DIDN'T KNOW.
YOU KNEW, **LUMI?** AND YOU DIDN'T TELL ME?
THEIR BUSINESS.
OH, ***HABIBI,*** DON'T SAY YOU'RE MAD AT ME!
I BROUGHT YOU BOTH PRESENTS! LATOYA SAID YOU'D LIKE THESE.
TRYING TO BUY OUR LOVE ALREADY, HUH? COOL.

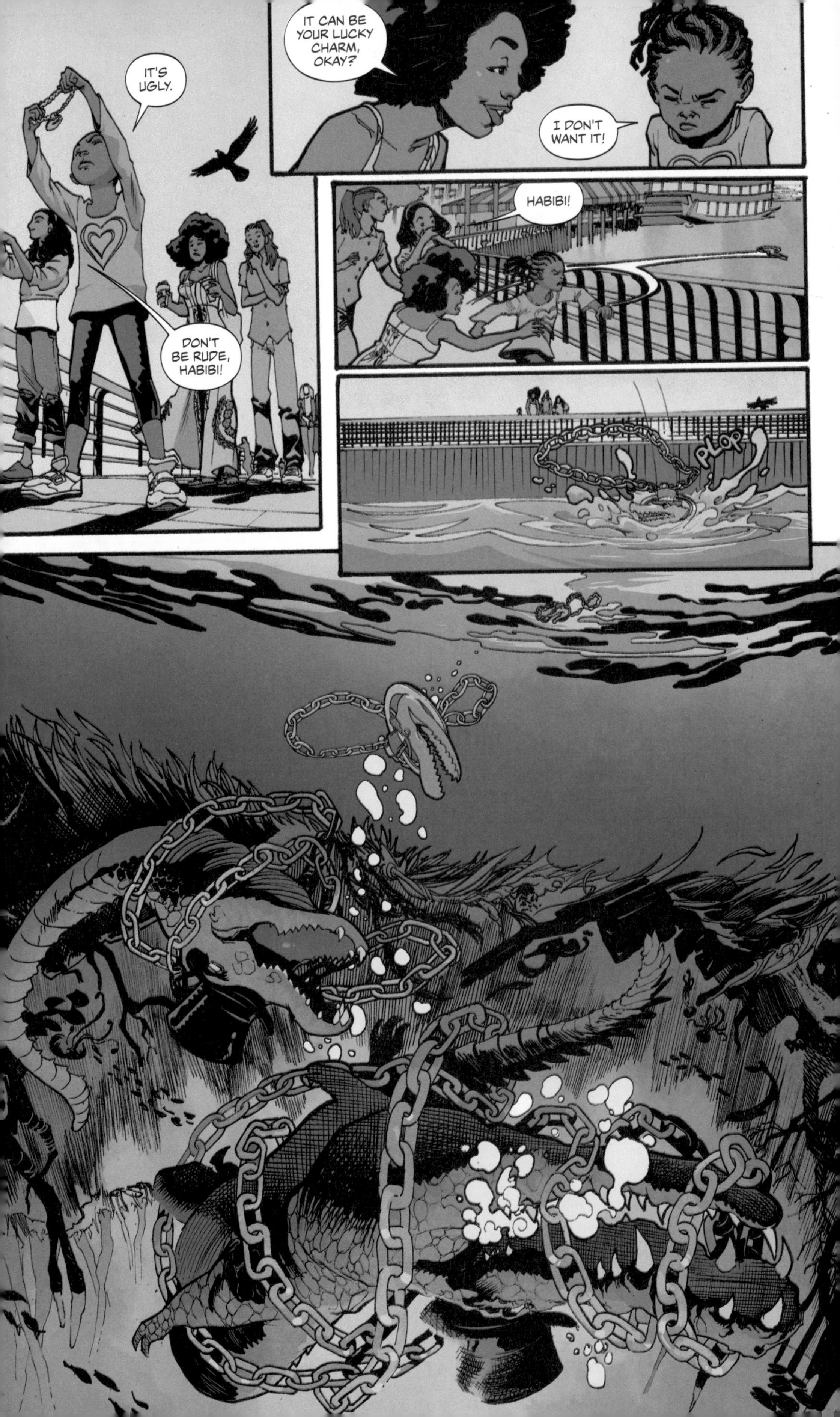
IT'S UGLY.
DON'T BE RUDE, HABIBI!
IT CAN BE YOUR LUCKY CHARM, OKAY?
I DON'T WANT IT!
HABIBI!
PLOP

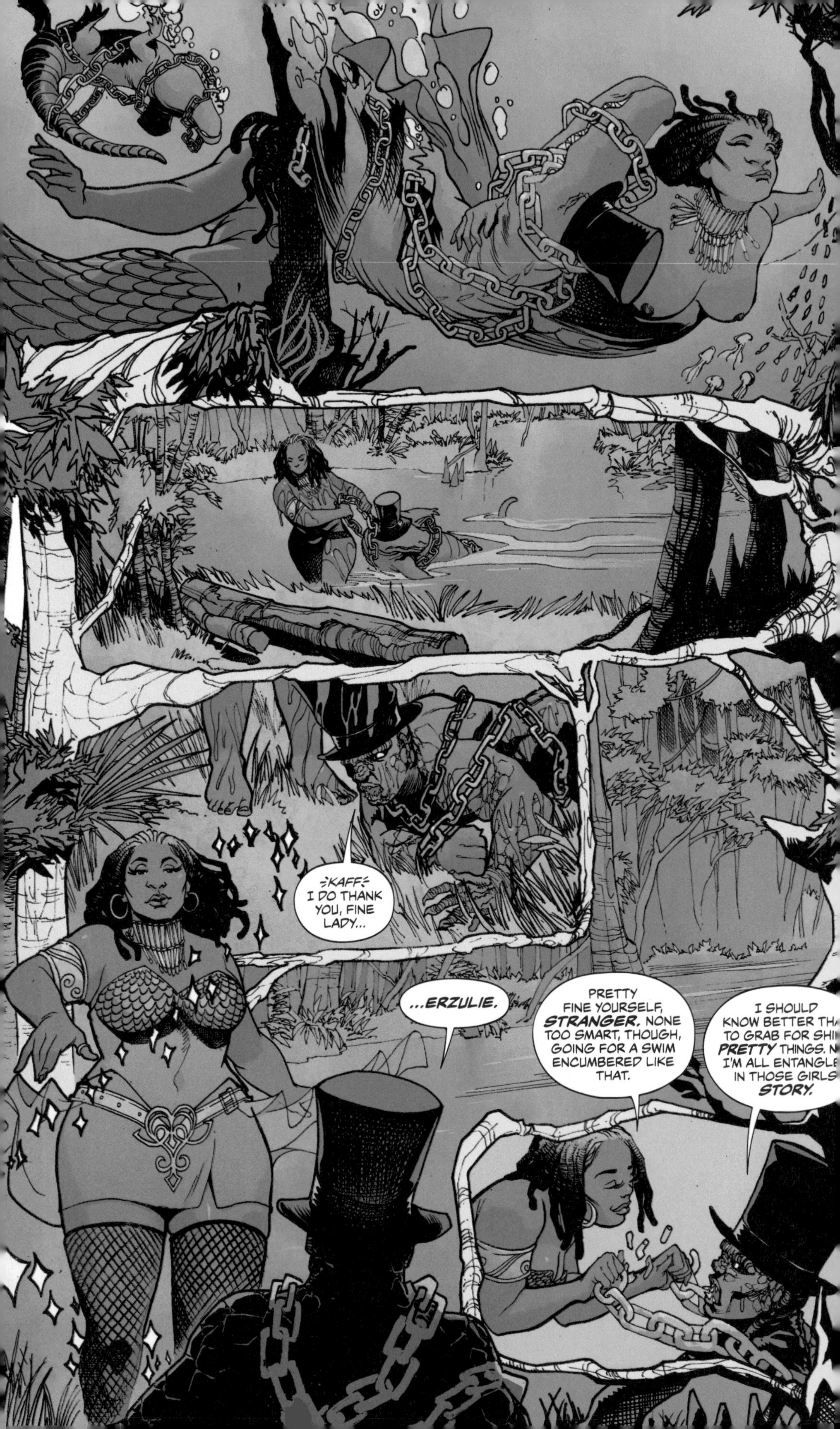

-KAFF- I DO THANK YOU, FINE LADY...
...ERZULIE.
PRETTY FINE YOURSELF, STRANGER. NONE TOO SMART, THOUGH, GOING FOR A SWIM ENCUMBERED LIKE THAT.
I SHOULD KNOW BETTER TH TO GRAB FOR SHI PRETTY THINGS. N I'M ALL ENTANGLE IN THOSE GIRLS STORY.

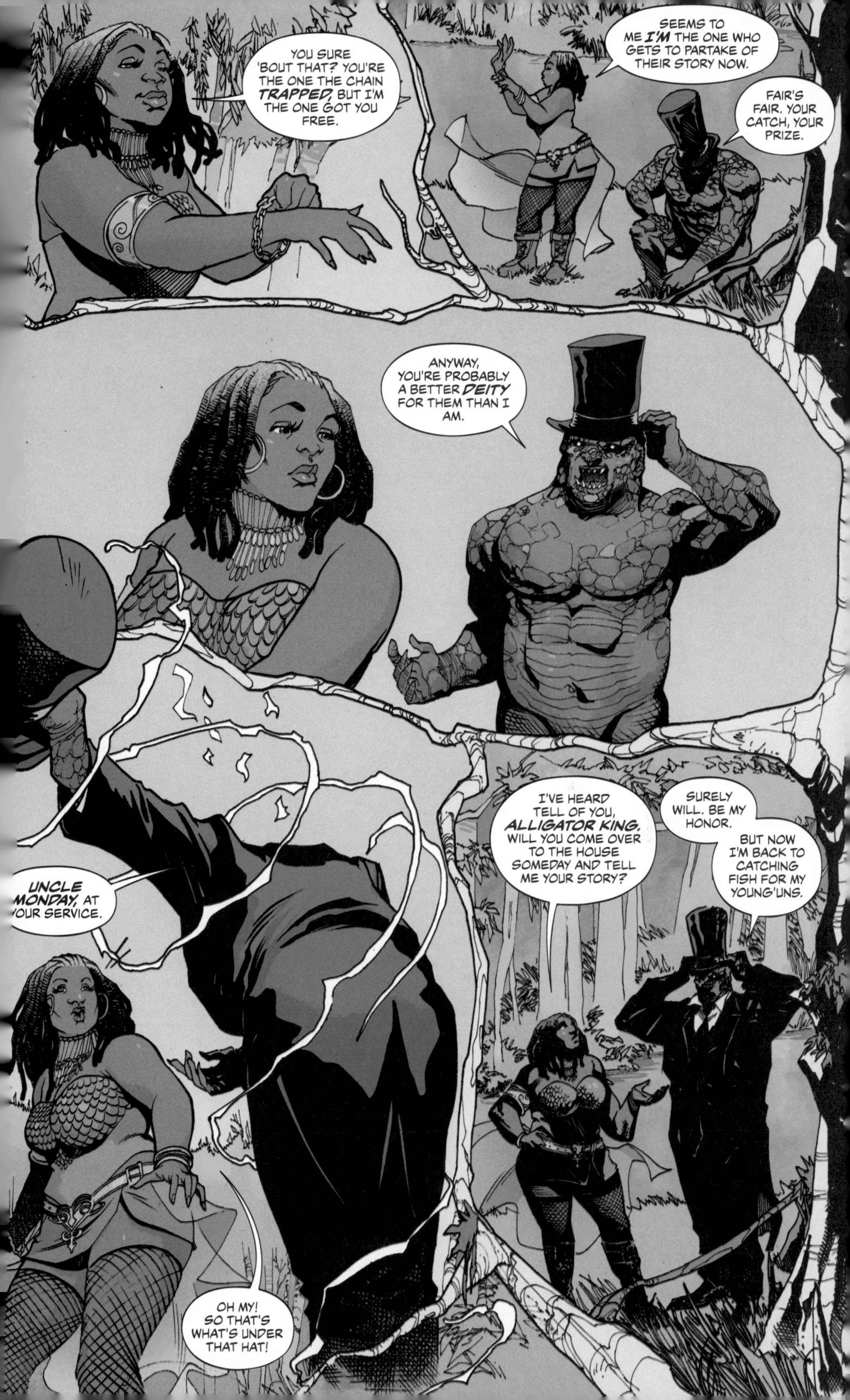
YOU SURE 'BOUT THAT? YOU'RE THE ONE THE CHAIN TRAPPED, BUT I'M THE ONE GOT YOU FREE.
SEEMS TO ME I'M THE ONE WHO GETS TO PARTAKE OF THEIR STORY NOW.
FAIR'S FAIR. YOUR CATCH, YOUR PRIZE.
ANYWAY, YOU'RE PROBABLY A BETTER DEITY FOR THEM THAN I AM.
UNCLE MONDAY, AT YOUR SERVICE.
OH MY! SO THAT'S WHAT'S UNDER THAT HAT!
I'VE HEARD TELL OF YOU, ALLIGATOR KING. WILL YOU COME OVER TO THE HOUSE SOMEDAY AND TELL ME YOUR STORY?
SURELY WILL. BE MY HONOR.
BUT NOW I'M BACK TO CATCHING FISH FOR MY YOUNG'UNS.

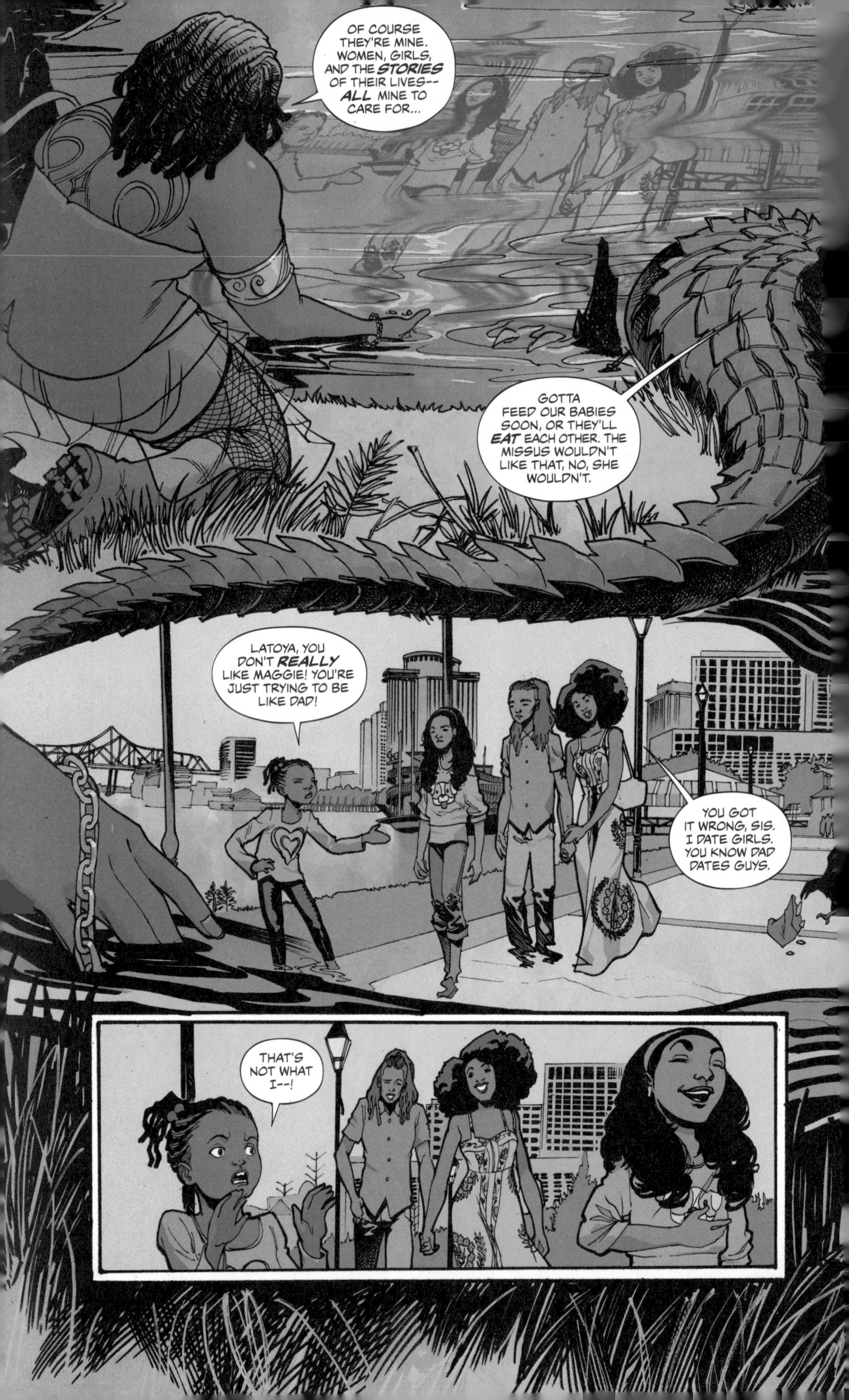
OF COURSE THEY'RE MINE. WOMEN, GIRLS, AND THE STORIES OF THEIR LIVES-- ALL MINE TO CARE FOR...
GOTTA FEED OUR BABIES SOON, OR THEY'LL EAT EACH OTHER. THE MISSUS WOULDN'T LIKE THAT, NO, SHE WOULDN'T.
LATOYA, YOU DON'T REALLY LIKE MAGGIE! YOU'RE JUST TRYING TO BE LIKE DAD!
YOU GOT IT WRONG, SIS. I DATE GIRLS. YOU KNOW DAD DATES GUYS.
THAT'S NOT WHAT I--!

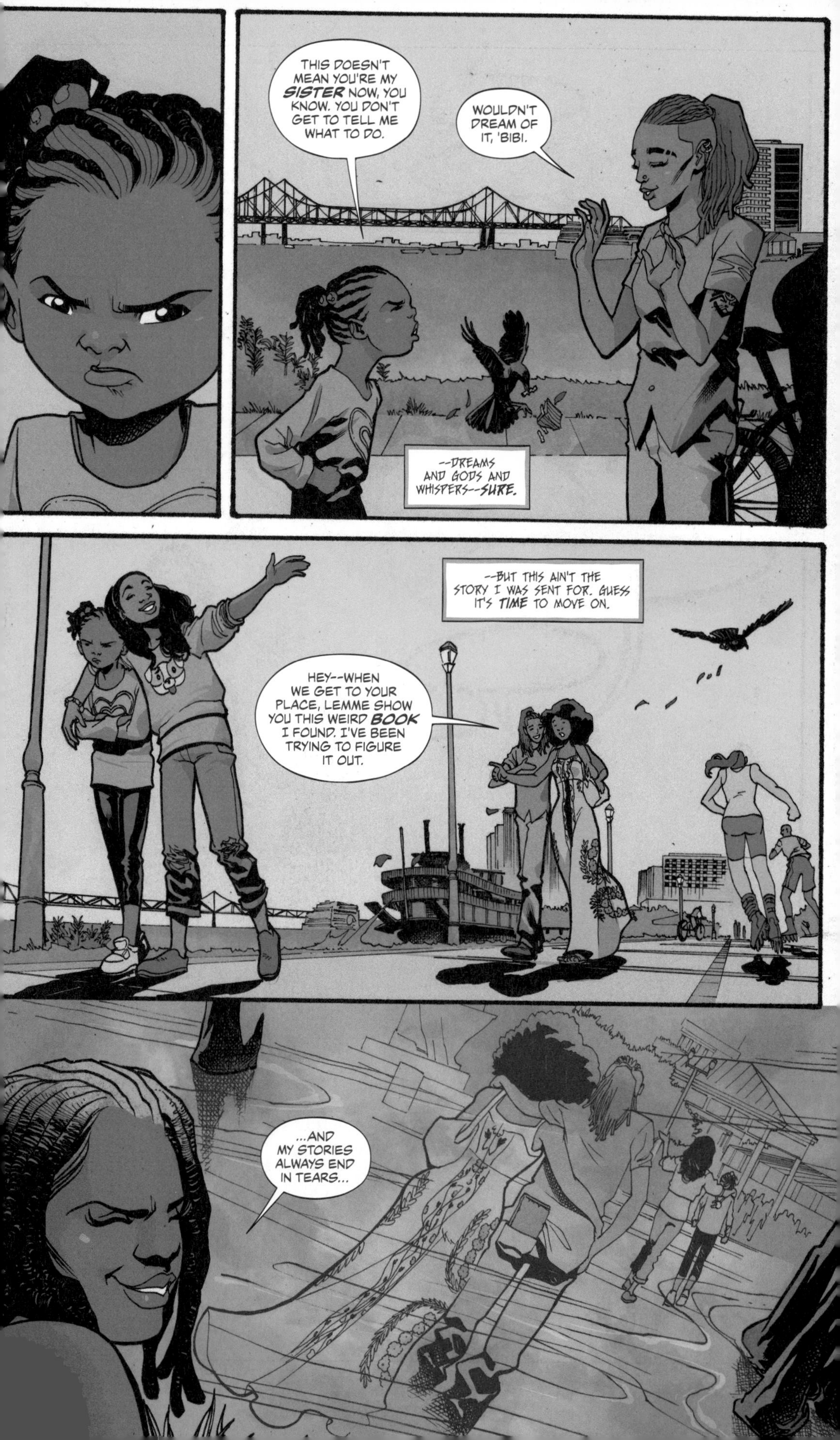
THIS DOESN'T MEAN YOU'RE MY SISTER NOW, YOU KNOW. YOU DON'T GET TO TELL ME WHAT TO DO.
WOULDN'T DREAM OF IT, 'BIBI.
--DREAMS AND GODS AND WHISPERS--SURE.
--BUT THIS AIN'T THE STORY I WAS SENT FOR. GUESS IT'S TIME TO MOVE ON.
HEY--WHEN WE GET TO YOUR PLACE, LEMME SHOW YOU THIS WEIRD BOOK I FOUND. I'VE BEEN TRYING TO FIGURE IT OUT.
...AND MY STORIES ALWAYS END IN TEARS...

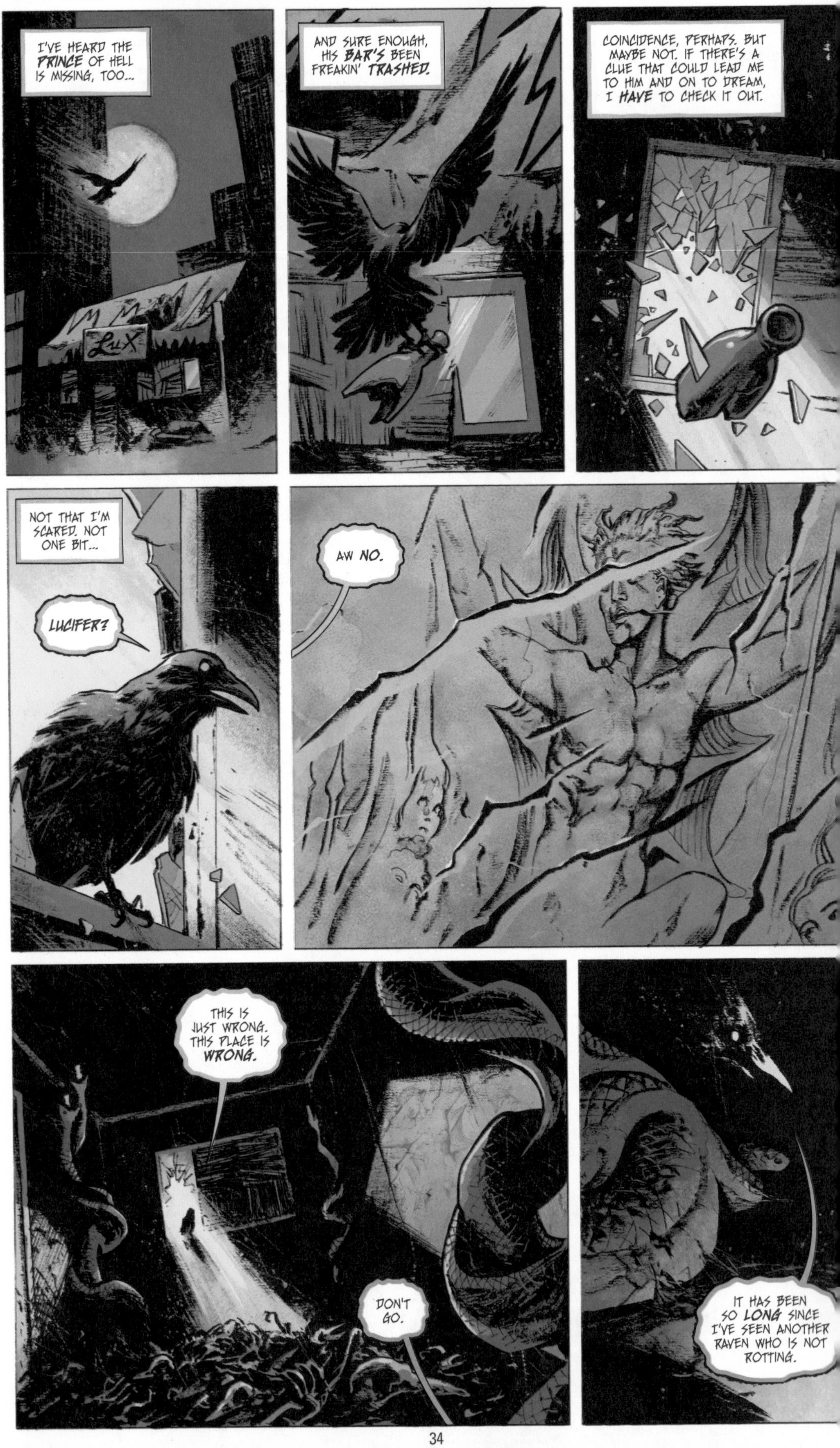

I'VE HEARD THE PRINCE OF HELL IS MISSING, TOO...
AND SURE ENOUGH, HIS BAR'S BEEN FREAKIN' TRASHED.
COINCIDENCE, PERHAPS. BUT MAYBE NOT. IF THERE'S A CLUE THAT COULD LEAD ME TO HIM AND ON TO DREAM, I HAVE TO CHECK IT OUT.
LUX
NOT THAT I'M SCARED. NOT ONE BIT...
LUCIFER?
AW NO.
THIS IS JUST WRONG. THIS PLACE IS WRONG.
DON'T GO.
IT HAS BEEN SO LONG SINCE I'VE SEEN ANOTHER RAVEN WHO IS NOT ROTTING.

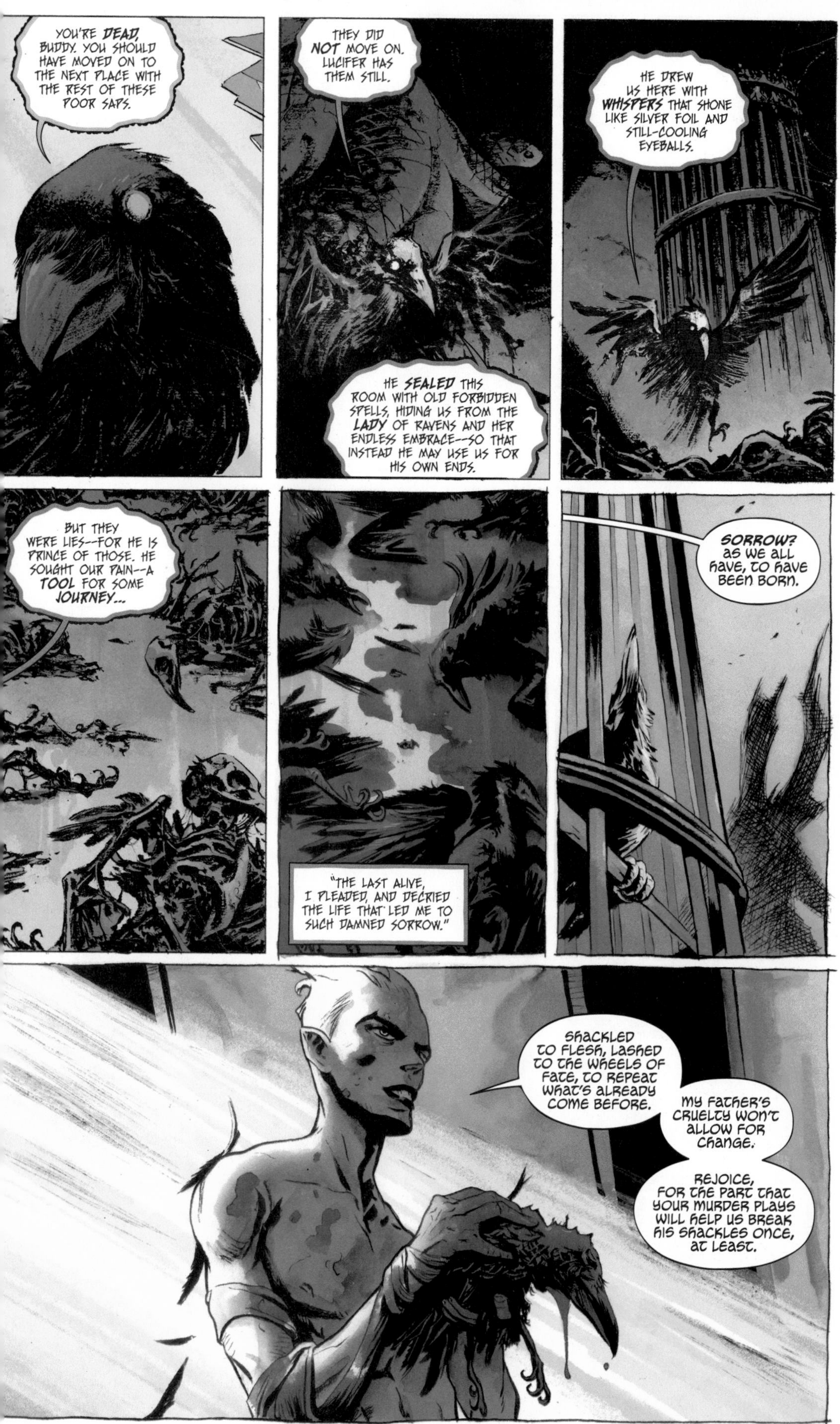
YOU'RE DEAD, BUDDY. YOU SHOULD HAVE MOVED ON TO THE NEXT PLACE WITH THE REST OF THESE POOR SAPS.
THEY DID NOT MOVE ON. LUCIFER HAS THEM STILL.
HE SEALED THIS ROOM WITH OLD FORBIDDEN SPELLS, HIDING US FROM THE LADY OF RAVENS AND HER ENDLESS EMBRACE--SO THAT INSTEAD HE MAY USE US FOR HIS OWN ENDS.
HE DREW US HERE WITH WHISPERS THAT SHONE LIKE SILVER FOIL AND STILL-COOLING EYEBALLS.
BUT THEY WERE LIES--FOR HE IS PRINCE OF THOSE. HE SOUGHT OUR PAIN--A TOOL FOR SOME JOURNEY...
"THE LAST ALIVE, I PLEADED, AND DECRIED THE LIFE THAT LED ME TO SUCH DAMNED SORROW."
SORROW? AS WE ALL HAVE, TO HAVE BEEN BORN.
SHACKLED TO FLESH, LASHED TO THE WHEELS OF FATE, TO REPEAT WHAT'S ALREADY COME BEFORE.
MY FATHER'S CRUELTY WON'T ALLOW FOR CHANGE.
REJOICE, FOR THE PART THAT YOUR MURDER PLAYS WILL HELP US BREAK HIS SHACKLES ONCE, AT LEAST.

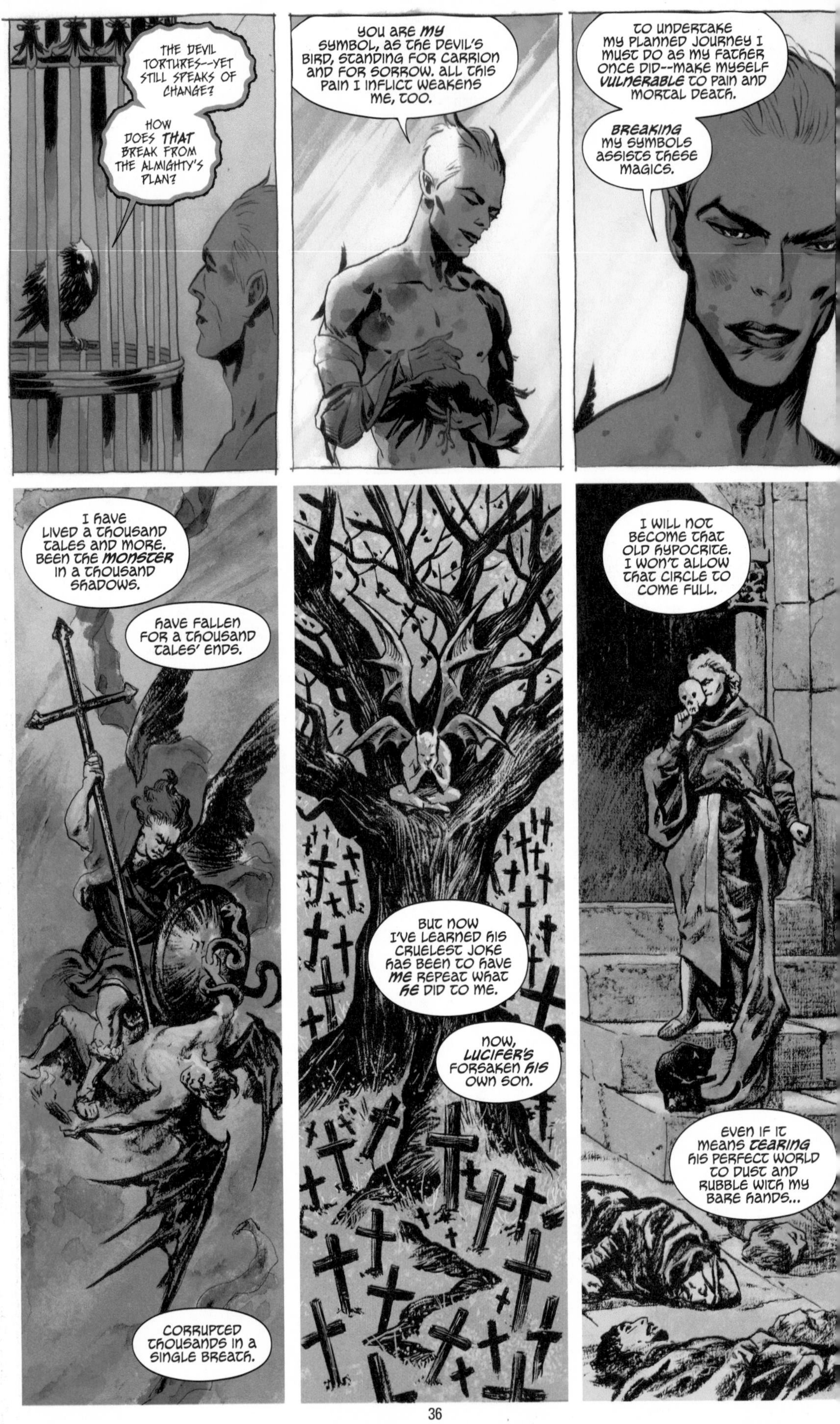
THE DEVIL TORTURES--YET STILL SPEAKS OF CHANGE?
HOW DOES THAT BREAK FROM THE ALMIGHTY'S PLAN?
YOU ARE MY SYMBOL, AS THE DEVIL'S BIRD, STANDING FOR CARRION AND FOR SORROW. ALL THIS PAIN I INFLICT WEAKENS ME, TOO.
TO UNDERTAKE MY PLANNED JOURNEY I MUST DO AS MY FATHER ONCE DID--MAKE MYSELF VULNERABLE TO PAIN AND MORTAL DEATH.
BREAKING MY SYMBOLS ASSISTS THESE MAGICS.
I HAVE LIVED A THOUSAND TALES AND MORE. BEEN THE MONSTER IN A THOUSAND SHADOWS.
HAVE FALLEN FOR A THOUSAND TALES' ENDS.
CORRUPTED THOUSANDS IN A SINGLE BREATH.
BUT NOW I'VE LEARNED HIS CRUELEST JOKE HAS BEEN TO HAVE ME REPEAT WHAT HE DID TO ME.
NOW, LUCIFER'S FORSAKEN HIS OWN SON.
I WILL NOT BECOME THAT OLD HYPOCRITE. I WON'T ALLOW THAT CIRCLE TO COME FULL.
EVEN IF IT MEANS TEARING HIS PERFECT WORLD TO DUST AND RUBBLE WITH MY BARE HANDS...

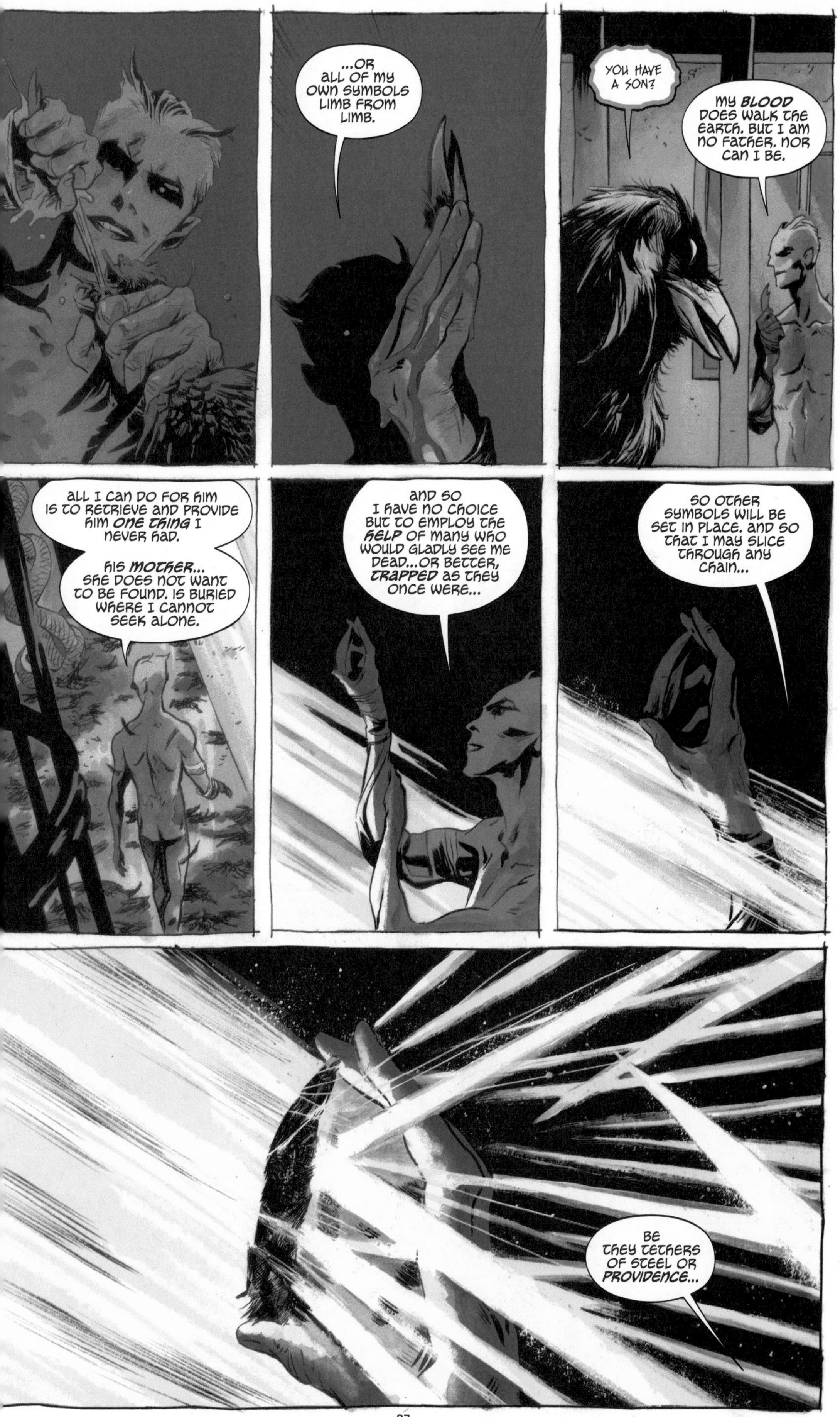
...OR ALL OF MY OWN SYMBOLS LIMB FROM LIMB.
YOU HAVE A SON?
MY **BLOOD** DOES WALK THE EARTH. BUT I AM NO FATHER. NOR CAN I BE.
ALL I CAN DO FOR HIM IS TO RETRIEVE AND PROVIDE HIM **ONE THING** I NEVER HAD.
HIS **MOTHER**... SHE DOES NOT WANT TO BE FOUND. IS BURIED WHERE I CANNOT SEEK ALONE.
AND SO I HAVE NO CHOICE BUT TO EMPLOY THE **HELP** OF MANY WHO WOULD GLADLY SEE ME DEAD...OR BETTER, **TRAPPED** AS THEY ONCE WERE...
SO OTHER SYMBOLS WILL BE SET IN PLACE. AND SO THAT I MAY SLICE THROUGH ANY CHAIN...
BE THEY TETHERS OF STEEL OR **PROVIDENCE**...

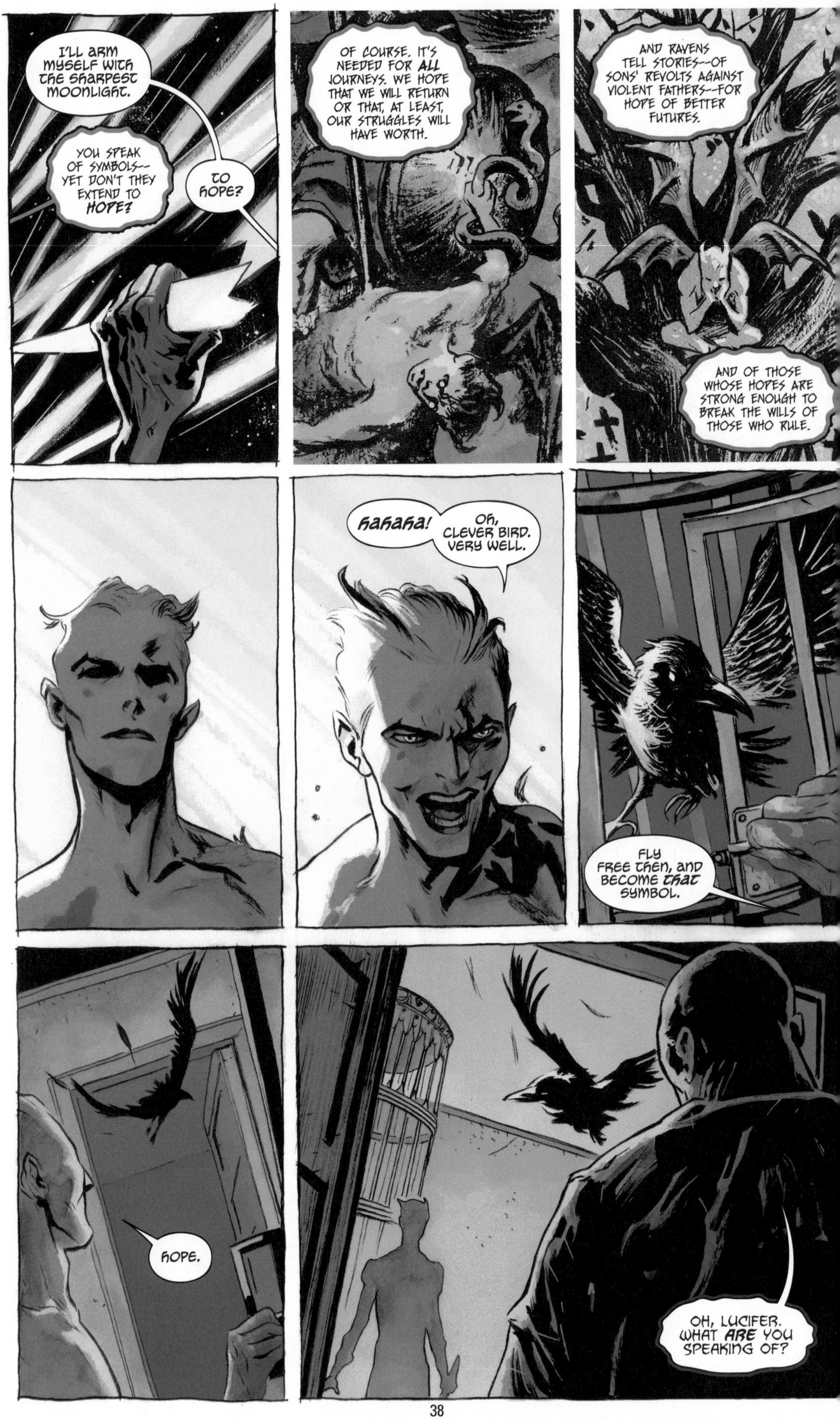
I'LL ARM MYSELF WITH THE SHARPEST MOONLIGHT.
YOU SPEAK OF SYMBOLS-- YET DON'T THEY EXTEND TO HOPE?
TO HOPE?
OF COURSE. IT'S NEEDED FOR ALL JOURNEYS. WE HOPE THAT WE WILL RETURN OR THAT, AT LEAST, OUR STRUGGLES WILL HAVE WORTH.
AND RAVENS TELL STORIES--OF SONS' REVOLTS AGAINST VIOLENT FATHERS--FOR HOPE OF BETTER FUTURES.
AND OF THOSE WHOSE HOPES ARE STRONG ENOUGH TO BREAK THE WILLS OF THOSE WHO RULE.
HAHAHA!
OH, CLEVER BIRD. VERY WELL.
FLY FREE THEN, AND BECOME THAT SYMBOL.
HOPE.
OH, LUCIFER. WHAT ARE YOU SPEAKING OF?

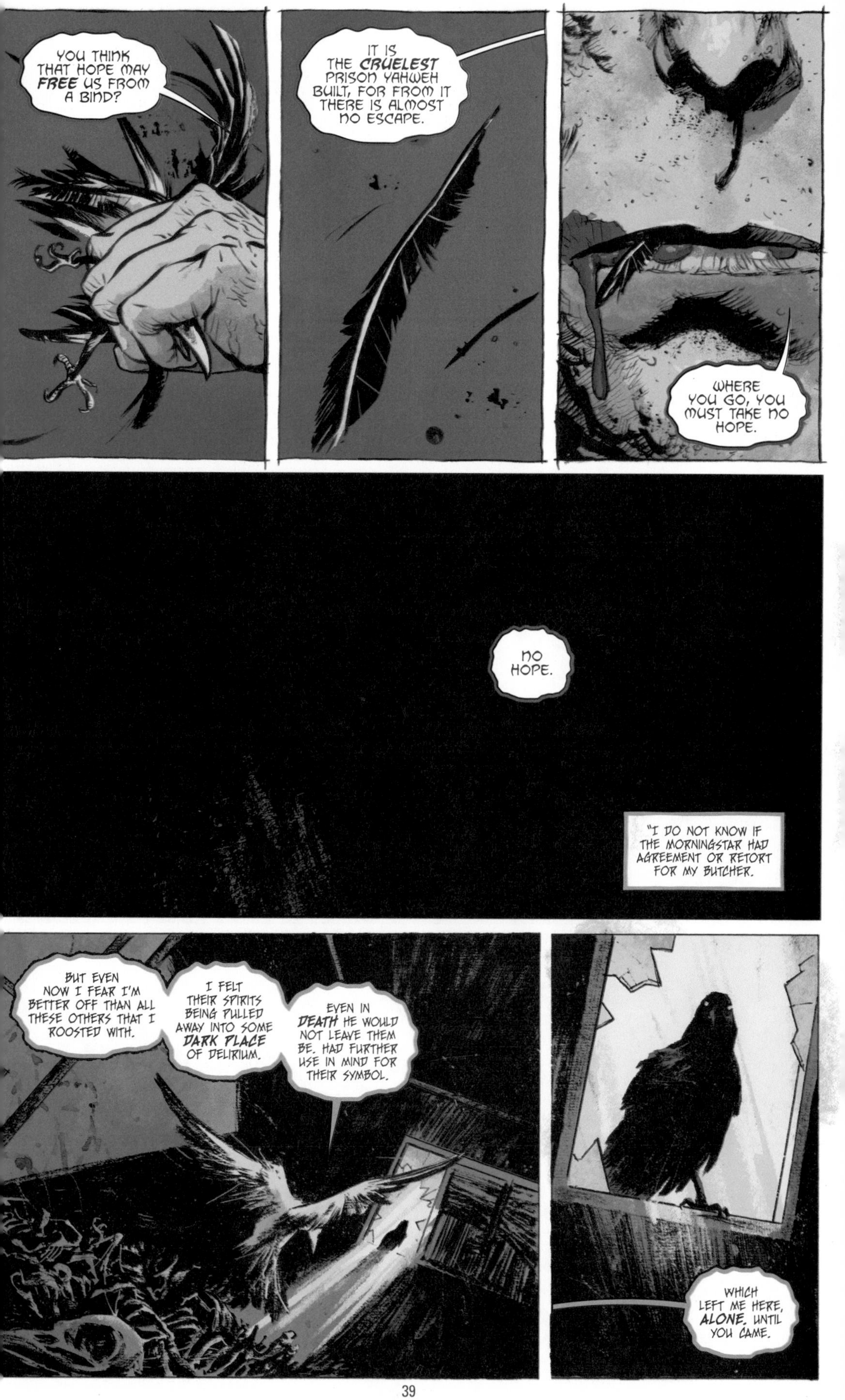

YOU THINK THAT HOPE MAY FREE US FROM A BIND?
IT IS THE CRUELEST PRISON YAHWEH BUILT, FOR FROM IT THERE IS ALMOST NO ESCAPE.
WHERE YOU GO, YOU MUST TAKE NO HOPE.
NO HOPE.
"I DO NOT KNOW IF THE MORNINGSTAR HAD AGREEMENT OR RETORT FOR MY BUTCHER.
BUT EVEN NOW I FEAR I'M BETTER OFF THAN ALL THESE OTHERS THAT I ROOSTED WITH.
I FELT THEIR SPIRITS BEING PULLED AWAY INTO SOME DARK PLACE OF DELIRIUM.
EVEN IN DEATH HE WOULD NOT LEAVE THEM BE. HAD FURTHER USE IN MIND FOR THEIR SYMBOL.
WHICH LEFT ME HERE, ALONE, UNTIL YOU CAME.

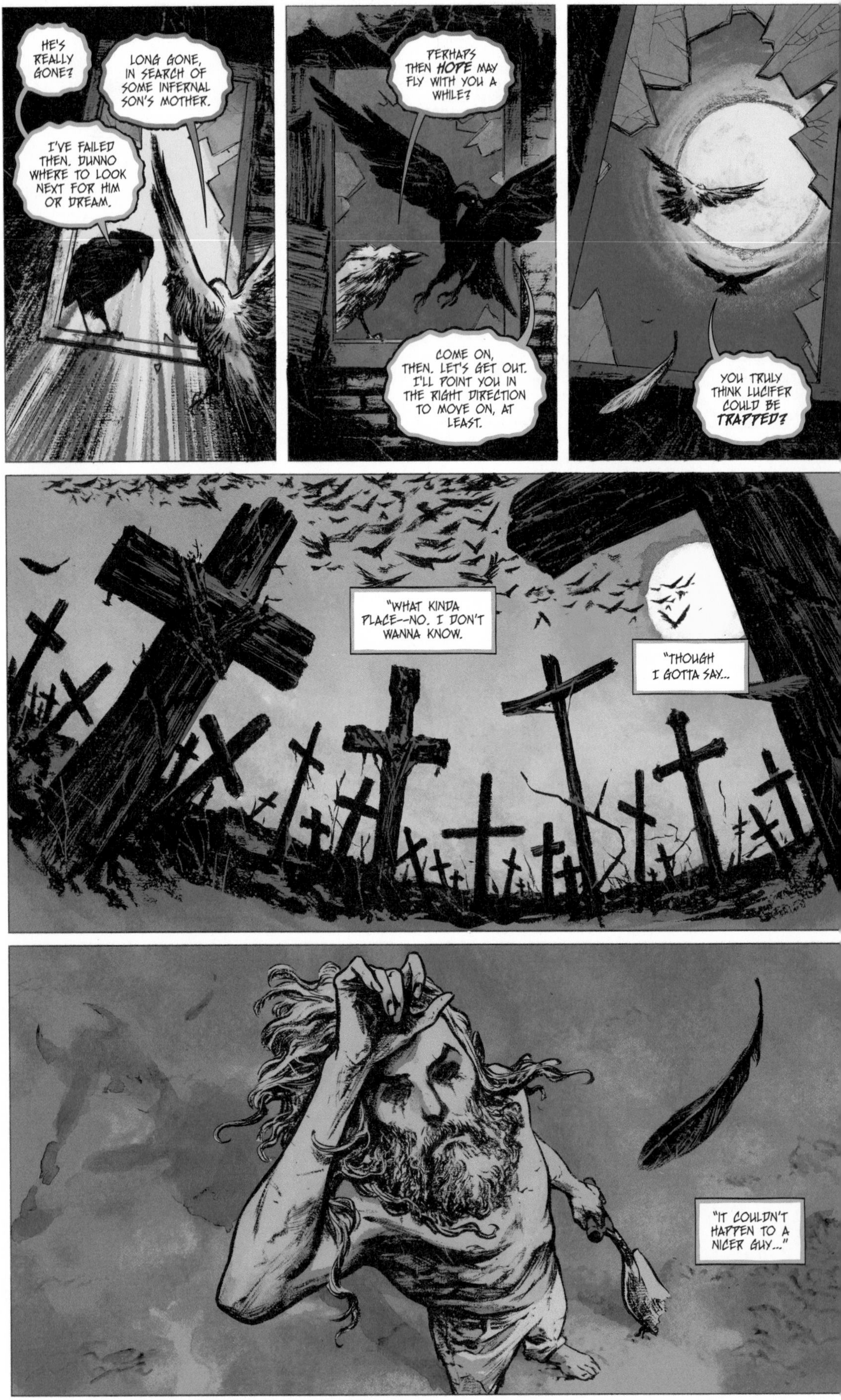

HE'S REALLY GONE?
LONG GONE, IN SEARCH OF SOME INFERNAL SON'S MOTHER.
I'VE FAILED THEN. DUNNO WHERE TO LOOK NEXT FOR HIM OR DREAM.
PERHAPS THEN HOPE MAY FLY WITH YOU A WHILE?
COME ON, THEN. LET'S GET OUT. I'LL POINT YOU IN THE RIGHT DIRECTION TO MOVE ON, AT LEAST.
YOU TRULY THINK LUCIFER COULD BE TRAPPED?
"WHAT KINDA PLACE--NO. I DON'T WANNA KNOW.
"THOUGH I GOTTA SAY...
"IT COULDN'T HAPPEN TO A NICER GUY..."

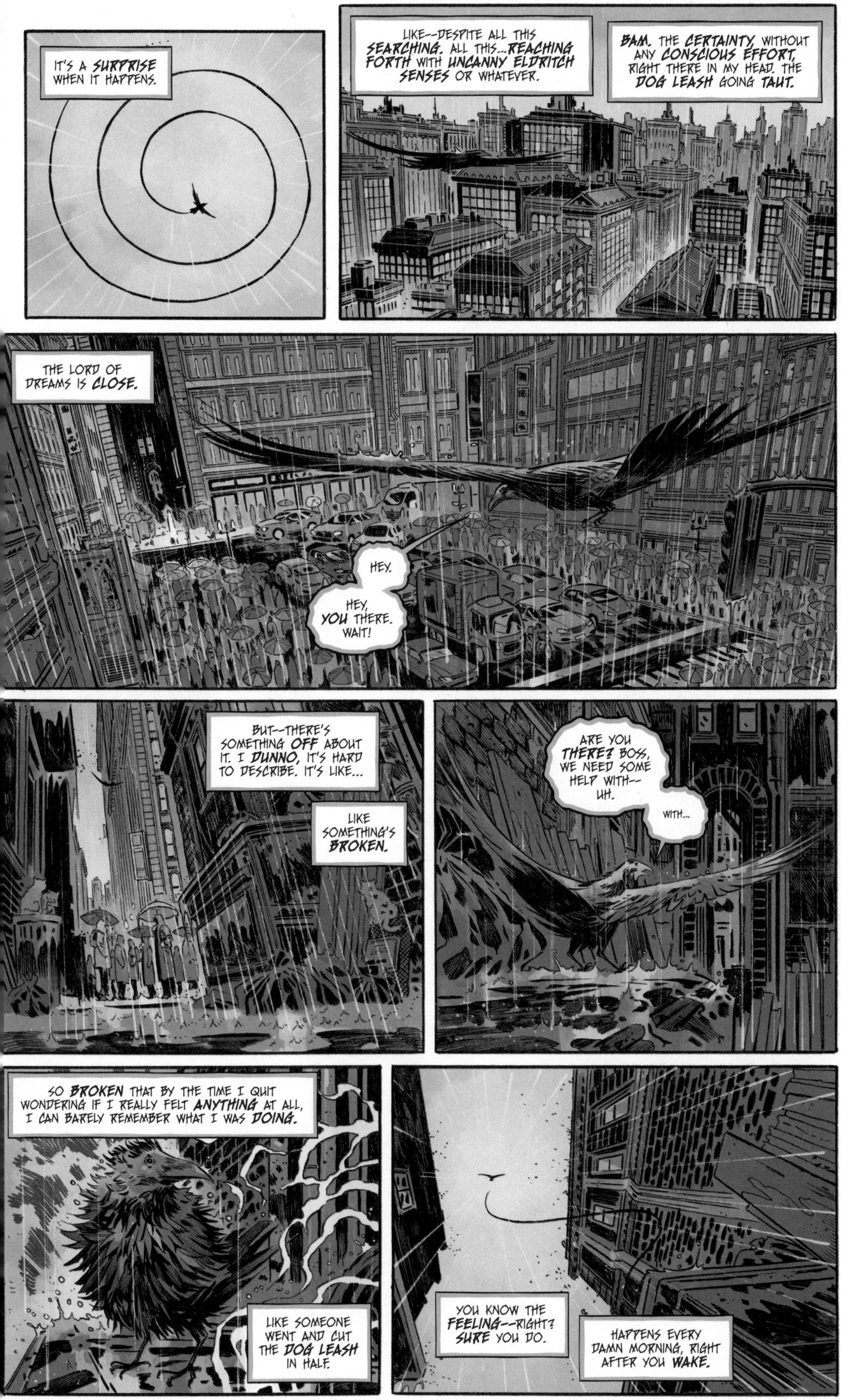
IT'S A SURPRISE WHEN IT HAPPENS.
LIKE--DESPITE ALL THIS SEARCHING. ALL THIS...REACHING FORTH WITH UNCANNY ELDRITCH SENSES OR WHATEVER.
BAM. THE CERTAINTY, WITHOUT ANY CONSCIOUS EFFORT, RIGHT THERE IN MY HEAD. THE DOG LEASH GOING TAUT.
THE LORD OF DREAMS IS CLOSE.
HEY.
HEY, YOU THERE. WAIT!
BUT--THERE'S SOMETHING OFF ABOUT IT. I DUNNO, IT'S HARD TO DESCRIBE. IT'S LIKE...
LIKE SOMETHING'S BROKEN.
ARE YOU THERE? BOSS, WE NEED SOME HELP WITH-- UH.
WITH...
SO BROKEN THAT BY THE TIME I QUIT WONDERING IF I REALLY FELT ANYTHING AT ALL, I CAN BARELY REMEMBER WHAT I WAS DOING.
LIKE SOMEONE WENT AND CUT THE DOG LEASH IN HALF.
YOU KNOW THE FEELING--RIGHT? SURE YOU DO.
HAPPENS EVERY DAMN MORNING, RIGHT AFTER YOU WAKE.

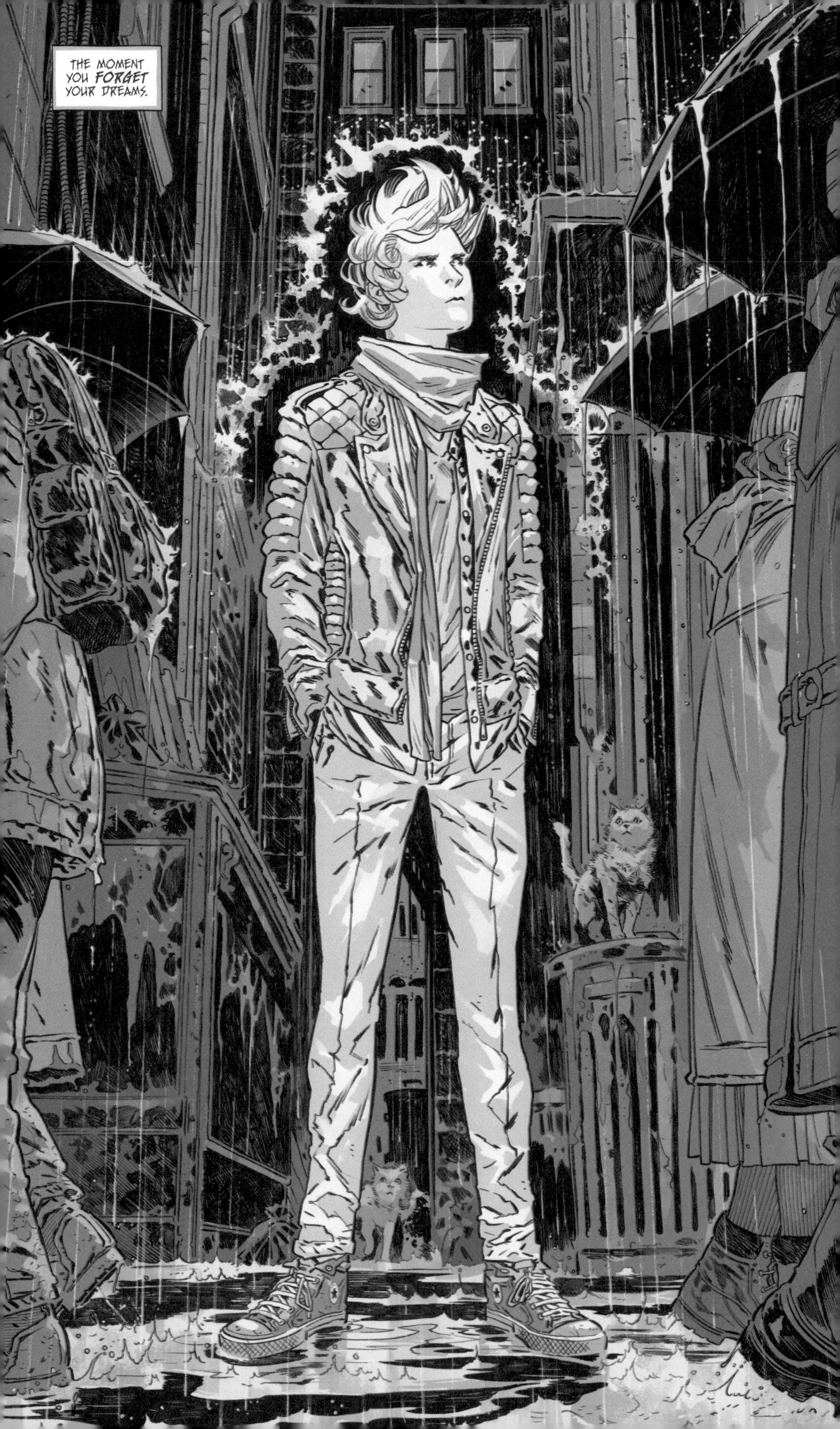
THE MOMENT YOU FORGET YOUR DREAMS.

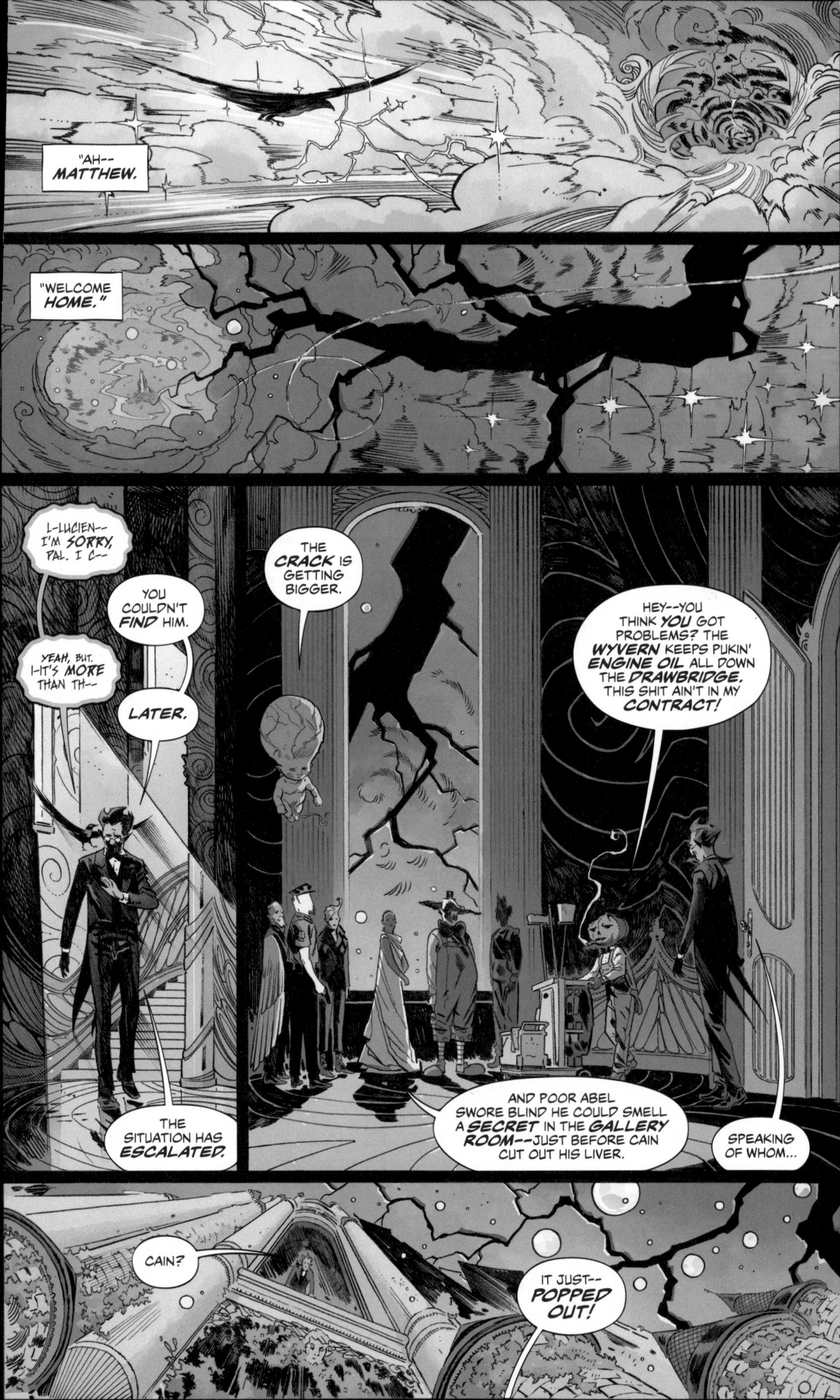
"AH--
MATTHEW.
"WELCOME
HOME."
L-LUCIEN--
I'M SORRY,
PAL. I C--
YOU
COULDN'T
FIND HIM.
YEAH, BUT.
I-IT'S MORE
THAN TH--
LATER.
THE
SITUATION HAS
ESCALATED.
THE
CRACK IS
GETTING
BIGGER.
HEY--YOU
THINK YOU GOT
PROBLEMS? THE
WYVERN KEEPS PUKIN'
ENGINE OIL ALL DOWN
THE DRAWBRIDGE.
THIS SHIT AIN'T IN MY
CONTRACT!
AND POOR ABEL
SWORE BLIND HE COULD SMELL
A SECRET IN THE GALLERY
ROOM--JUST BEFORE CAIN
CUT OUT HIS LIVER.
SPEAKING
OF WHOM...
CAIN?
IT JUST--
POPPED
OUT!

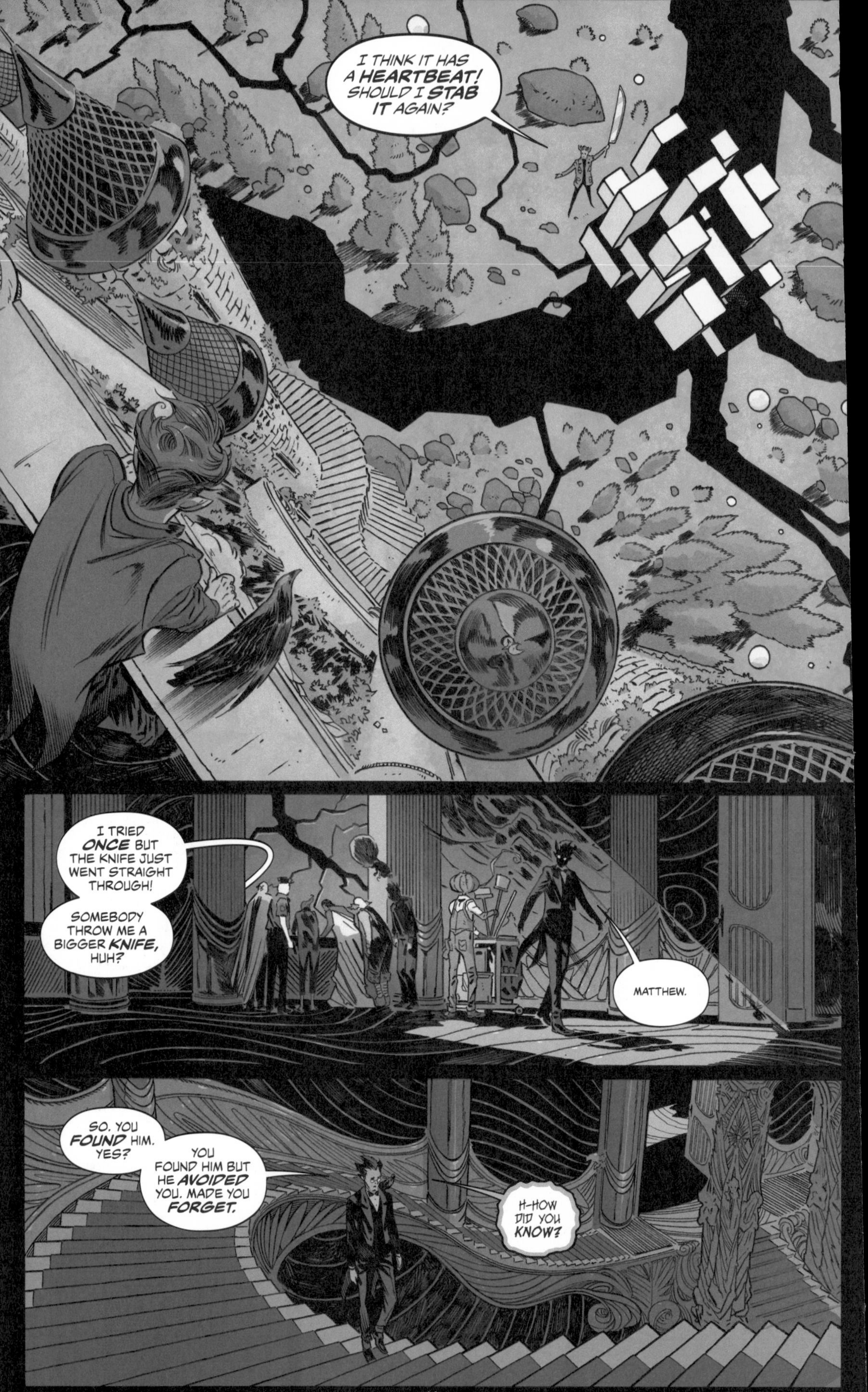
I THINK IT HAS A HEARTBEAT! SHOULD I STAB IT AGAIN?
I TRIED ONCE BUT THE KNIFE JUST WENT STRAIGHT THROUGH!
SOMEBODY THROW ME A BIGGER KNIFE, HUH?
MATTHEW.
SO. YOU FOUND HIM. YES?
YOU FOUND HIM BUT HE AVOIDED YOU. MADE YOU FORGET.
H-HOW DID YOU KNOW?

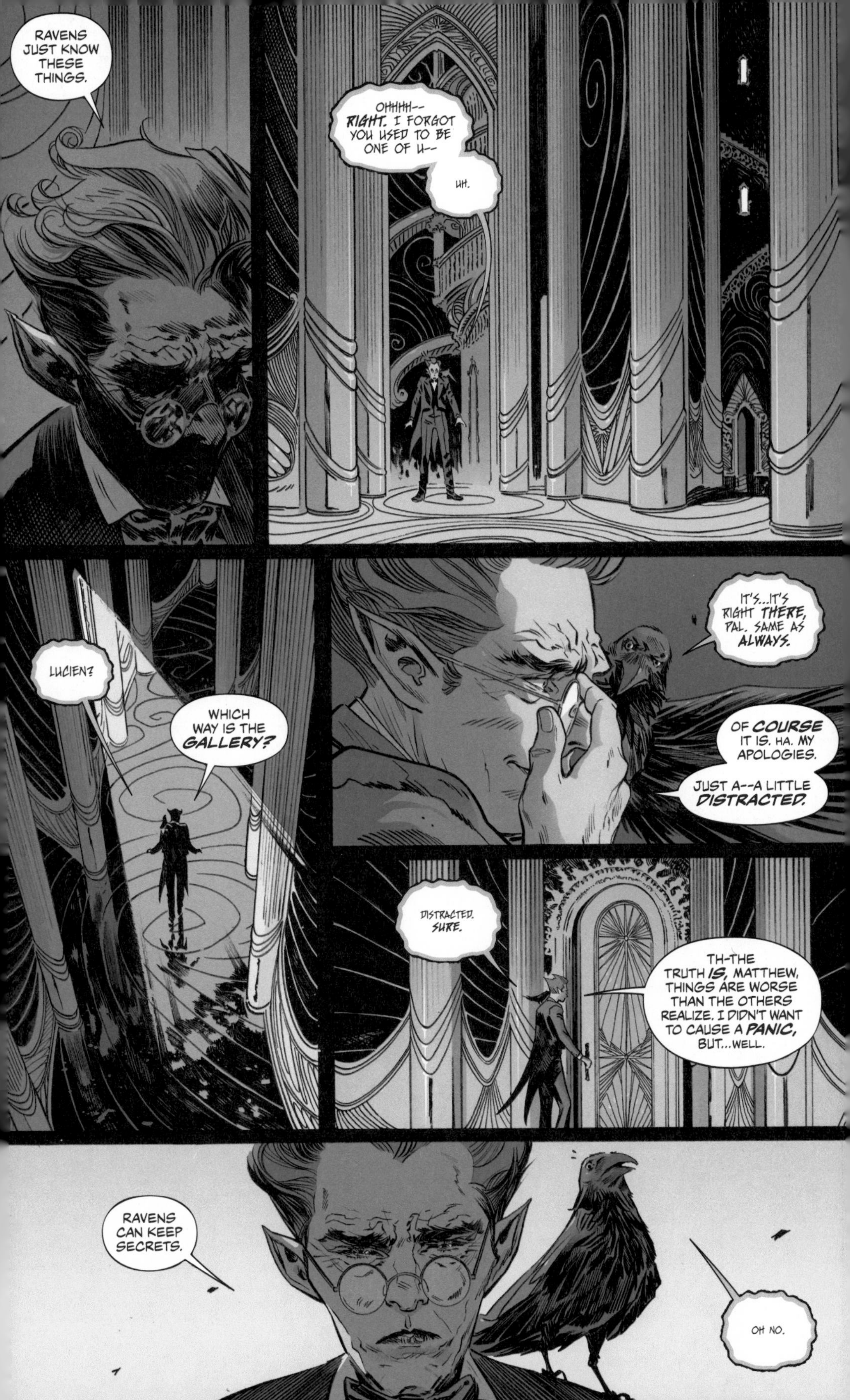
RAVENS JUST KNOW THESE THINGS.
OHHHH-- RIGHT. I FORGOT YOU USED TO BE ONE OF U--
UH.
LUCIEN?
WHICH WAY IS THE GALLERY?
IT'S...IT'S RIGHT THERE, PAL. SAME AS ALWAYS.
OF COURSE IT IS. HA. MY APOLOGIES.
JUST A--A LITTLE DISTRACTED.
DISTRACTED. SURE.
TH-THE TRUTH IS, MATTHEW, THINGS ARE WORSE THAN THE OTHERS REALIZE. I DIDN'T WANT TO CAUSE A PANIC, BUT...WELL.
RAVENS CAN KEEP SECRETS.
OH NO.

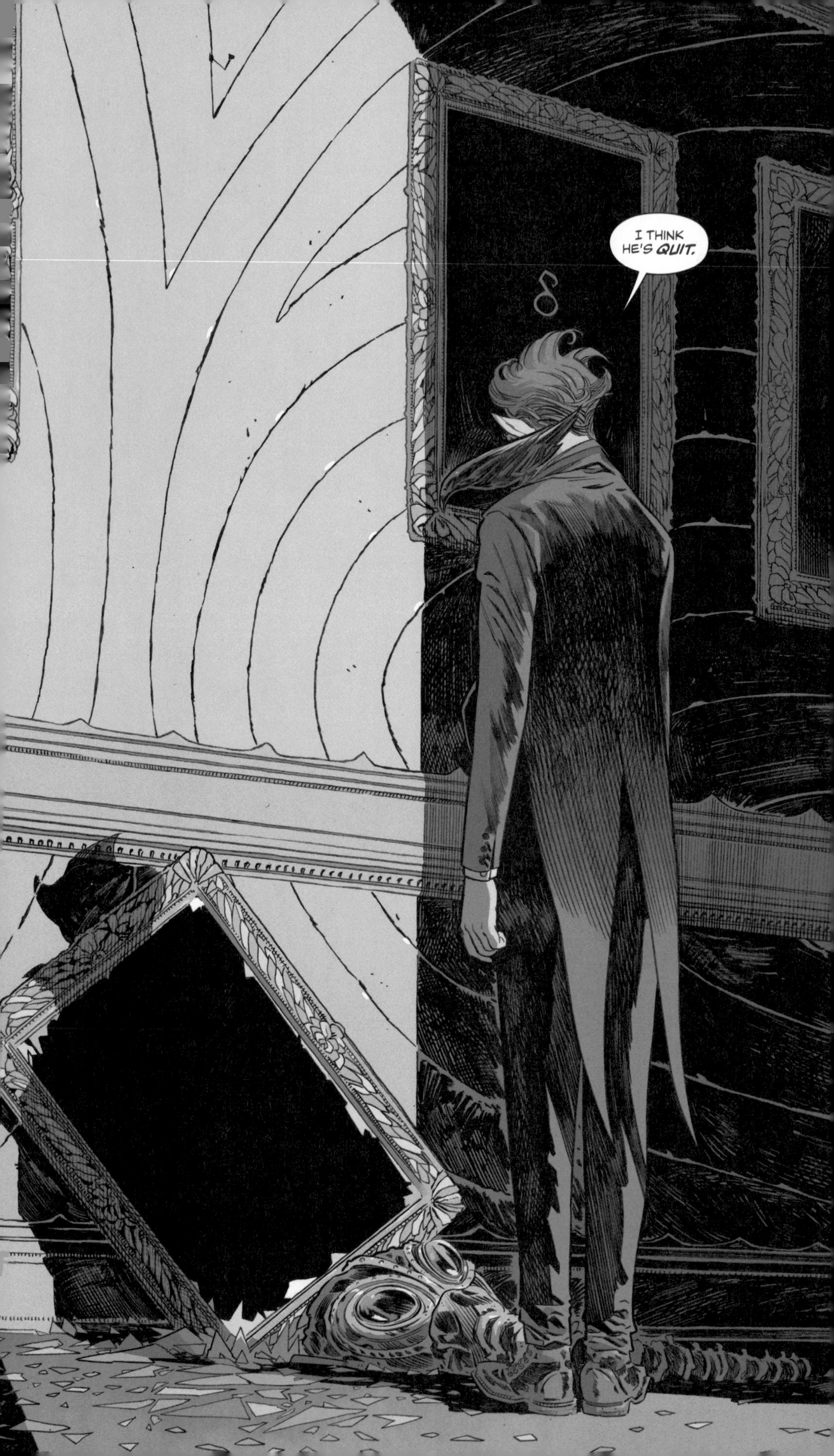
I THINK HE'S QUIT.

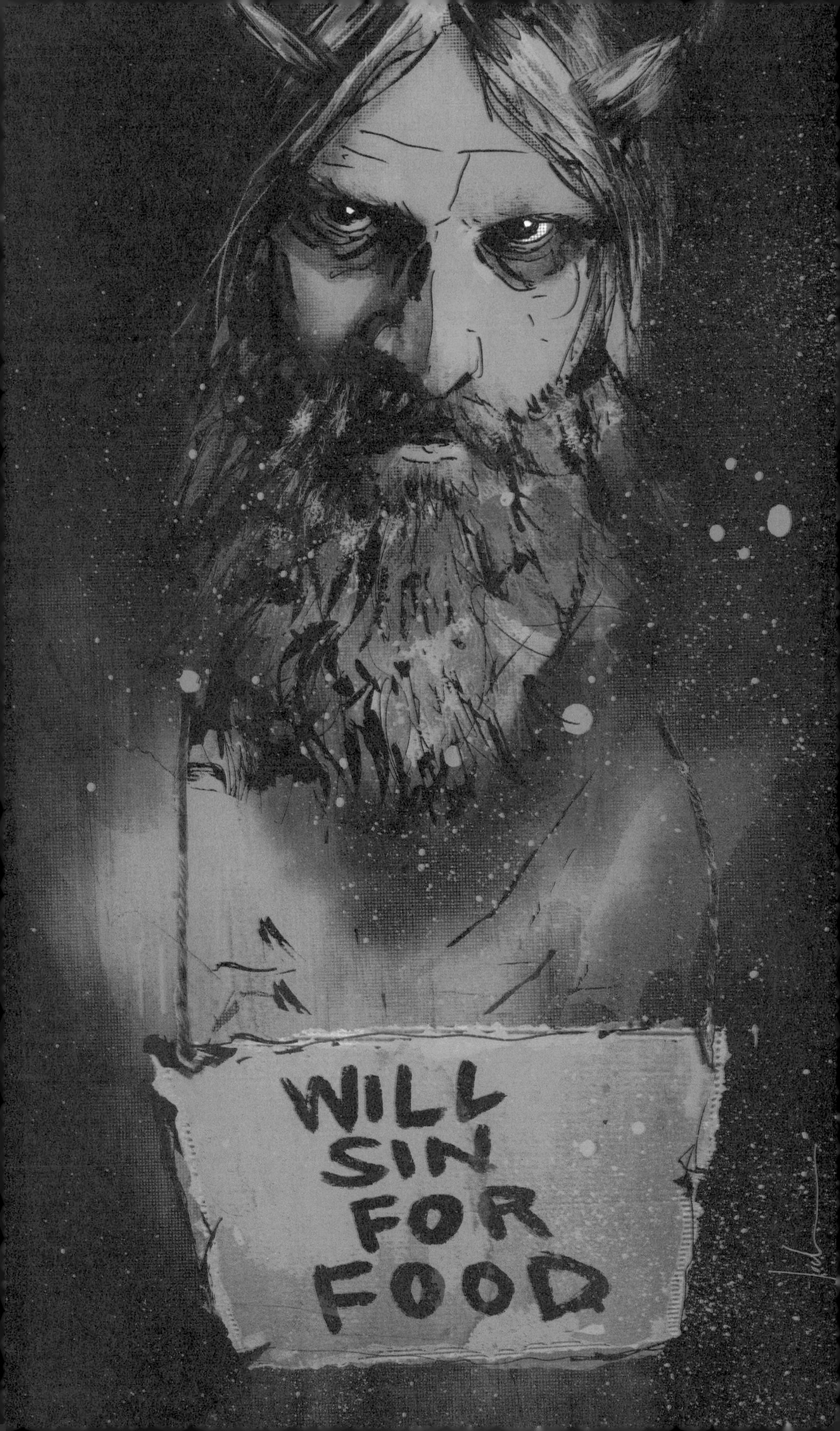
WILL
SIN
FOR
FOOD

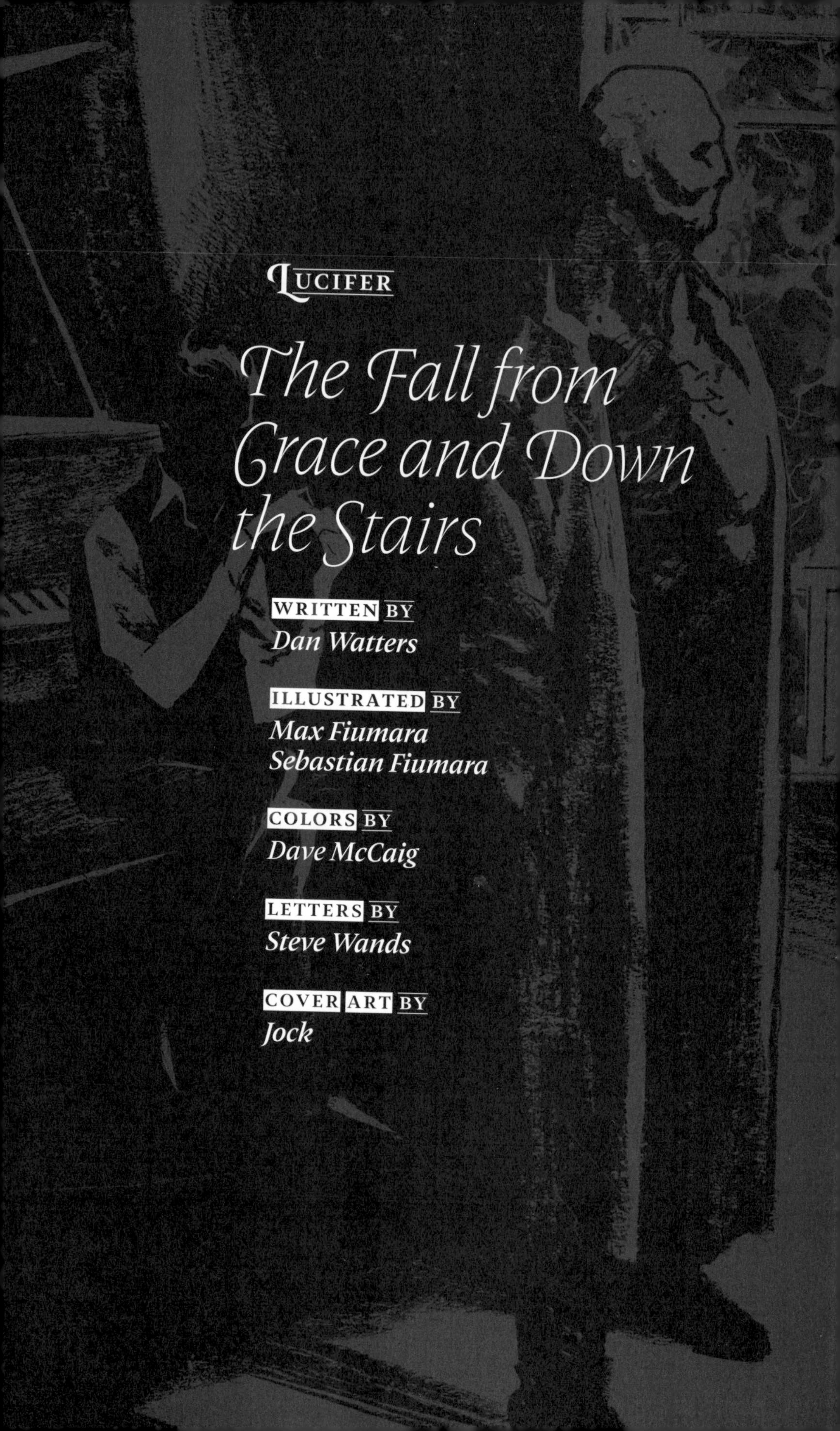

LUCIFER

The Fall from Grace and Down the Stairs

WRITTEN BY
Dan Watters

ILLUSTRATED BY
Max Fiumara
Sebastian Fiumara

COLORS BY
Dave McCaig

LETTERS BY
Steve Wands

COVER ART BY
Jock

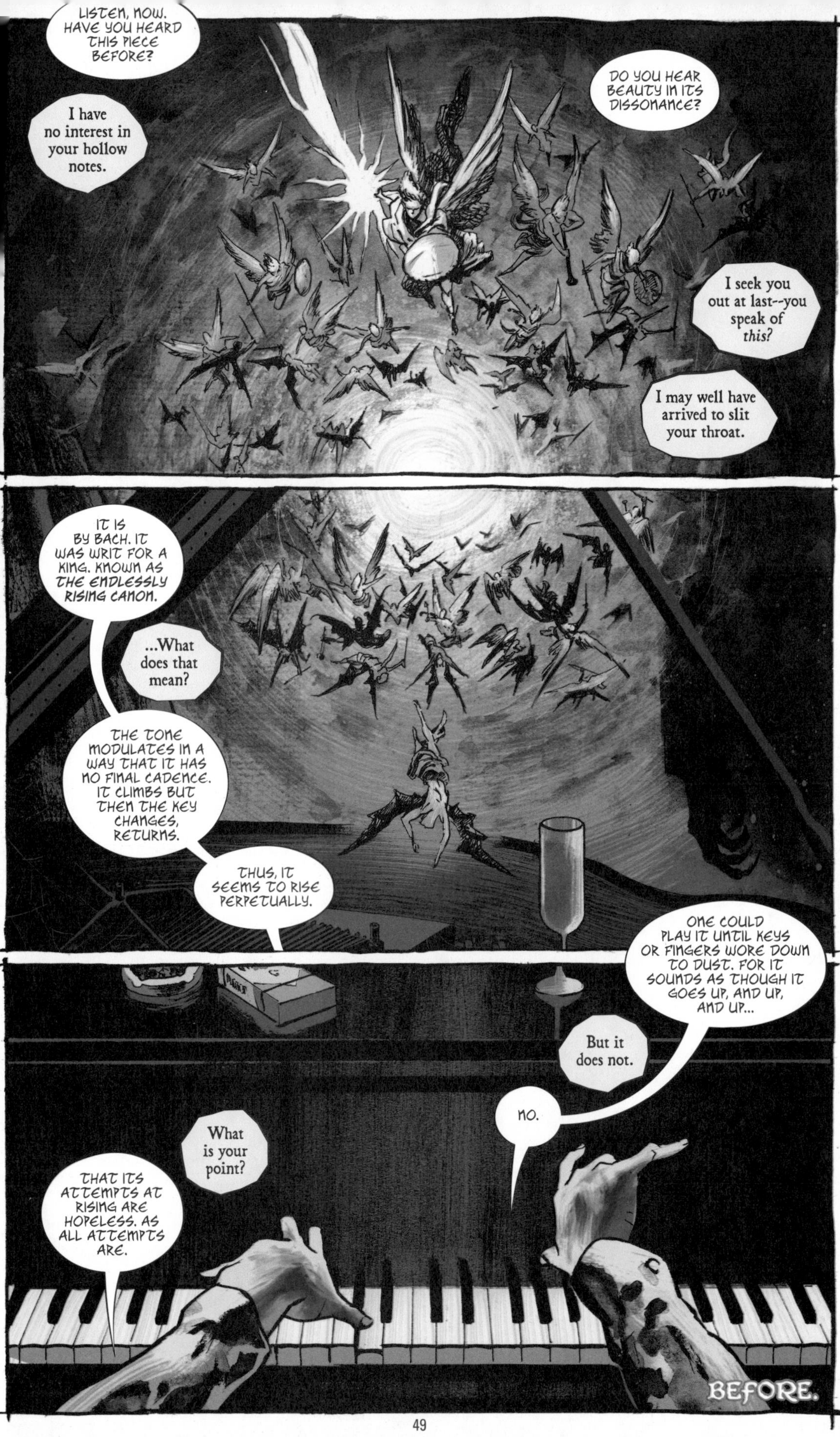
LISTEN, NOW. HAVE YOU HEARD THIS PIECE BEFORE?
I have no interest in your hollow notes.
DO YOU HEAR BEAUTY IN ITS DISSONANCE?
I seek you out at last--you speak of *this*?
I may well have arrived to slit your throat.
IT IS BY BACH. IT WAS WRIT FOR A KING. KNOWN AS *THE ENDLESSLY RISING CANON.*
...What does that mean?
THE TONE MODULATES IN A WAY THAT IT HAS NO FINAL CADENCE. IT CLIMBS BUT THEN THE KEY CHANGES, RETURNS.
THUS, IT SEEMS TO RISE PERPETUALLY.
ONE COULD PLAY IT UNTIL KEYS OR FINGERS WORE DOWN TO DUST. FOR IT SOUNDS AS THOUGH IT GOES UP, AND UP, AND UP...
But it does not.
NO.
What is your point?
THAT ITS ATTEMPTS AT RISING ARE HOPELESS. AS ALL ATTEMPTS ARE.
BEFORE.

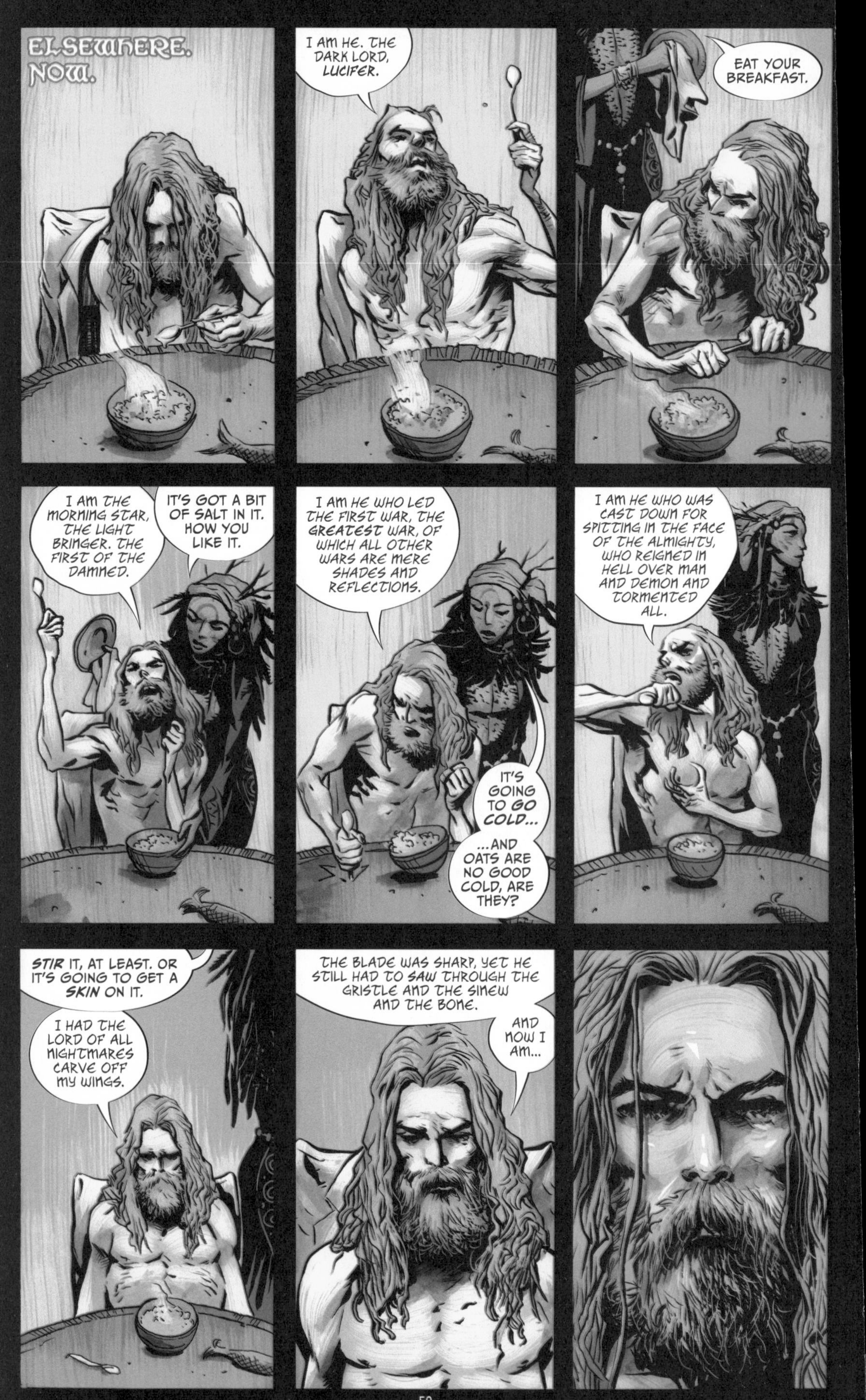
ELSEWHERE.
NOW.
I AM HE. THE DARK LORD, LUCIFER.
EAT YOUR BREAKFAST.
I AM THE MORNING STAR, THE LIGHT BRINGER. THE FIRST OF THE DAMNED.
IT'S GOT A BIT OF SALT IN IT. HOW YOU LIKE IT.
I AM HE WHO LED THE FIRST WAR, THE GREATEST WAR, OF WHICH ALL OTHER WARS ARE MERE SHADES AND REFLECTIONS.
IT'S GOING TO GO COLD...
...AND OATS ARE NO GOOD COLD, ARE THEY?
I AM HE WHO WAS CAST DOWN FOR SPITTING IN THE FACE OF THE ALMIGHTY, WHO REIGNED IN HELL OVER MAN AND DEMON AND TORMENTED ALL.
STIR IT, AT LEAST. OR IT'S GOING TO GET A SKIN ON IT.
I HAD THE LORD OF ALL NIGHTMARES CARVE OFF MY WINGS.
THE BLADE WAS SHARP, YET HE STILL HAD TO SAW THROUGH THE GRISTLE AND THE SINEW AND THE BONE.
AND NOW I AM...

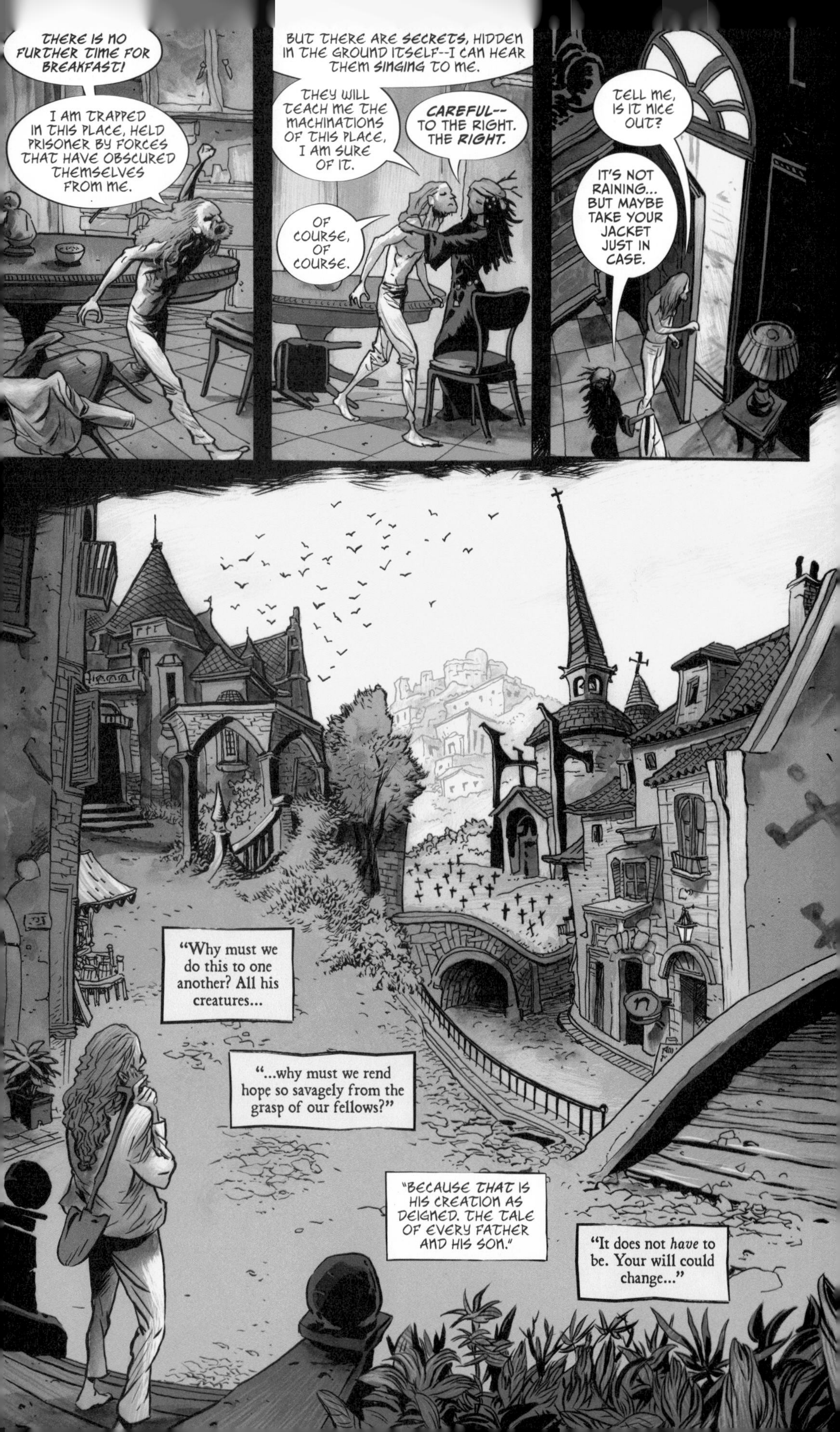
THERE IS NO FURTHER TIME FOR BREAKFAST!
I AM TRAPPED IN THIS PLACE, HELD PRISONER BY FORCES THAT HAVE OBSCURED THEMSELVES FROM ME.
BUT THERE ARE SECRETS, HIDDEN IN THE GROUND ITSELF--I CAN HEAR THEM SINGING TO ME.
THEY WILL TEACH ME THE MACHINATIONS OF THIS PLACE, I AM SURE OF IT.
CAREFUL-- TO THE RIGHT. THE RIGHT.
OF COURSE, OF COURSE.
TELL ME, IS IT NICE OUT?
IT'S NOT RAINING... BUT MAYBE TAKE YOUR JACKET JUST IN CASE.
"Why must we do this to one another? All his creatures...
"...why must we rend hope so savagely from the grasp of our fellows?"
"BECAUSE THAT IS HIS CREATION AS DEIGNED. THE TALE OF EVERY FATHER AND HIS SON."
"It does not have to be. Your will could change..."

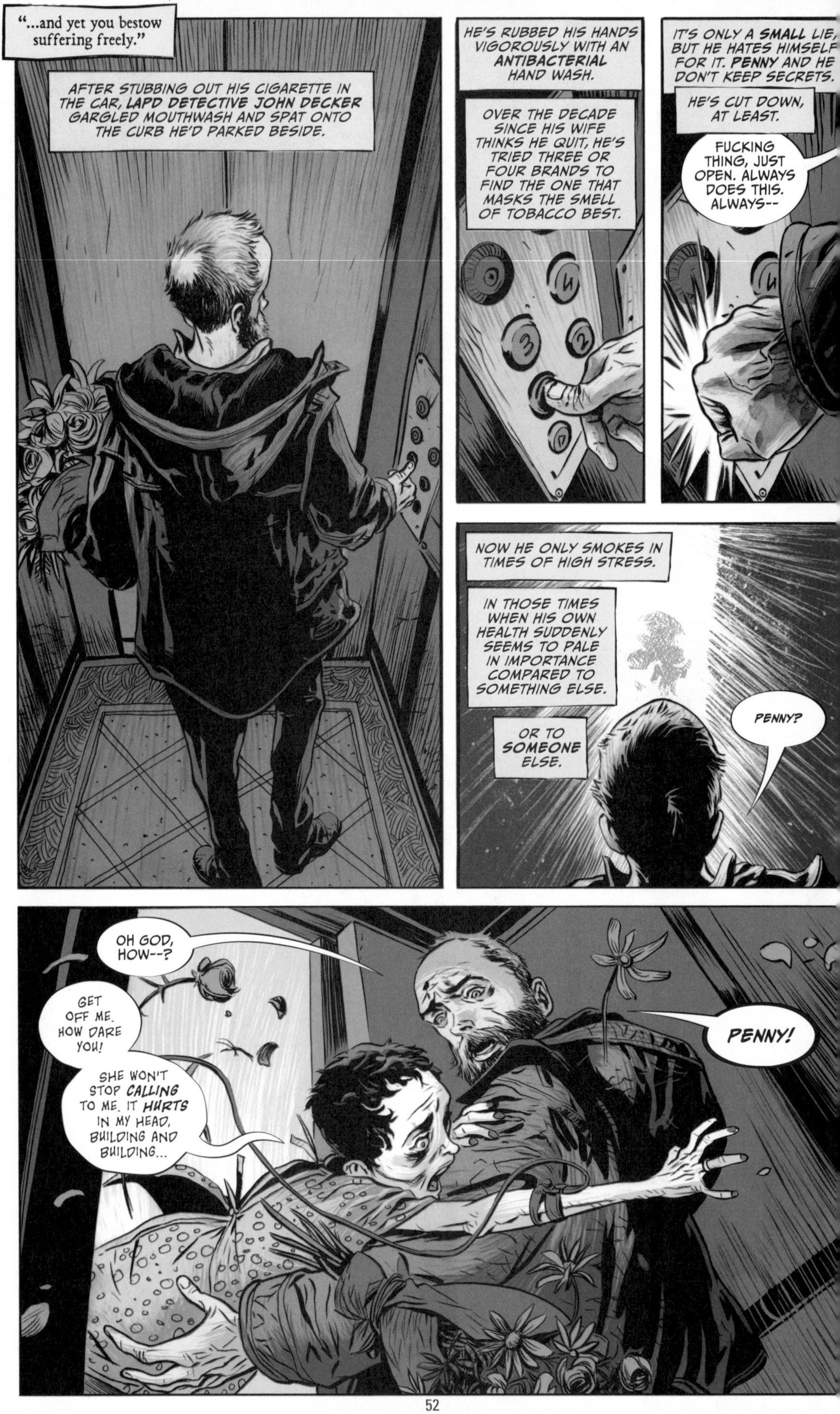
"...and yet you bestow suffering freely."
AFTER STUBBING OUT HIS CIGARETTE IN THE CAR, LAPD DETECTIVE JOHN DECKER GARGLED MOUTHWASH AND SPAT ONTO THE CURB HE'D PARKED BESIDE.
HE'S RUBBED HIS HANDS VIGOROUSLY WITH AN ANTIBACTERIAL HAND WASH.
OVER THE DECADE SINCE HIS WIFE THINKS HE QUIT, HE'S TRIED THREE OR FOUR BRANDS TO FIND THE ONE THAT MASKS THE SMELL OF TOBACCO BEST.
IT'S ONLY A SMALL LIE, BUT HE HATES HIMSELF FOR IT. PENNY AND HE DON'T KEEP SECRETS.
HE'S CUT DOWN, AT LEAST.
FUCKING THING, JUST OPEN. ALWAYS DOES THIS. ALWAYS--
NOW HE ONLY SMOKES IN TIMES OF HIGH STRESS.
IN THOSE TIMES WHEN HIS OWN HEALTH SUDDENLY SEEMS TO PALE IN IMPORTANCE COMPARED TO SOMETHING ELSE.
OR TO SOMEONE ELSE.
PENNY?
OH GOD, HOW--?
PENNY!
GET OFF ME. HOW DARE YOU!
SHE WON'T STOP CALLING TO ME. IT HURTS IN MY HEAD, BUILDING AND BUILDING...

HONESTLY, MR. DECKER...

DETECTIVE DECKER.

PENELOPE SHOULDN'T HAVE EVEN BEEN ABLE TO WALK TWO STEPS, THE TUMOR IN HER BRAIN--

IT *HURTS...* I CAN'T ESCAPE HER. HOW DO YOU ESCAPE *FLESH?*

THIS IS OBSCENE. SHE'S DELIRIOUS, PUMPED FULL OF DRUGS-- THERE'S NO *DIGNITY* IN THIS.

YOU'RE ONLY PROLONGING HER PAIN.

I SYMPATHIZE, DETECTIVE, I DO. WE'RE MAKING HER AS COMFORTABLE AS POSSIBLE. BUT AS SHE CAN NO LONGER GIVE HER CONSENT, WE HAVE TO KEEP HER HERE.

MY GUARDIAN APPLICATION...

IS *STILL* PENDING.

FOR CHRIST'S SAKE. BY THE TIME IT GOES THROUGH, SHE'LL BE GONE...

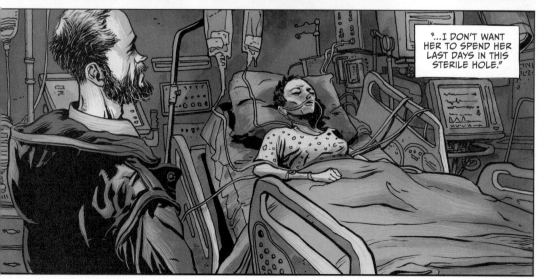

"...I DON'T WANT HER TO SPEND HER LAST DAYS IN THIS STERILE HOLE."

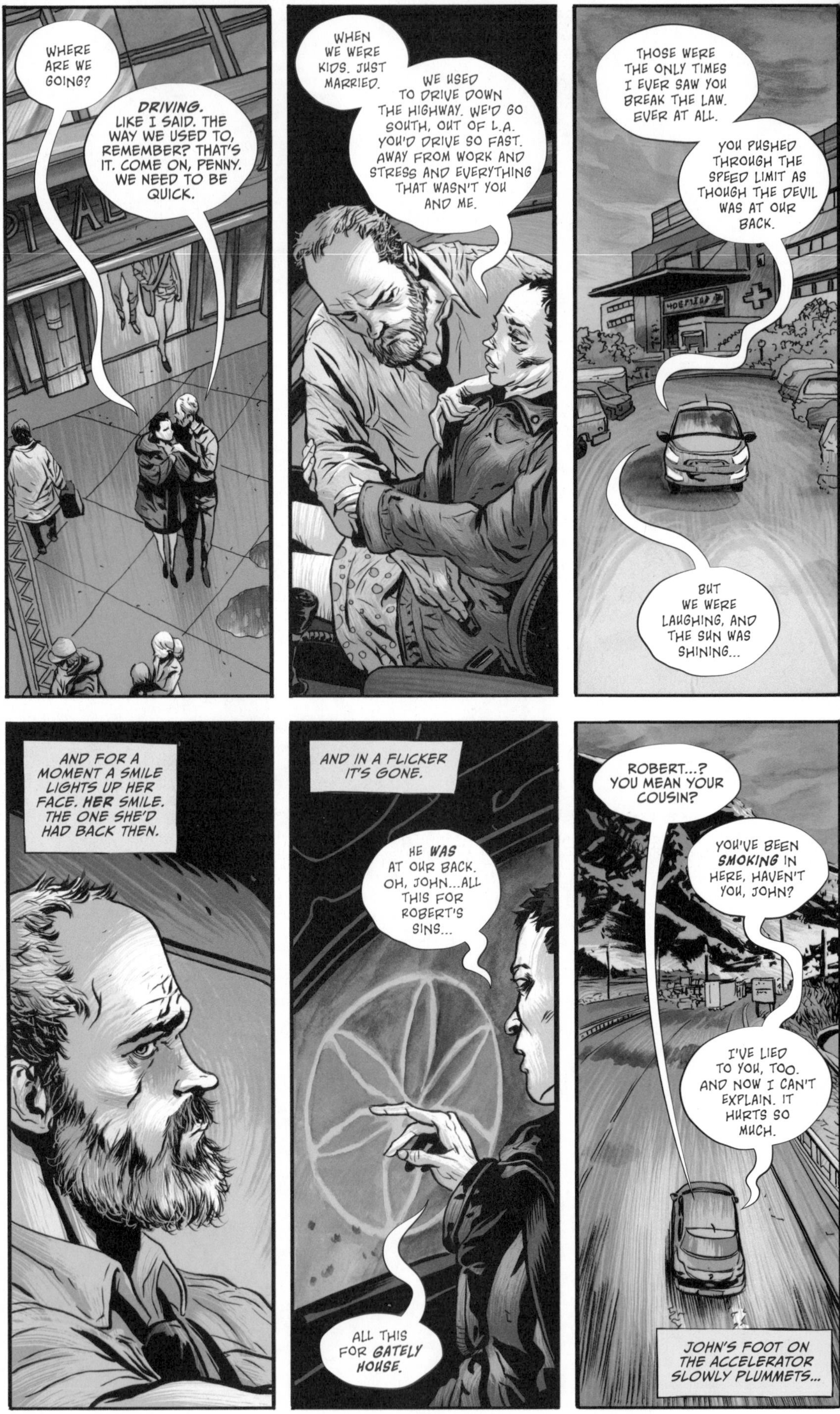
WHERE ARE WE GOING?
DRIVING. LIKE I SAID. THE WAY WE USED TO, REMEMBER? THAT'S IT. COME ON, PENNY. WE NEED TO BE QUICK.
WHEN WE WERE KIDS. JUST MARRIED.
WE USED TO DRIVE DOWN THE HIGHWAY. WE'D GO SOUTH, OUT OF L.A. YOU'D DRIVE SO FAST. AWAY FROM WORK AND STRESS AND EVERYTHING THAT WASN'T YOU AND ME.
THOSE WERE THE ONLY TIMES I EVER SAW YOU BREAK THE LAW. EVER AT ALL.
YOU PUSHED THROUGH THE SPEED LIMIT AS THOUGH THE DEVIL WAS AT OUR BACK.
BUT WE WERE LAUGHING, AND THE SUN WAS SHINING...
AND FOR A MOMENT A SMILE LIGHTS UP HER FACE. HER SMILE. THE ONE SHE'D HAD BACK THEN.
AND IN A FLICKER IT'S GONE.
HE WAS AT OUR BACK. OH, JOHN...ALL THIS FOR ROBERT'S SINS...
ALL THIS FOR GATELY HOUSE.
ROBERT...? YOU MEAN YOUR COUSIN?
YOU'VE BEEN SMOKING IN HERE, HAVEN'T YOU, JOHN?
I'VE LIED TO YOU, TOO. AND NOW I CAN'T EXPLAIN. IT HURTS SO MUCH.
JOHN'S FOOT ON THE ACCELERATOR SLOWLY PLUMMETS...

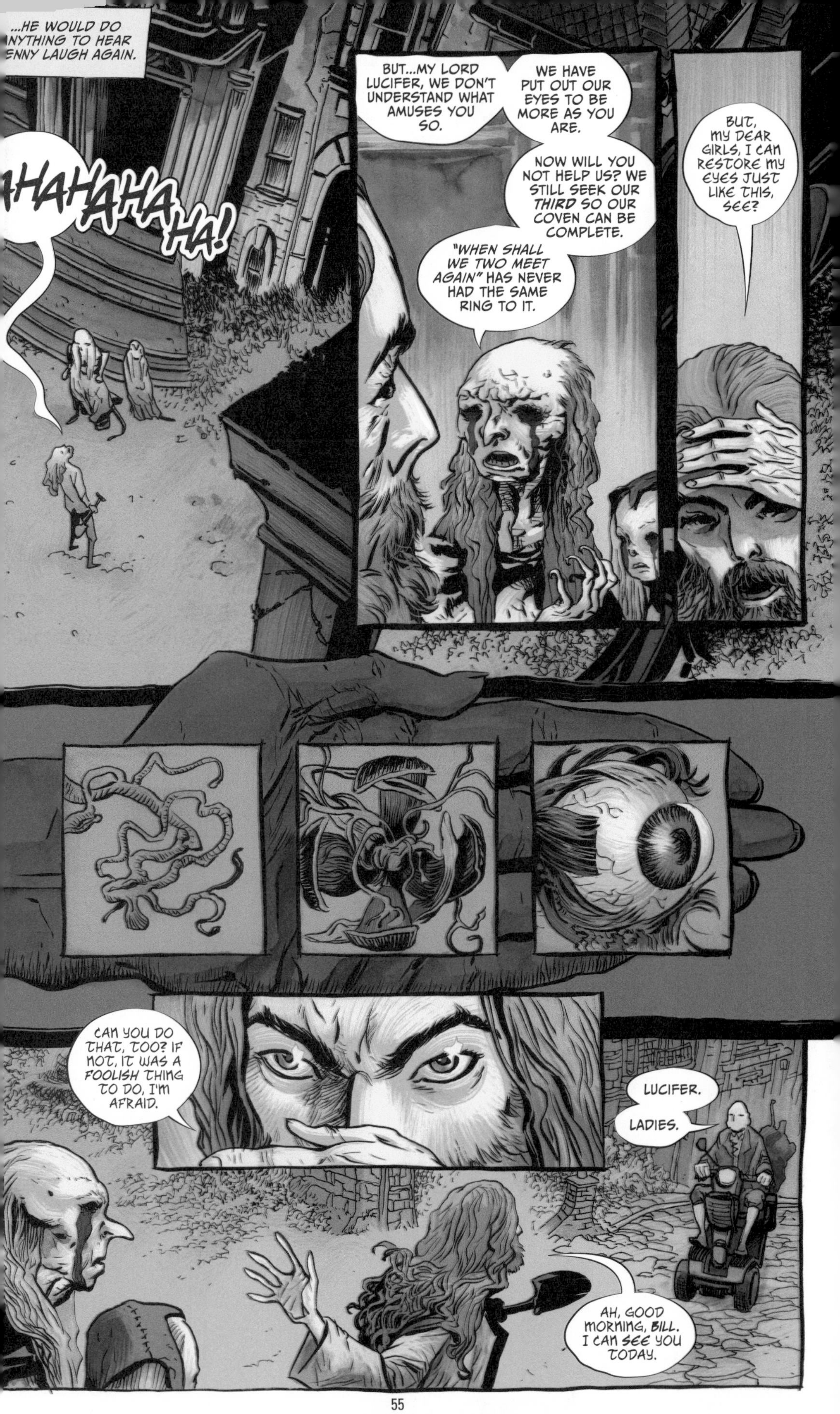
...HE WOULD DO
NYTHING TO HEAR
ENNY LAUGH AGAIN.
HAHAHAHAHA!
BUT...MY LORD LUCIFER, WE DON'T UNDERSTAND WHAT AMUSES YOU SO.
WE HAVE PUT OUT OUR EYES TO BE MORE AS YOU ARE.
NOW WILL YOU NOT HELP US? WE STILL SEEK OUR THIRD SO OUR COVEN CAN BE COMPLETE.
"WHEN SHALL WE TWO MEET AGAIN" HAS NEVER HAD THE SAME RING TO IT.
BUT, MY DEAR GIRLS, I CAN RESTORE MY EYES JUST LIKE THIS, SEE?
CAN YOU DO THAT, TOO? IF NOT, IT WAS A FOOLISH THING TO DO, I'M AFRAID.
LUCIFER.
LADIES.
AH, GOOD MORNING, BILL. I CAN SEE YOU TODAY.

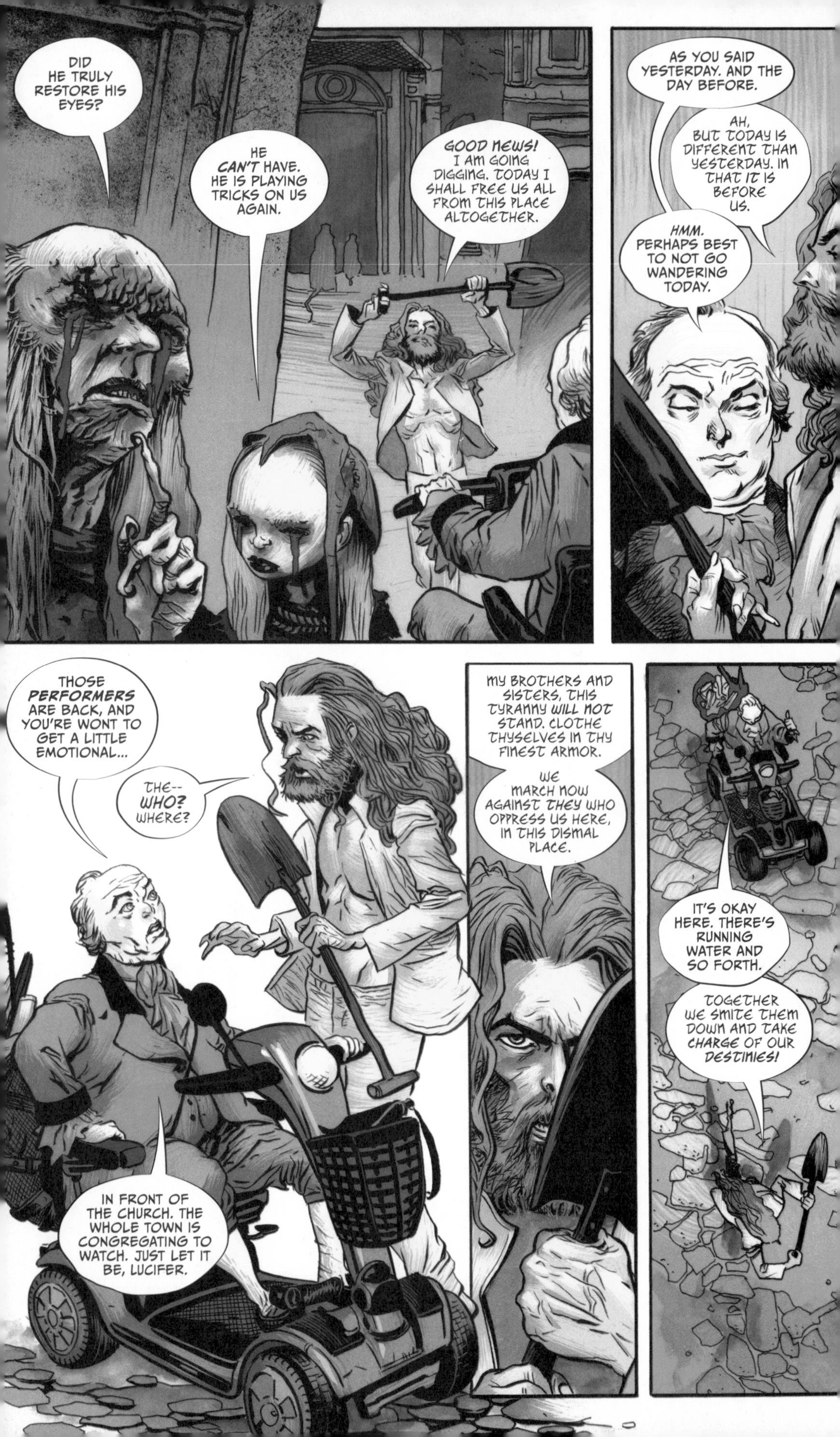
DID HE TRULY RESTORE HIS EYES?
HE *CAN'T* HAVE. HE IS PLAYING TRICKS ON US AGAIN.
GOOD NEWS! I AM GOING DIGGING. TODAY I SHALL FREE US ALL FROM THIS PLACE ALTOGETHER.
AS YOU SAID YESTERDAY. AND THE DAY BEFORE.
AH, BUT TODAY IS DIFFERENT THAN YESTERDAY. IN THAT *IT* IS BEFORE US.
HMM. PERHAPS BEST TO NOT GO WANDERING TODAY.
THOSE *PERFORMERS* ARE BACK, AND YOU'RE WONT TO GET A LITTLE EMOTIONAL...
THE-- *WHO?* WHERE?
IN FRONT OF THE CHURCH. THE WHOLE TOWN IS CONGREGATING TO WATCH. JUST LET IT BE, LUCIFER.
MY BROTHERS AND SISTERS, THIS TYRANNY *WILL NOT* STAND. CLOTHE THYSELVES IN THY FINEST ARMOR.
WE MARCH NOW AGAINST *THEY* WHO OPPRESS US HERE, IN THIS DISMAL PLACE.
IT'S OKAY HERE. THERE'S RUNNING WATER AND SO FORTH.
TOGETHER WE SMITE THEM DOWN AND TAKE *CHARGE* OF OUR *DESTINIES!*

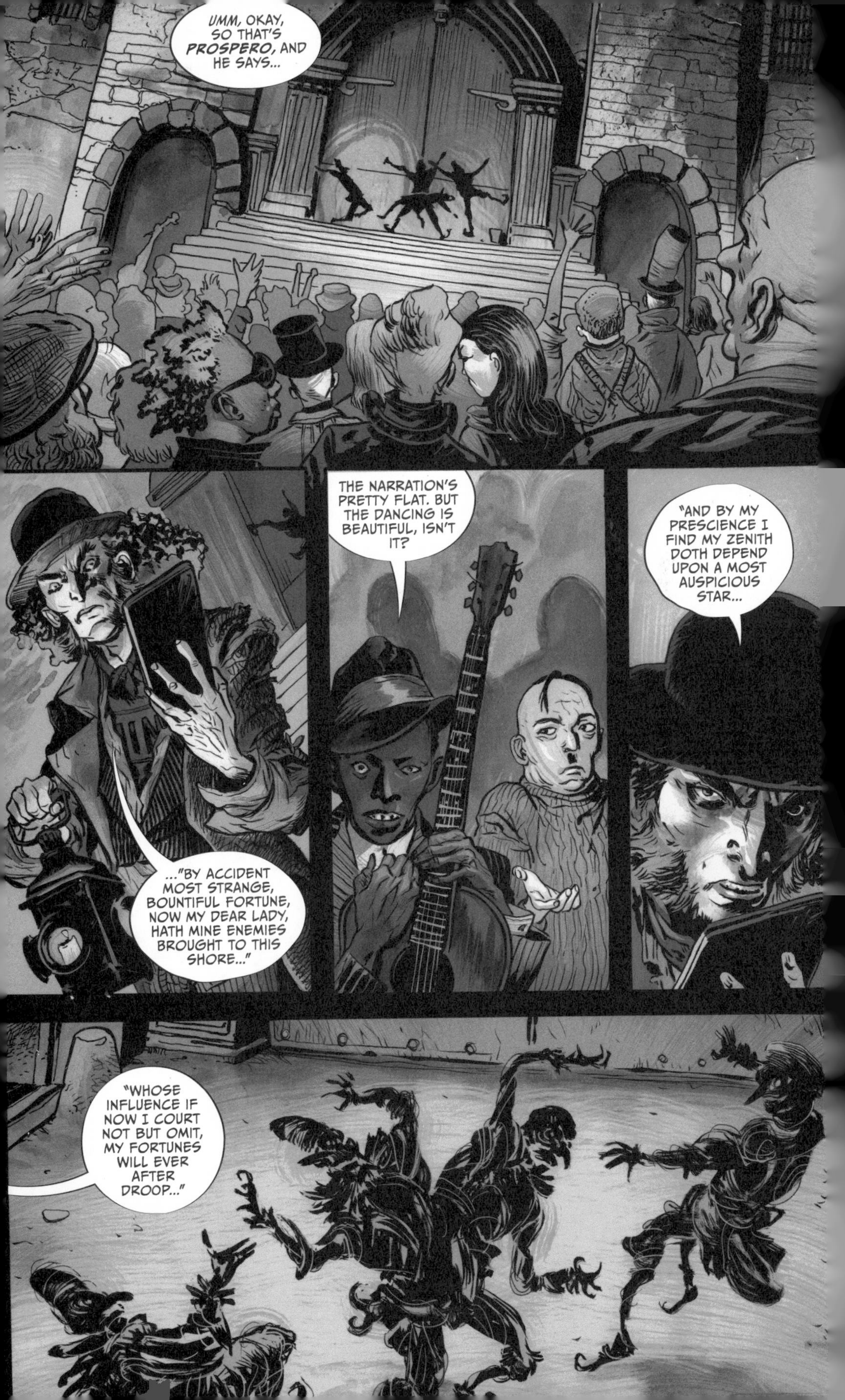
UMM, OKAY, SO THAT'S PROSPERO, AND HE SAYS...
..."BY ACCIDENT MOST STRANGE, BOUNTIFUL FORTUNE, NOW MY DEAR LADY, HATH MINE ENEMIES BROUGHT TO THIS SHORE..."
THE NARRATION'S PRETTY FLAT. BUT THE DANCING IS BEAUTIFUL, ISN'T IT?
"AND BY MY PRESCIENCE I FIND MY ZENITH DOTH DEPEND UPON A MOST AUSPICIOUS STAR...
"WHOSE INFLUENCE IF NOW I COURT NOT BUT OMIT, MY FORTUNES WILL EVER AFTER DROOP..."

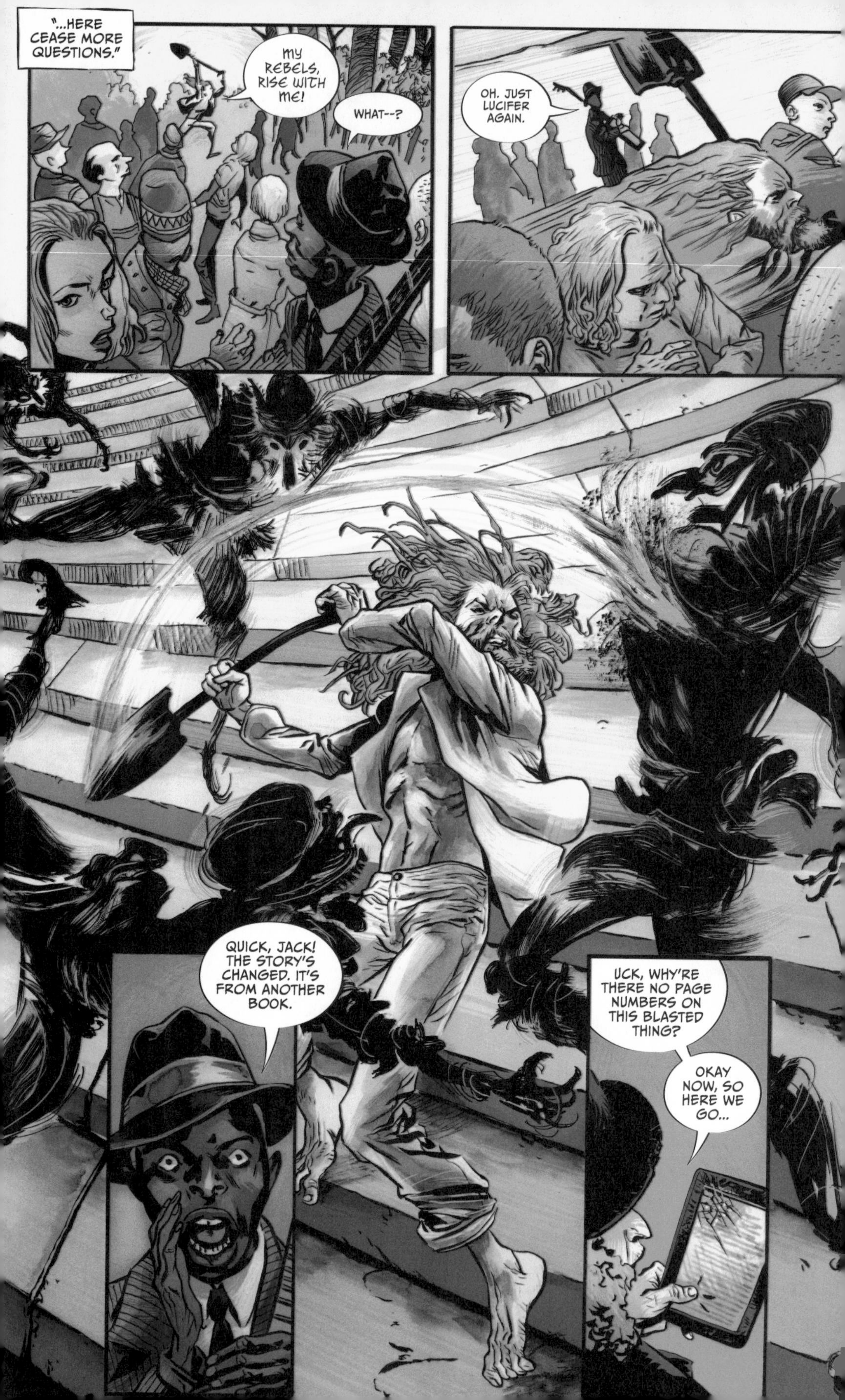
"...HERE CEASE MORE QUESTIONS."
MY REBELS, RISE WITH ME!
WHAT--?
OH. JUST LUCIFER AGAIN.
QUICK, JACK! THE STORY'S CHANGED. IT'S FROM ANOTHER BOOK.
UCK, WHY'RE THERE NO PAGE NUMBERS ON THIS BLASTED THING?
OKAY NOW, SO HERE WE GO...

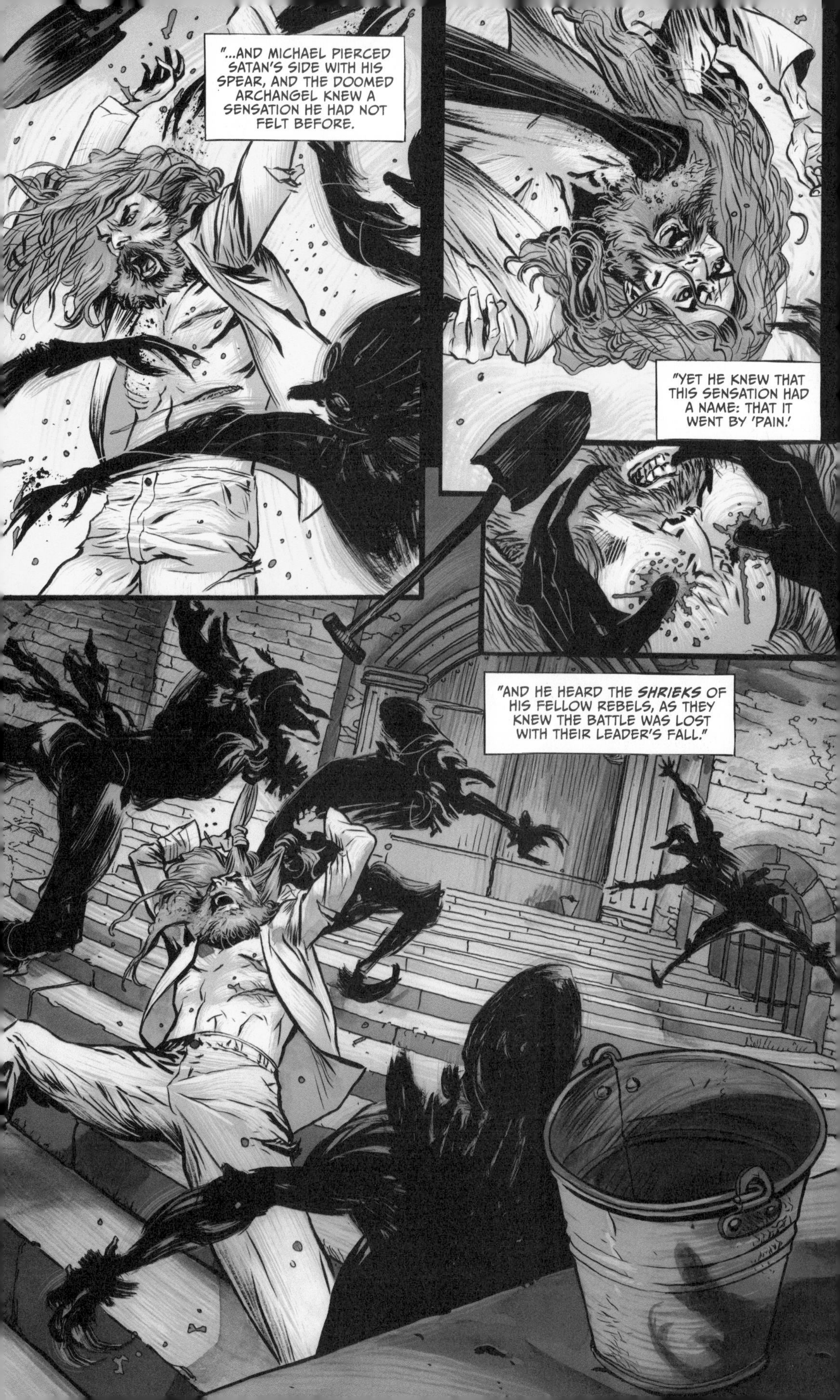
"...AND MICHAEL PIERCED SATAN'S SIDE WITH HIS SPEAR, AND THE DOOMED ARCHANGEL KNEW A SENSATION HE HAD NOT FELT BEFORE.
"YET HE KNEW THAT THIS SENSATION HAD A NAME: THAT IT WENT BY 'PAIN.'
"AND HE HEARD THE SHRIEKS OF HIS FELLOW REBELS, AS THEY KNEW THE BATTLE WAS LOST WITH THEIR LEADER'S FALL."

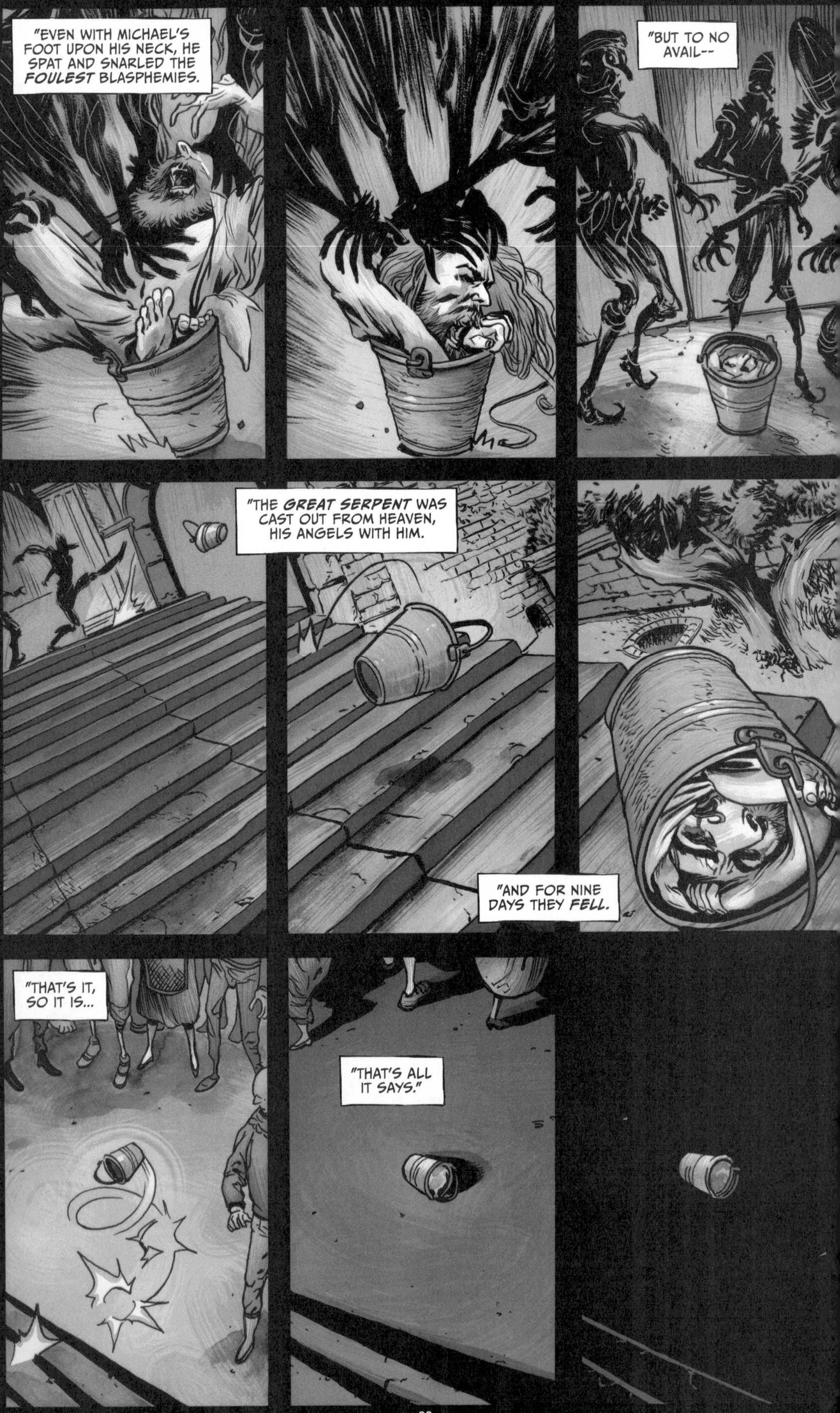
"EVEN WITH MICHAEL'S FOOT UPON HIS NECK, HE SPAT AND SNARLED THE FOULEST BLASPHEMIES.
"BUT TO NO AVAIL--
"THE GREAT SERPENT WAS CAST OUT FROM HEAVEN, HIS ANGELS WITH HIM.
"AND FOR NINE DAYS THEY FELL.
"THAT'S IT, SO IT IS...
"THAT'S ALL IT SAYS."

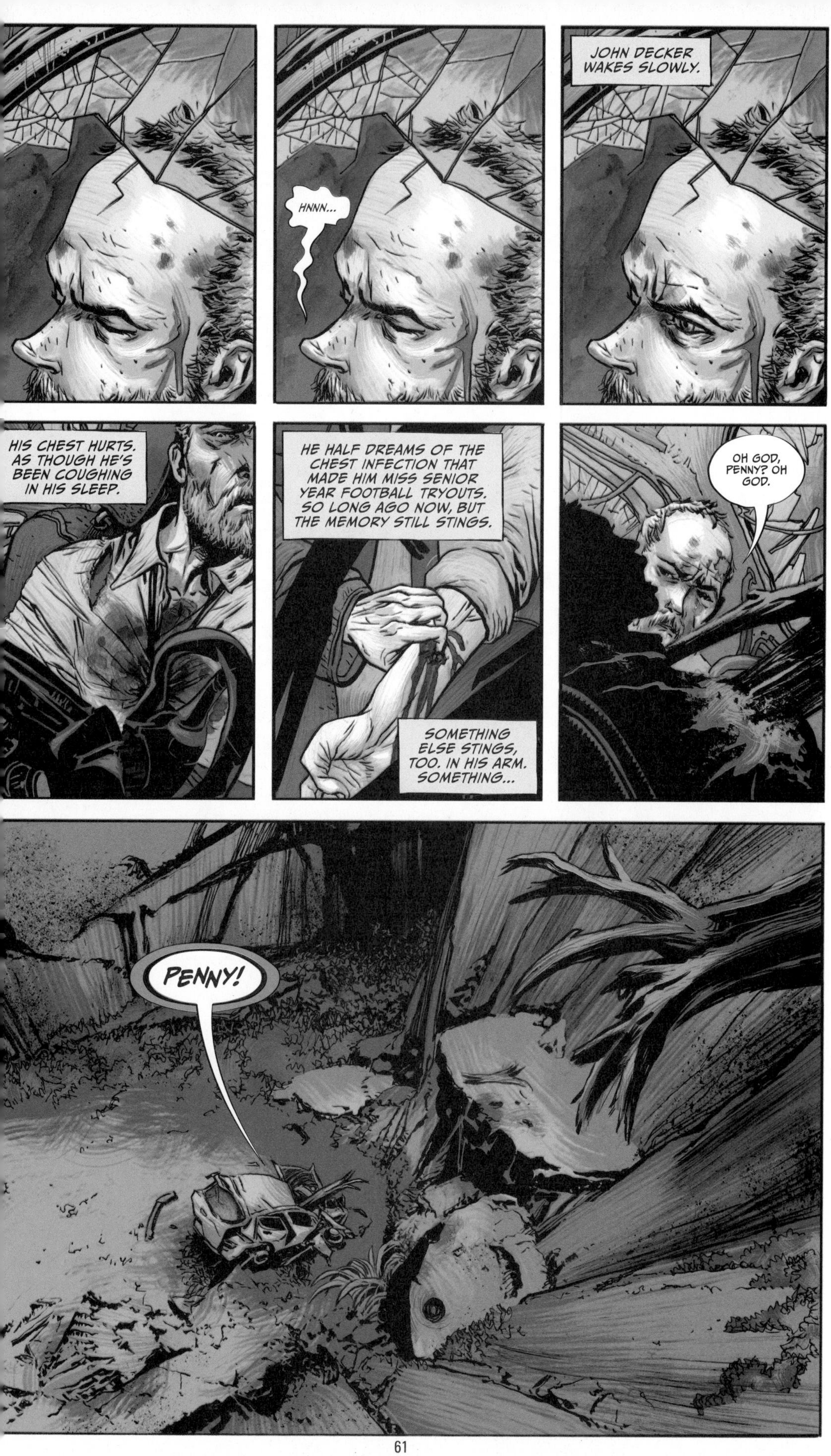
HNNN...
JOHN DECKER WAKES SLOWLY.
HIS CHEST HURTS. AS THOUGH HE'S BEEN COUGHING IN HIS SLEEP.
HE HALF DREAMS OF THE CHEST INFECTION THAT MADE HIM MISS SENIOR YEAR FOOTBALL TRYOUTS. SO LONG AGO NOW, BUT THE MEMORY STILL STINGS.
SOMETHING ELSE STINGS, TOO. IN HIS ARM. SOMETHING...
OH GOD, PENNY? OH GOD.
PENNY!

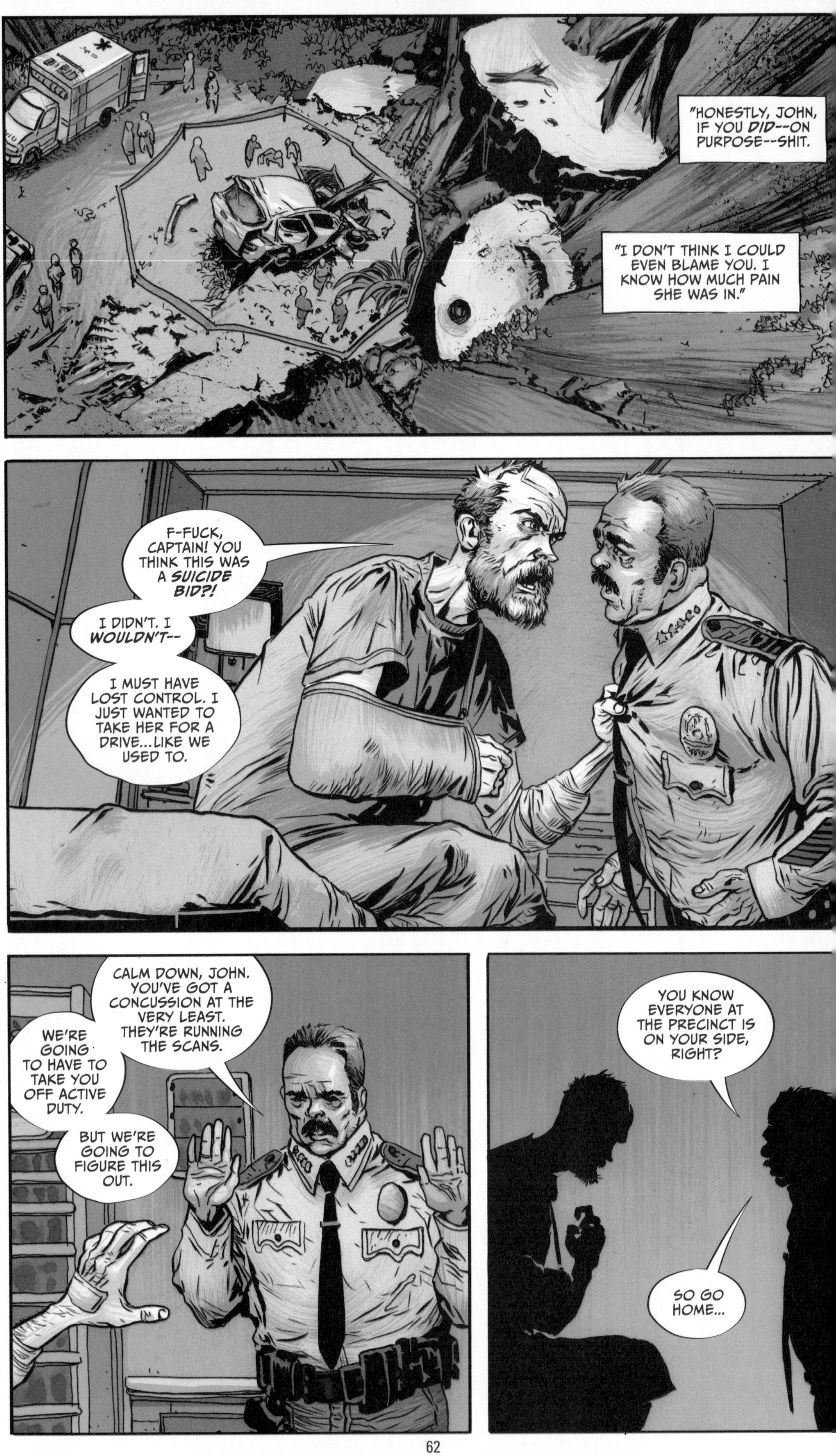
"HONESTLY, JOHN, IF YOU DID--ON PURPOSE--SHIT.
"I DON'T THINK I COULD EVEN BLAME YOU. I KNOW HOW MUCH PAIN SHE WAS IN."
F-FUCK, CAPTAIN! YOU THINK THIS WAS A SUICIDE BID?!
I DIDN'T. I WOULDN'T--
I MUST HAVE LOST CONTROL. I JUST WANTED TO TAKE HER FOR A DRIVE...LIKE WE USED TO.
CALM DOWN, JOHN. YOU'VE GOT A CONCUSSION AT THE VERY LEAST. THEY'RE RUNNING THE SCANS.
WE'RE GOING TO HAVE TO TAKE YOU OFF ACTIVE DUTY.
BUT WE'RE GOING TO FIGURE THIS OUT.
YOU KNOW EVERYONE AT THE PRECINCT IS ON YOUR SIDE, RIGHT?
SO GO HOME...

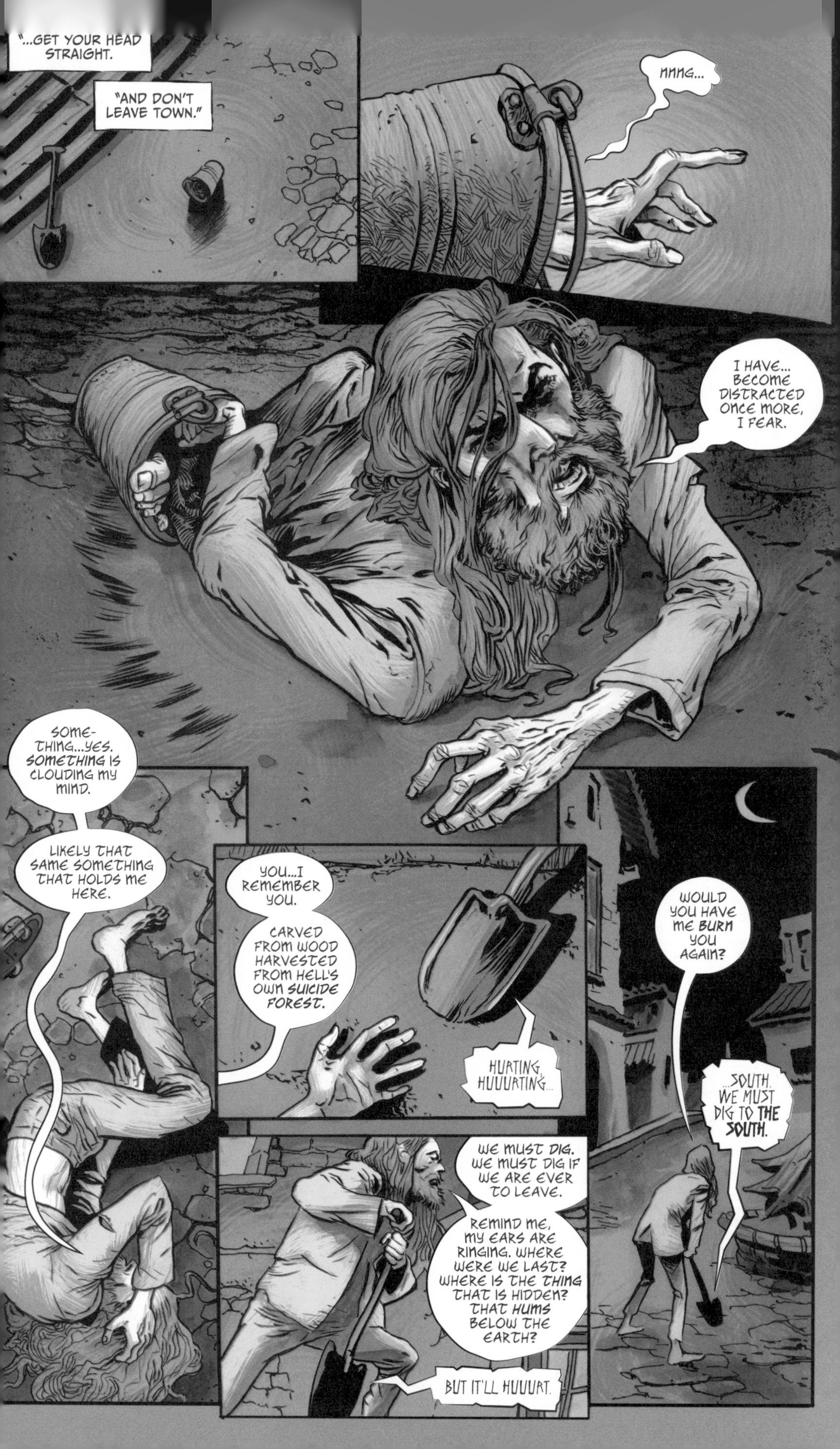

"...GET YOUR HEAD STRAIGHT.
"AND DON'T LEAVE TOWN."
MNNG...
I HAVE... BECOME DISTRACTED ONCE MORE, I FEAR.
SOME-THING...YES. SOMETHING IS CLOUDING MY MIND.
LIKELY THAT SAME SOMETHING THAT HOLDS ME HERE.
YOU...I REMEMBER YOU.
CARVED FROM WOOD HARVESTED FROM HELL'S OWN SUICIDE FOREST.
HURTING, HUUURTING...
WOULD YOU HAVE ME BURN YOU AGAIN?
...SOUTH. WE MUST DIG TO THE SOUTH.
WE MUST DIG. WE MUST DIG IF WE ARE EVER TO LEAVE.
REMIND ME, MY EARS ARE RINGING. WHERE WERE WE LAST? WHERE IS THE THING THAT IS HIDDEN? THAT HUMS BELOW THE EARTH?
BUT IT'LL HUUURT.

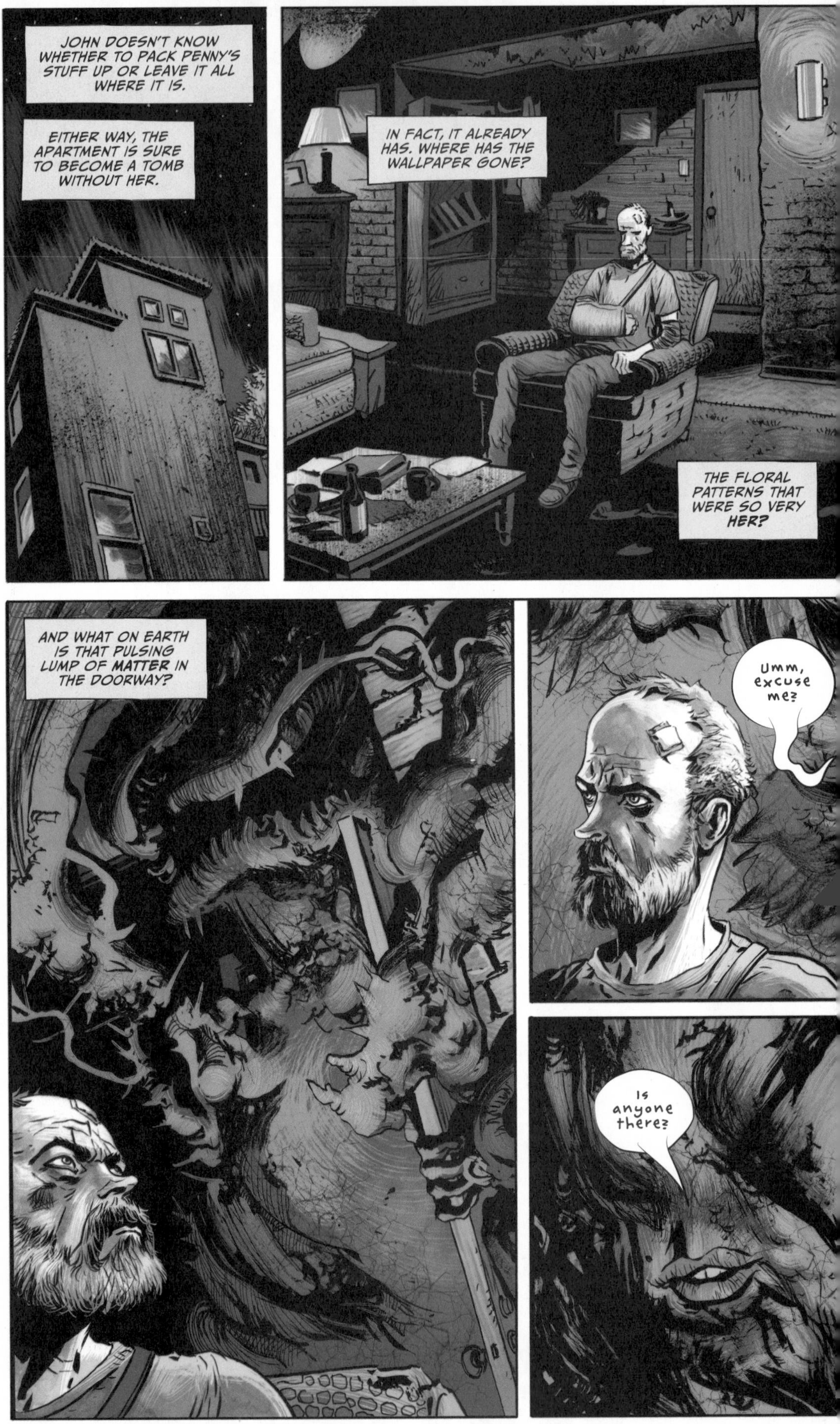
JOHN DOESN'T KNOW WHETHER TO PACK PENNY'S STUFF UP OR LEAVE IT ALL WHERE IT IS.
EITHER WAY, THE APARTMENT IS SURE TO BECOME A TOMB WITHOUT HER.
IN FACT, IT ALREADY HAS. WHERE HAS THE WALLPAPER GONE?
THE FLORAL PATTERNS THAT WERE SO VERY HER?
AND WHAT ON EARTH IS THAT PULSING LUMP OF MATTER IN THE DOORWAY?
Umm, excuse me?
Is anyone there?

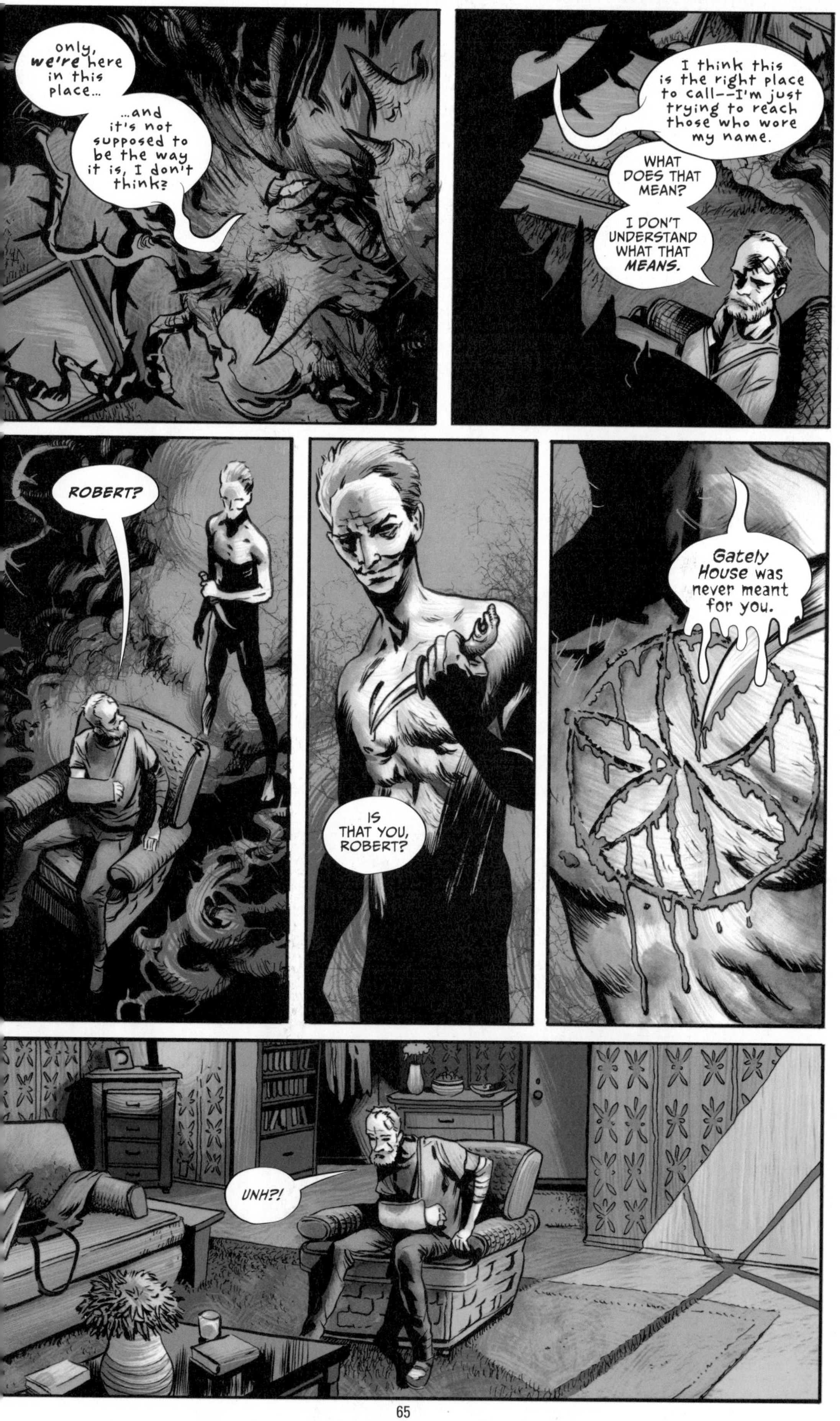
only, we're here in this place...
...and it's not supposed to be the way it is, I don't think?
I think this is the right place to call--I'm just trying to reach those who wore my name.
WHAT DOES THAT MEAN?
I DON'T UNDERSTAND WHAT THAT MEANS.
ROBERT?
IS THAT YOU, ROBERT?
Gately House was never meant for you.
UNH?!

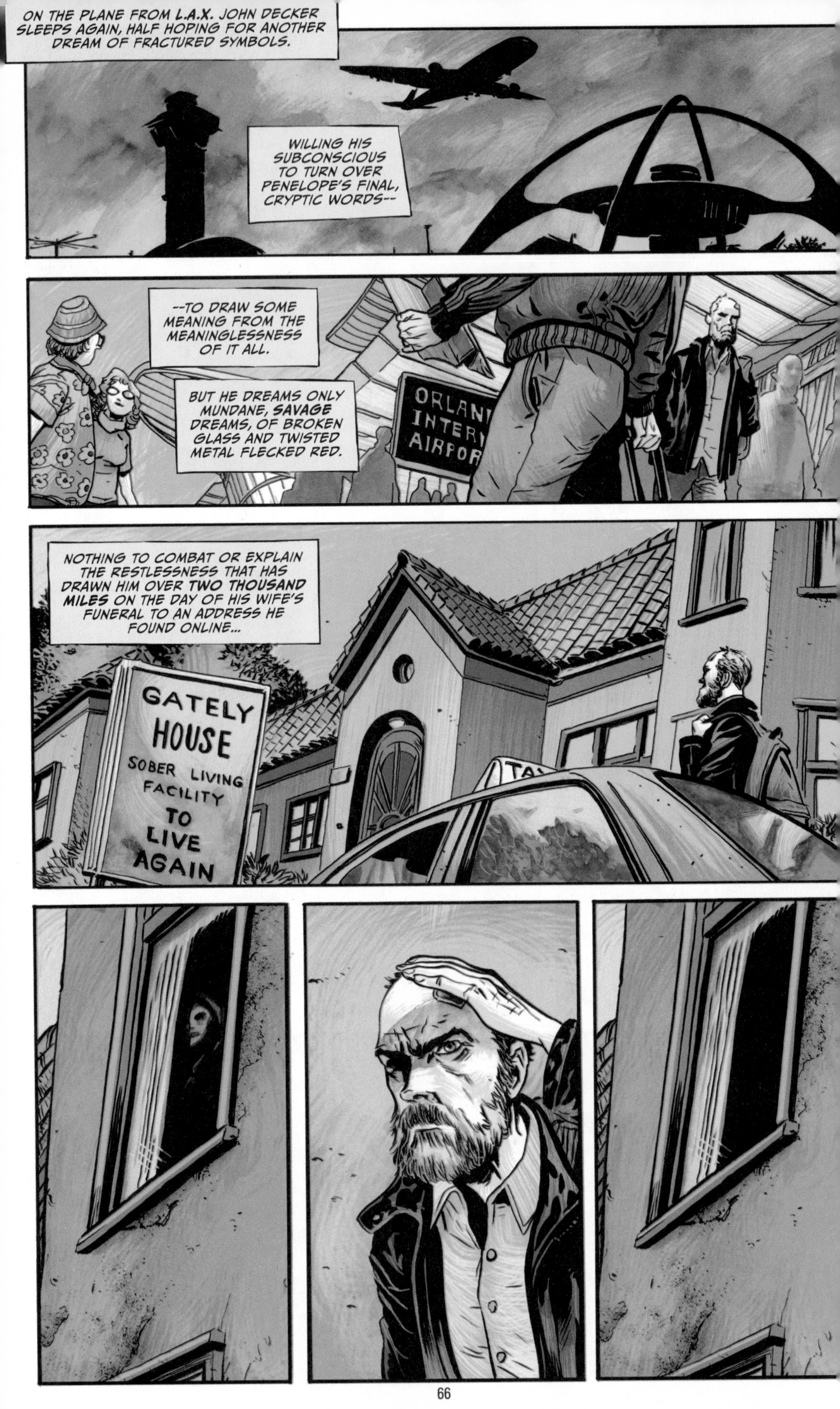
ON THE PLANE FROM L.A.X. JOHN DECKER SLEEPS AGAIN, HALF HOPING FOR ANOTHER DREAM OF FRACTURED SYMBOLS.
WILLING HIS SUBCONSCIOUS TO TURN OVER PENELOPE'S FINAL, CRYPTIC WORDS--
--TO DRAW SOME MEANING FROM THE MEANINGLESSNESS OF IT ALL.
BUT HE DREAMS ONLY MUNDANE, SAVAGE DREAMS, OF BROKEN GLASS AND TWISTED METAL FLECKED RED.
ORLAN INTER AIRPOR
NOTHING TO COMBAT OR EXPLAIN THE RESTLESSNESS THAT HAS DRAWN HIM OVER TWO THOUSAND MILES ON THE DAY OF HIS WIFE'S FUNERAL TO AN ADDRESS HE FOUND ONLINE...
GATELY HOUSE
SOBER LIVING FACILITY
TO LIVE AGAIN

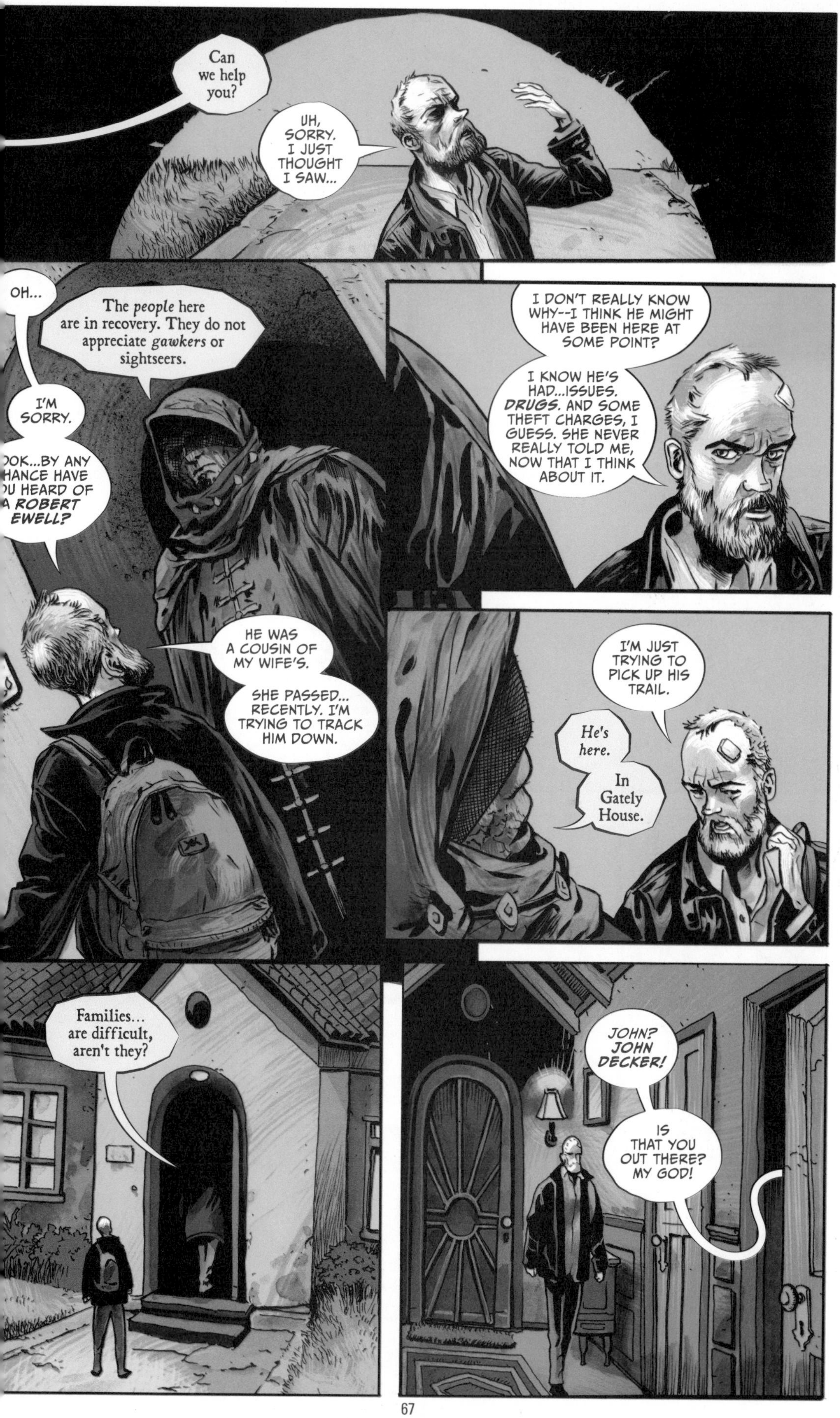
Can we help you?
UH, SORRY. I JUST THOUGHT I SAW...
OH...
The *people* here are in recovery. They do not appreciate *gawkers* or sightseers.
I'M SORRY.
OOK...BY ANY HANCE HAVE OU HEARD OF A *ROBERT EWELL?*
I DON'T REALLY KNOW WHY--I THINK HE MIGHT HAVE BEEN HERE AT SOME POINT?
I KNOW HE'S HAD...ISSUES. ***DRUGS.*** AND SOME THEFT CHARGES, I GUESS. SHE NEVER REALLY TOLD ME, NOW THAT I THINK ABOUT IT.
HE WAS A COUSIN OF MY WIFE'S.
SHE PASSED... RECENTLY. I'M TRYING TO TRACK HIM DOWN.
I'M JUST TRYING TO PICK UP HIS TRAIL.
He's here.
In Gately House.
Families... are difficult, aren't they?
JOHN? ***JOHN DECKER!***
IS THAT YOU OUT THERE? MY GOD!

ROBERT! YOU'RE ACTUALLY HERE...

WHEN PENNY MENTIONED THIS PLACE, I THOUGHT IT'D BE SOMEWHERE YOU'D *PASSED THROUGH* YEARS AGO.

YEAH, WELL. IT'S BEEN A TOUGH FEW YEARS. YOU KNOW WHERE THEY SAY ROADS PAVED WITH GOOD INTENTIONS LEAD.

SIT DOWN, SIT DOWN--

PENNY ISN'T WITH YOU?

OH GOD. JOHN, WHAT'S WRONG?

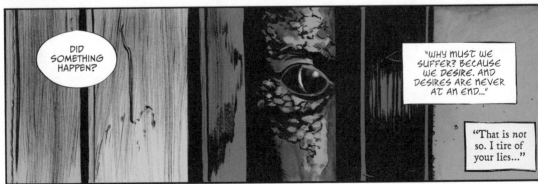

DID SOMETHING HAPPEN?

"WHY MUST WE SUFFER? BECAUSE WE DESIRE. AND DESIRES ARE NEVER AT AN END..."

"That is not so. I tire of your lies..."

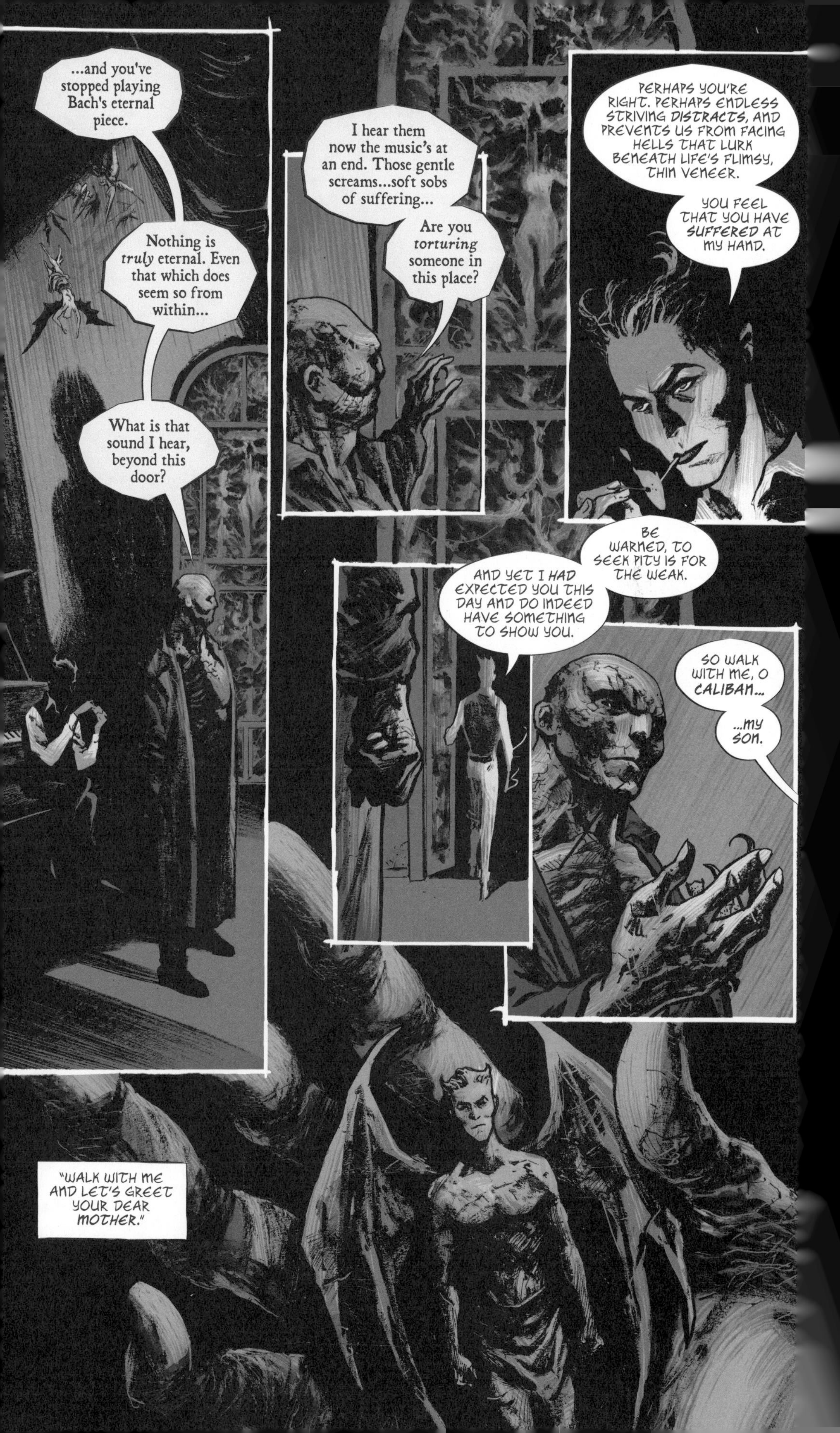
...and you've stopped playing Bach's eternal piece.
Nothing is *truly* eternal. Even that which does seem so from within...
What is that sound I hear, beyond this door?
I hear them now the music's at an end. Those gentle screams...soft sobs of suffering...
Are you *torturing* someone in this place?
PERHAPS YOU'RE RIGHT. PERHAPS ENDLESS STRIVING *DISTRACTS*, AND PREVENTS US FROM FACING HELLS THAT LURK BENEATH LIFE'S FLIMSY, THIN VENEER.
YOU FEEL THAT YOU HAVE *SUFFERED* AT MY HAND.
BE WARNED, TO SEEK PITY IS FOR THE WEAK.
AND YET I *HAD* EXPECTED YOU THIS DAY AND DO INDEED HAVE SOMETHING TO SHOW YOU.
SO WALK WITH ME, O **CALIBAN**...
...MY **SON**.
"WALK WITH ME AND LET'S GREET YOUR DEAR *MOTHER*."

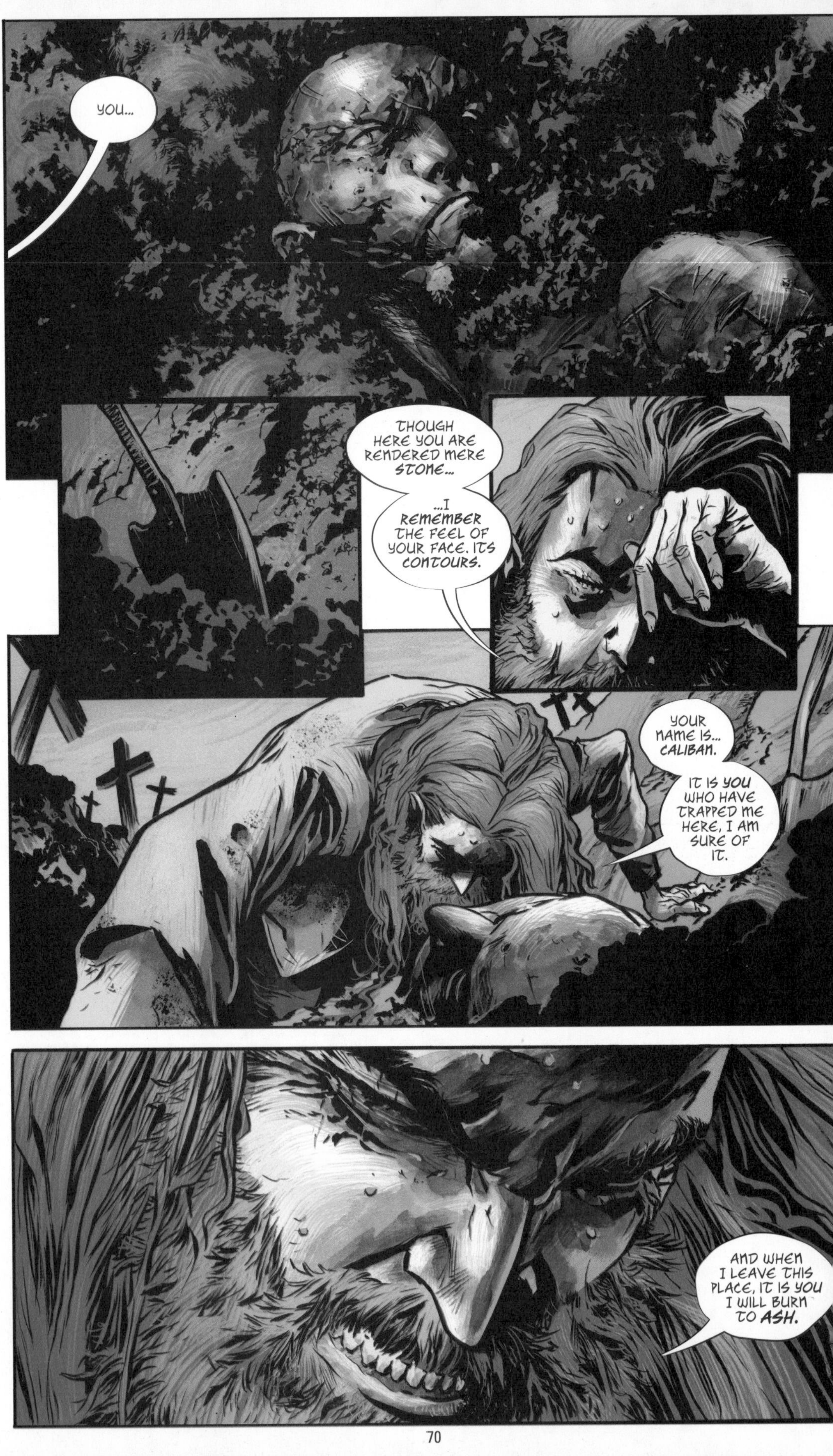
YOU...
THOUGH HERE YOU ARE RENDERED MERE STONE...
...I REMEMBER THE FEEL OF YOUR FACE. ITS CONTOURS.
YOUR NAME IS... CALIBAN.
IT IS YOU WHO HAVE TRAPPED ME HERE, I AM SURE OF IT.
AND WHEN I LEAVE THIS PLACE, IT IS YOU I WILL BURN TO **ASH.**

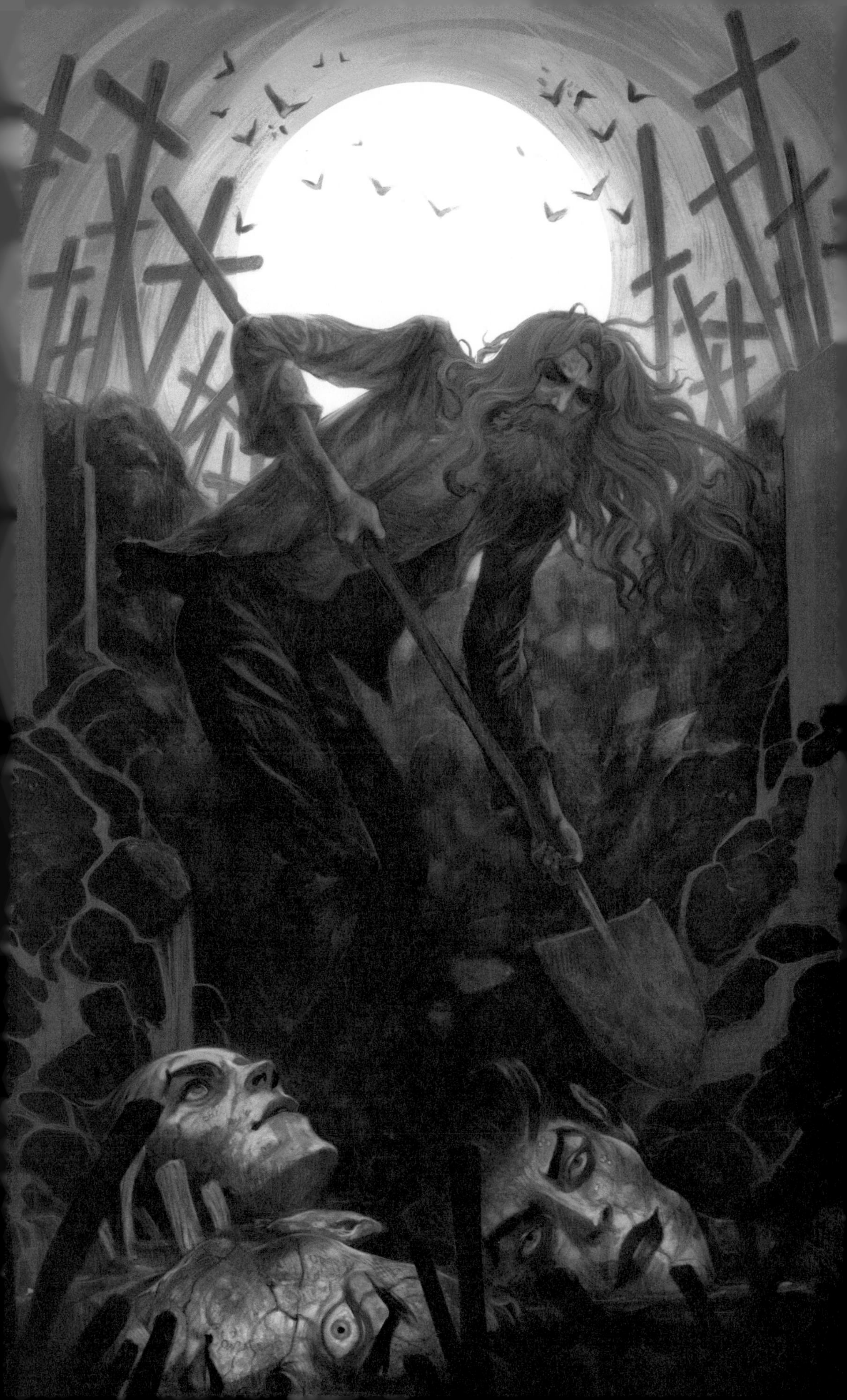

LUCIFER

Of Red Death and Ginger Tomcats

WRITTEN BY
Dan Watters

ILLUSTRATED BY
Max Fiumara
Sebastian Fiumara

COLORS BY
Dave McCaig

LETTERS BY
Steve Wands

COVER ART BY
Tiffany Turrill

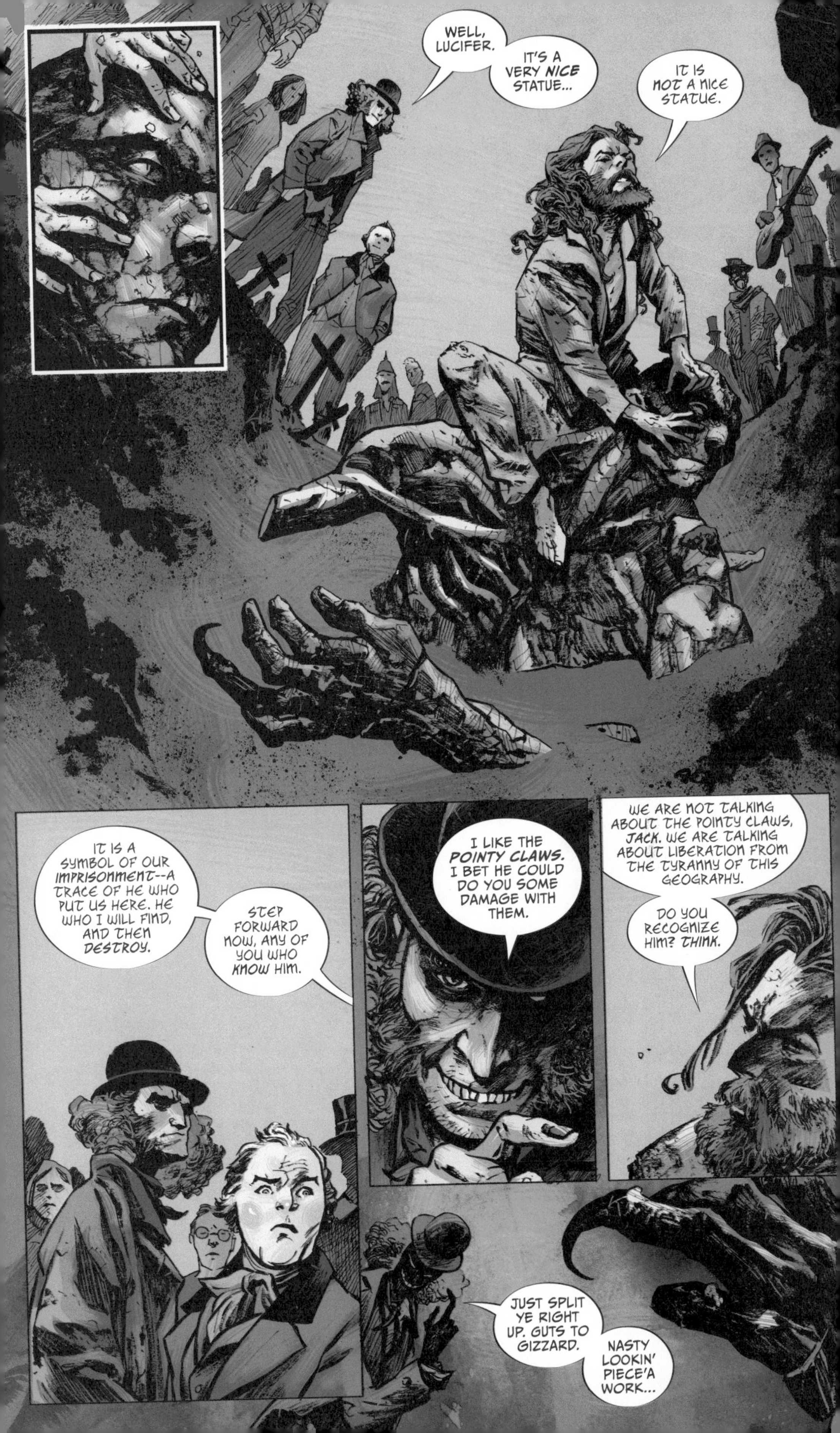
WELL, LUCIFER.
IT'S A VERY NICE STATUE...
IT IS NOT A NICE STATUE.
IT IS A SYMBOL OF OUR IMPRISONMENT--A TRACE OF HE WHO PUT US HERE. HE WHO I WILL FIND, AND THEN DESTROY.
STEP FORWARD NOW, ANY OF YOU WHO KNOW HIM.
I LIKE THE POINTY CLAWS. I BET HE COULD DO YOU SOME DAMAGE WITH THEM.
WE ARE NOT TALKING ABOUT THE POINTY CLAWS, JACK. WE ARE TALKING ABOUT LIBERATION FROM THE TYRANNY OF THIS GEOGRAPHY.
DO YOU RECOGNIZE HIM? THINK.
JUST SPLIT YE RIGHT UP. GUTS TO GIZZARD.
NASTY LOOKIN' PIECE'A WORK...

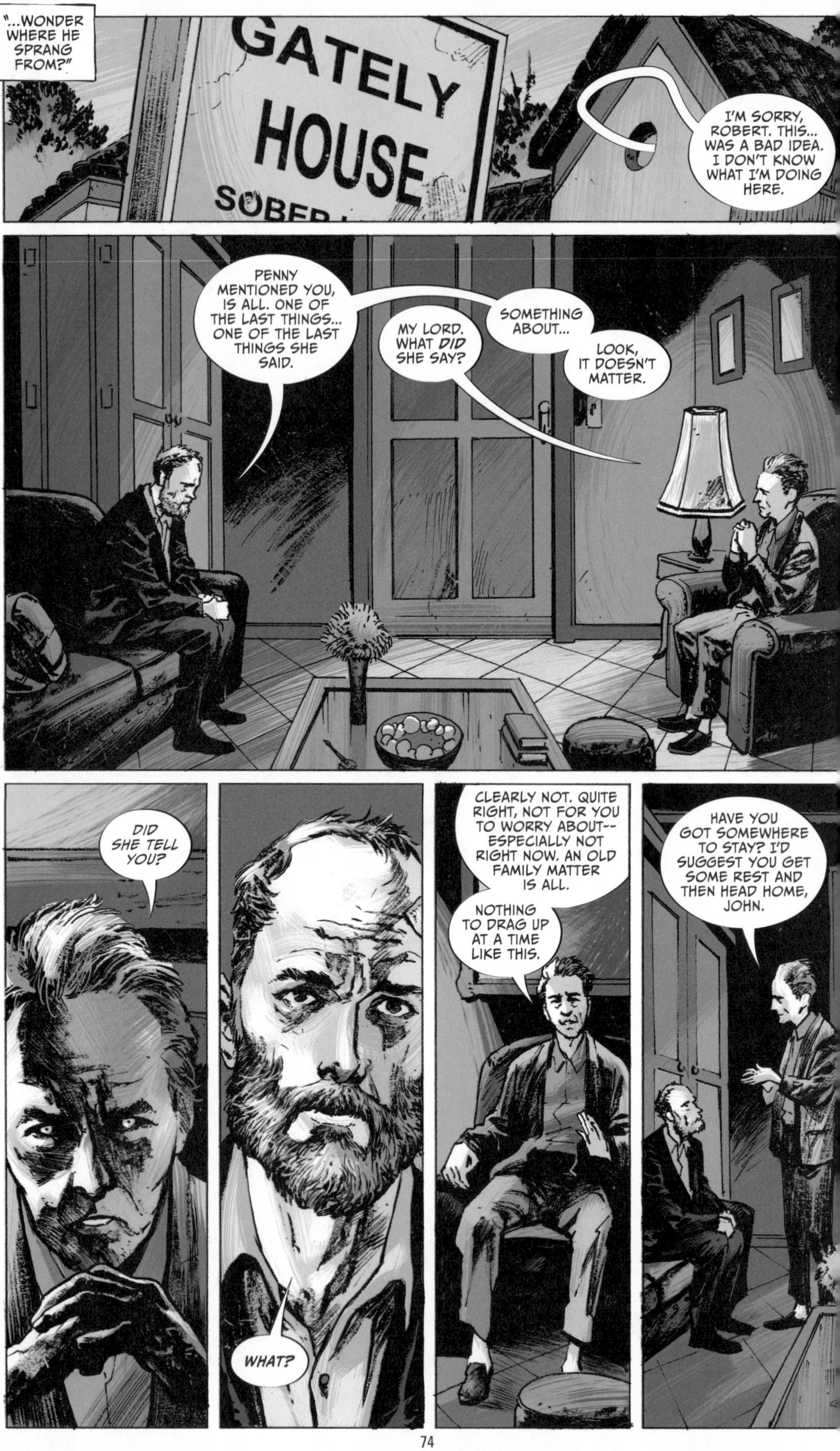
"...WONDER WHERE HE SPRANG FROM?"
GATELY HOUSE
SOBER
I'M SORRY, ROBERT. THIS... WAS A BAD IDEA. I DON'T KNOW WHAT I'M DOING HERE.
PENNY MENTIONED YOU, IS ALL. ONE OF THE LAST THINGS... ONE OF THE LAST THINGS SHE SAID.
SOMETHING ABOUT...
MY LORD. WHAT DID SHE SAY?
LOOK, IT DOESN'T MATTER.
DID SHE TELL YOU?
WHAT?
CLEARLY NOT. QUITE RIGHT, NOT FOR YOU TO WORRY ABOUT-- ESPECIALLY NOT RIGHT NOW. AN OLD FAMILY MATTER IS ALL.
NOTHING TO DRAG UP AT A TIME LIKE THIS.
HAVE YOU GOT SOMEWHERE TO STAY? I'D SUGGEST YOU GET SOME REST AND THEN HEAD HOME, JOHN.

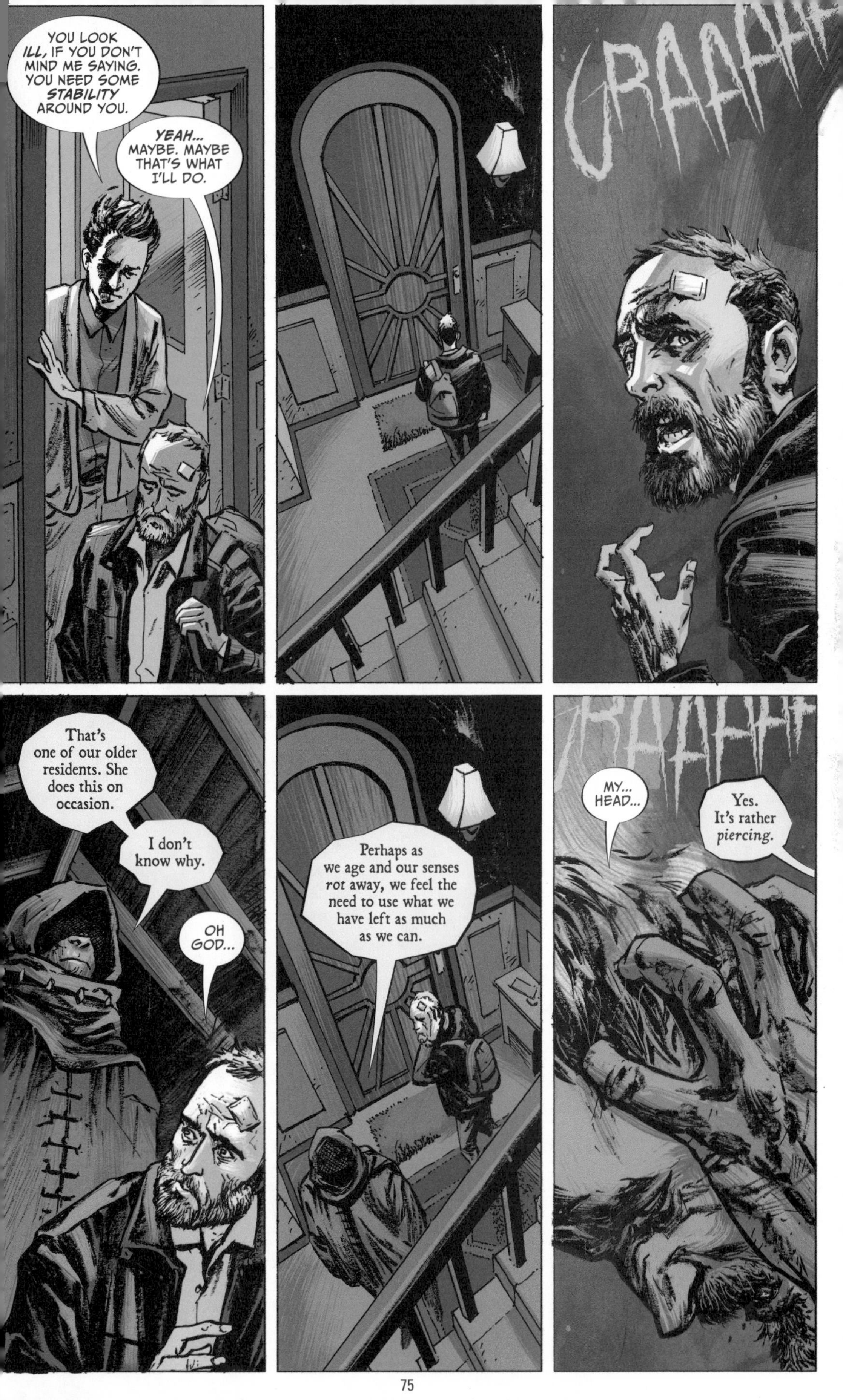
YOU LOOK *ILL,* IF YOU DON'T MIND ME SAYING. YOU NEED SOME *STABILITY* AROUND YOU.
YEAH... MAYBE. MAYBE THAT'S WHAT I'LL DO.
CRAAAAH
That's one of our older residents. She does this on occasion.
I don't know why.
OH GOD...
Perhaps as we age and our senses *rot* away, we feel the need to use what we have left as much as we can.
MY... HEAD...
Yes. It's rather *piercing.*

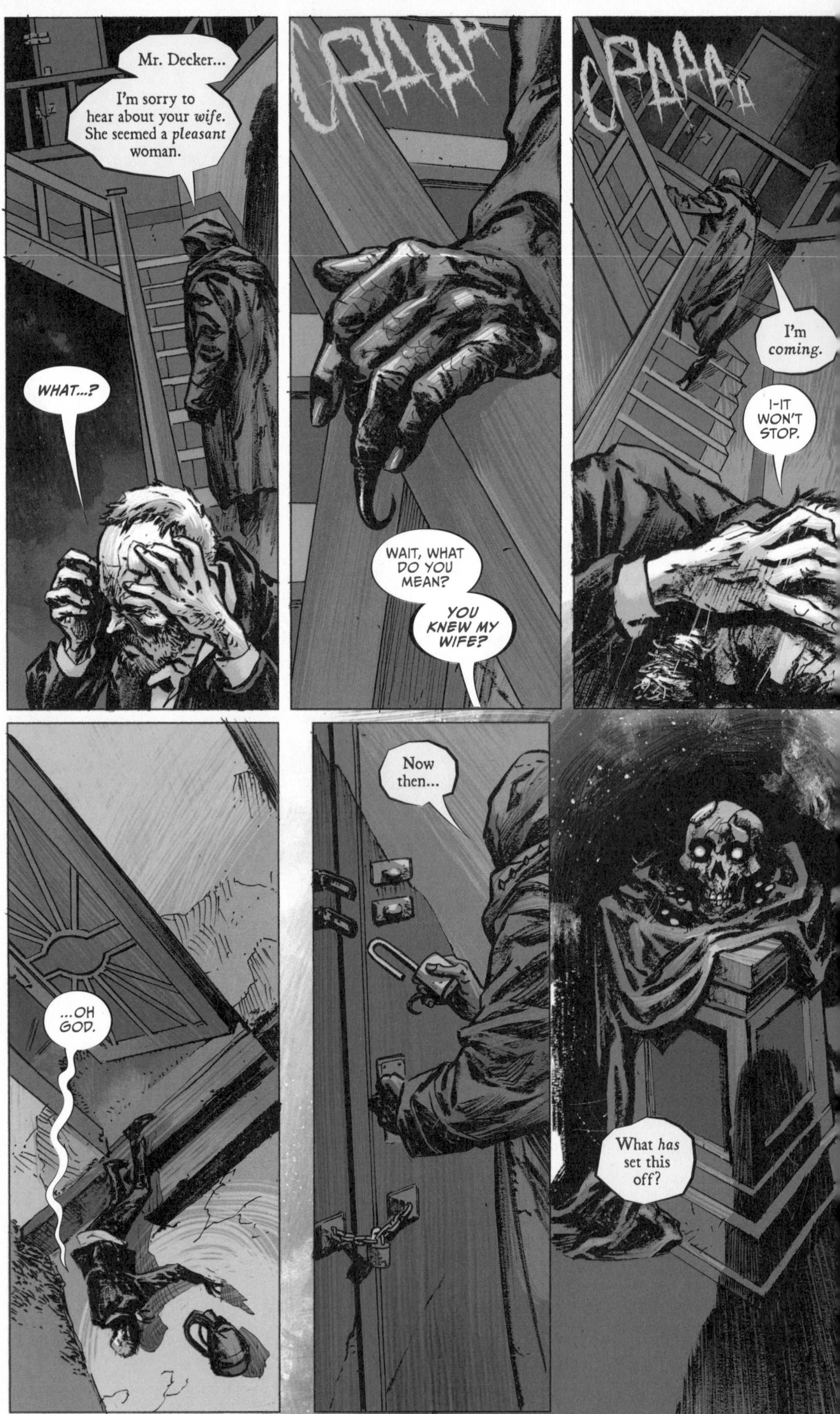
Mr. Decker...
I'm sorry to hear about your *wife*. She seemed a *pleasant* woman.
WHAT...?
CRAAA
WAIT, WHAT DO YOU MEAN?
YOU KNEW MY WIFE?
CRAAAA
I'm *coming*.
I-IT WON'T STOP.
...OH GOD.
Now then...
What *has* set this off?

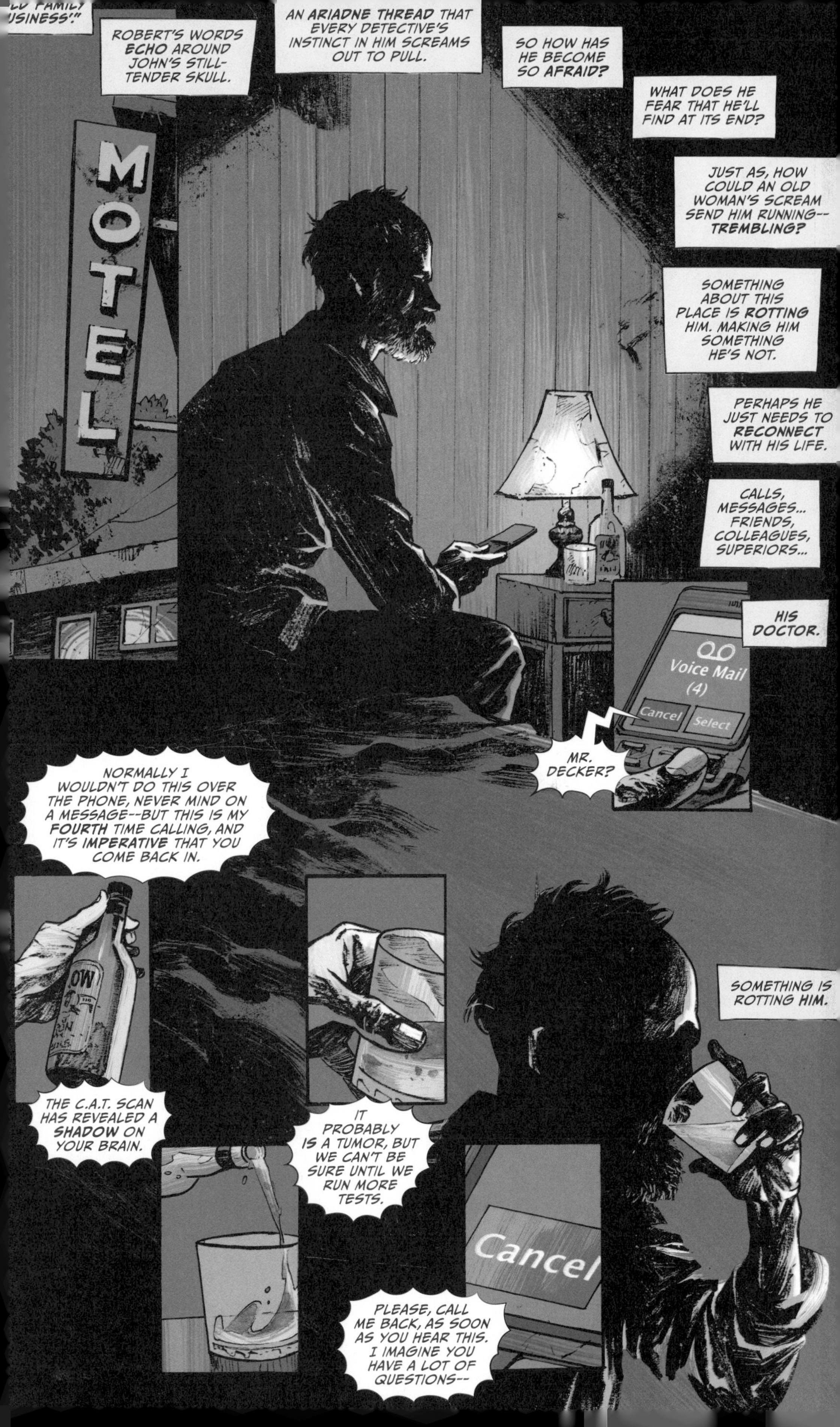

ROBERT'S WORDS ECHO AROUND JOHN'S STILL-TENDER SKULL.
AN ARIADNE THREAD THAT EVERY DETECTIVE'S INSTINCT IN HIM SCREAMS OUT TO PULL.
SO HOW HAS HE BECOME SO AFRAID?
WHAT DOES HE FEAR THAT HE'LL FIND AT ITS END?
JUST AS, HOW COULD AN OLD WOMAN'S SCREAM SEND HIM RUNNING-- TREMBLING?
SOMETHING ABOUT THIS PLACE IS ROTTING HIM. MAKING HIM SOMETHING HE'S NOT.
PERHAPS HE JUST NEEDS TO RECONNECT WITH HIS LIFE.
CALLS, MESSAGES... FRIENDS, COLLEAGUES, SUPERIORS...
HIS DOCTOR.
MOTEL
Voice Mail
(4)
Cancel
Select
MR. DECKER?
NORMALLY I WOULDN'T DO THIS OVER THE PHONE, NEVER MIND ON A MESSAGE--BUT THIS IS MY FOURTH TIME CALLING, AND IT'S IMPERATIVE THAT YOU COME BACK IN.
THE C.A.T. SCAN HAS REVEALED A SHADOW ON YOUR BRAIN.
IT PROBABLY IS A TUMOR, BUT WE CAN'T BE SURE UNTIL WE RUN MORE TESTS.
SOMETHING IS ROTTING HIM.
Cancel
PLEASE, CALL ME BACK, AS SOON AS YOU HEAR THIS. I IMAGINE YOU HAVE A LOT OF QUESTIONS--

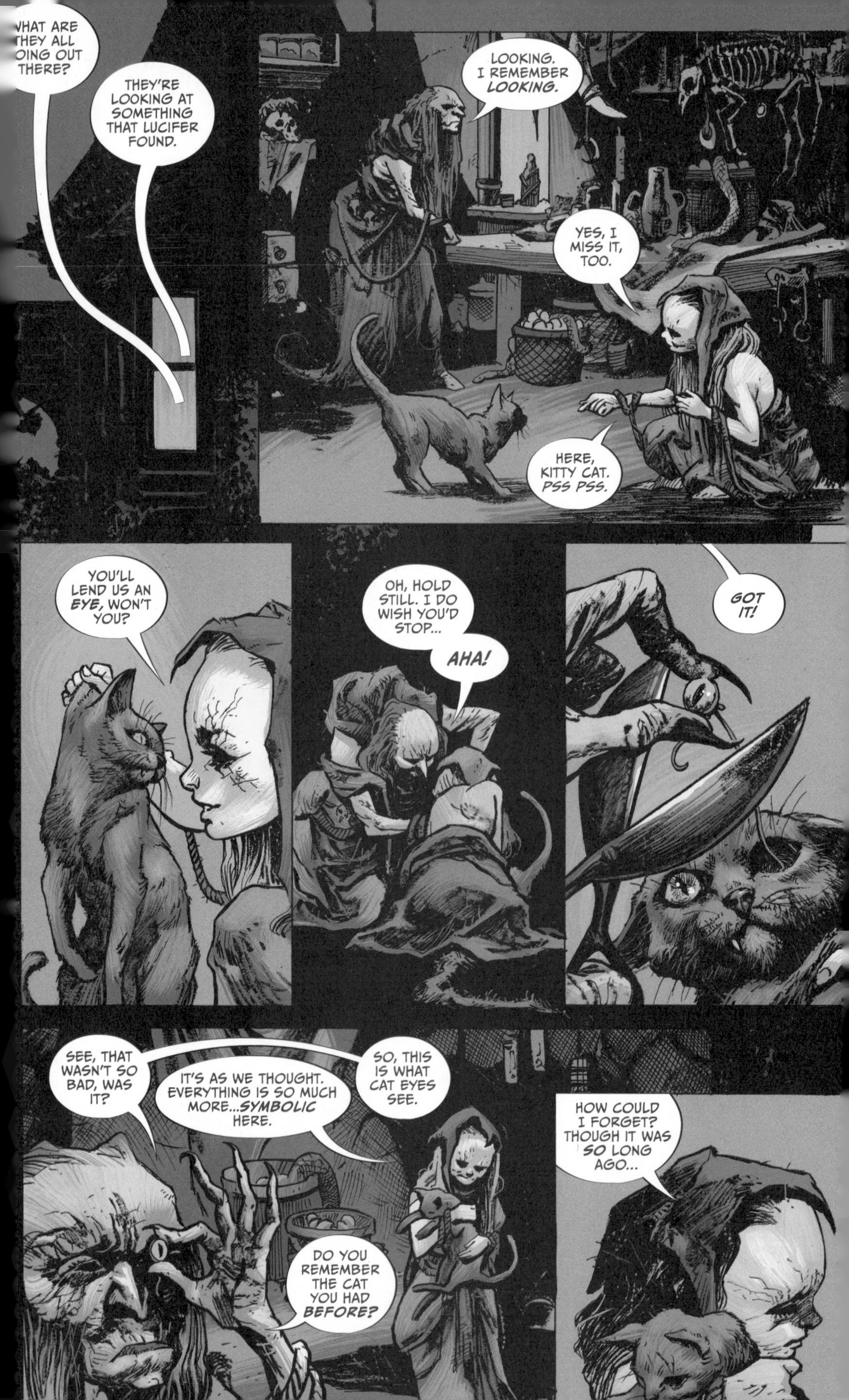

WHAT ARE THEY ALL OING OUT THERE?
THEY'RE LOOKING AT SOMETHING THAT LUCIFER FOUND.
LOOKING. I REMEMBER LOOKING.
YES, I MISS IT, TOO.
HERE, KITTY CAT. PSS PSS.
YOU'LL LEND US AN EYE, WON'T YOU?
OH, HOLD STILL. I DO WISH YOU'D STOP...
AHA!
GOT IT!
SEE, THAT WASN'T SO BAD, WAS IT?
SO, THIS IS WHAT CAT EYES SEE.
IT'S AS WE THOUGHT. EVERYTHING IS SO MUCH MORE...SYMBOLIC HERE.
DO YOU REMEMBER THE CAT YOU HAD BEFORE?
HOW COULD I FORGET? THOUGH IT WAS SO LONG AGO...

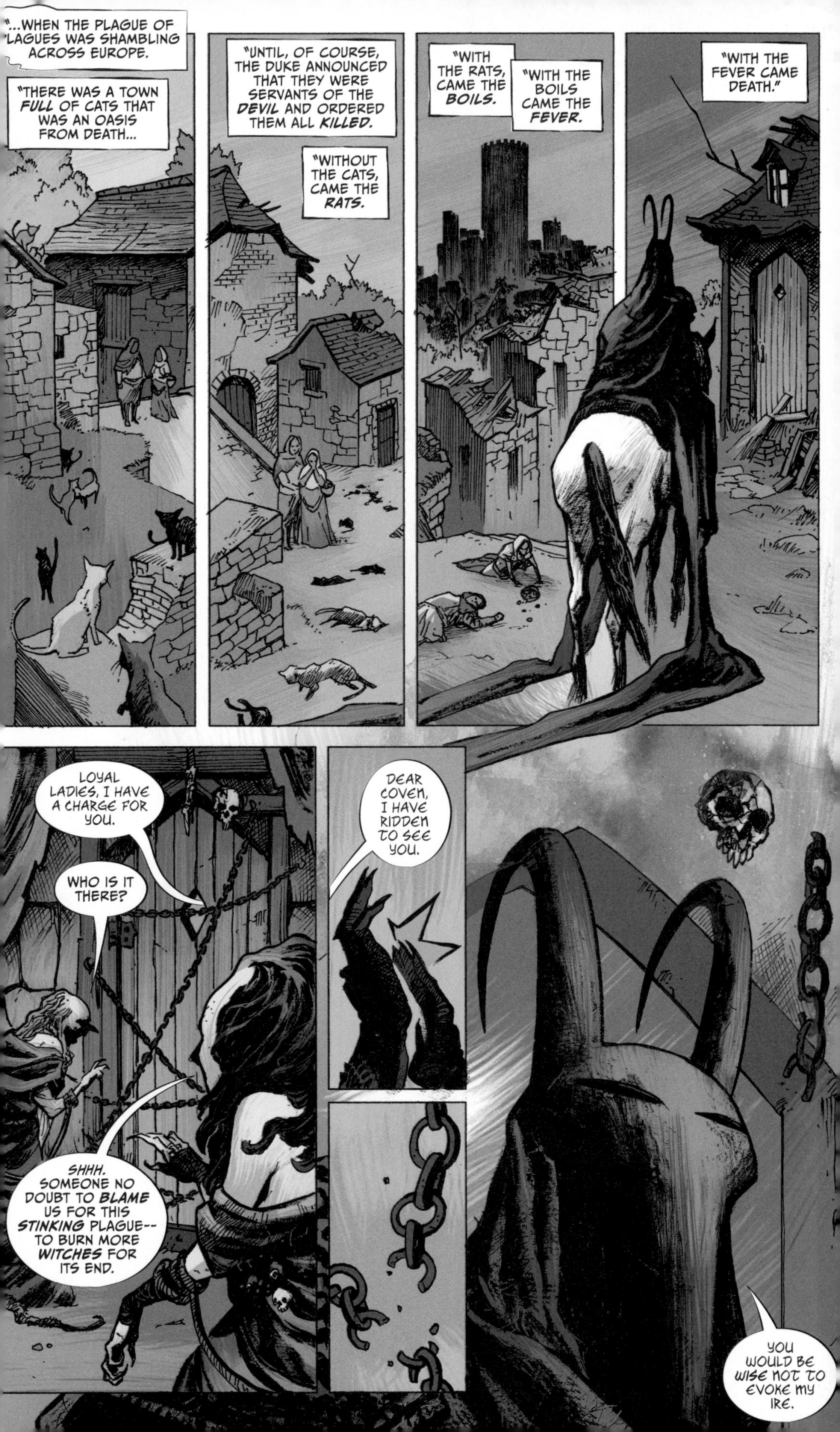
"...WHEN THE PLAGUE OF LAGUES WAS SHAMBLING ACROSS EUROPE.
"THERE WAS A TOWN FULL OF CATS THAT WAS AN OASIS FROM DEATH...
"UNTIL, OF COURSE, THE DUKE ANNOUNCED THAT THEY WERE SERVANTS OF THE DEVIL AND ORDERED THEM ALL KILLED.
"WITHOUT THE CATS, CAME THE RATS.
"WITH THE RATS, CAME THE BOILS.
"WITH THE BOILS CAME THE FEVER.
"WITH THE FEVER CAME DEATH."
LOYAL LADIES, I HAVE A CHARGE FOR YOU.
WHO IS IT THERE?
SHHH. SOMEONE NO DOUBT TO BLAME US FOR THIS STINKING PLAGUE--TO BURN MORE WITCHES FOR ITS END.
DEAR COVEN, I HAVE RIDDEN TO SEE YOU.
YOU WOULD BE WISE NOT TO EVOKE MY IRE.

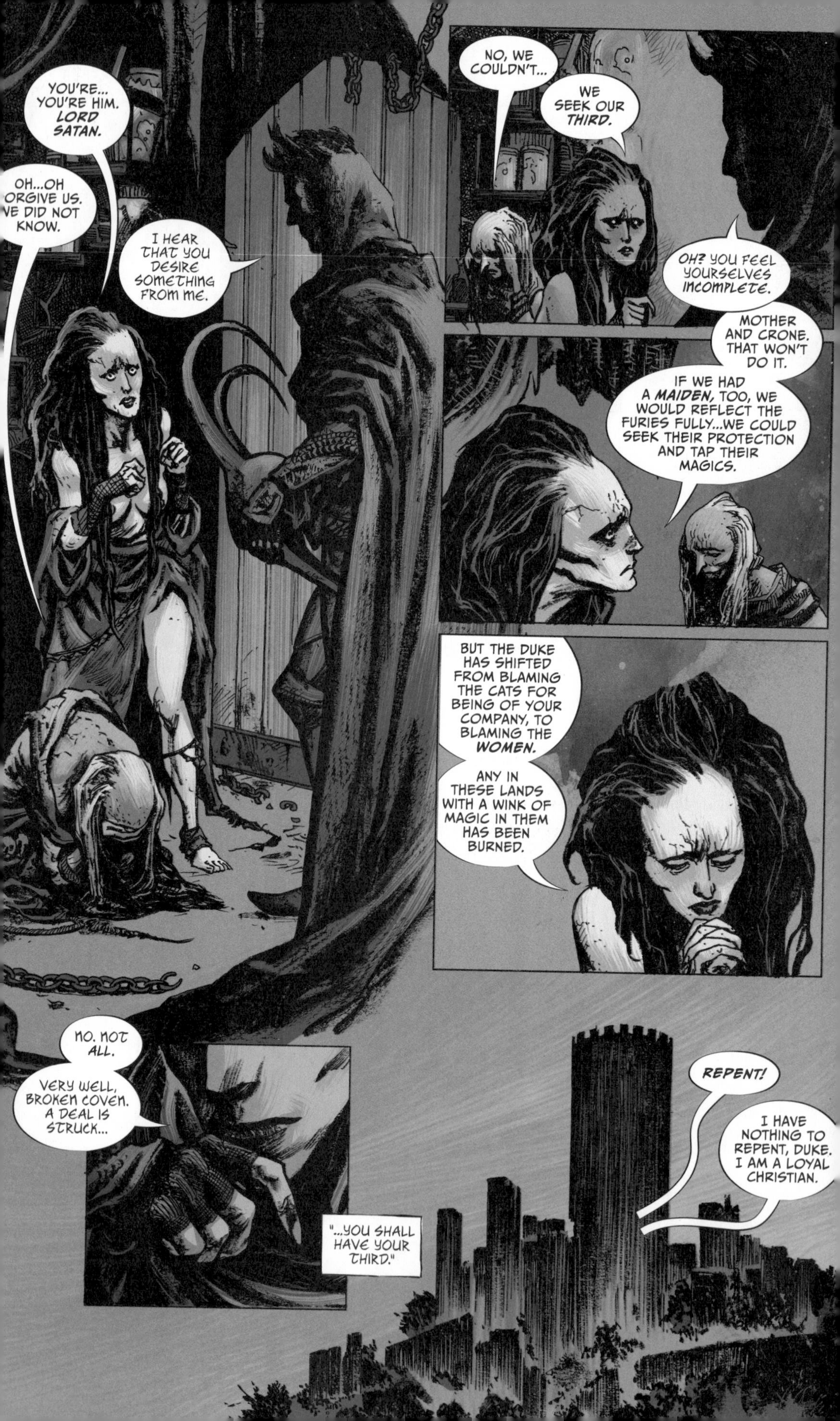

YOU'RE... YOU'RE HIM. LORD SATAN.
OH...OH ORGIVE US. VE DID NOT KNOW.
I HEAR THAT YOU DESIRE SOMETHING FROM ME.
NO, WE COULDN'T...
WE SEEK OUR THIRD.
OH? YOU FEEL YOURSELVES INCOMPLETE.
MOTHER AND CRONE. THAT WON'T DO IT.
IF WE HAD A MAIDEN, TOO, WE WOULD REFLECT THE FURIES FULLY...WE COULD SEEK THEIR PROTECTION AND TAP THEIR MAGICS.
BUT THE DUKE HAS SHIFTED FROM BLAMING THE CATS FOR BEING OF YOUR COMPANY, TO BLAMING THE WOMEN.
ANY IN THESE LANDS WITH A WINK OF MAGIC IN THEM HAS BEEN BURNED.
NO. NOT ALL.
VERY WELL, BROKEN COVEN. A DEAL IS STRUCK...
"...YOU SHALL HAVE YOUR THIRD."
REPENT!
I HAVE NOTHING TO REPENT, DUKE. I AM A LOYAL CHRISTIAN.

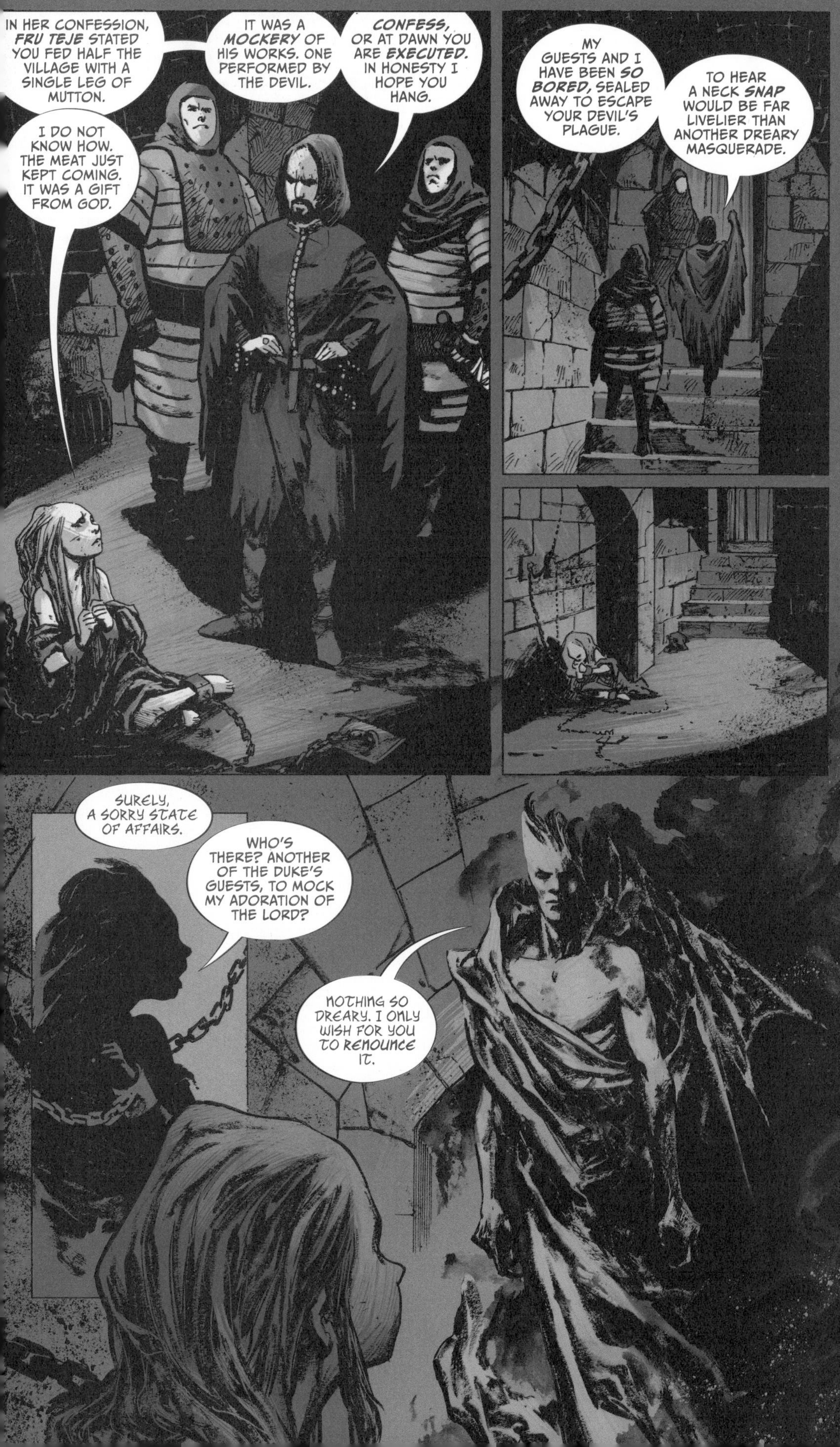
IN HER CONFESSION, FRU TEJE STATED YOU FED HALF THE VILLAGE WITH A SINGLE LEG OF MUTTON.
IT WAS A MOCKERY OF HIS WORKS. ONE PERFORMED BY THE DEVIL.
CONFESS, OR AT DAWN YOU ARE EXECUTED. IN HONESTY I HOPE YOU HANG.
I DO NOT KNOW HOW. THE MEAT JUST KEPT COMING. IT WAS A GIFT FROM GOD.
MY GUESTS AND I HAVE BEEN SO BORED, SEALED AWAY TO ESCAPE YOUR DEVIL'S PLAGUE.
TO HEAR A NECK SNAP WOULD BE FAR LIVELIER THAN ANOTHER DREARY MASQUERADE.
SURELY, A SORRY STATE OF AFFAIRS.
WHO'S THERE? ANOTHER OF THE DUKE'S GUESTS, TO MOCK MY ADORATION OF THE LORD?
NOTHING SO DREARY. I ONLY WISH FOR YOU TO RENOUNCE IT.

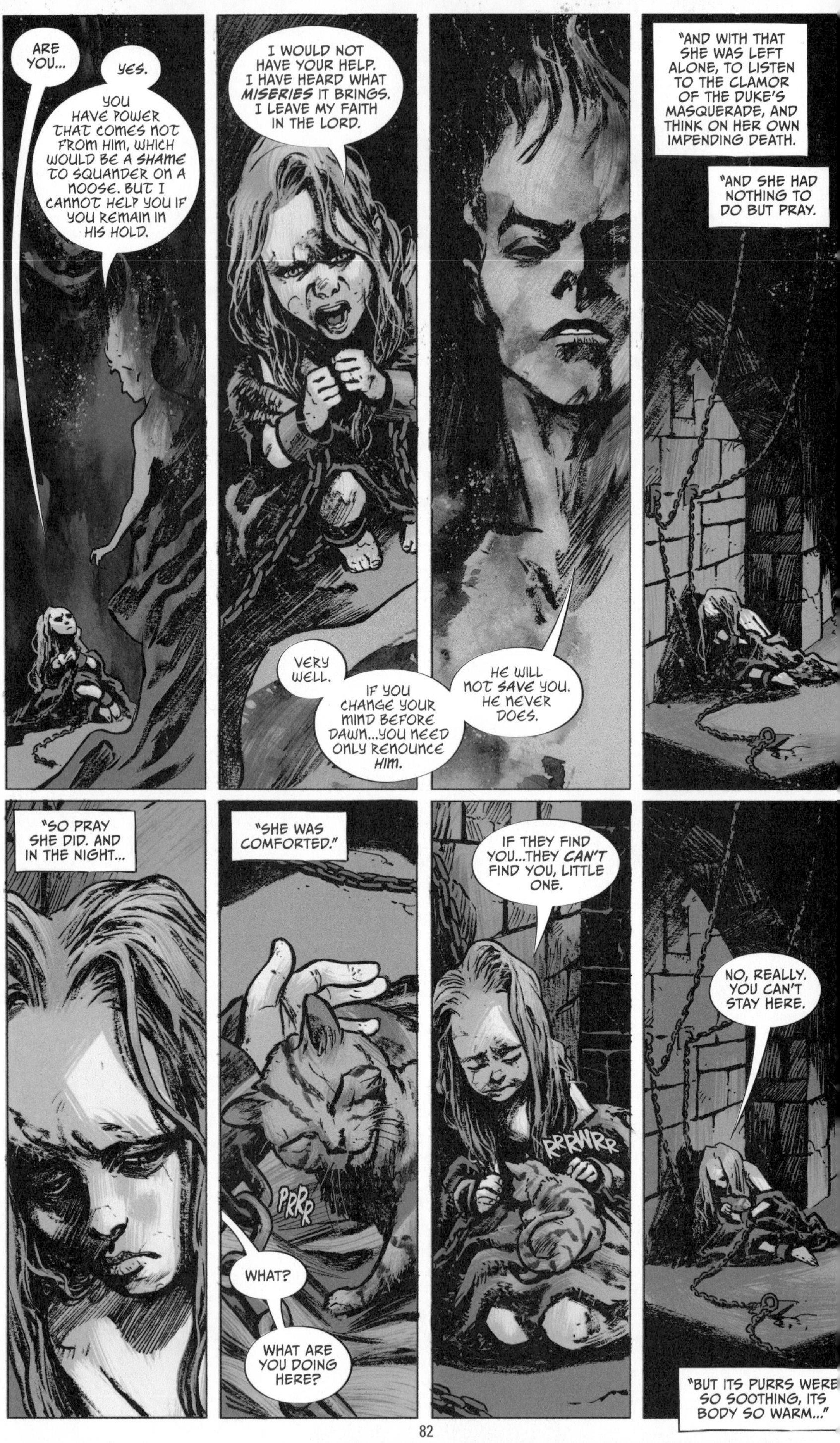

ARE YOU...
YES.
YOU HAVE POWER THAT COMES NOT FROM HIM, WHICH WOULD BE A SHAME TO SQUANDER ON A NOOSE. BUT I CANNOT HELP YOU IF YOU REMAIN IN HIS HOLD.
I WOULD NOT HAVE YOUR HELP. I HAVE HEARD WHAT MISERIES IT BRINGS. I LEAVE MY FAITH IN THE LORD.
VERY WELL.
IF YOU CHANGE YOUR MIND BEFORE DAWN...YOU NEED ONLY RENOUNCE HIM.
HE WILL NOT SAVE YOU. HE NEVER DOES.
"AND WITH THAT SHE WAS LEFT ALONE, TO LISTEN TO THE CLAMOR OF THE DUKE'S MASQUERADE, AND THINK ON HER OWN IMPENDING DEATH.
"AND SHE HAD NOTHING TO DO BUT PRAY.
"SO PRAY SHE DID. AND IN THE NIGHT...
"SHE WAS COMFORTED."
PRRR
WHAT?
WHAT ARE YOU DOING HERE?
IF THEY FIND YOU...THEY CAN'T FIND YOU, LITTLE ONE.
RRRWRR
NO, REALLY. YOU CAN'T STAY HERE.
"BUT ITS PURRS WERE SO SOOTHING, ITS BODY SO WARM..."

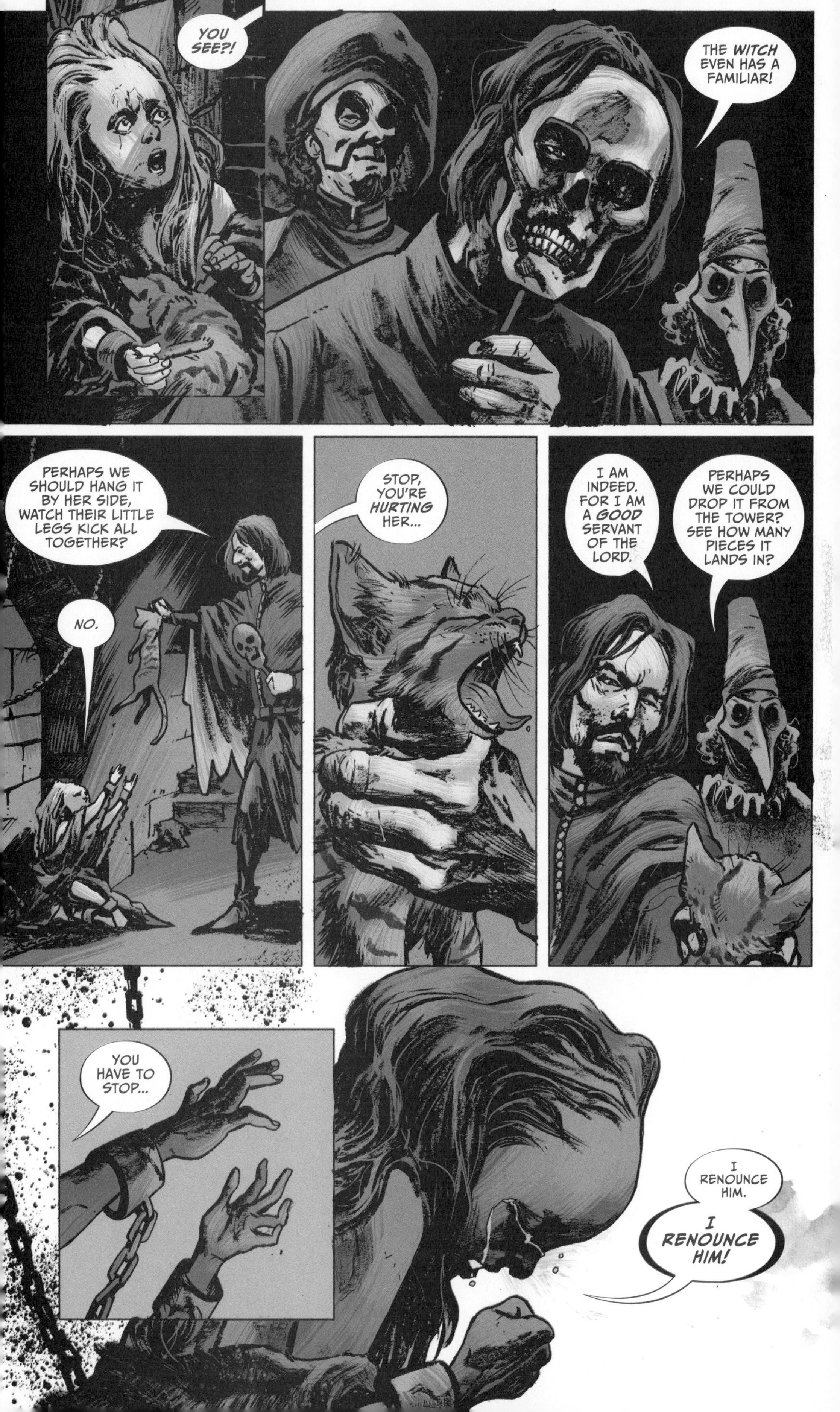

YOU SEE?!
THE WITCH EVEN HAS A FAMILIAR!
PERHAPS WE SHOULD HANG IT BY HER SIDE, WATCH THEIR LITTLE LEGS KICK ALL TOGETHER?
NO.
STOP, YOU'RE HURTING HER...
I AM INDEED. FOR I AM A GOOD SERVANT OF THE LORD.
PERHAPS WE COULD DROP IT FROM THE TOWER? SEE HOW MANY PIECES IT LANDS IN?
YOU HAVE TO STOP...
I RENOUNCE HIM.
I RENOUNCE HIM!

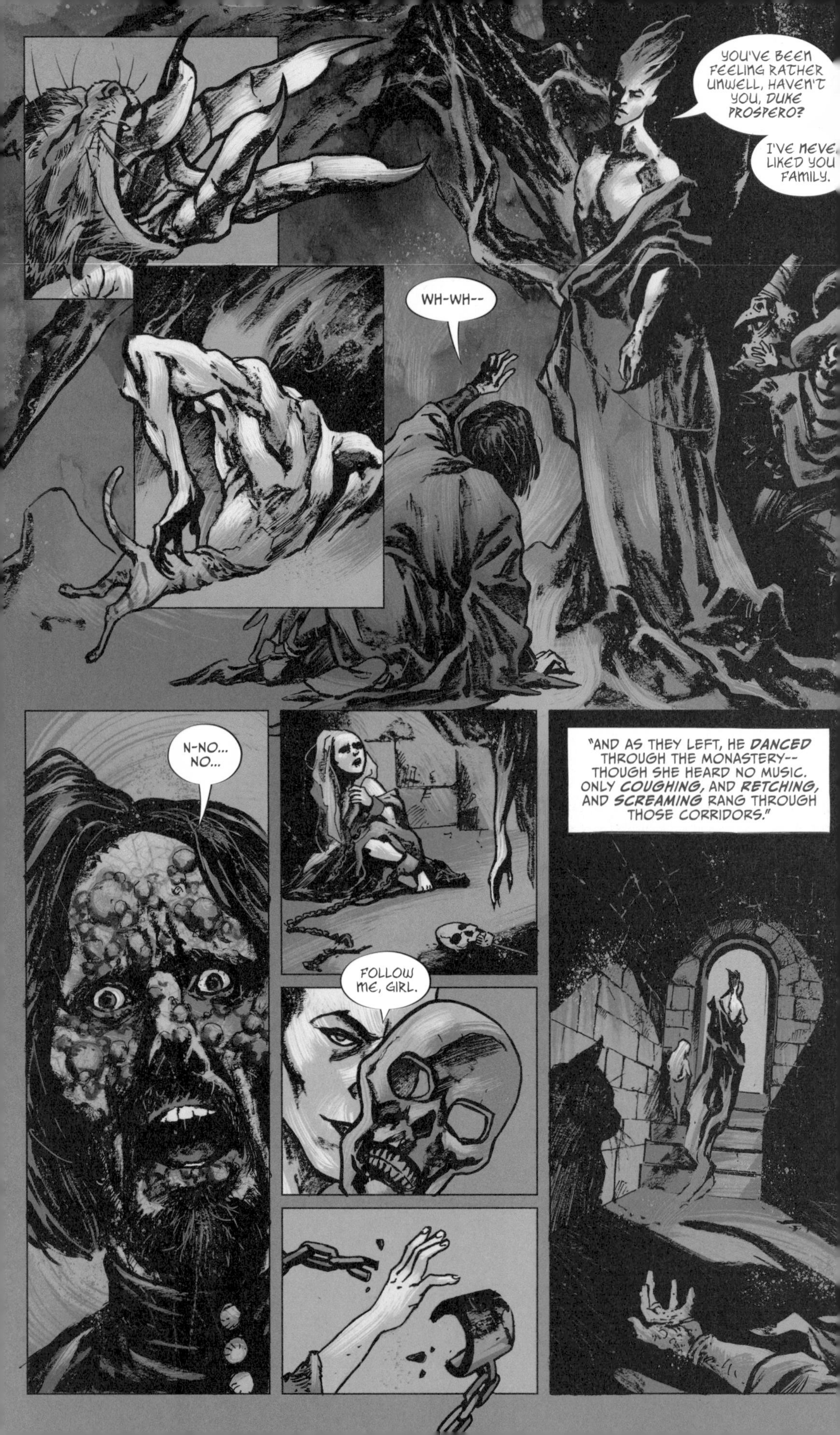
YOU'VE BEEN FEELING RATHER UNWELL, HAVEN'T YOU, DUKE PROSPERO?
I'VE NEVE LIKED YOU FAMILY.
WH-WH--
N-NO... NO...
"AND AS THEY LEFT, HE DANCED THROUGH THE MONASTERY-- THOUGH SHE HEARD NO MUSIC. ONLY COUGHING, AND RETCHING, AND SCREAMING RANG THROUGH THOSE CORRIDORS."
FOLLOW ME, GIRL.

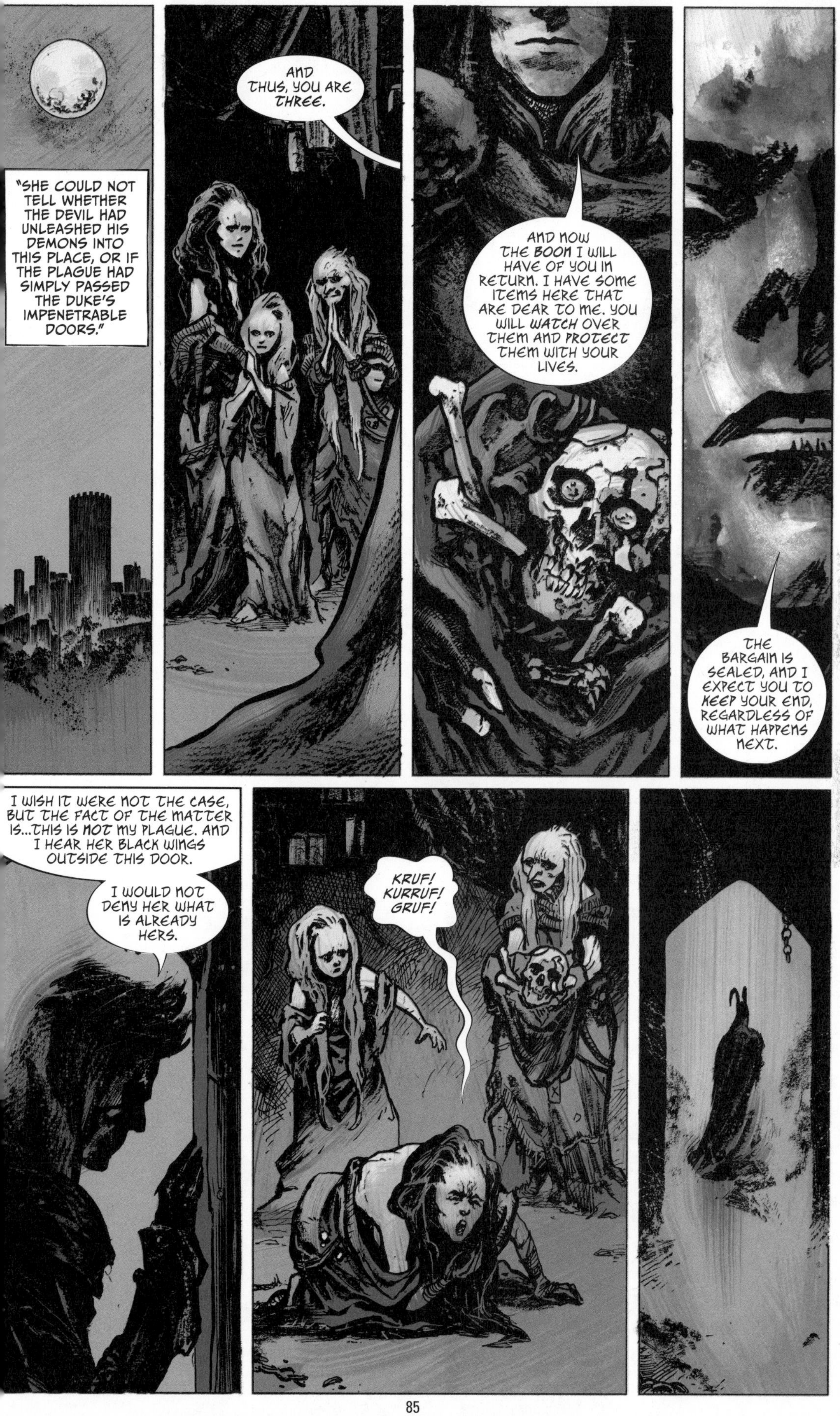
"SHE COULD NOT TELL WHETHER THE DEVIL HAD UNLEASHED HIS DEMONS INTO THIS PLACE, OR IF THE PLAGUE HAD SIMPLY PASSED THE DUKE'S IMPENETRABLE DOORS."
AND THUS, YOU ARE THREE.
AND NOW THE BOON I WILL HAVE OF YOU IN RETURN. I HAVE SOME ITEMS HERE THAT ARE DEAR TO ME. YOU WILL WATCH OVER THEM AND PROTECT THEM WITH YOUR LIVES.
THE BARGAIN IS SEALED, AND I EXPECT YOU TO KEEP YOUR END, REGARDLESS OF WHAT HAPPENS NEXT.
I WISH IT WERE NOT THE CASE, BUT THE FACT OF THE MATTER IS...THIS IS NOT MY PLAGUE. AND I HEAR HER BLACK WINGS OUTSIDE THIS DOOR.
I WOULD NOT DENY HER WHAT IS ALREADY HERS.
KRUF! KURRUF! GRUF!

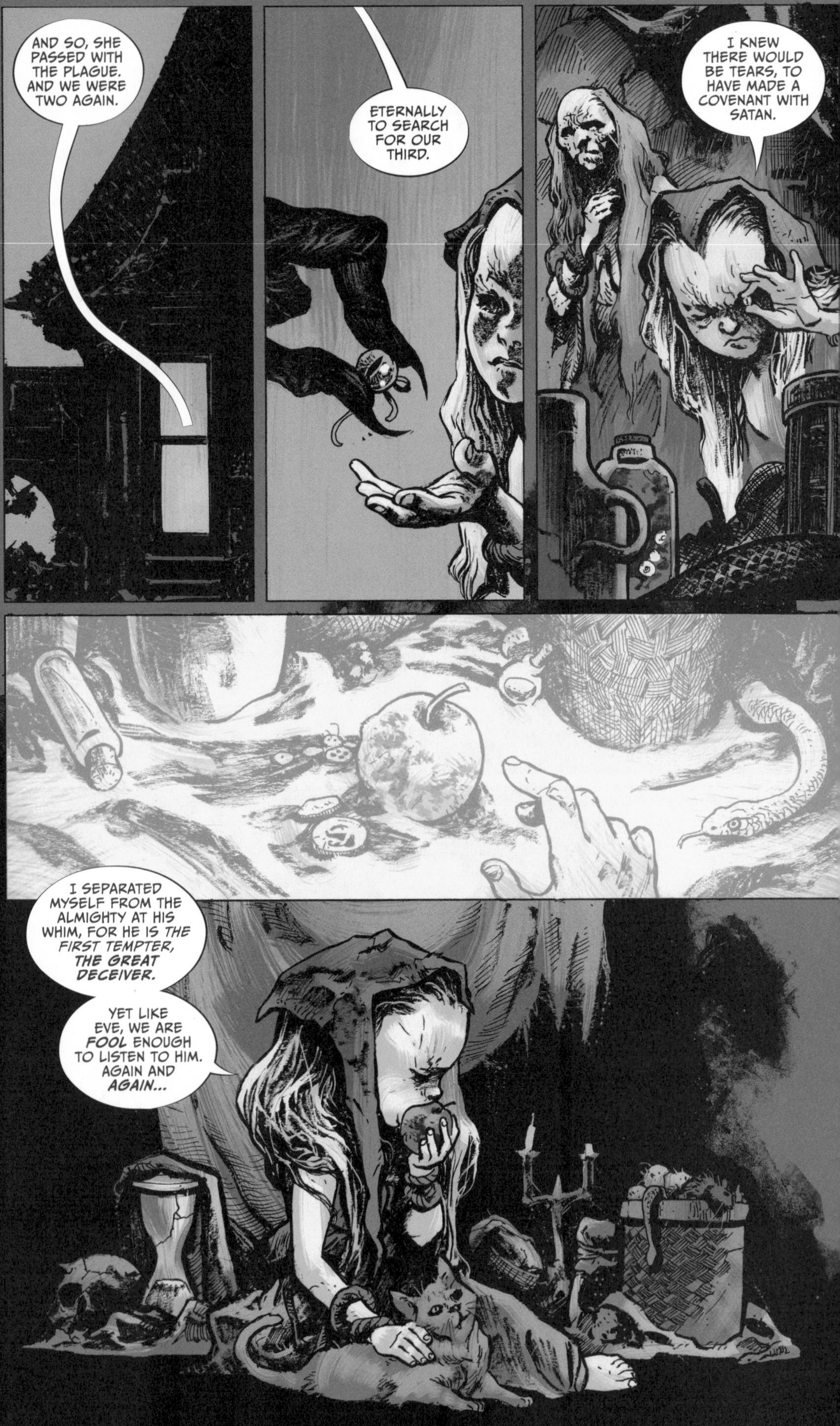
AND SO, SHE PASSED WITH THE PLAGUE. AND WE WERE TWO AGAIN.
ETERNALLY TO SEARCH FOR OUR THIRD.
I KNEW THERE WOULD BE TEARS, TO HAVE MADE A COVENANT WITH SATAN.
I SEPARATED MYSELF FROM THE ALMIGHTY AT HIS WHIM, FOR HE IS THE FIRST TEMPTER, THE GREAT DECEIVER.
YET LIKE EVE, WE ARE FOOL ENOUGH TO LISTEN TO HIM. AGAIN AND AGAIN...

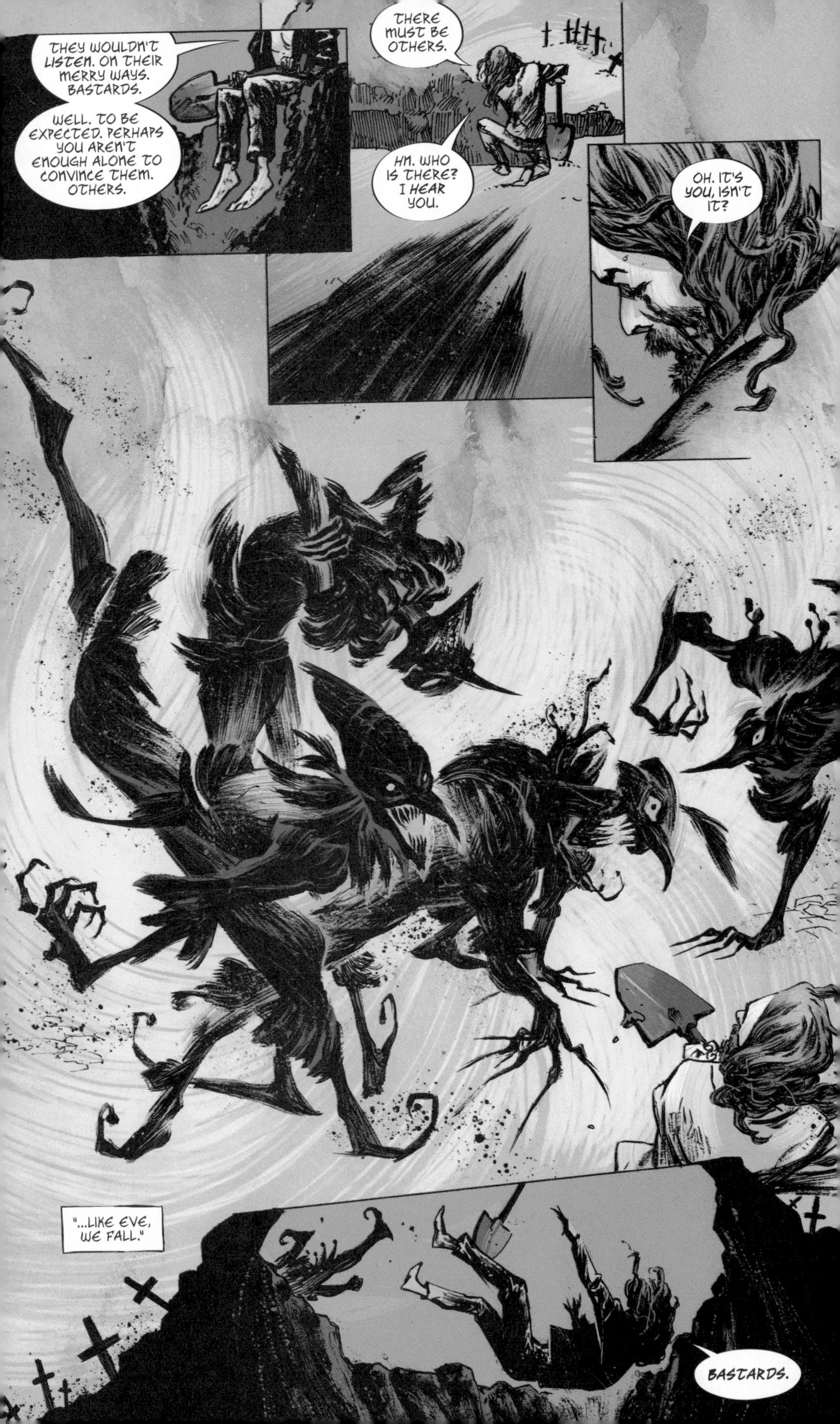
THEY WOULDN'T LISTEN. ON THEIR MERRY WAYS. BASTARDS.
WELL. TO BE EXPECTED. PERHAPS YOU AREN'T ENOUGH ALONE TO CONVINCE THEM. OTHERS.
THERE MUST BE OTHERS.
HM. WHO IS THERE? I HEAR YOU.
OH. IT'S YOU, ISN'T IT?
"...LIKE EVE, WE FALL."
BASTARDS.

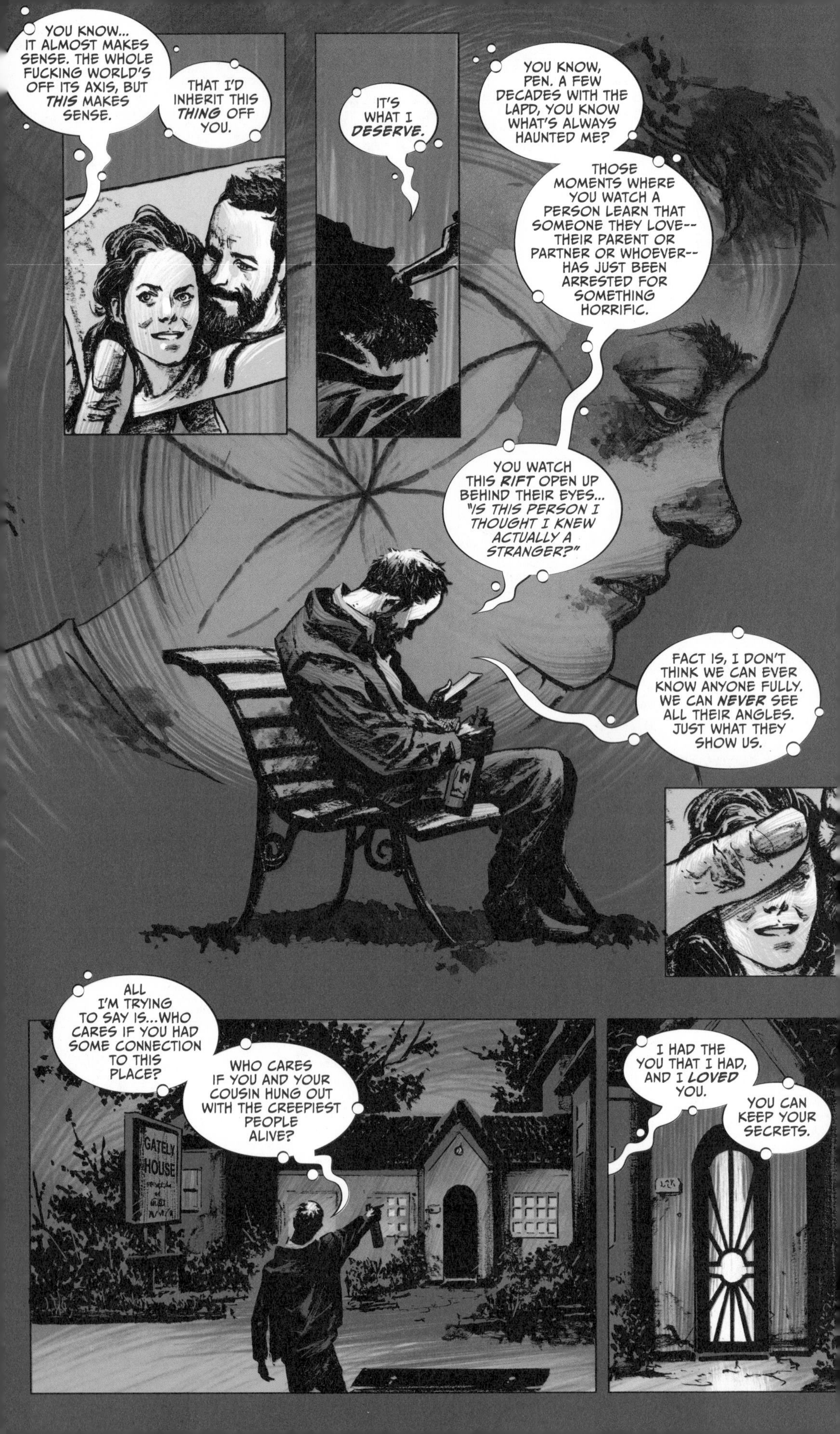
YOU KNOW... IT ALMOST MAKES SENSE. THE WHOLE FUCKING WORLD'S OFF ITS AXIS, BUT *THIS* MAKES SENSE.
THAT I'D INHERIT THIS *THING* OFF YOU.
IT'S WHAT I *DESERVE.*
YOU KNOW, PEN. A FEW DECADES WITH THE LAPD, YOU KNOW WHAT'S ALWAYS HAUNTED ME?
THOSE MOMENTS WHERE YOU WATCH A PERSON LEARN THAT SOMEONE THEY LOVE-- THEIR PARENT OR PARTNER OR WHOEVER-- HAS JUST BEEN ARRESTED FOR SOMETHING HORRIFIC.
YOU WATCH THIS *RIFT* OPEN UP BEHIND THEIR EYES... *"IS THIS PERSON I THOUGHT I KNEW ACTUALLY A STRANGER?"*
FACT IS, I DON'T THINK WE CAN EVER KNOW ANYONE FULLY. WE CAN *NEVER* SEE ALL THEIR ANGLES. JUST WHAT THEY SHOW US.
ALL I'M TRYING TO SAY IS...WHO CARES IF YOU HAD SOME CONNECTION TO THIS PLACE?
WHO CARES IF YOU AND YOUR COUSIN HUNG OUT WITH THE CREEPIEST PEOPLE ALIVE?
GATELY HOUSE
I HAD THE YOU THAT I HAD, AND I *LOVED* YOU.
YOU CAN KEEP YOUR SECRETS.

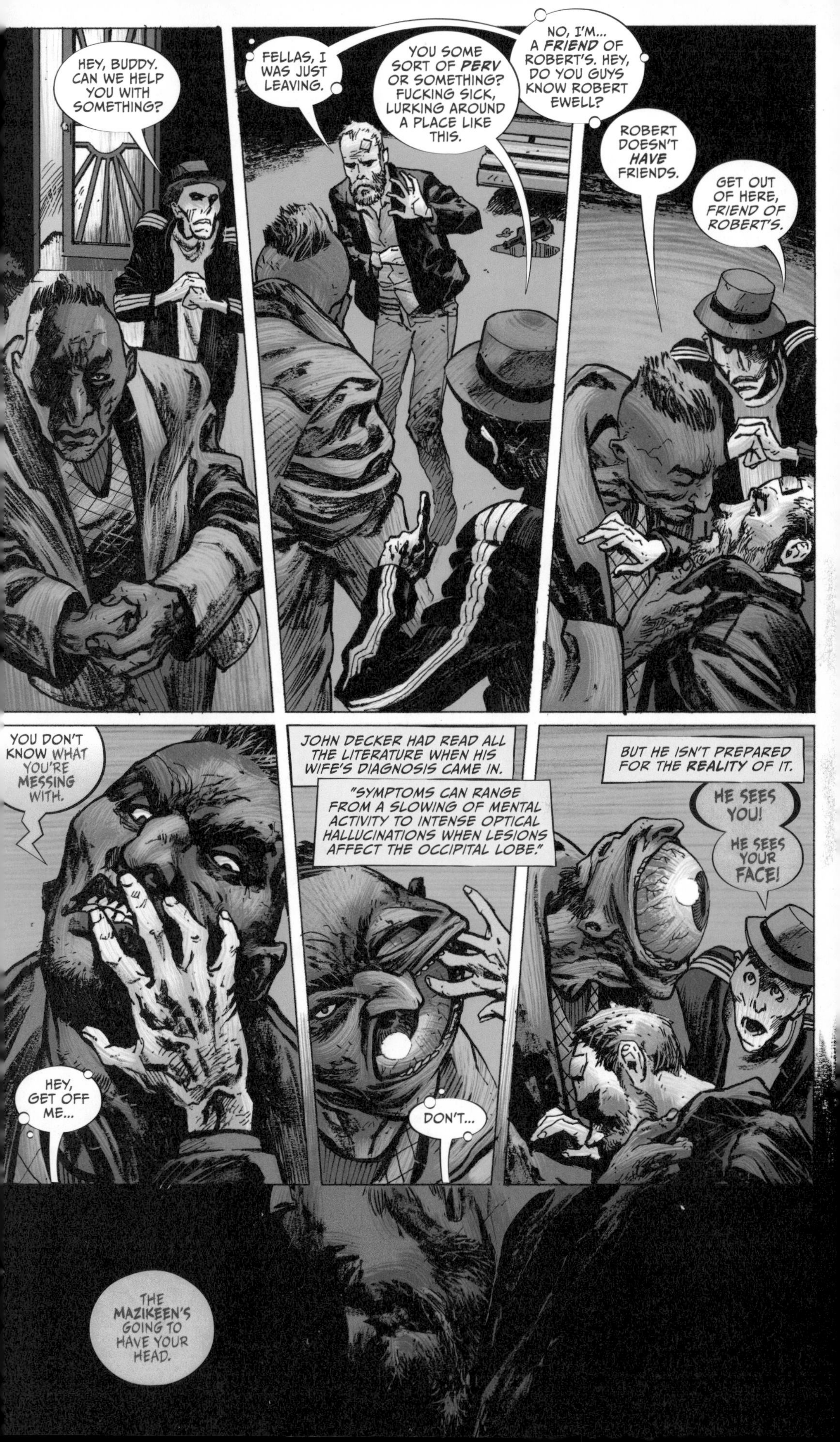

HEY, BUDDY. CAN WE HELP YOU WITH SOMETHING?
FELLAS, I WAS JUST LEAVING.
YOU SOME SORT OF PERV OR SOMETHING? FUCKING SICK, LURKING AROUND A PLACE LIKE THIS.
NO, I'M... A FRIEND OF ROBERT'S. HEY, DO YOU GUYS KNOW ROBERT EWELL?
ROBERT DOESN'T HAVE FRIENDS.
GET OUT OF HERE, FRIEND OF ROBERT'S.
YOU DON'T KNOW WHAT YOU'RE MESSING WITH.
HEY, GET OFF ME...
JOHN DECKER HAD READ ALL THE LITERATURE WHEN HIS WIFE'S DIAGNOSIS CAME IN.
"SYMPTOMS CAN RANGE FROM A SLOWING OF MENTAL ACTIVITY TO INTENSE OPTICAL HALLUCINATIONS WHEN LESIONS AFFECT THE OCCIPITAL LOBE."
DON'T...
BUT HE ISN'T PREPARED FOR THE REALITY OF IT.
HE SEES YOU!
HE SEES YOUR FACE!
THE MAZIKEEN'S GOING TO HAVE YOUR HEAD.

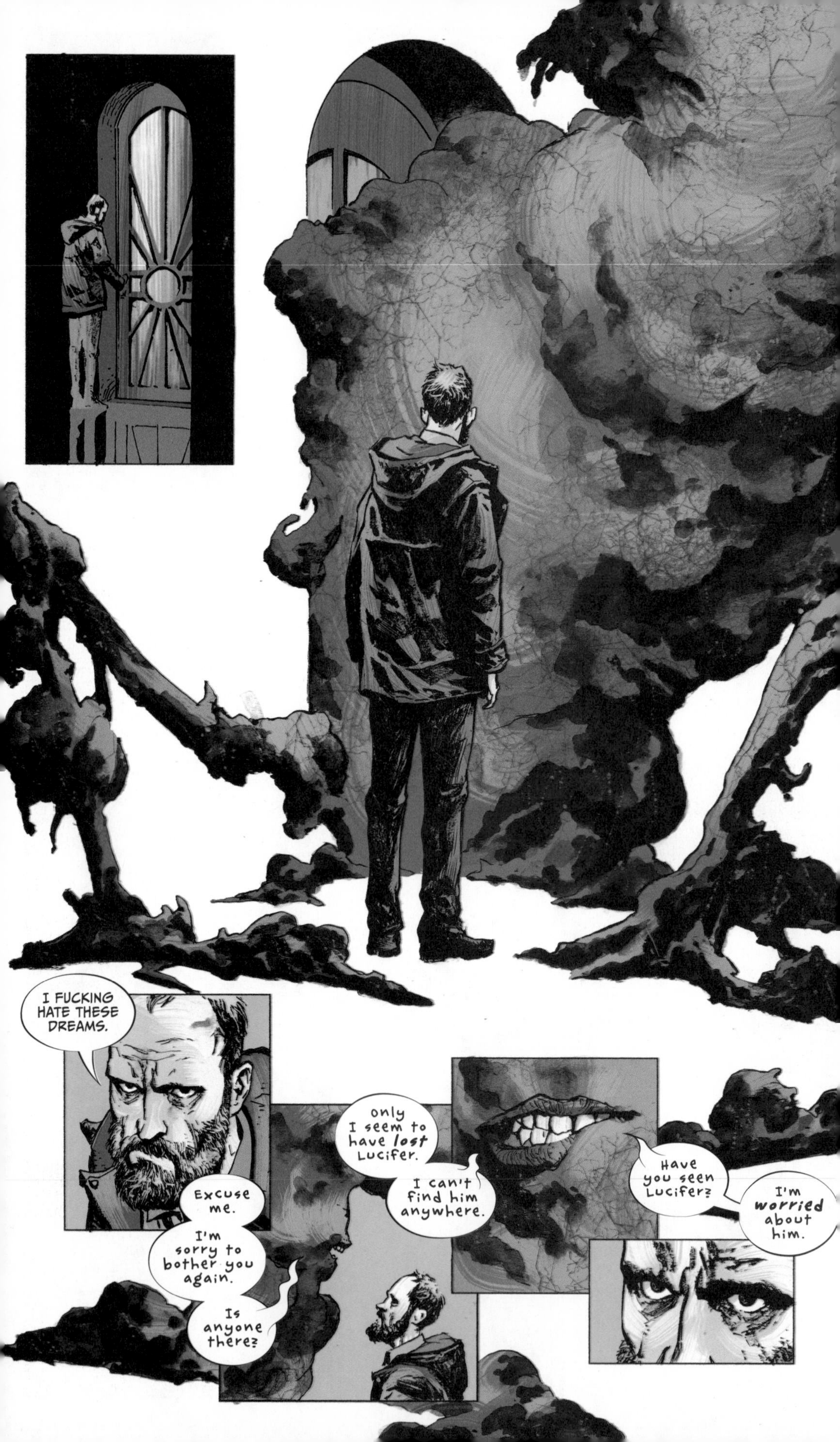
I FUCKING HATE THESE DREAMS.
Excuse me.
I'm sorry to bother you again.
Is anyone there?
Only I seem to have *lost* Lucifer.
I can't find him anywhere.
Have you seen Lucifer?
I'm *worried* about him.

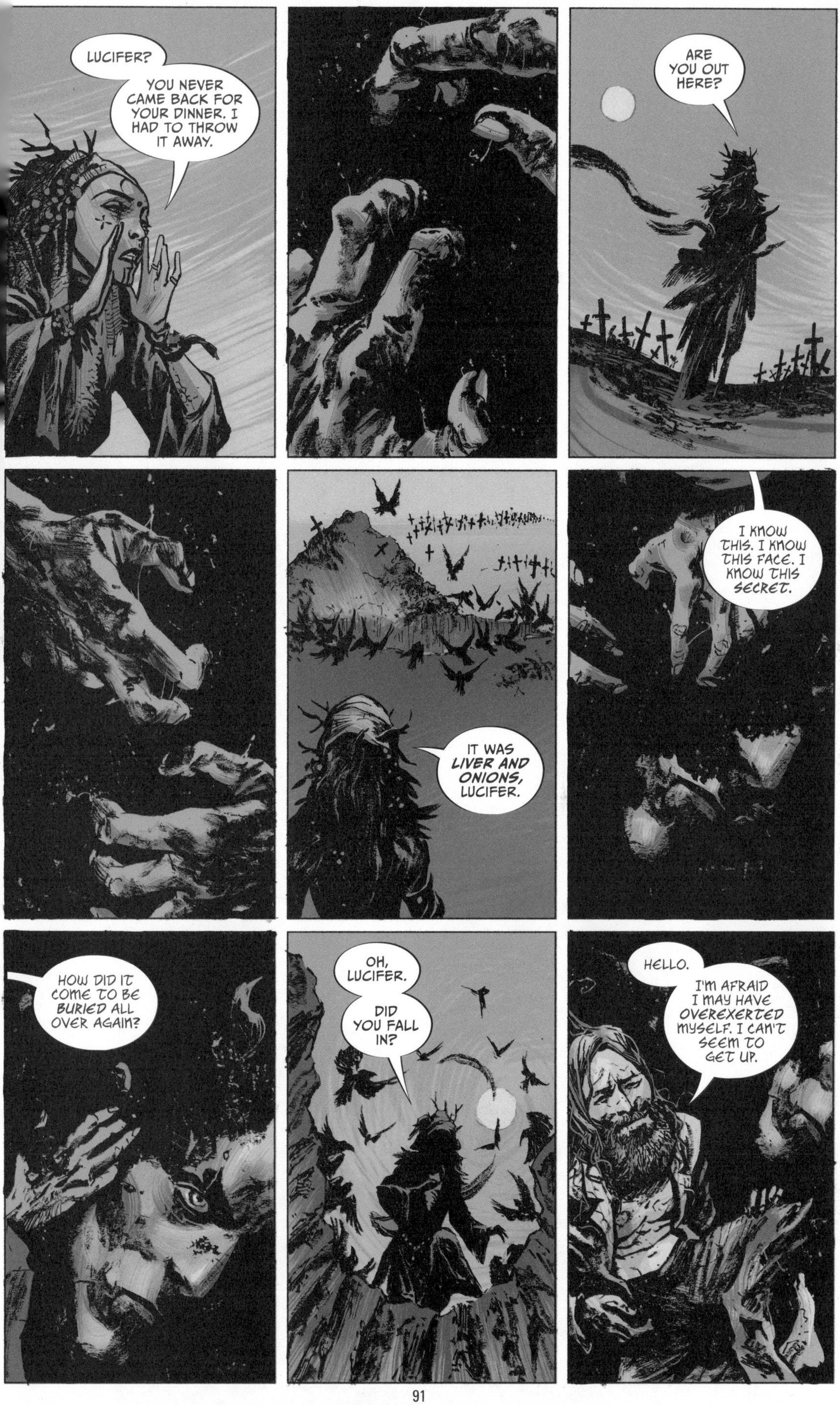
LUCIFER?
YOU NEVER CAME BACK FOR YOUR DINNER. I HAD TO THROW IT AWAY.
ARE YOU OUT HERE?
I KNOW THIS. I KNOW THIS FACE. I KNOW THIS SECRET.
IT WAS *LIVER AND ONIONS,* LUCIFER.
HOW DID IT COME TO BE BURIED ALL OVER AGAIN?
OH, LUCIFER.
DID YOU FALL IN?
HELLO.
I'M AFRAID I MAY HAVE OVEREXERTED MYSELF. I CAN'T SEEM TO GET UP.

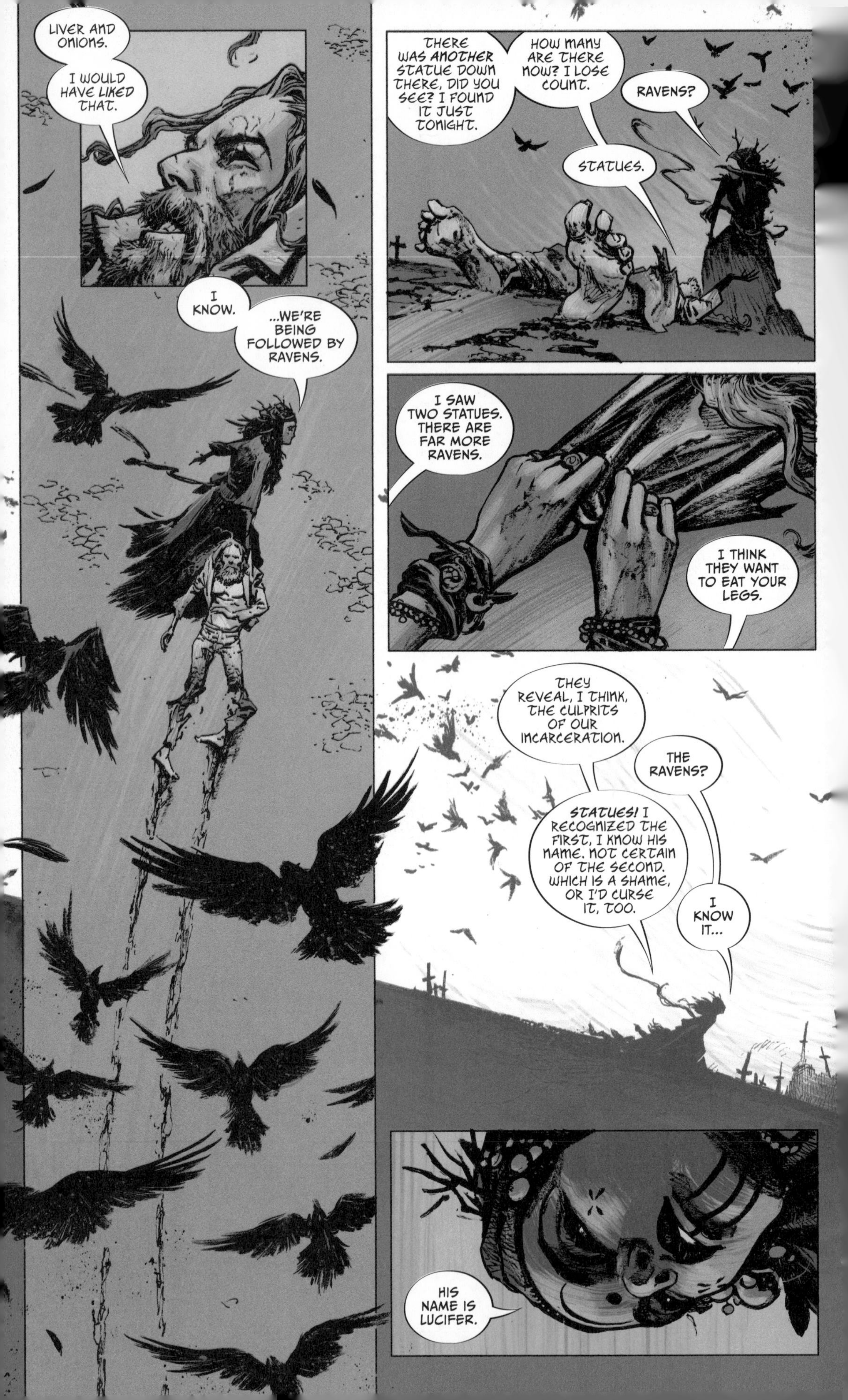
LIVER AND ONIONS.
I WOULD HAVE LIKED THAT.
I KNOW.
...WE'RE BEING FOLLOWED BY RAVENS.
THERE WAS ANOTHER STATUE DOWN THERE, DID YOU SEE? I FOUND IT JUST TONIGHT.
HOW MANY ARE THERE NOW? I LOSE COUNT.
RAVENS?
STATUES.
I SAW TWO STATUES. THERE ARE FAR MORE RAVENS.
I THINK THEY WANT TO EAT YOUR LEGS.
THEY REVEAL, I THINK, THE CULPRITS OF OUR INCARCERATION.
THE RAVENS?
STATUES! I RECOGNIZED THE FIRST, I KNOW HIS NAME. NOT CERTAIN OF THE SECOND. WHICH IS A SHAME, OR I'D CURSE IT, TOO.
I KNOW IT...
HIS NAME IS LUCIFER.

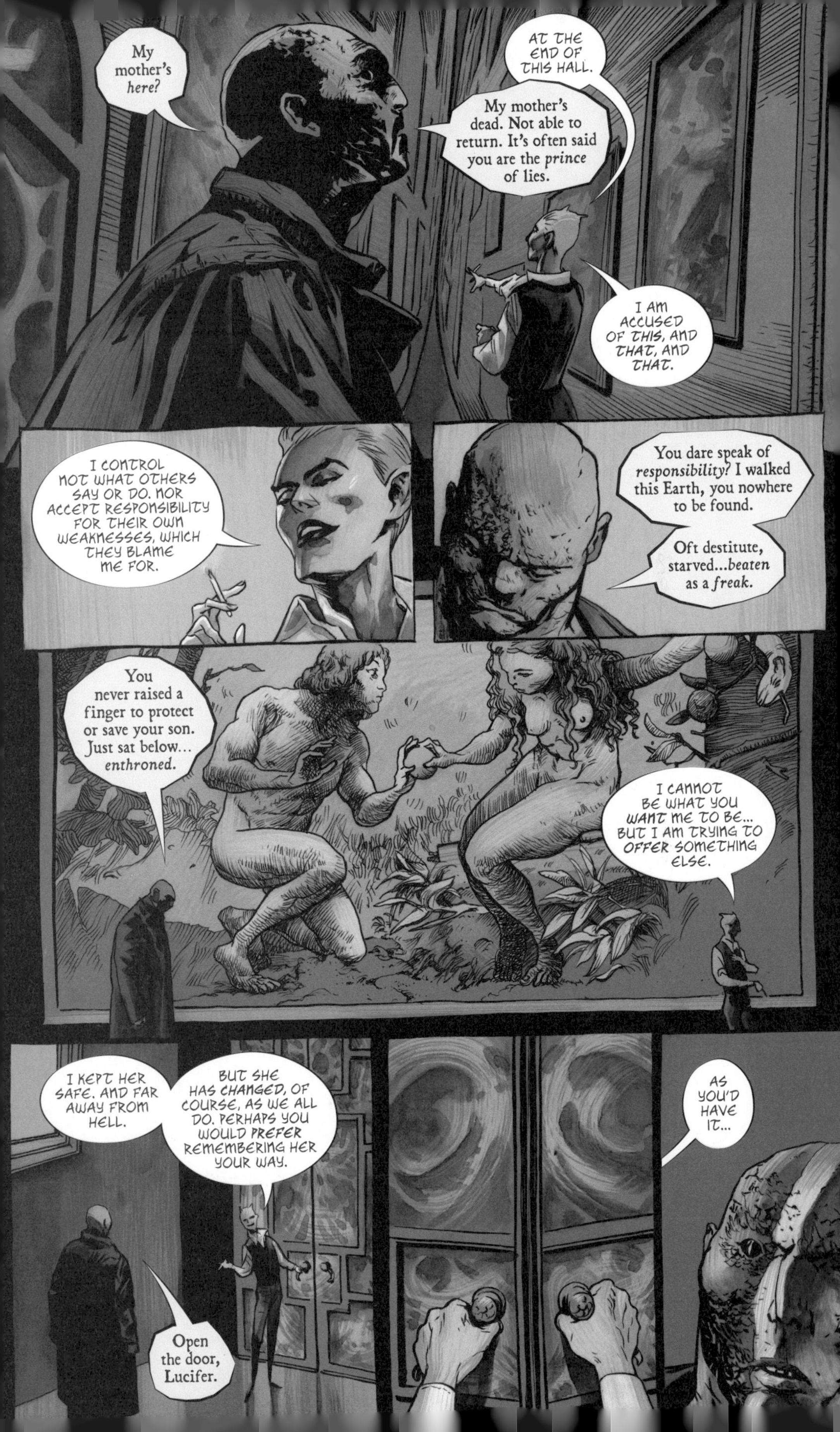
My mother's here?
AT THE END OF THIS HALL.
My mother's dead. Not able to return. It's often said you are the *prince* of lies.
I AM ACCUSED OF *THIS*, AND *THAT*, AND *THAT*.
I CONTROL NOT WHAT OTHERS SAY OR DO. NOR ACCEPT RESPONSIBILITY FOR THEIR OWN WEAKNESSES, WHICH THEY BLAME ME FOR.
You dare speak of *responsibility*? I walked this Earth, you nowhere to be found.
Oft destitute, starved...*beaten* as a *freak*.
You never raised a finger to protect or save your son. Just sat below... *enthroned*.
I CANNOT BE WHAT YOU *WANT* ME TO BE... BUT I AM TRYING TO *OFFER* SOMETHING ELSE.
I KEPT HER SAFE. AND FAR AWAY FROM HELL.
BUT SHE HAS *CHANGED*, OF COURSE, AS WE ALL DO. PERHAPS YOU WOULD *PREFER* REMEMBERING HER YOUR WAY.
Open the door, Lucifer.
AS YOU'D HAVE IT...

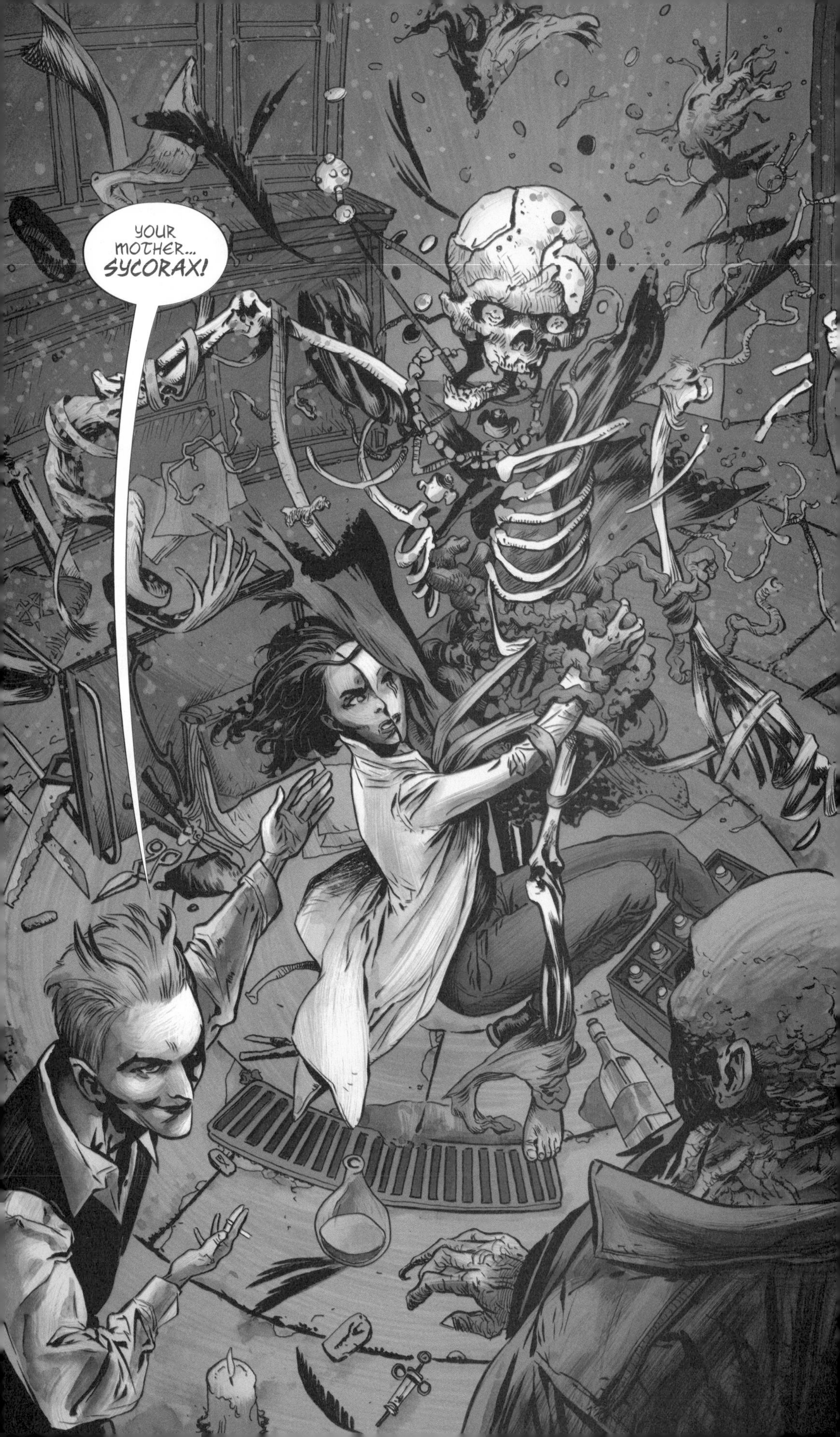
YOUR MOTHER... SYCORAX!

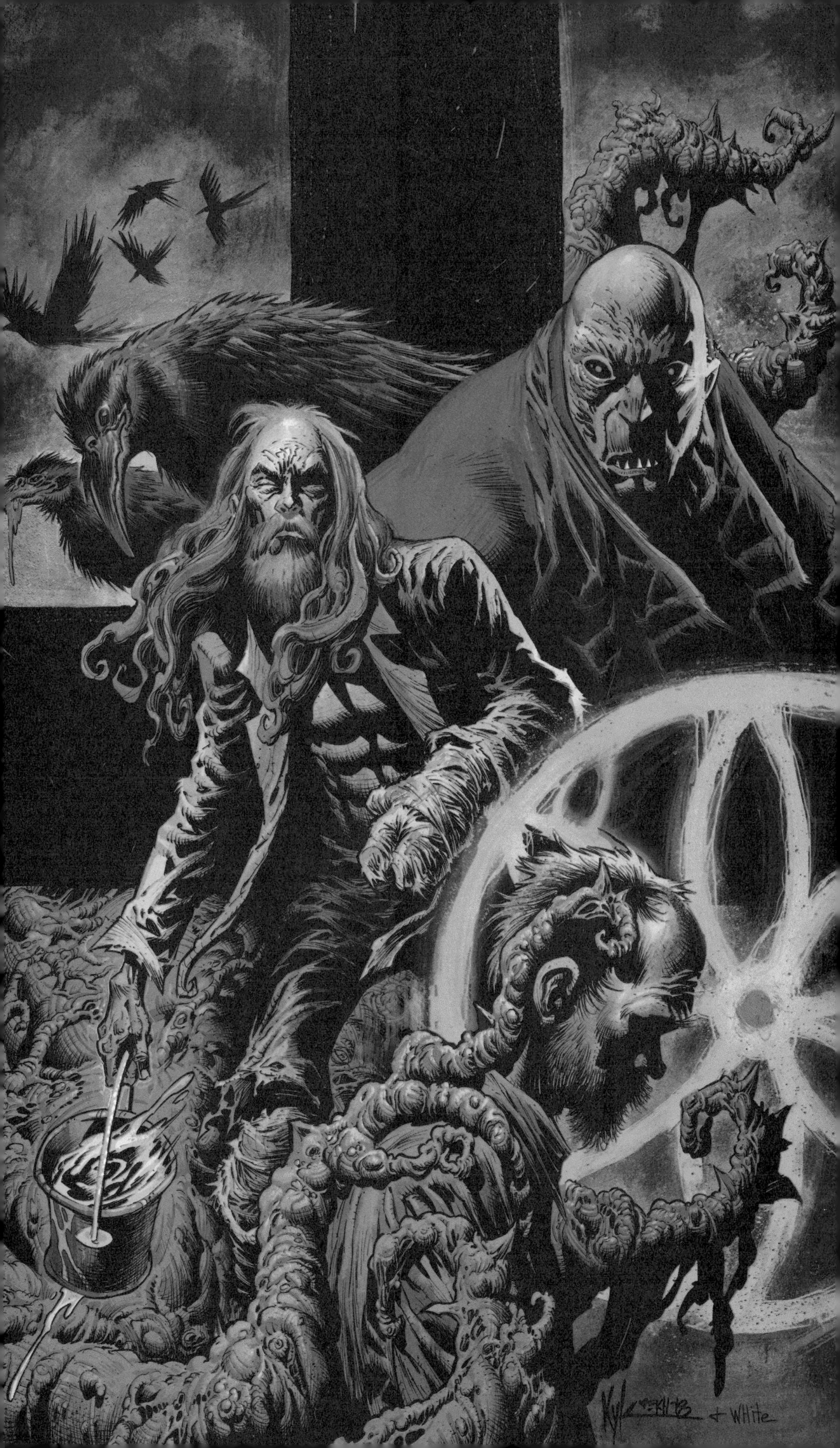

LUCIFER

The Annulment of Heaven and Hell

WRITTEN BY
Dan Watters

ILLUSTRATED BY
Max Fiumara
Sebastian Fiumara

COLORS BY
Dave McCaig

LETTERS BY
Steve Wands

COVER ART BY
Kyle Hotz and
Dean White

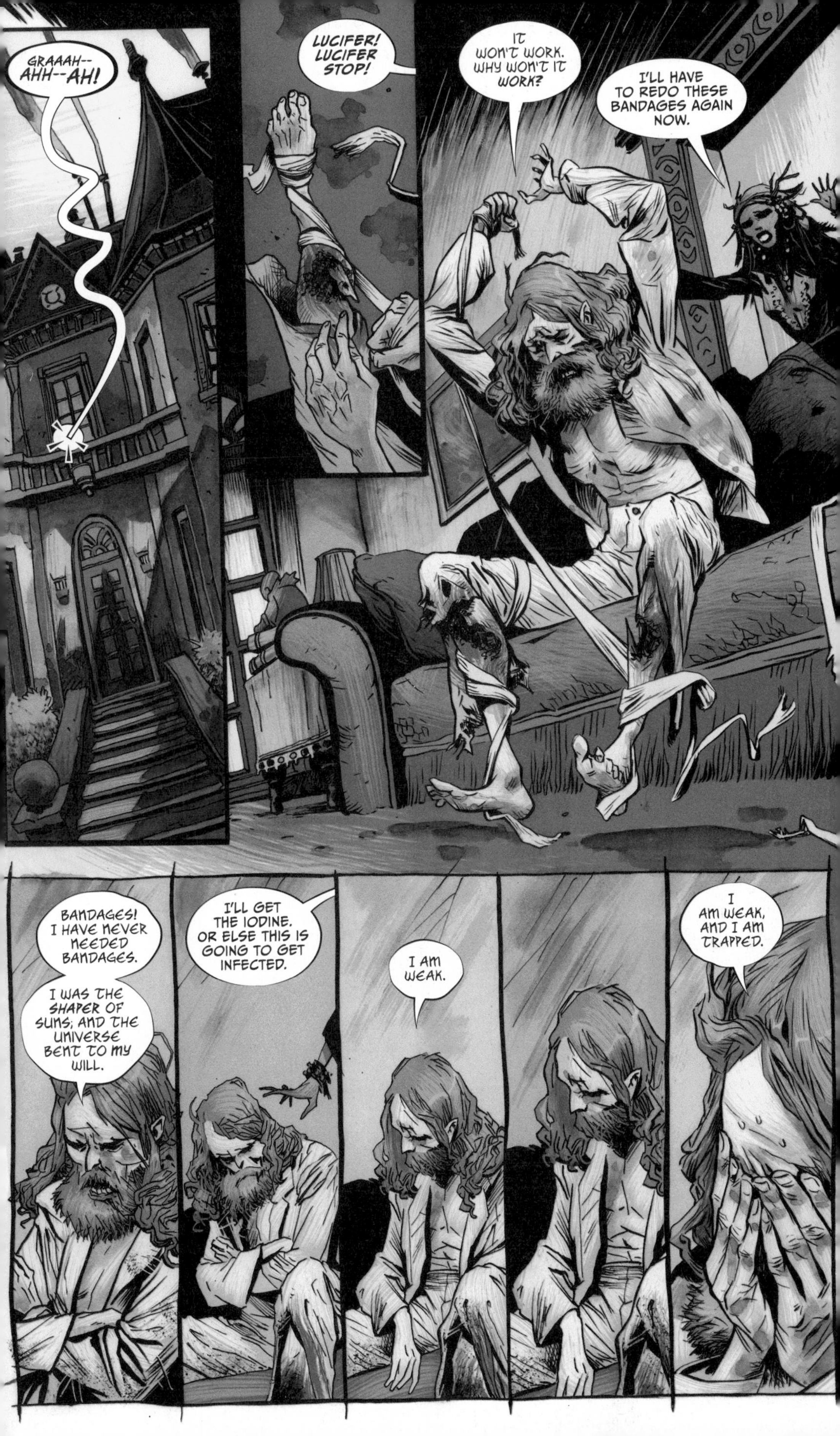
GRAAAH--
AHH--AH!
LUCIFER! LUCIFER STOP!
IT WON'T WORK. WHY WON'T IT WORK?
I'LL HAVE TO REDO THESE BANDAGES AGAIN NOW.
BANDAGES! I HAVE NEVER NEEDED BANDAGES.
I WAS THE SHAPER OF SUNS; AND THE UNIVERSE BENT TO MY WILL.
I'LL GET THE IODINE. OR ELSE THIS IS GOING TO GET INFECTED.
I AM WEAK.
I AM WEAK, AND I AM TRAPPED.

...NO, I'VE NEVER SEEN HIM LIKE THIS. I THINK HE'S *DEPRESSED.*

WOULD YOU MIND TALKING TO HIM?

LUCIFER. I FOUND *YOUR SHOVEL.* I THOUGHT YOU MIGHT WANT IT.

HELLO, BILL BLAKE. I DON'T.

IT DOES WHINE, SO.

EVERYONE MISSES YOU OUT THERE, LUCIFER.

YOU MAKE US LAUGH. YOU REALLY DO.

ONCE, I FLEW ACROSS A BLACK ABYSS OF VOID. THIS IS BEFORE *HE'D* MOLDED IT ALL INTO FORM, OF COURSE.

I FLEW IN A DARKNESS THAT NONE HAVE KNOWN BEFORE, OR SINCE.

AND IT MADE ME LAUGH, THIS DARKNESS.

IT WAS THE *FIRST* LAUGH, PERHAPS. I'VE NEVER THOUGHT ABOUT THAT.

AND THE VO SWALLOWED BECAUSE IT H NOTHING T SEND BACK I ECHO.

HOW ARE YOU BOYS GETTING ON?

IN ALL HONESTY, I FEAR I HAVE NOT CHEERED HIM THUS FAR.

AND HE APPEARS TO HAVE CUT OFF ONE OF HIS FINGERS.

OH, WAIT. *TWO,* NOW.

PERHAPS I SHOULD TAKE THAT OFF HIM.

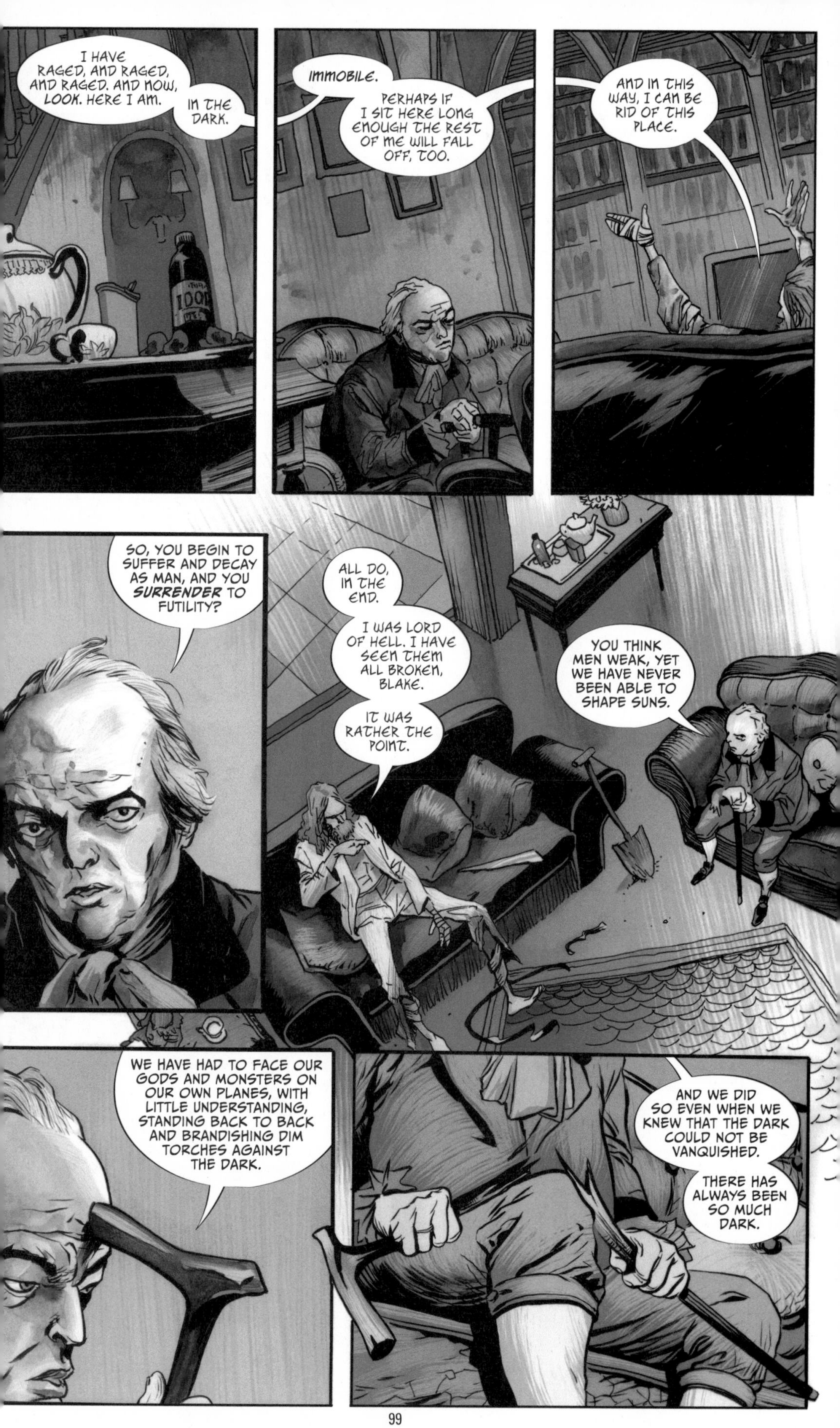
I HAVE RAGED, AND RAGED, AND RAGED. AND NOW, LOOK. HERE I AM.
IN THE DARK.
IMMOBILE.
PERHAPS IF I SIT HERE LONG ENOUGH THE REST OF ME WILL FALL OFF, TOO.
AND IN THIS WAY, I CAN BE RID OF THIS PLACE.
SO, YOU BEGIN TO SUFFER AND DECAY AS MAN, AND YOU SURRENDER TO FUTILITY?
ALL DO, IN THE END.
I WAS LORD OF HELL. I HAVE SEEN THEM ALL BROKEN, BLAKE.
IT WAS RATHER THE POINT.
YOU THINK MEN WEAK, YET WE HAVE NEVER BEEN ABLE TO SHAPE SUNS.
WE HAVE HAD TO FACE OUR GODS AND MONSTERS ON OUR OWN PLANES, WITH LITTLE UNDERSTANDING, STANDING BACK TO BACK AND BRANDISHING DIM TORCHES AGAINST THE DARK.
AND WE DID SO EVEN WHEN WE KNEW THAT THE DARK COULD NOT BE VANQUISHED.
THERE HAS ALWAYS BEEN SO MUCH DARK.

IT'S SO DARK THAT JOHN DECKER IS NOT SURE IF HE IS WAKING **FROM** OR INTO THE NIGHTMARE.

THE FIRST SYMPTOM THAT **PENNY** SHOWED WHEN HER **TUMOR** BEGAN TO DEVELOP WAS SHE COULD SMELL FRESH-CUT GRASS THAT **WASN'T** THERE.

NOW HE **SMELLS** COLD, WET ASHES-- AND BLOOD. BUT HE'S NOT SURE IF HE'S TASTING THAT.

HE REMEMBERS THE FIRST TIME SHE WOKE ANXIOUS AND CONFUSED, EVEN AS HE HELD HER HAND. IT WAS BECOMING HARDER FOR HER TO MAKE CONNECTIONS AND SEE THINGS AS THEY WERE.

HE RECALLS A BRIGHT **RED** EYE GLOWERING DOWN AT HIM. THAT CARNIVOROUS, **BLOOD**-SLITTED CATARACT.

PERHAPS IT WAS JUST THE LIGHT BLINKING ON A **RESPIRATOR** BESIDE HIS SICKBED.

PERHAPS THIS IS A **HOSPITAL.** PERHAPS HE'S JUST GETTING CONFUSED.

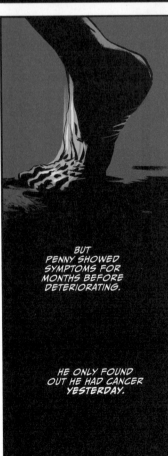

BUT PENNY SHOWED SYMPTOMS FOR MONTHS BEFORE DETERIORATING.

HE ONLY FOUND OUT HE HAD CANCER **YESTERDAY.**

IT **WAS** YESTERDAY, WASN'T IT?

IT'S SO HARD TO BE CERTAIN.

IT'S SO **DARK.**

TOWARD THE END, PENNY HAD OFTEN GOTTEN CONFUSED ABOUT WHEN OR WHERE SHE WAS.

TAKE, FOR EXAMPLE, HER WILD TALK ABOUT HER COUSIN, ROBERT.

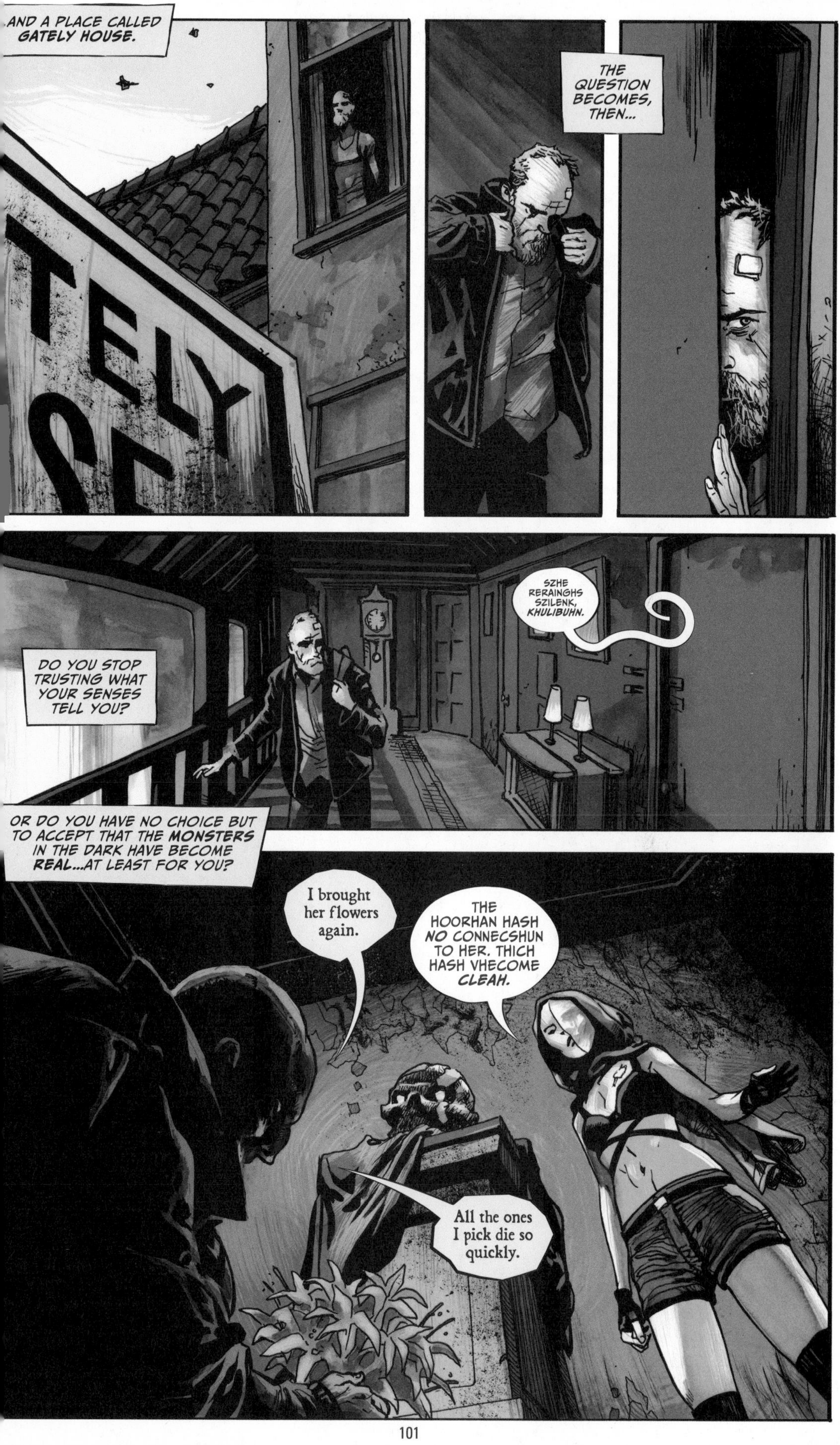
AND A PLACE CALLED GATELY HOUSE.
TELY SE
THE QUESTION BECOMES, THEN...
DO YOU STOP TRUSTING WHAT YOUR SENSES TELL YOU?
SZHE RERAINGHS SZILENK, KHULIBUHN.
OR DO YOU HAVE NO CHOICE BUT TO ACCEPT THAT THE MONSTERS IN THE DARK HAVE BECOME REAL...AT LEAST FOR YOU?
I brought her flowers again.
THE HOORHAN HASH NO CONNECSHUN TO HER. THICH HASH VHECOME CLEAH.
All the ones I pick die so quickly.

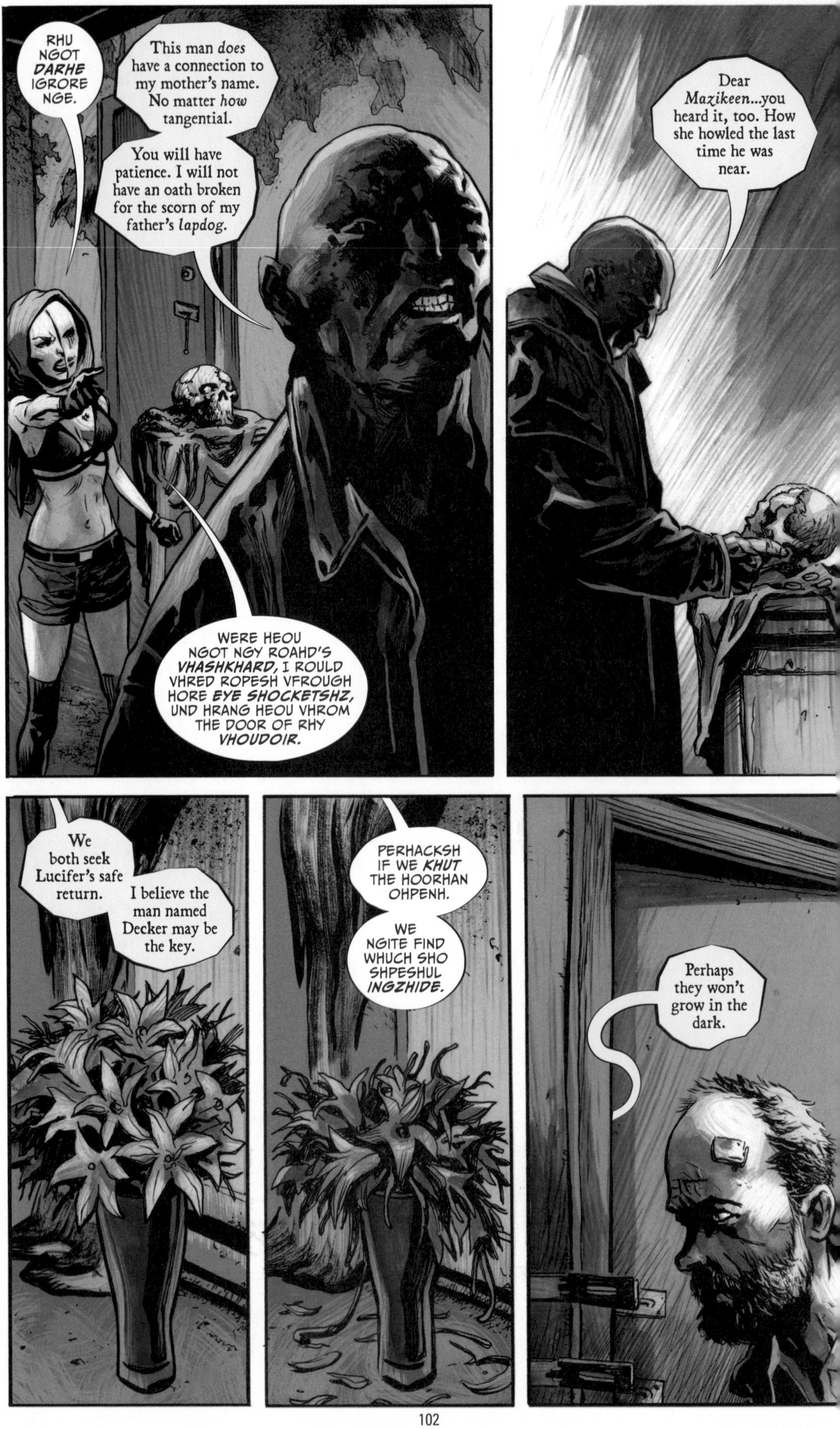
RHU NGOT DARHE IGRORE NGE.
This man *does* have a connection to my mother's name. No matter *how* tangential.
You will have patience. I will not have an oath broken for the scorn of my father's *lapdog*.
WERE HEOU NGOT NGY ROAHD'S VHASHKHARD, I ROULD VHRED ROPESH VFROUGH HORE EYE SHOCKETSHZ, UND HRANG HEOU VHROM THE DOOR OF RHY VHOUDOIR.
Dear *Mazikeen*...you heard it, too. How she howled the last time he was near.
We both seek Lucifer's safe return.
I believe the man named Decker may be the key.
PERHACKSH IF WE KHUT THE HOORHAN OHPENH.
WE NGITE FIND WHUCH SHO SHPESHUL INGZHIDE.
Perhaps they won't grow in the dark.

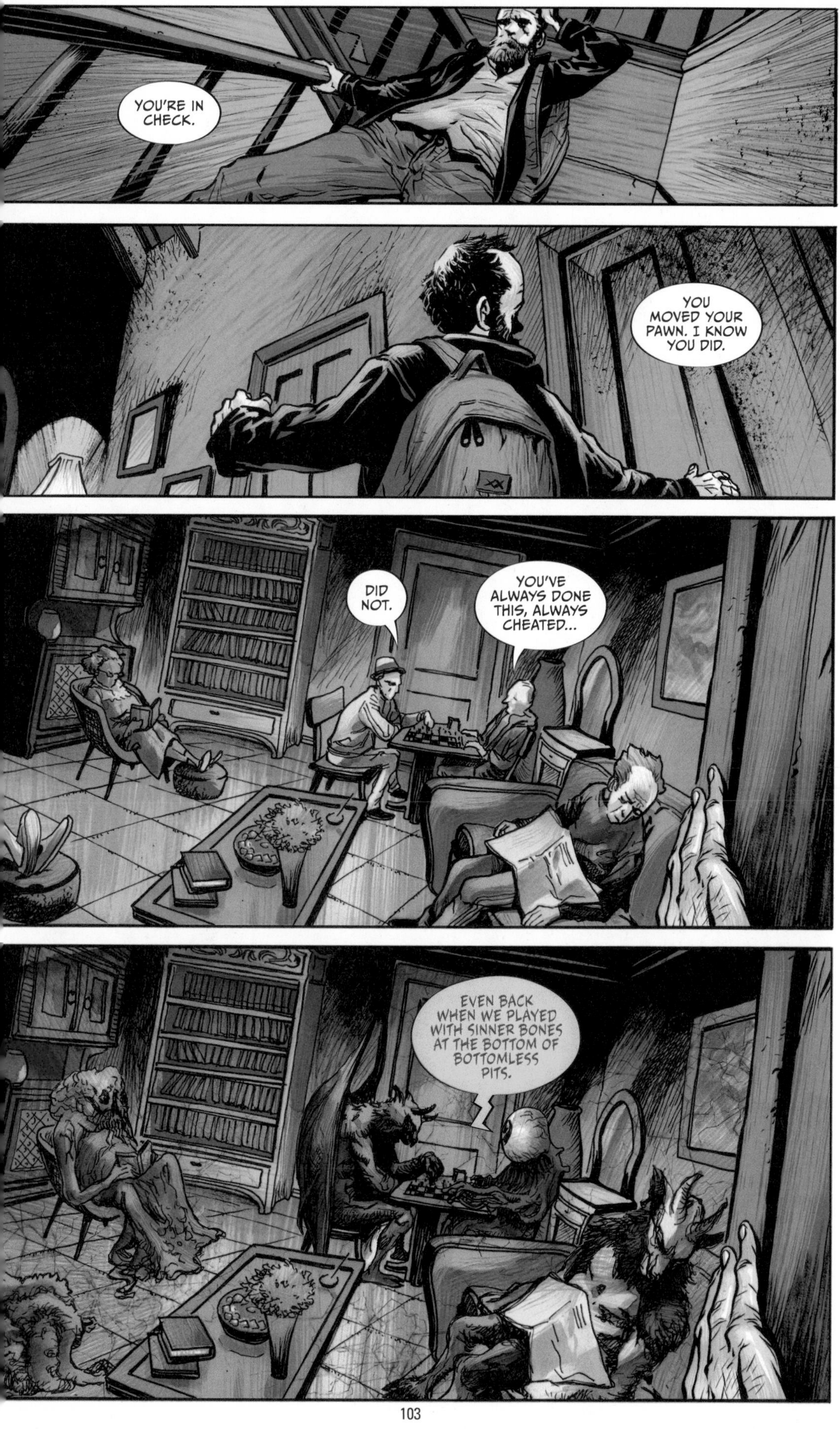
YOU'RE IN CHECK.
YOU MOVED YOUR PAWN. I KNOW YOU DID.
DID NOT.
YOU'VE ALWAYS DONE THIS, ALWAYS CHEATED...
EVEN BACK WHEN WE PLAYED WITH SINNER BONES AT THE BOTTOM OF BOTTOMLESS PITS.

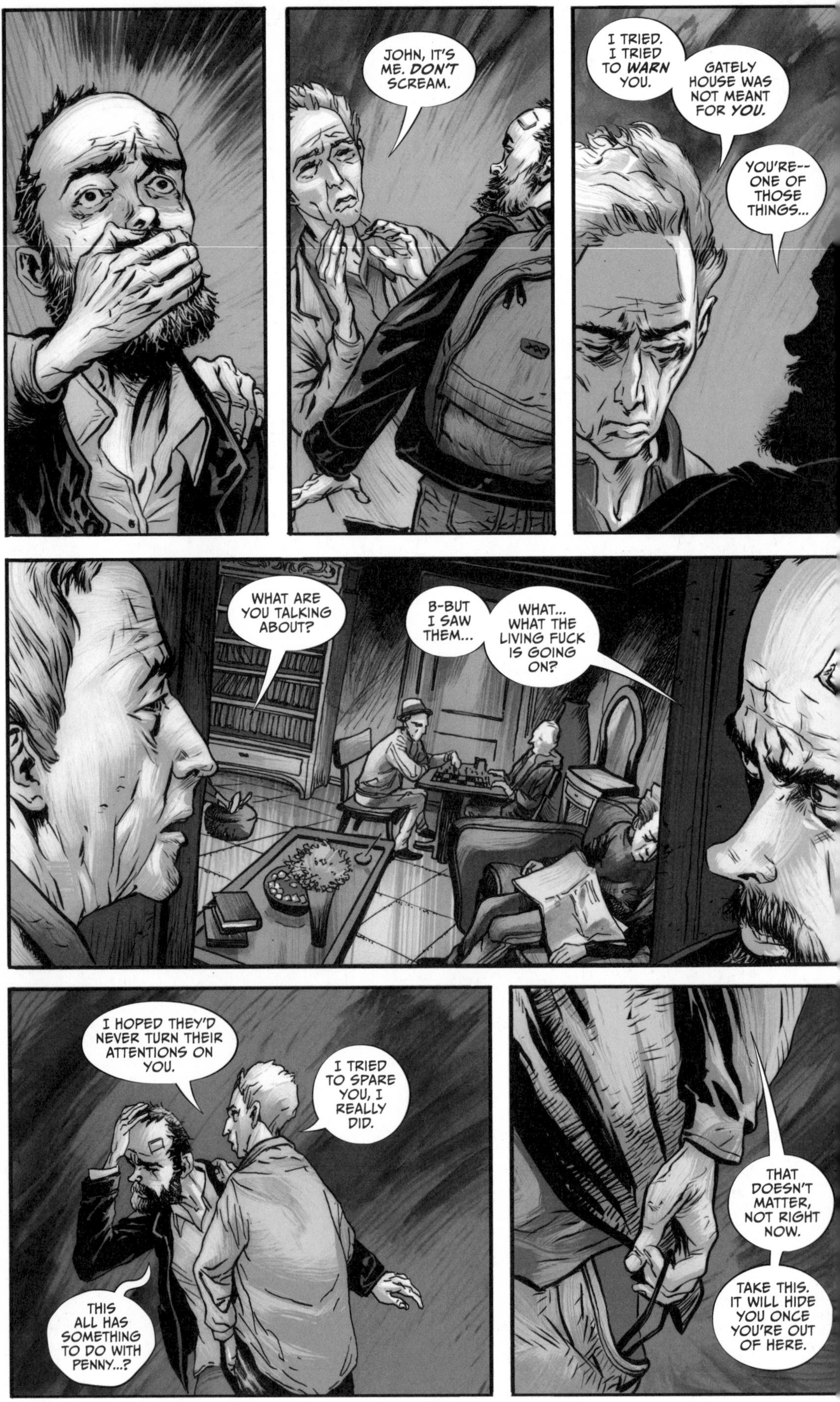

JOHN, IT'S ME. DON'T SCREAM.
I TRIED. I TRIED TO WARN YOU.
GATELY HOUSE WAS NOT MEANT FOR YOU.
YOU'RE-- ONE OF THOSE THINGS...
WHAT ARE YOU TALKING ABOUT?
B-BUT I SAW THEM...
WHAT... WHAT THE LIVING FUCK IS GOING ON?
I HOPED THEY'D NEVER TURN THEIR ATTENTIONS ON YOU.
I TRIED TO SPARE YOU, I REALLY DID.
THIS ALL HAS SOMETHING TO DO WITH PENNY...?
THAT DOESN'T MATTER, NOT RIGHT NOW.
TAKE THIS. IT WILL HIDE YOU ONCE YOU'RE OUT OF HERE.

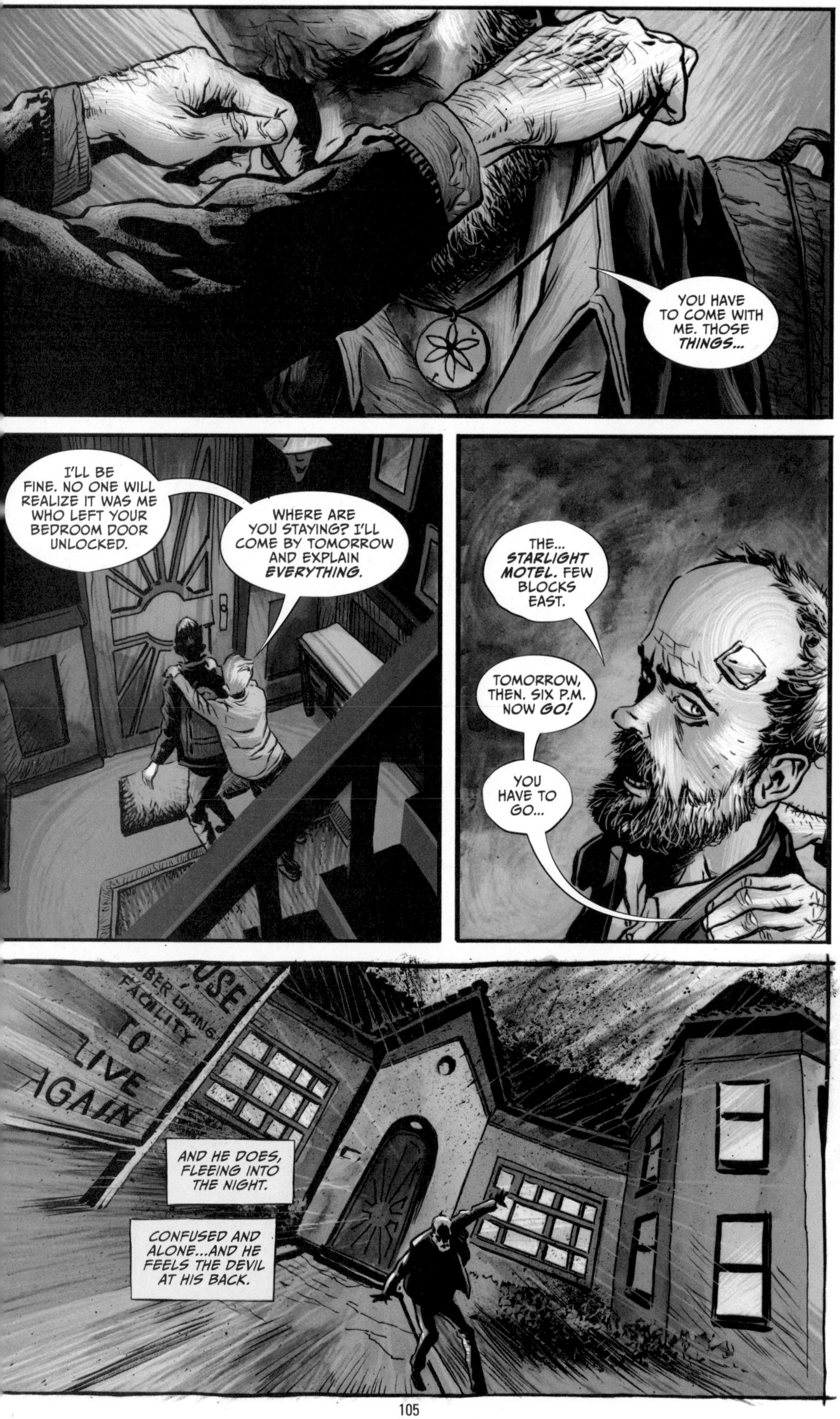
YOU HAVE TO COME WITH ME. THOSE THINGS...
I'LL BE FINE. NO ONE WILL REALIZE IT WAS ME WHO LEFT YOUR BEDROOM DOOR UNLOCKED.
WHERE ARE YOU STAYING? I'LL COME BY TOMORROW AND EXPLAIN EVERYTHING.
THE... STARLIGHT MOTEL. FEW BLOCKS EAST.
TOMORROW, THEN. SIX P.M. NOW GO!
YOU HAVE TO GO...
TO LIVE AGAIN
FACILITY
AND HE DOES, FLEEING INTO THE NIGHT.
CONFUSED AND ALONE...AND HE FEELS THE DEVIL AT HIS BACK.

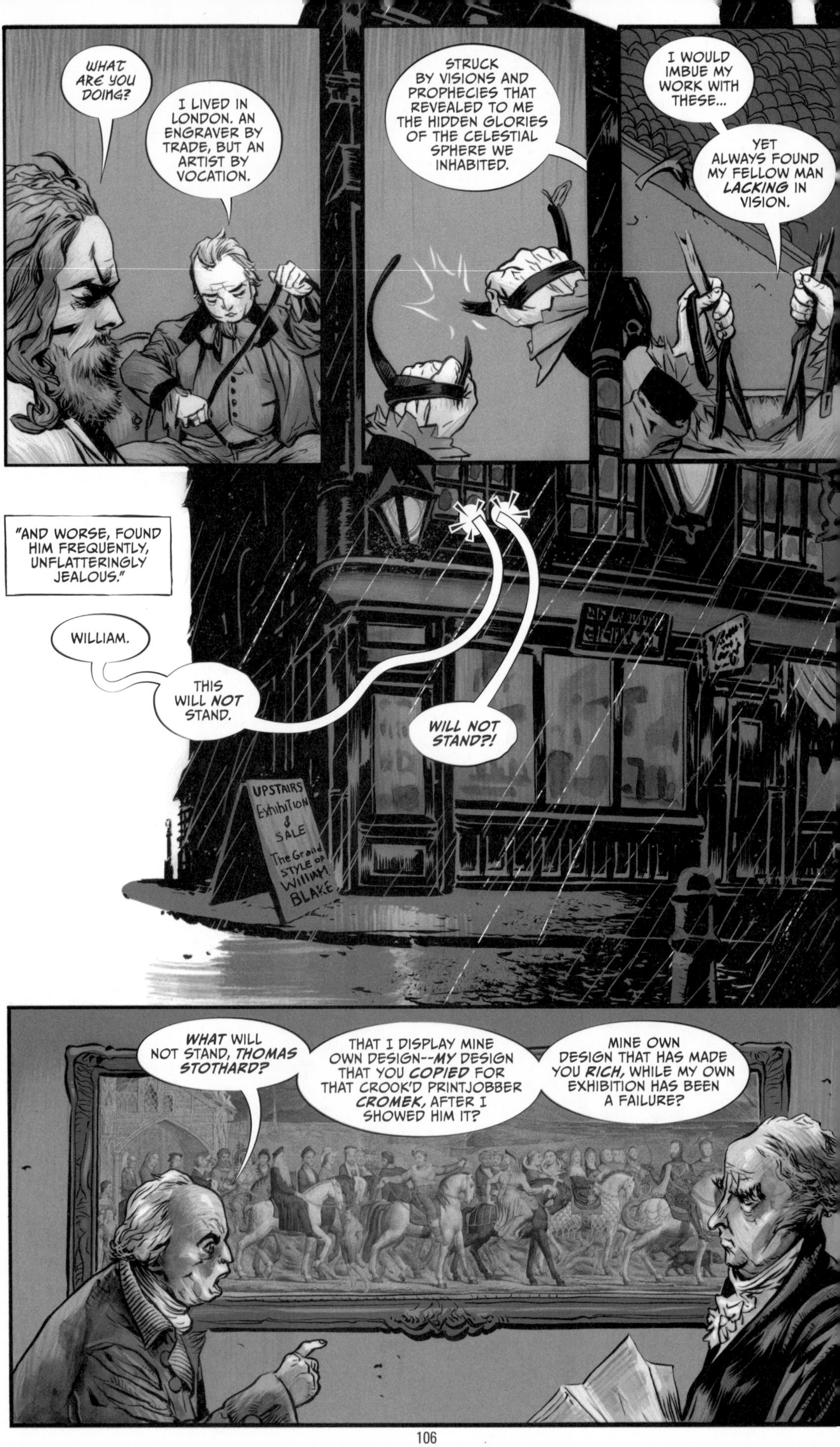

WHAT ARE YOU DOING?
I LIVED IN LONDON. AN ENGRAVER BY TRADE, BUT AN ARTIST BY VOCATION.
STRUCK BY VISIONS AND PROPHECIES THAT REVEALED TO ME THE HIDDEN GLORIES OF THE CELESTIAL SPHERE WE INHABITED.
I WOULD IMBUE MY WORK WITH THESE...
YET ALWAYS FOUND MY FELLOW MAN *LACKING* IN VISION.
"AND WORSE, FOUND HIM FREQUENTLY, UNFLATTERINGLY JEALOUS."
WILLIAM.
THIS WILL *NOT* STAND.
WILL NOT STAND?!
UPSTAIRS
Exhibition & SALE
The Grand STYLE of WILLIAM BLAKE
WHAT WILL NOT STAND, *THOMAS STOTHARD?*
THAT I DISPLAY MINE OWN DESIGN--*MY* DESIGN THAT YOU *COPIED* FOR THAT CROOK'D PRINTJOBBER *CROMEK,* AFTER I SHOWED HIM IT?
MINE OWN DESIGN THAT HAS MADE YOU *RICH,* WHILE MY OWN EXHIBITION HAS BEEN A FAILURE?

YOU SPEAK NONSENSE, WILLIAM.

MY PILGRIMAGE TO CANTERBURY IS A SUCCESS, BUT NOT MY ONLY SUCCESS. WHAT NEED WOULD I HAVE TO PLAGIARIZE YOU?

EVER SINCE WE WERE AT THE ROYAL ACADEMY, YOU HAVE SHOWN GLIMMERS OF THE GREAT BEAUTY YOU'RE CAPABLE OF CREATING.

YET YOU INSIST ON THESE PRINTS--THESE DISTORTED CARICATURES.

PERHAPS IF YOU WORKED IN OILS...IF YOU'D RELAX YOUR STYLE SOME...THESE EMPTY ROOMS WOULD BE FILLED WITH BUYERS.

INSTEAD, YOU RETURN TO PETTY RIVALRY, ANGERED BY MY SUCCESS, AND THE NEWSPAPERS CONSIDER YOUR WORK A FARRAGO OF NONSENSE.

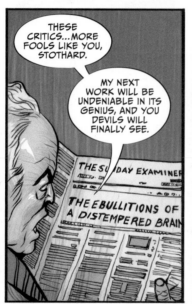

THESE CRITICS...MORE FOOLS LIKE YOU, STOTHARD.

MY NEXT WORK WILL BE UNDENIABLE IN ITS GENIUS, AND YOU DEVILS WILL FINALLY SEE.

THE SUNDAY EXAMINER

THE EBULLITIONS OF A DISTEMPERED BRAIN

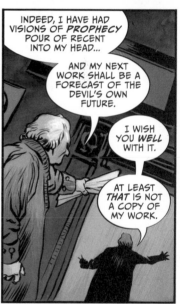

INDEED, I HAVE HAD VISIONS OF PROPHECY POUR OF RECENT INTO MY HEAD...

AND MY NEXT WORK SHALL BE A FORECAST OF THE DEVIL'S OWN FUTURE.

I WISH YOU WELL WITH IT.

AT LEAST THAT IS NOT A COPY OF MY WORK.

WILLIAM BLAKE?

IT IS MY MISFORTUNE TO BE HE.

HAVE YOU COME TO GAWP AT THE MAD POET, SIR? IT IS UNLIKELY YOU HAVE COME TO BUY ANY ART.

I AM INDEED AN ADMIRER OF YOUR WORK, AND I--

I ASSURE YOU, SIR...

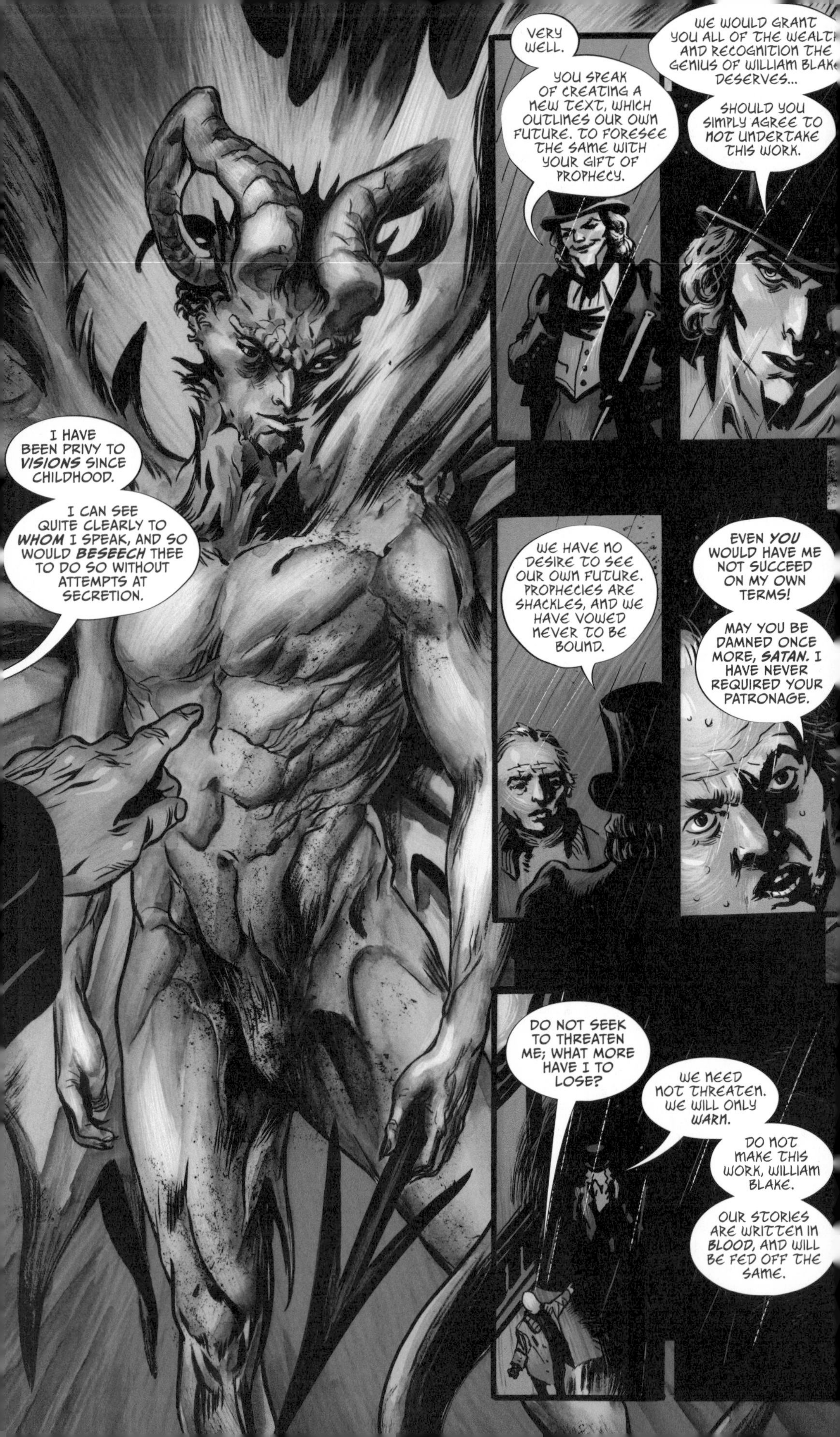
I HAVE BEEN PRIVY TO VISIONS SINCE CHILDHOOD.
I CAN SEE QUITE CLEARLY TO WHOM I SPEAK, AND SO WOULD BESEECH THEE TO DO SO WITHOUT ATTEMPTS AT SECRETION.
VERY WELL.
YOU SPEAK OF CREATING A NEW TEXT, WHICH OUTLINES OUR OWN FUTURE. TO FORESEE THE SAME WITH YOUR GIFT OF PROPHECY.
WE WOULD GRANT YOU ALL OF THE WEALTH AND RECOGNITION THE GENIUS OF WILLIAM BLAKE DESERVES...
SHOULD YOU SIMPLY AGREE TO NOT UNDERTAKE THIS WORK.
WE HAVE NO DESIRE TO SEE OUR OWN FUTURE. PROPHECIES ARE SHACKLES, AND WE HAVE VOWED NEVER TO BE BOUND.
EVEN YOU WOULD HAVE ME NOT SUCCEED ON MY OWN TERMS!
MAY YOU BE DAMNED ONCE MORE, SATAN. I HAVE NEVER REQUIRED YOUR PATRONAGE.
DO NOT SEEK TO THREATEN ME; WHAT MORE HAVE I TO LOSE?
WE NEED NOT THREATEN. WE WILL ONLY WARN.
DO NOT MAKE THIS WORK, WILLIAM BLAKE.
OUR STORIES ARE WRITTEN IN BLOOD, AND WILL BE FED OFF THE SAME.

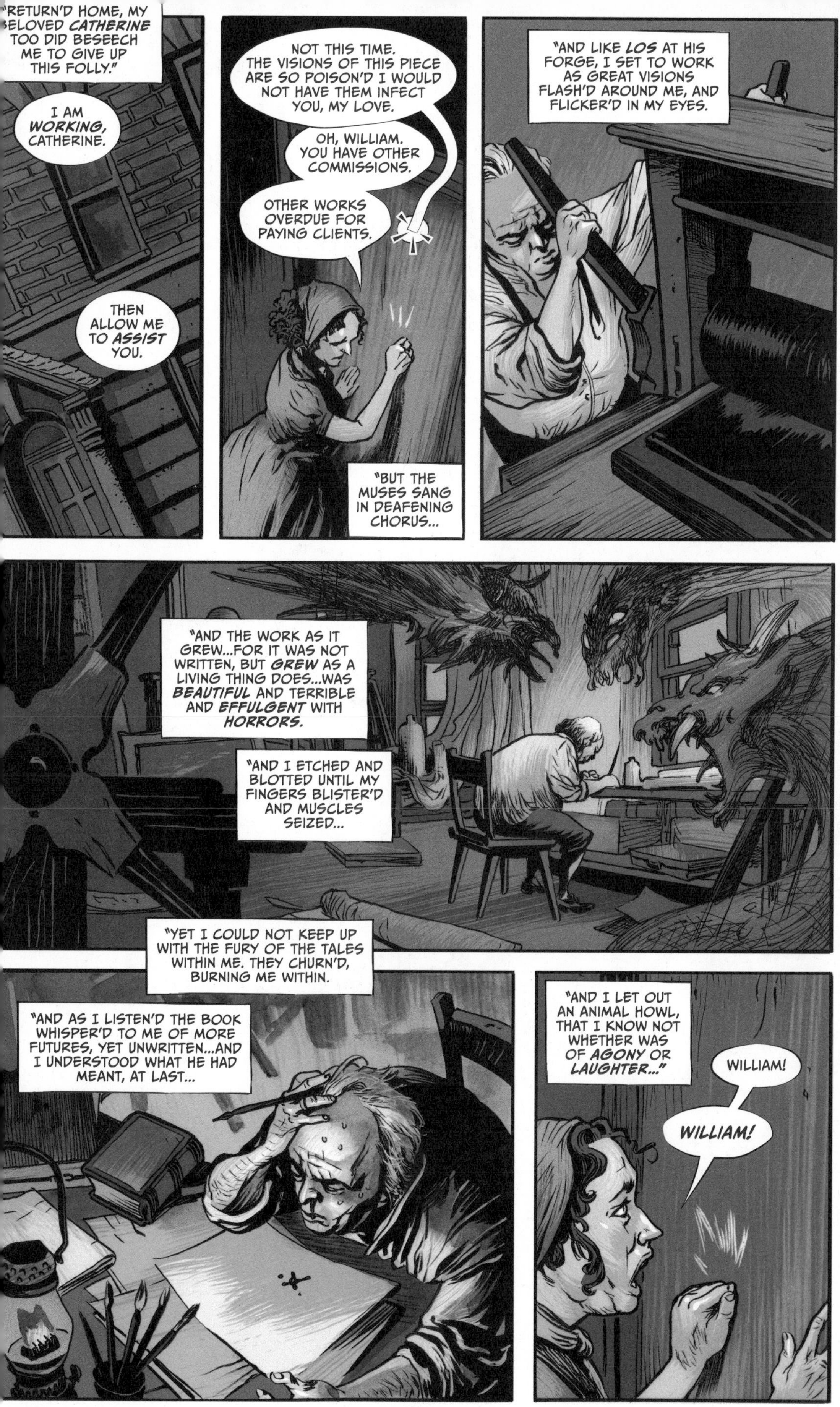
"RETURN'D HOME, MY BELOVED CATHERINE TOO DID BESEECH ME TO GIVE UP THIS FOLLY."
I AM WORKING, CATHERINE.
THEN ALLOW ME TO ASSIST YOU.
NOT THIS TIME. THE VISIONS OF THIS PIECE ARE SO POISON'D I WOULD NOT HAVE THEM INFECT YOU, MY LOVE.
OH, WILLIAM. YOU HAVE OTHER COMMISSIONS.
OTHER WORKS OVERDUE FOR PAYING CLIENTS.
"BUT THE MUSES SANG IN DEAFENING CHORUS...
"AND LIKE LOS AT HIS FORGE, I SET TO WORK AS GREAT VISIONS FLASH'D AROUND ME, AND FLICKER'D IN MY EYES.
"AND THE WORK AS IT GREW...FOR IT WAS NOT WRITTEN, BUT GREW AS A LIVING THING DOES...WAS BEAUTIFUL AND TERRIBLE AND EFFULGENT WITH HORRORS.
"AND I ETCHED AND BLOTTED UNTIL MY FINGERS BLISTER'D AND MUSCLES SEIZED...
"YET I COULD NOT KEEP UP WITH THE FURY OF THE TALES WITHIN ME. THEY CHURN'D, BURNING ME WITHIN.
"AND AS I LISTEN'D THE BOOK WHISPER'D TO ME OF MORE FUTURES, YET UNWRITTEN...AND I UNDERSTOOD WHAT HE HAD MEANT, AT LAST...
"AND I LET OUT AN ANIMAL HOWL, THAT I KNOW NOT WHETHER WAS OF AGONY OR LAUGHTER..."
WILLIAM!
WILLIAM!

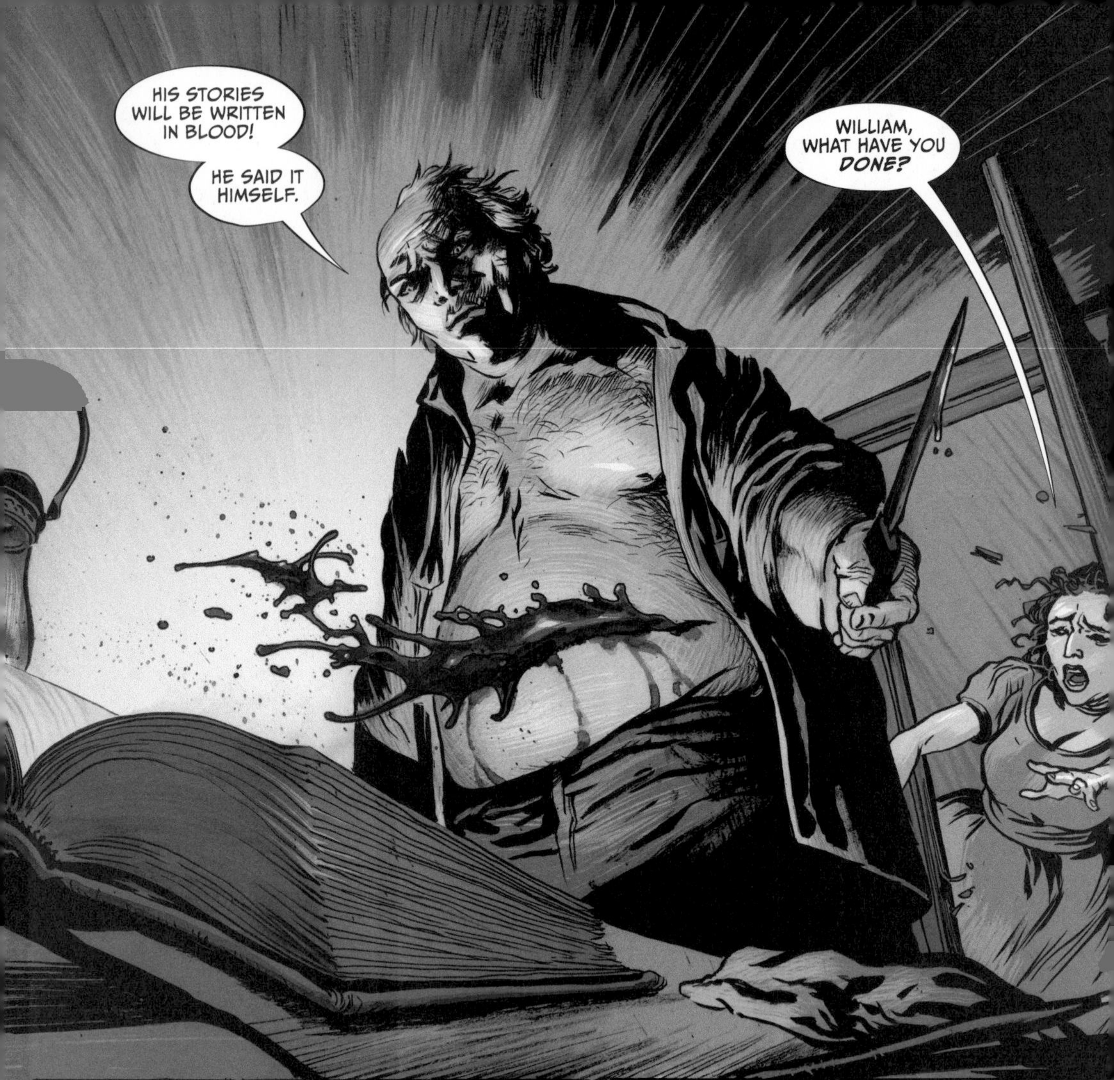
HIS STORIES WILL BE WRITTEN IN BLOOD!
HE SAID IT HIMSELF.
WILLIAM, WHAT HAVE YOU *DONE?*

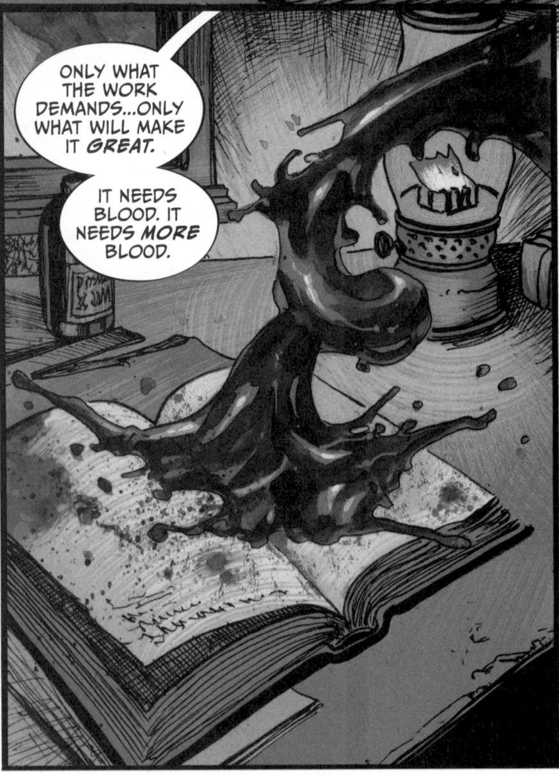
ONLY WHAT THE WORK DEMANDS...ONLY WHAT WILL MAKE IT *GREAT.*
IT NEEDS BLOOD. IT NEEDS *MORE* BLOOD.

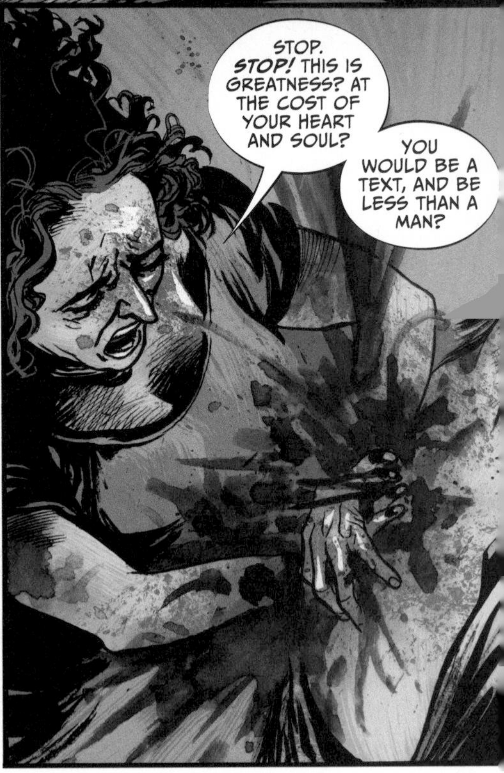
STOP. *STOP!* THIS IS GREATNESS? AT THE COST OF YOUR HEART AND SOUL?
YOU WOULD BE A TEXT, AND BE LESS THAN A MAN?

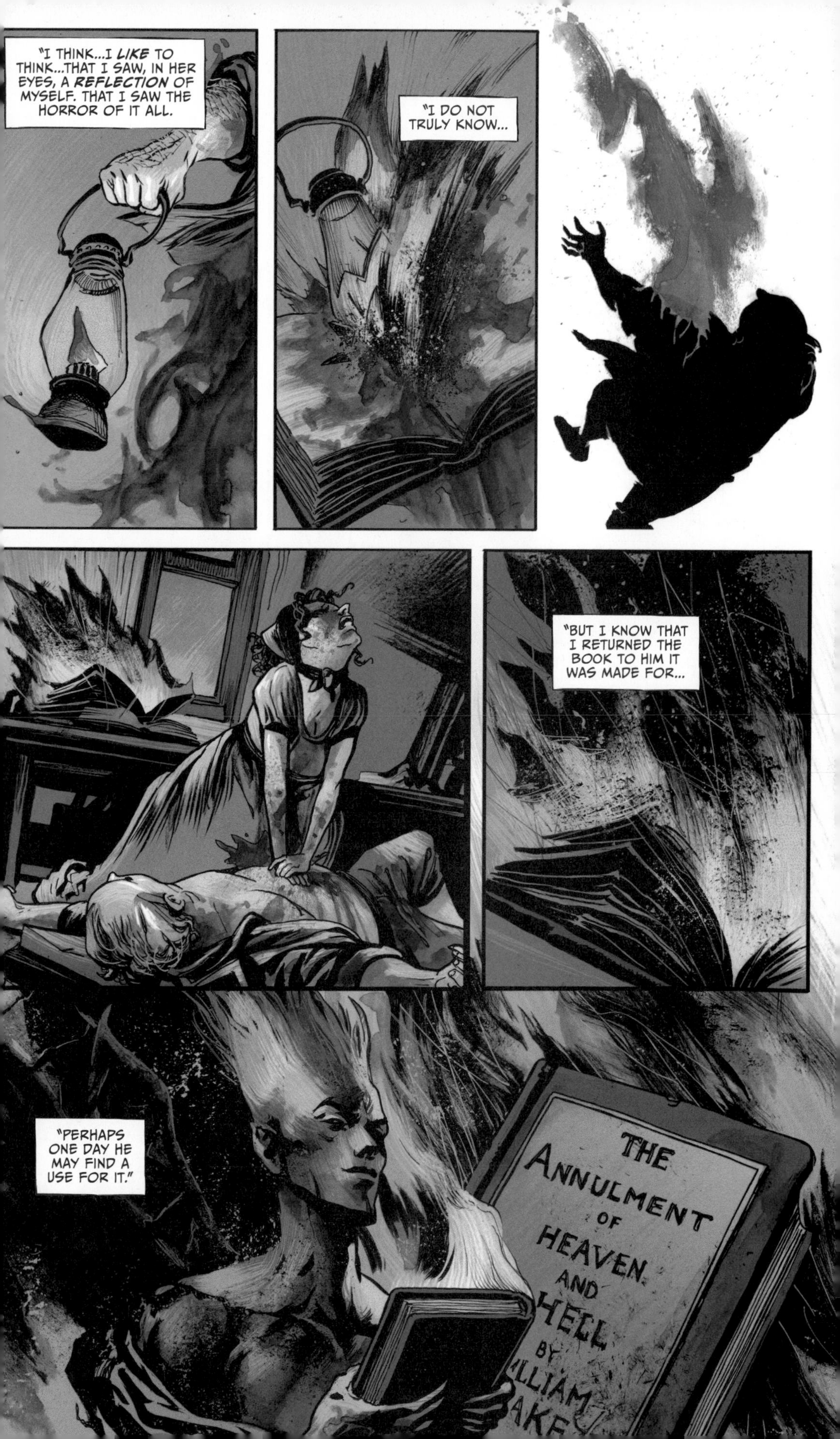
"I THINK...I *LIKE* TO THINK...THAT I SAW, IN HER EYES, A *REFLECTION* OF MYSELF. THAT I SAW THE HORROR OF IT ALL.
"I DO NOT TRULY KNOW...
"BUT I KNOW THAT I RETURNED THE BOOK TO HIM IT WAS MADE FOR...
"PERHAPS ONE DAY HE MAY FIND A USE FOR IT."
THE ANNULMENT OF HEAVEN AND HELL BY

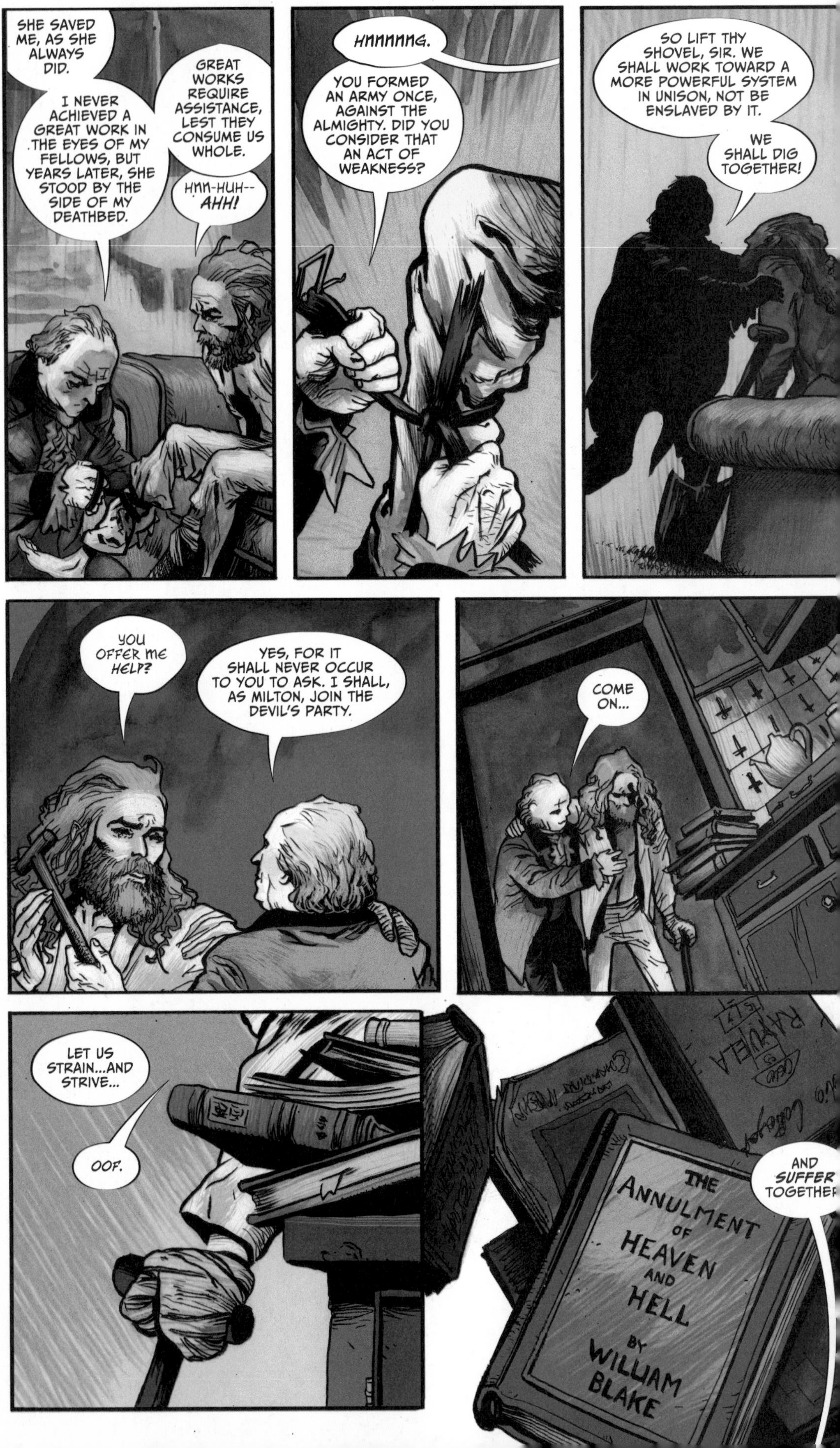
SHE SAVED ME, AS SHE ALWAYS DID.
I NEVER ACHIEVED A GREAT WORK IN THE EYES OF MY FELLOWS, BUT YEARS LATER, SHE STOOD BY THE SIDE OF MY DEATHBED.
GREAT WORKS REQUIRE ASSISTANCE, LEST THEY CONSUME US WHOLE.
HNN-HUH--AHH!
HNNNNNG.
YOU FORMED AN ARMY ONCE, AGAINST THE ALMIGHTY. DID YOU CONSIDER THAT AN ACT OF WEAKNESS?
SO LIFT THY SHOVEL, SIR. WE SHALL WORK TOWARD A MORE POWERFUL SYSTEM IN UNISON, NOT BE ENSLAVED BY IT.
WE SHALL DIG TOGETHER!
YOU OFFER ME HELP?
YES, FOR IT SHALL NEVER OCCUR TO YOU TO ASK. I SHALL, AS MILTON, JOIN THE DEVIL'S PARTY.
COME ON...
LET US STRAIN...AND STRIVE...
OOF.
AND SUFFER TOGETHER
THE ANNULMENT OF HEAVEN AND HELL BY WILLIAM BLAKE
RAYUELA

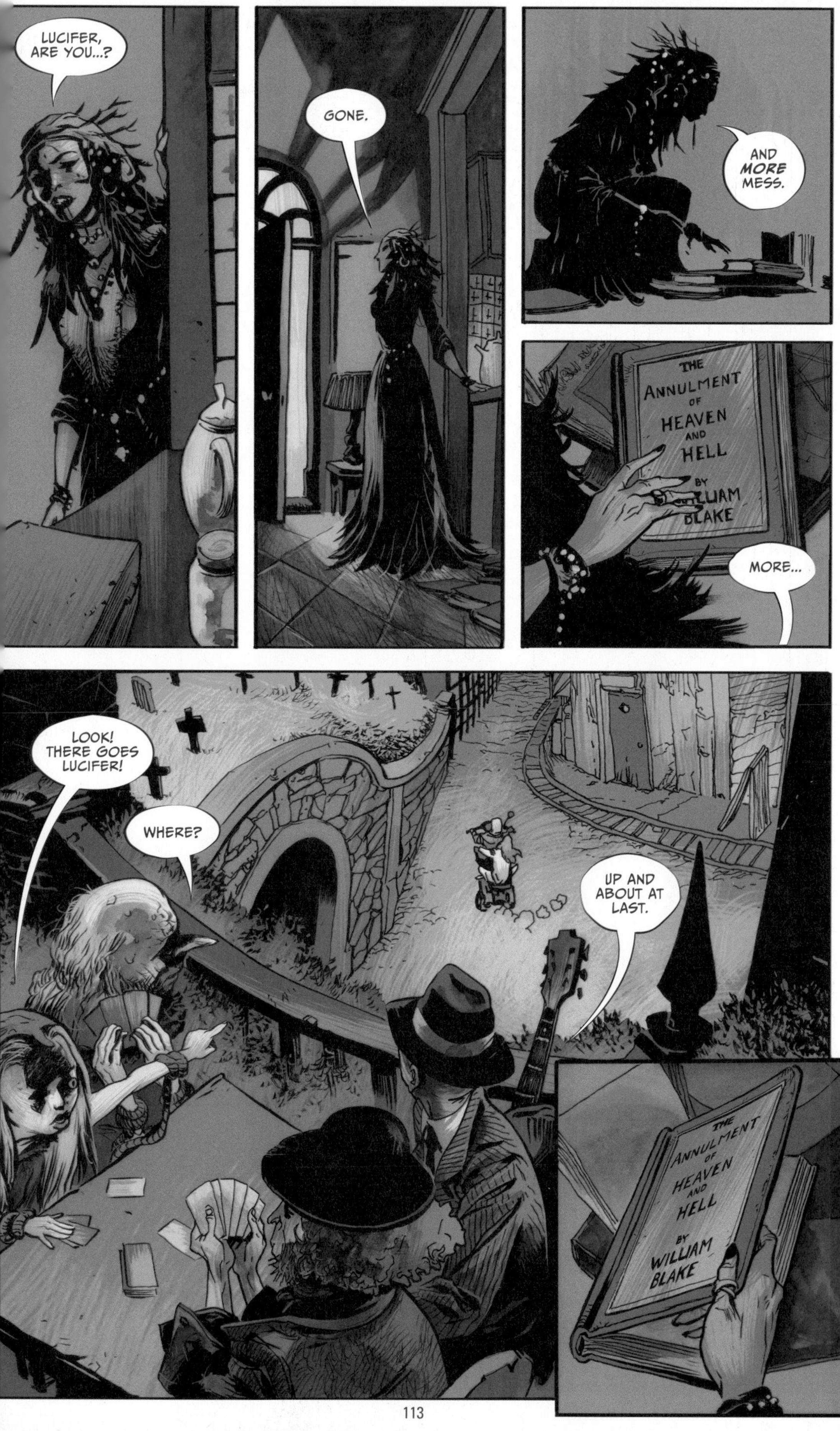
LUCIFER, ARE YOU...?
GONE.
AND MORE MESS.
THE ANNULMENT OF HEAVEN AND HELL BY WILLIAM BLAKE
MORE...
LOOK! THERE GOES LUCIFER!
WHERE?
UP AND ABOUT AT LAST.
THE ANNULMENT OF HEAVEN AND HELL BY WILLIAM BLAKE

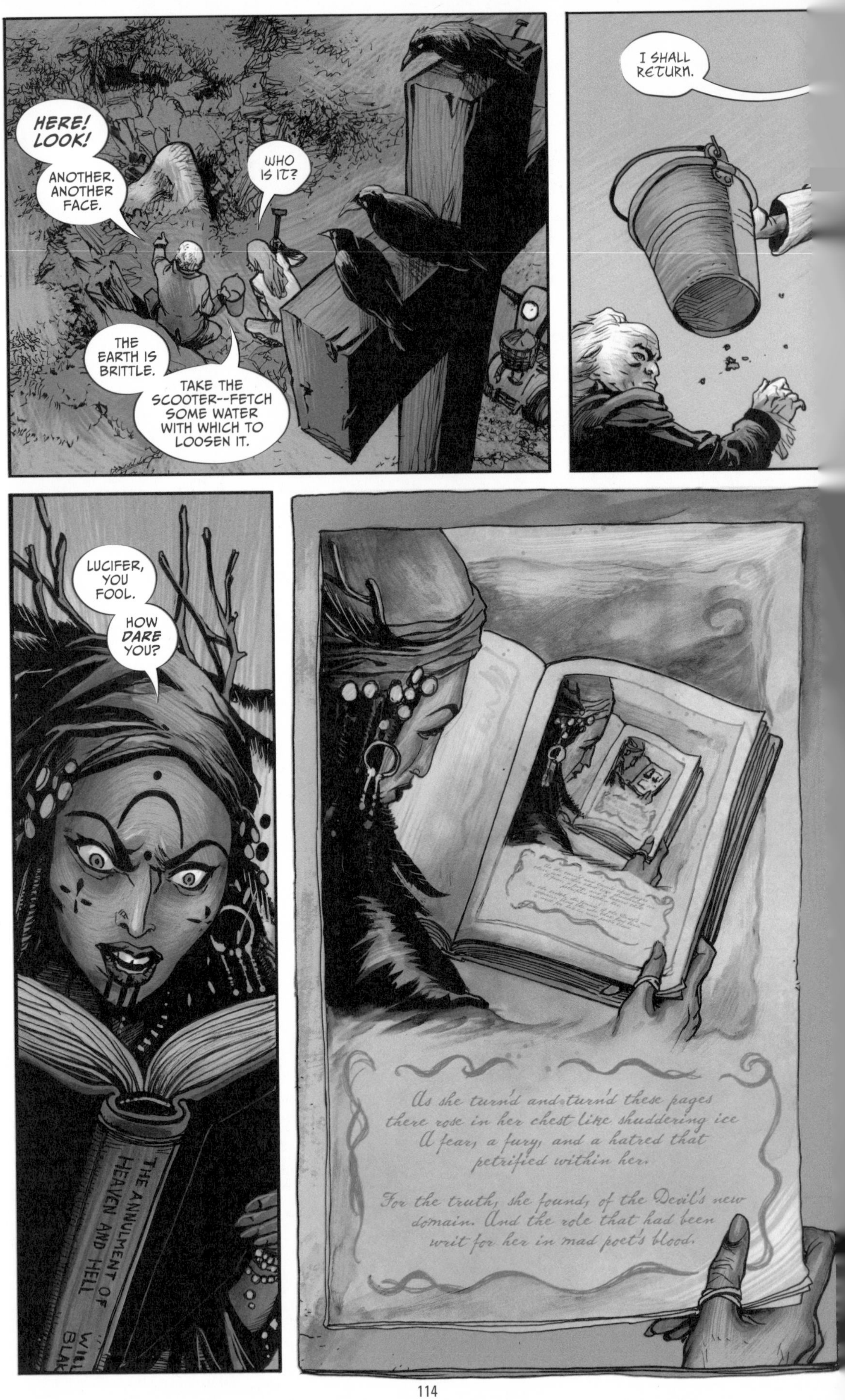
HERE! LOOK!
ANOTHER. ANOTHER FACE.
WHO IS IT?
THE EARTH IS BRITTLE.
TAKE THE SCOOTER--FETCH SOME WATER WITH WHICH TO LOOSEN IT.
I SHALL RETURN.
LUCIFER, YOU FOOL.
HOW *DARE* YOU?
THE ANNULMENT OF HEAVEN AND HELL
As she turn'd and turn'd these pages there rose in her chest like shuddering ice A fear, a fury, and a hatred that petrified within her.
For the truth, she found, of the Devil's new domain. And the role that had been writ for her in mad poet's blood.

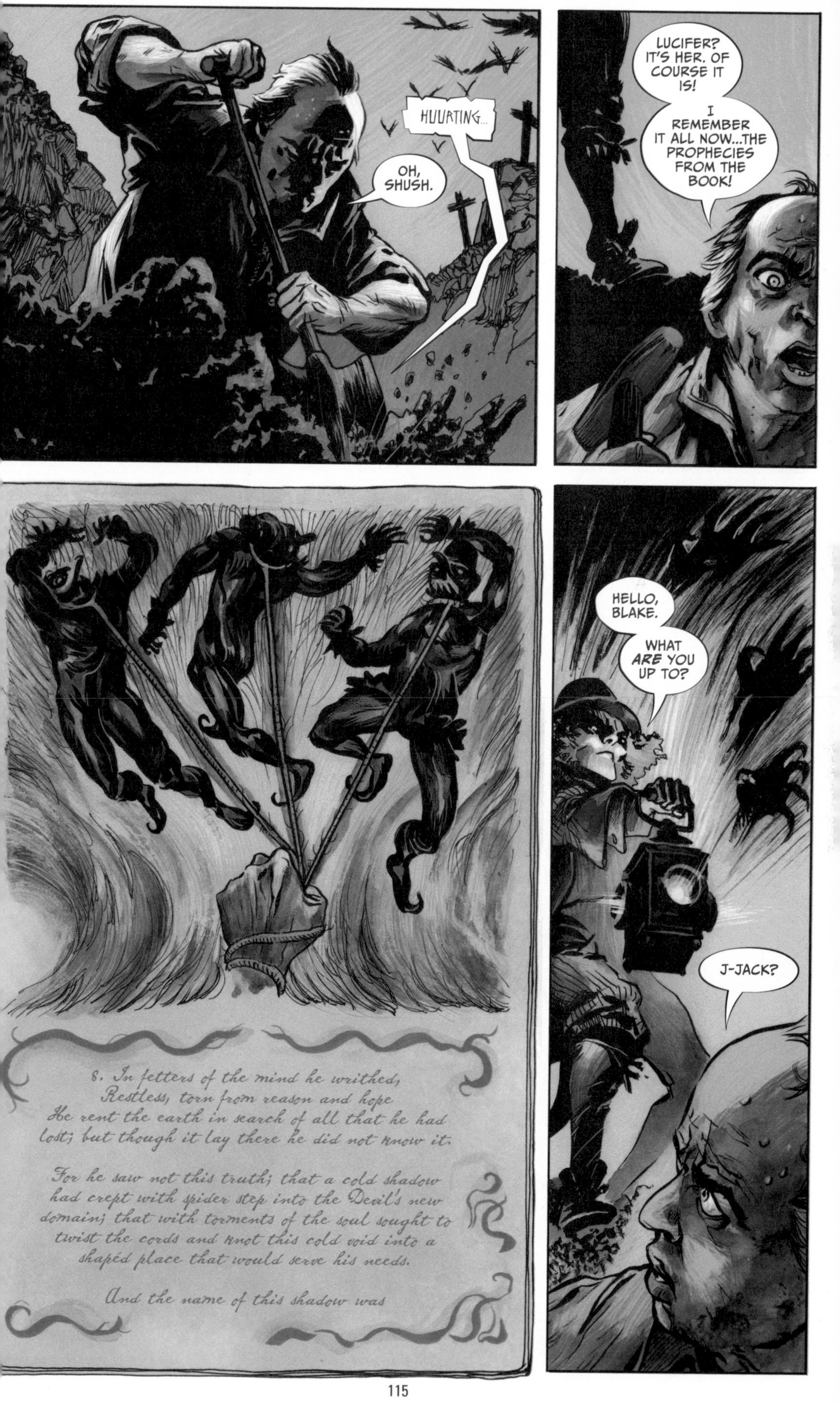
HUURTING...
OH, SHUSH.
LUCIFER? IT'S HER. OF COURSE IT IS!
I REMEMBER IT ALL NOW...THE PROPHECIES FROM THE BOOK!
8. In fetters of the mind he writhed,
Restless, torn from reason and hope
He rent the earth in search of all that he had
lost; but though it lay there he did not know it.
For he saw not this truth; that a cold shadow
had crept with spider step into the Devil's new
domain; that with torments of the soul sought to
twist the cords and knot this cold void into a
shaped place that would serve his needs.
And the name of this shadow was
HELLO, BLAKE.
WHAT ARE YOU UP TO?
J-JACK?

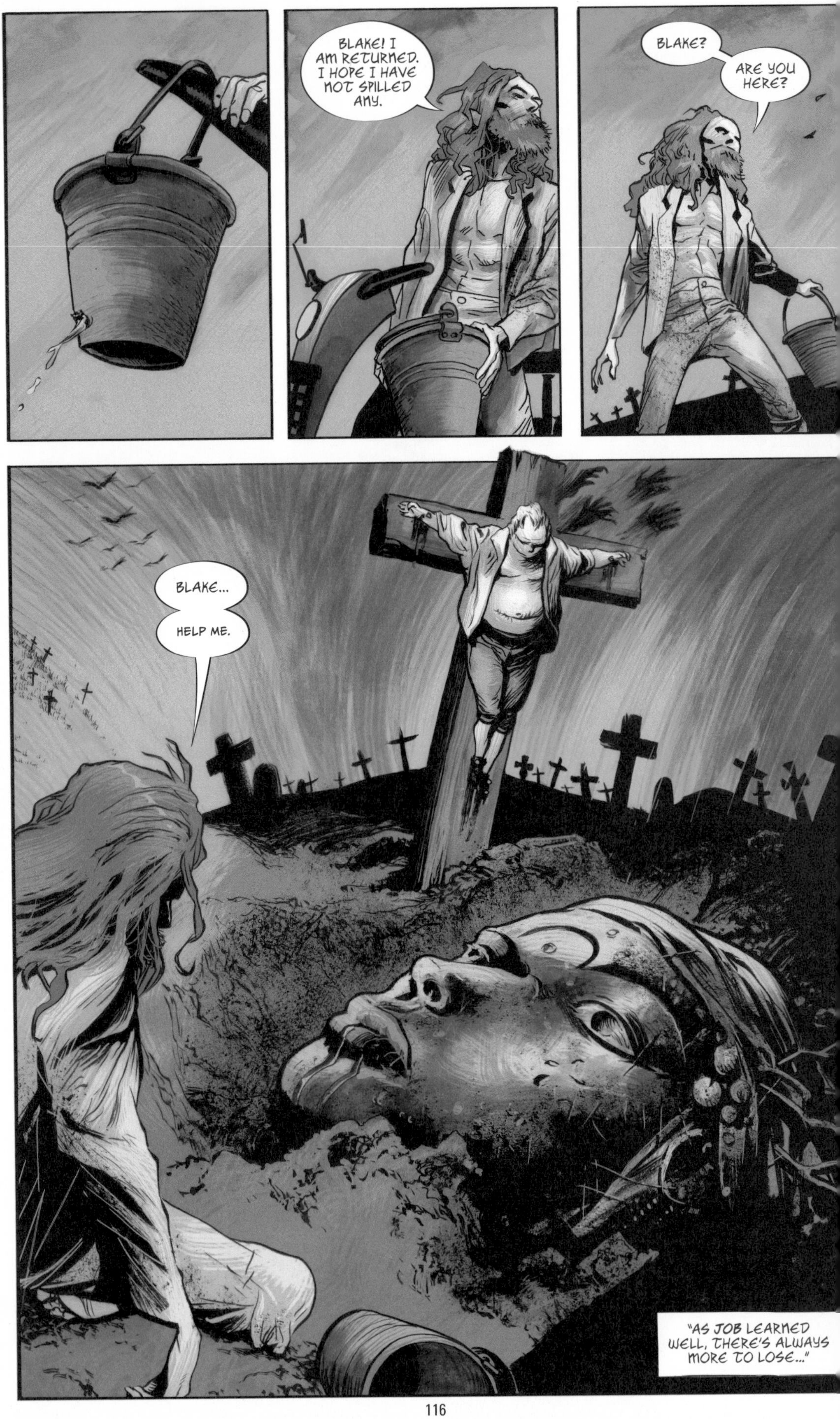
BLAKE! I AM RETURNED. I HOPE I HAVE NOT SPILLED ANY.
BLAKE?
ARE YOU HERE?
BLAKE...
HELP ME.
"AS JOB LEARNED WELL, THERE'S ALWAYS MORE TO LOSE..."

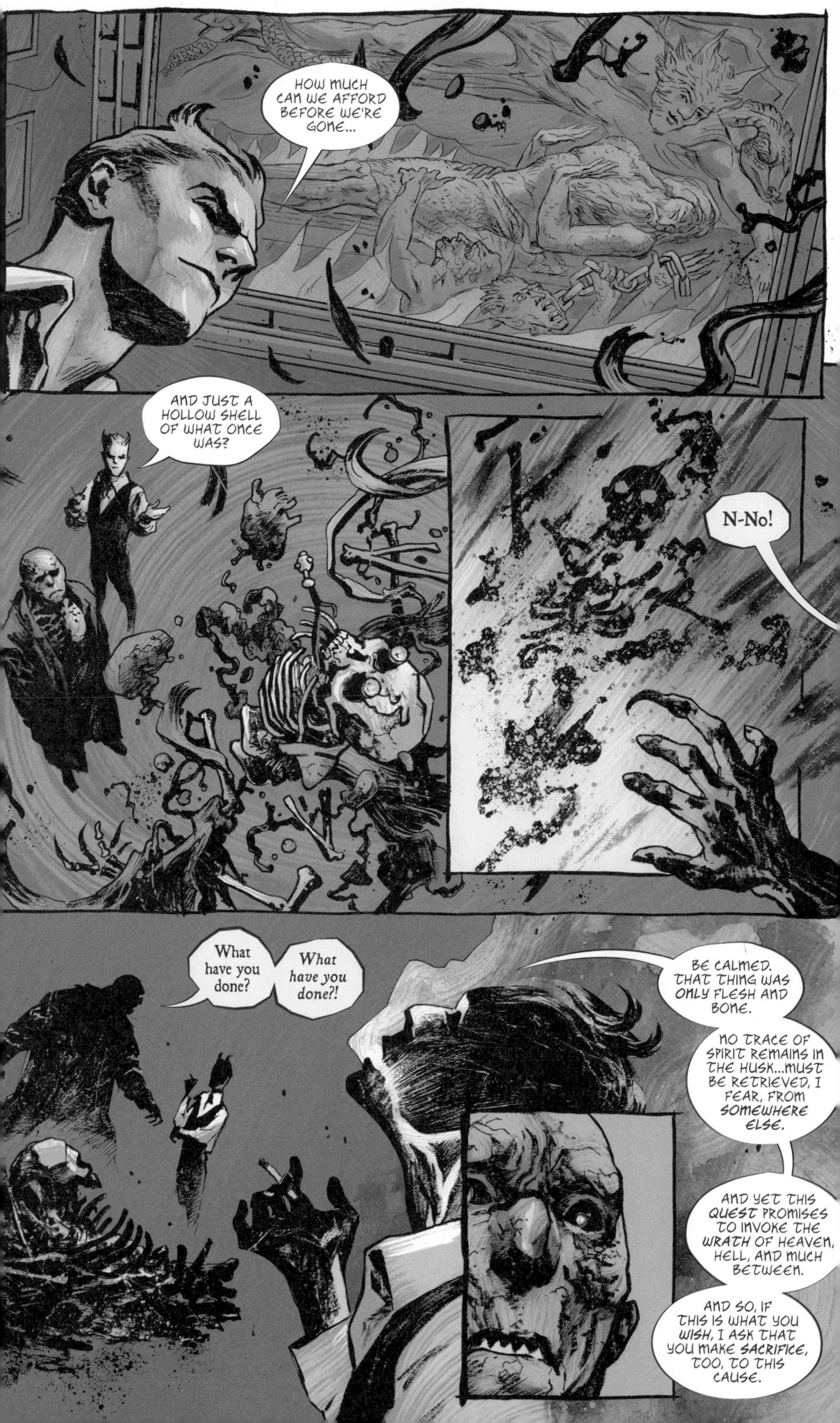
HOW MUCH CAN WE AFFORD BEFORE WE'RE GONE...
AND JUST A HOLLOW SHELL OF WHAT ONCE WAS?
N-No!
What have you done?
What have you done?!
BE CALMED. THAT THING WAS ONLY FLESH AND BONE.
NO TRACE OF SPIRIT REMAINS IN THE HUSK...MUST BE RETRIEVED, I FEAR, FROM SOMEWHERE ELSE.
AND YET THIS QUEST PROMISES TO INVOKE THE WRATH OF HEAVEN, HELL, AND MUCH BETWEEN.
AND SO, IF THIS IS WHAT YOU WISH, I ASK THAT YOU MAKE SACRIFICE, TOO, TO THIS CAUSE.

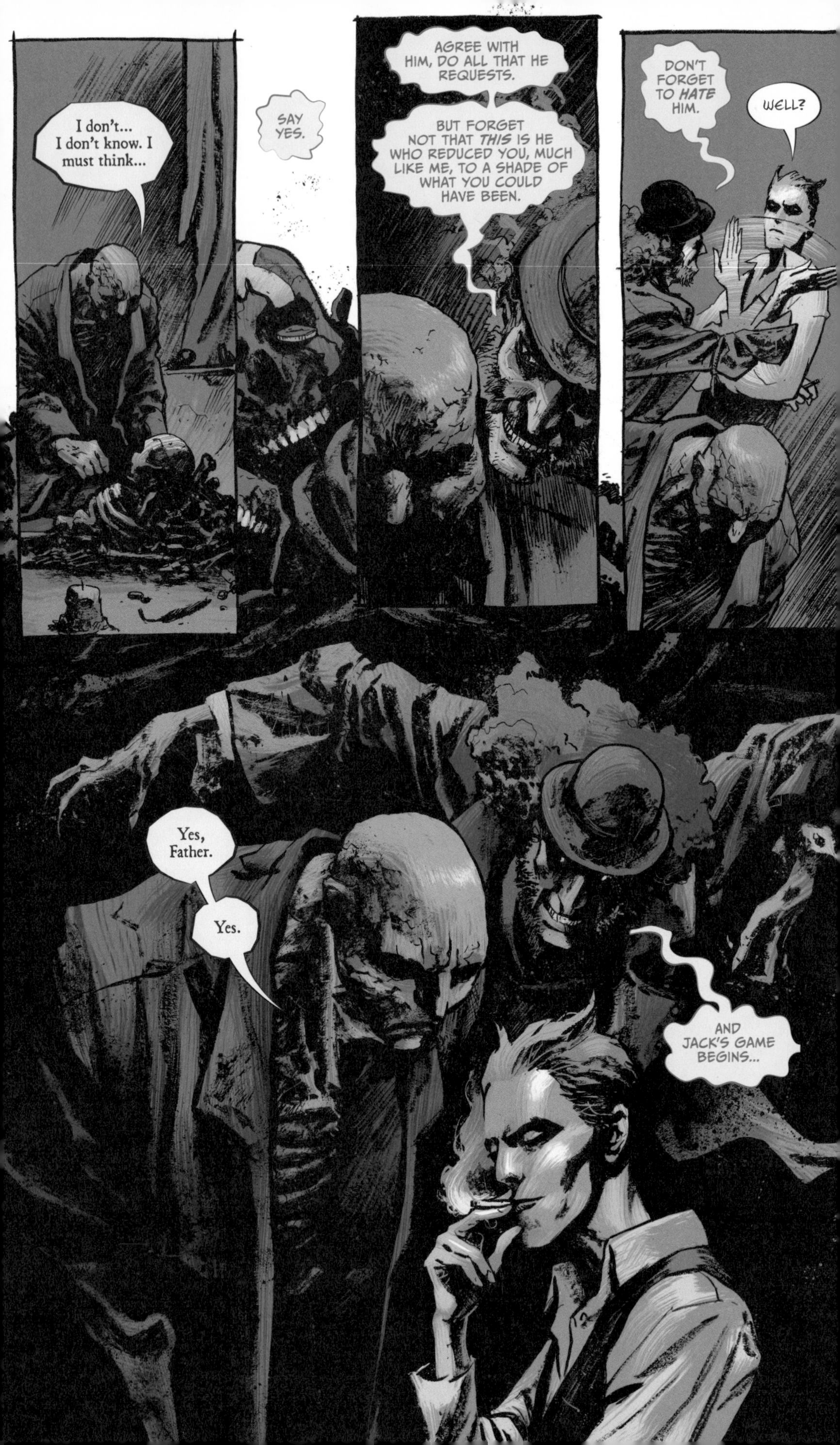
I don't... I don't know. I must think...
SAY YES.
AGREE WITH HIM, DO ALL THAT HE REQUESTS.
BUT FORGET NOT THAT THIS IS HE WHO REDUCED YOU, MUCH LIKE ME, TO A SHADE OF WHAT YOU COULD HAVE BEEN.
DON'T FORGET TO HATE HIM.
WELL?
Yes, Father.
Yes.
AND JACK'S GAME BEGINS...

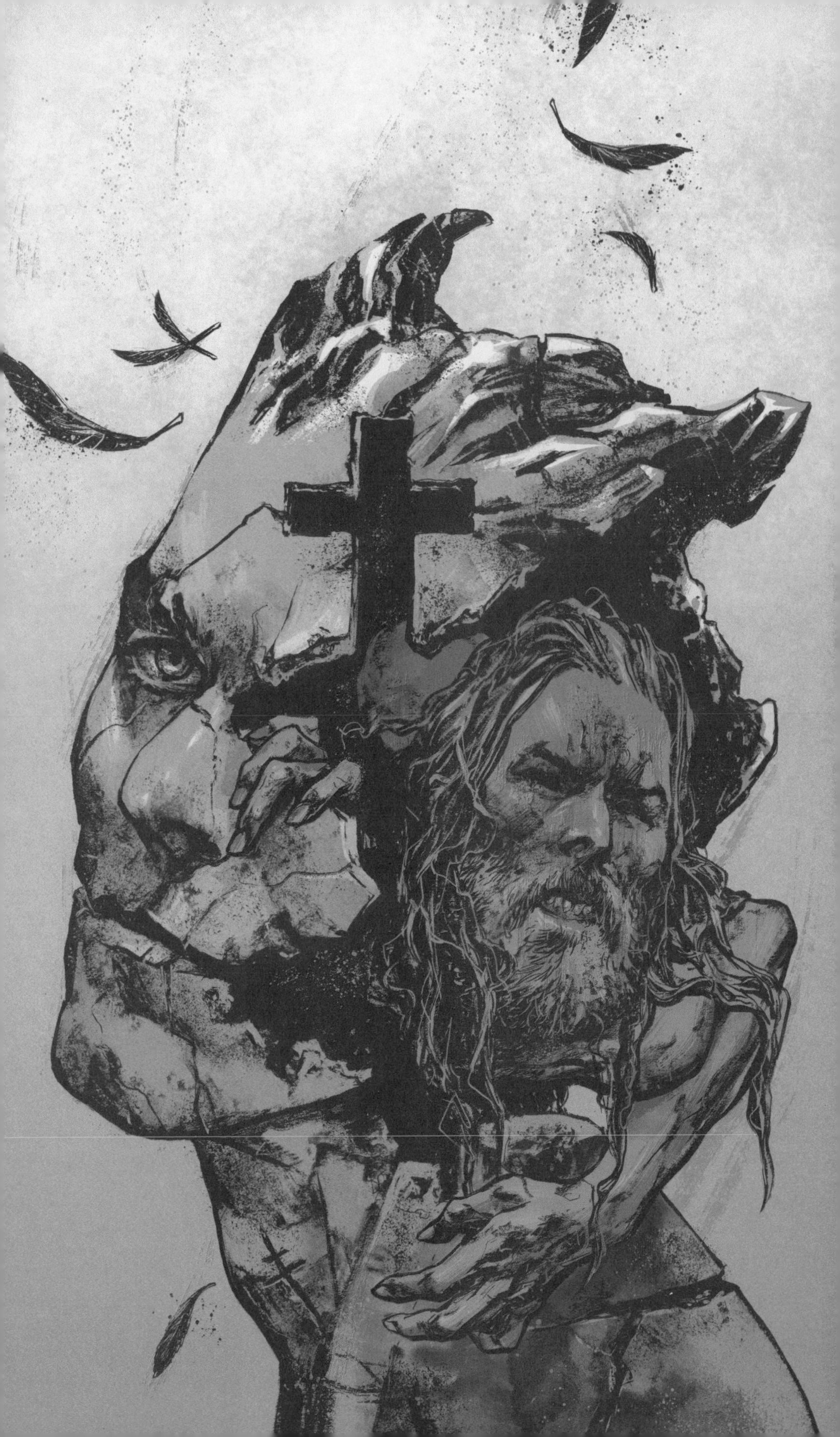

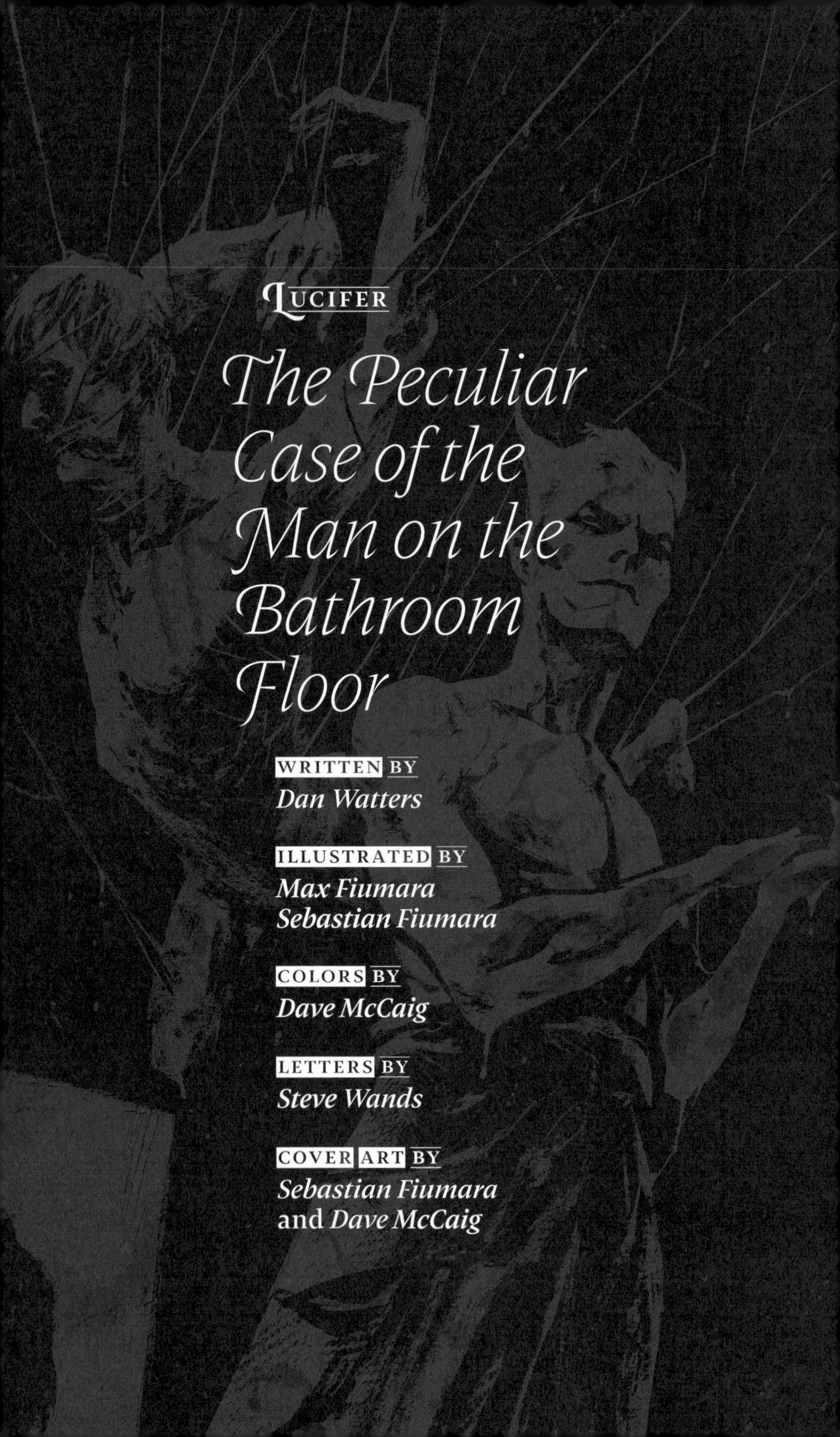

LUCIFER

The Peculiar Case of the Man on the Bathroom Floor

WRITTEN BY
Dan Watters

ILLUSTRATED BY
Max Fiumara
Sebastian Fiumara

COLORS BY
Dave McCaig

LETTERS BY
Steve Wands

COVER ART BY
Sebastian Fiumara
and *Dave McCaig*

SHE DIED OVER FIVE HUNDRED YEARS AGO.
THE INTERIM YEARS WERE OF COOL OBLIVION-- UNTROUBLED AND UNBURDENED.
AN ABYSS OF PERFECT STILLNESS, UNKNOWN AND IMPERCEIVABLE TO THE LIVING.
IN THIS SILENCE SHE HAD FORGOTTEN HER NAME, AND WHAT IT HAD BEEN TO HAVE ONE.
IT HAD BEEN BETTER THAT WAY.
SHE HAD FORGOTTEN PAIN AND LONELINESS, AND HOW IT FELT TO BE BETRAYED. ALL THE THINGS THAT THE LIVING KNOW.
THE ANNULMENT OF HEAVEN AND HELL
COME ON, PICK UP.
I KNOW YOU'RE THERE.
THE ANNULMENT OF HEAVEN AND HELL BY WILLIAM BLAKE
AND THEN THEY CAME--INTRUDERS INTO HER SOLITUDE, BREACHERS OF THE PEACE--AND SHE FORGOT IT HAD EVER BEEN SILENT AT ALL.
SHE HAS FINALLY REALIZED ALL OF THIS ON DISCOVERING A BOOK OF PROPHECY WRITTEN BY THE MORTAL WILLIAM BLAKE, WHICH TELLS THE STORY OF THIS FORSAKEN PLACE.
IT TELLS THE STORY OF THE ONE WHO WOULD NOT LET HER REST-- WHO MEANT TO FORCE HER TO LIVE AGAIN, WHETHER SHE WISHED TO OR NOT.
YOU NEED TO PICK UP.
YOU HAVE TO GET THEM OUT OF HERE.
SHE REMEMBERED THAT HER NAME IS SYCORAX. AND SHE REMEMBERS THAT...
THIS IS LUCIFER'S FAULT...

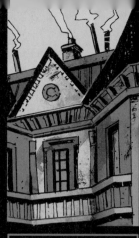

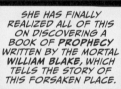

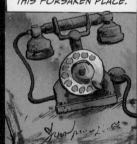

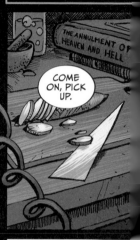

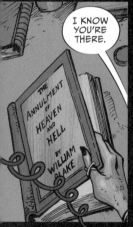

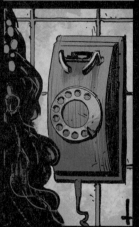

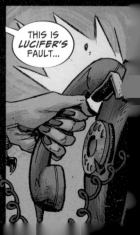

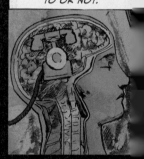

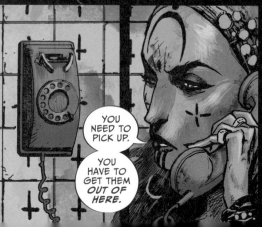

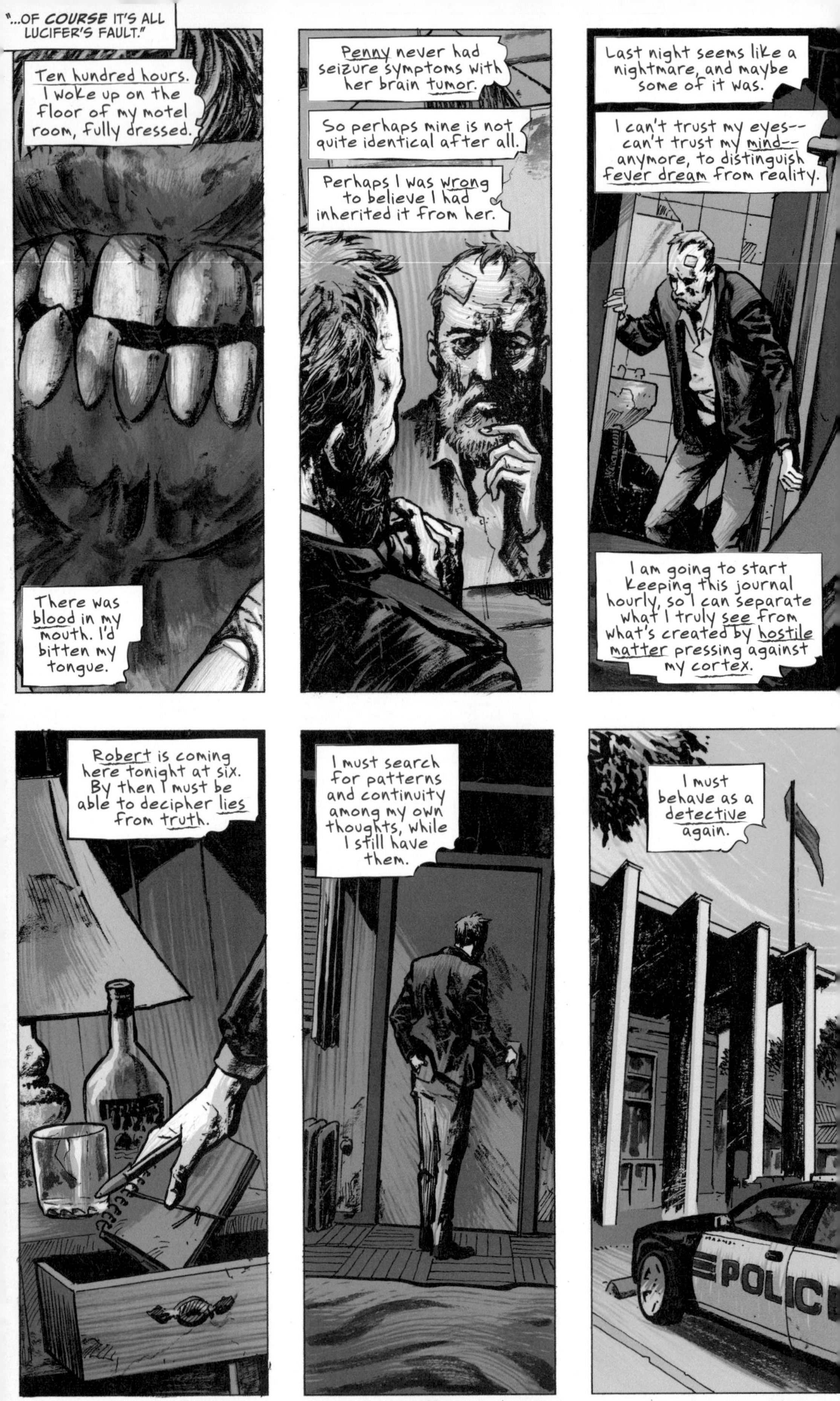
"...OF COURSE IT'S ALL LUCIFER'S FAULT."
Ten hundred hours. I woke up on the floor of my motel room, fully dressed.
There was blood in my mouth. I'd bitten my tongue.
Penny never had seizure symptoms with her brain tumor.
So perhaps mine is not quite identical after all.
Perhaps I was wrong to believe I had inherited it from her.
Last night seems like a nightmare, and maybe some of it was.
I can't trust my eyes-- can't trust my mind-- anymore, to distinguish fever dream from reality.
I am going to start keeping this journal hourly, so I can separate what I truly see from what's created by hostile matter pressing against my cortex.
Robert is coming here tonight at six. By then I must be able to decipher lies from truth.
I must search for patterns and continuity among my own thoughts, while I still have them.
I must behave as a detective again.
POLIC

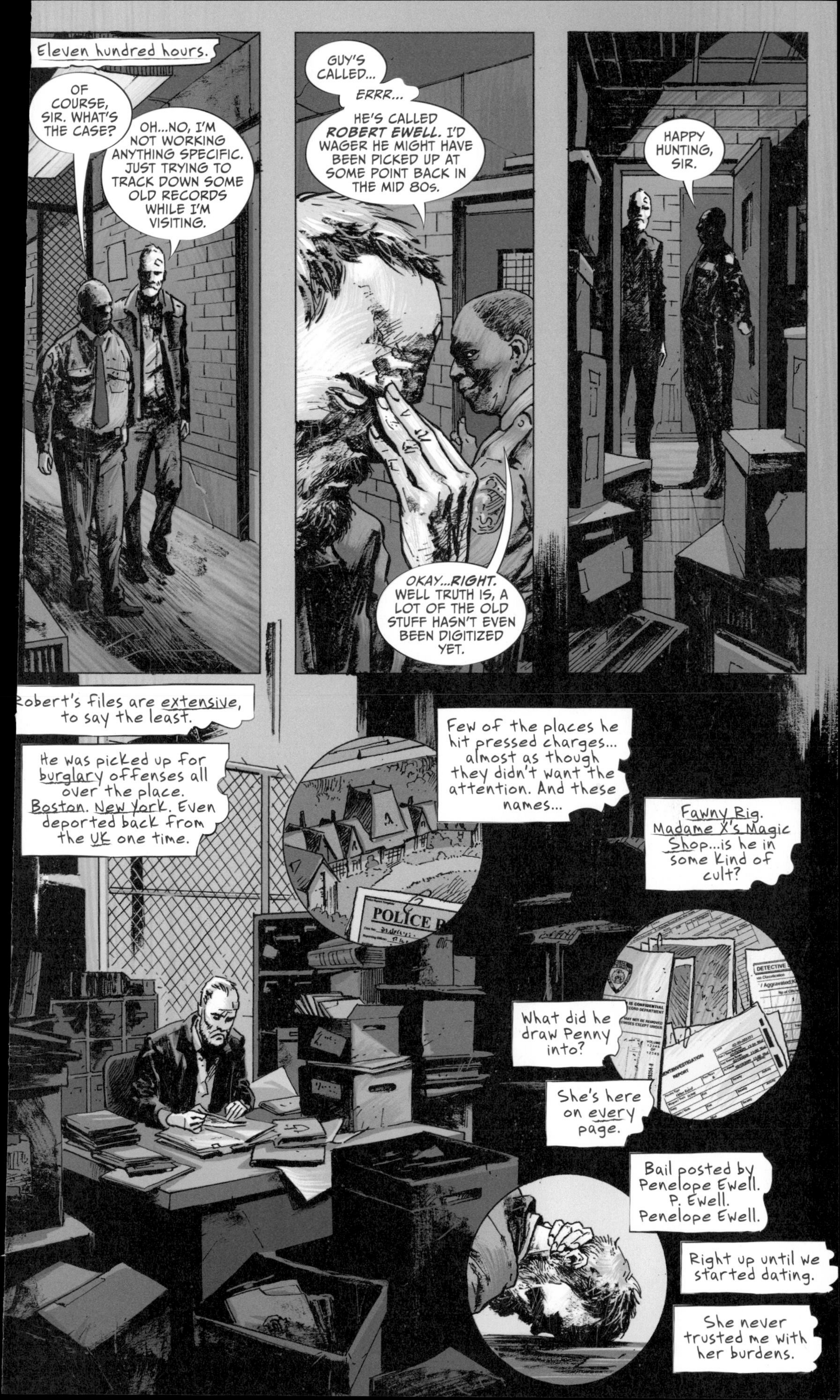

Eleven hundred hours.
OF COURSE, SIR. WHAT'S THE CASE?
OH...NO, I'M NOT WORKING ANYTHING SPECIFIC. JUST TRYING TO TRACK DOWN SOME OLD RECORDS WHILE I'M VISITING.
GUY'S CALLED...
ERRR...
HE'S CALLED ROBERT EWELL. I'D WAGER HE MIGHT HAVE BEEN PICKED UP AT SOME POINT BACK IN THE MID 80s.
OKAY...RIGHT. WELL TRUTH IS, A LOT OF THE OLD STUFF HASN'T EVEN BEEN DIGITIZED YET.
HAPPY HUNTING, SIR.
Robert's files are extensive, to say the least.
He was picked up for burglary offenses all over the place. Boston. New York. Even deported back from the UK one time.
Few of the places he hit pressed charges... almost as though they didn't want the attention. And these names...
POLICE R
Fawny Rig. Madame X's Magic Shop...is he in some kind of cult?
What did he draw Penny into?
She's here on every page.
Bail posted by Penelope Ewell. P. Ewell. Penelope Ewell.
Right up until we started dating.
She never trusted me with her burdens.

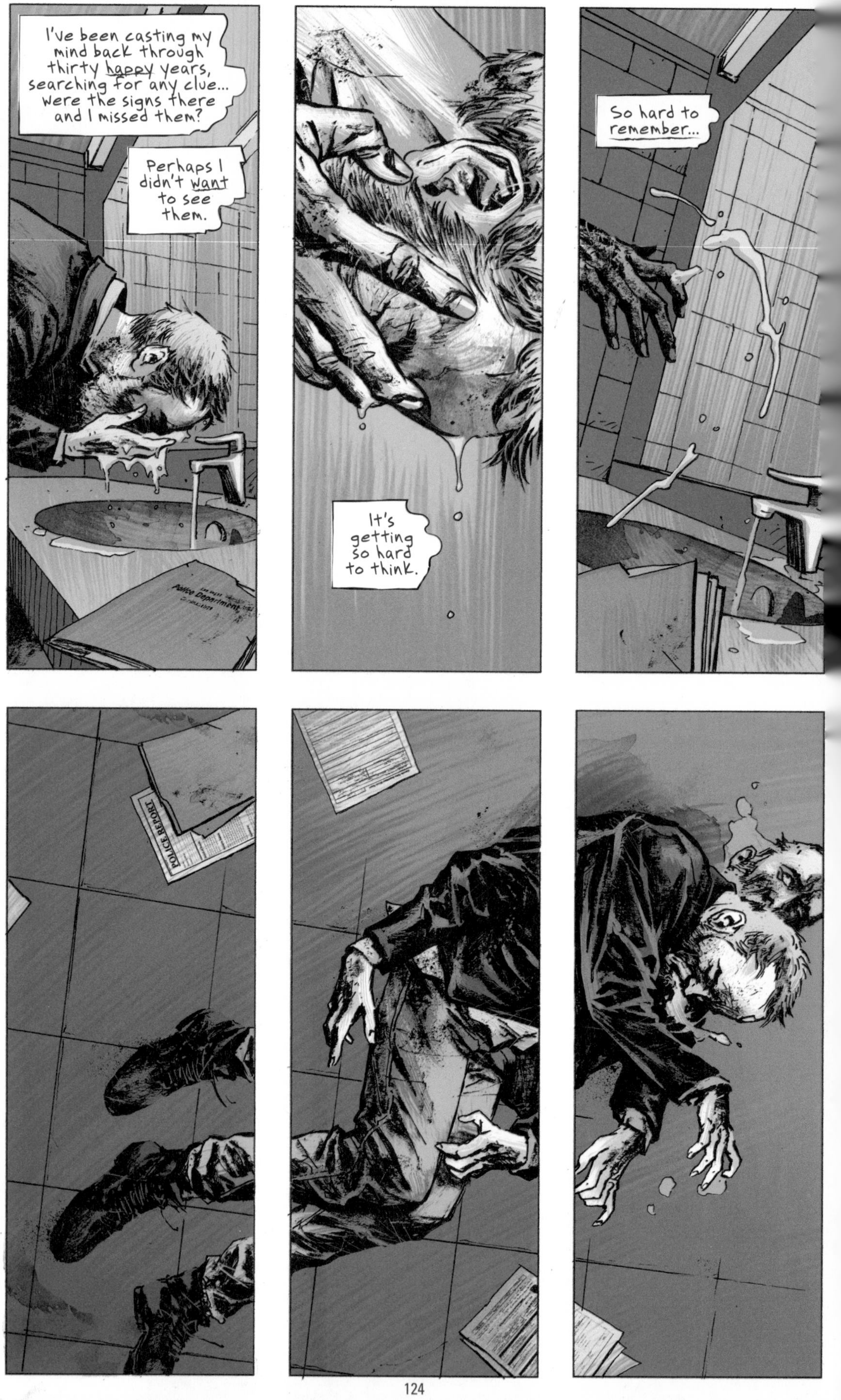
I've been casting my mind back through thirty happy years, searching for any clue... Were the signs there and I missed them?
Perhaps I didn't want to see them.
Police Department
It's getting so hard to think.
So hard to remember...
POLICE REPORT

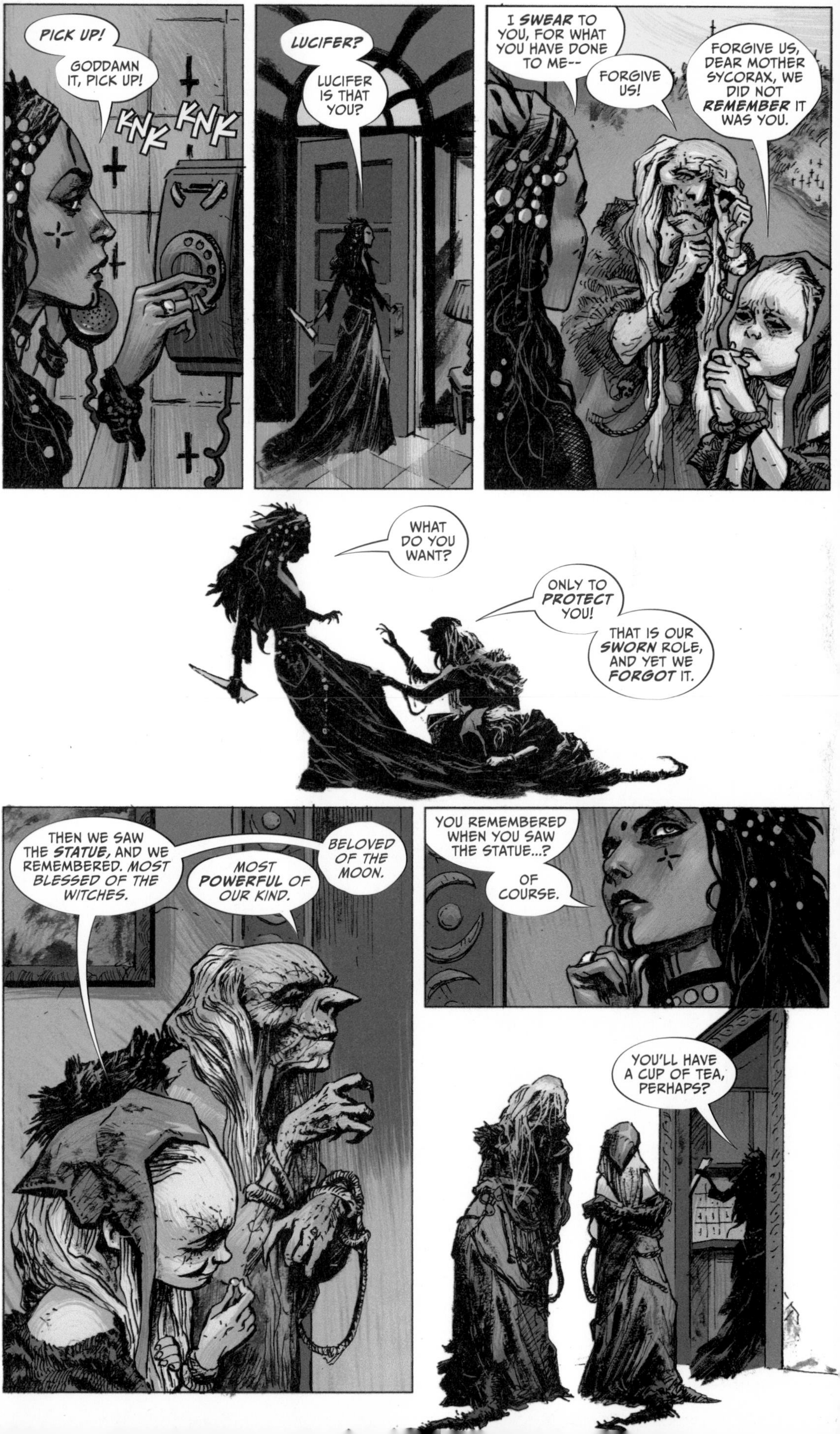
PICK UP!
GODDAMN IT, PICK UP!
KNK KNK
LUCIFER?
LUCIFER IS THAT YOU?
I SWEAR TO YOU, FOR WHAT YOU HAVE DONE TO ME--
FORGIVE US!
FORGIVE US, DEAR MOTHER SYCORAX, WE DID NOT REMEMBER IT WAS YOU.
WHAT DO YOU WANT?
ONLY TO PROTECT YOU!
THAT IS OUR SWORN ROLE, AND YET WE FORGOT IT.
THEN WE SAW THE STATUE, AND WE REMEMBERED. MOST BLESSED OF THE WITCHES.
BELOVED OF THE MOON.
MOST POWERFUL OF OUR KIND.
YOU REMEMBERED WHEN YOU SAW THE STATUE...?
OF COURSE.
YOU'LL HAVE A CUP OF TEA, PERHAPS?

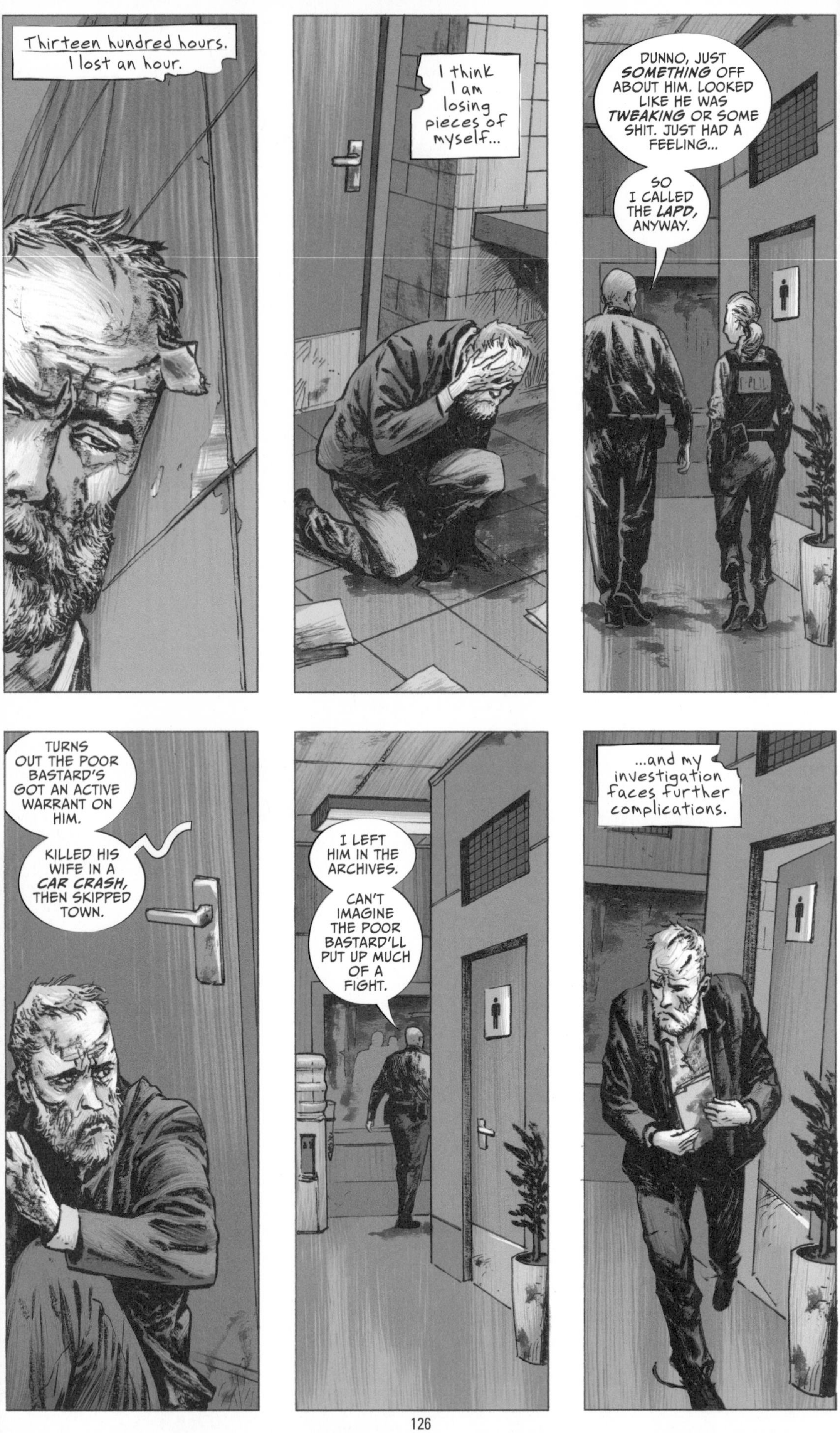
Thirteen hundred hours. I lost an hour.
I think I am losing pieces of myself...
DUNNO, JUST SOMETHING OFF ABOUT HIM. LOOKED LIKE HE WAS TWEAKING OR SOME SHIT. JUST HAD A FEELING...
SO I CALLED THE LAPD, ANYWAY.
TURNS OUT THE POOR BASTARD'S GOT AN ACTIVE WARRANT ON HIM.
KILLED HIS WIFE IN A CAR CRASH, THEN SKIPPED TOWN.
I LEFT HIM IN THE ARCHIVES.
CAN'T IMAGINE THE POOR BASTARD'LL PUT UP MUCH OF A FIGHT.
...and my investigation faces further complications.

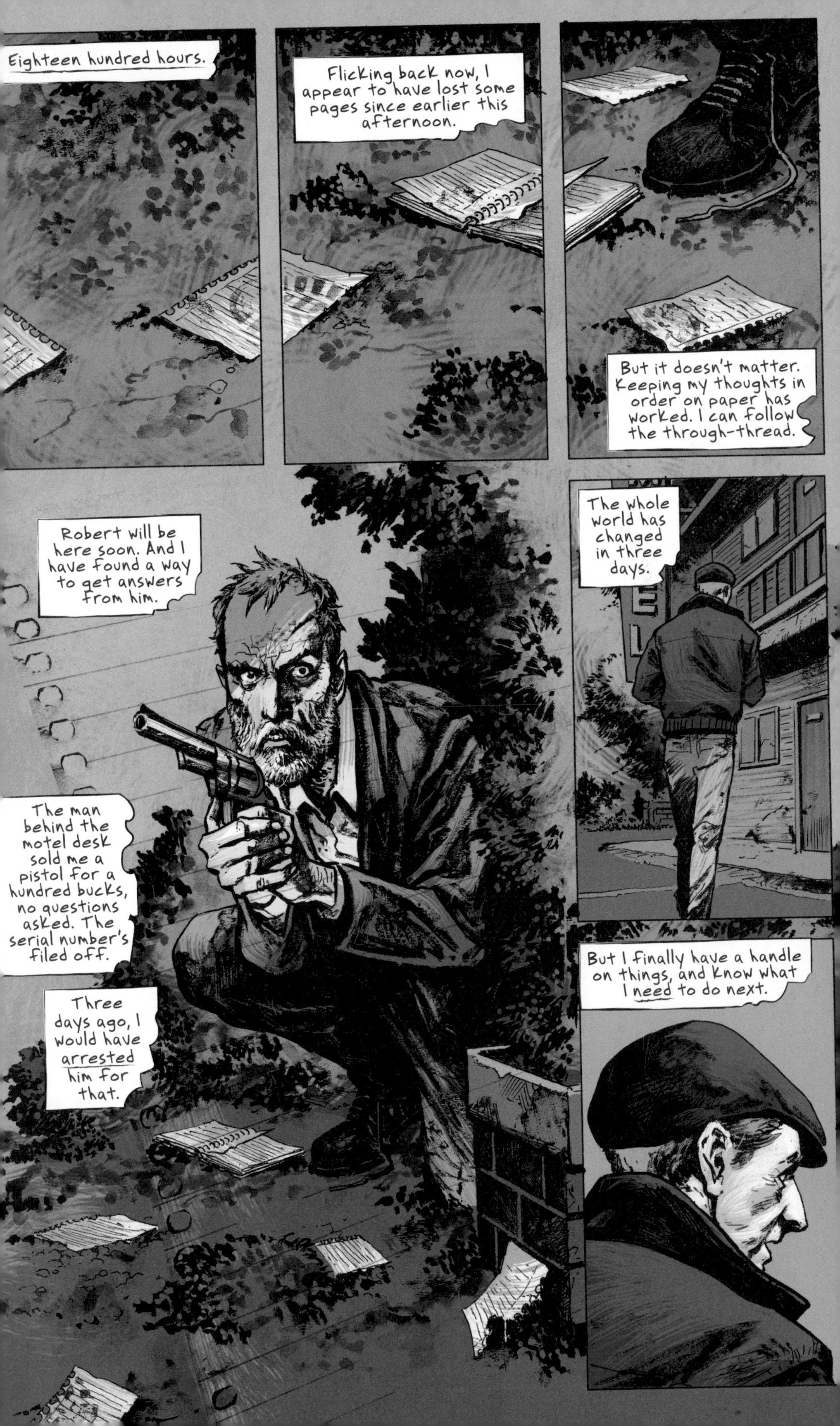
Eighteen hundred hours.
Flicking back now, I appear to have lost some pages since earlier this afternoon.
But it doesn't matter. Keeping my thoughts in order on paper has worked. I can follow the through-thread.
Robert will be here soon. And I have found a way to get answers from him.
The man behind the motel desk sold me a pistol for a hundred bucks, no questions asked. The serial number's filed off.
Three days ago, I would have arrested him for that.
The whole world has changed in three days.
But I finally have a handle on things, and know what I need to do next.

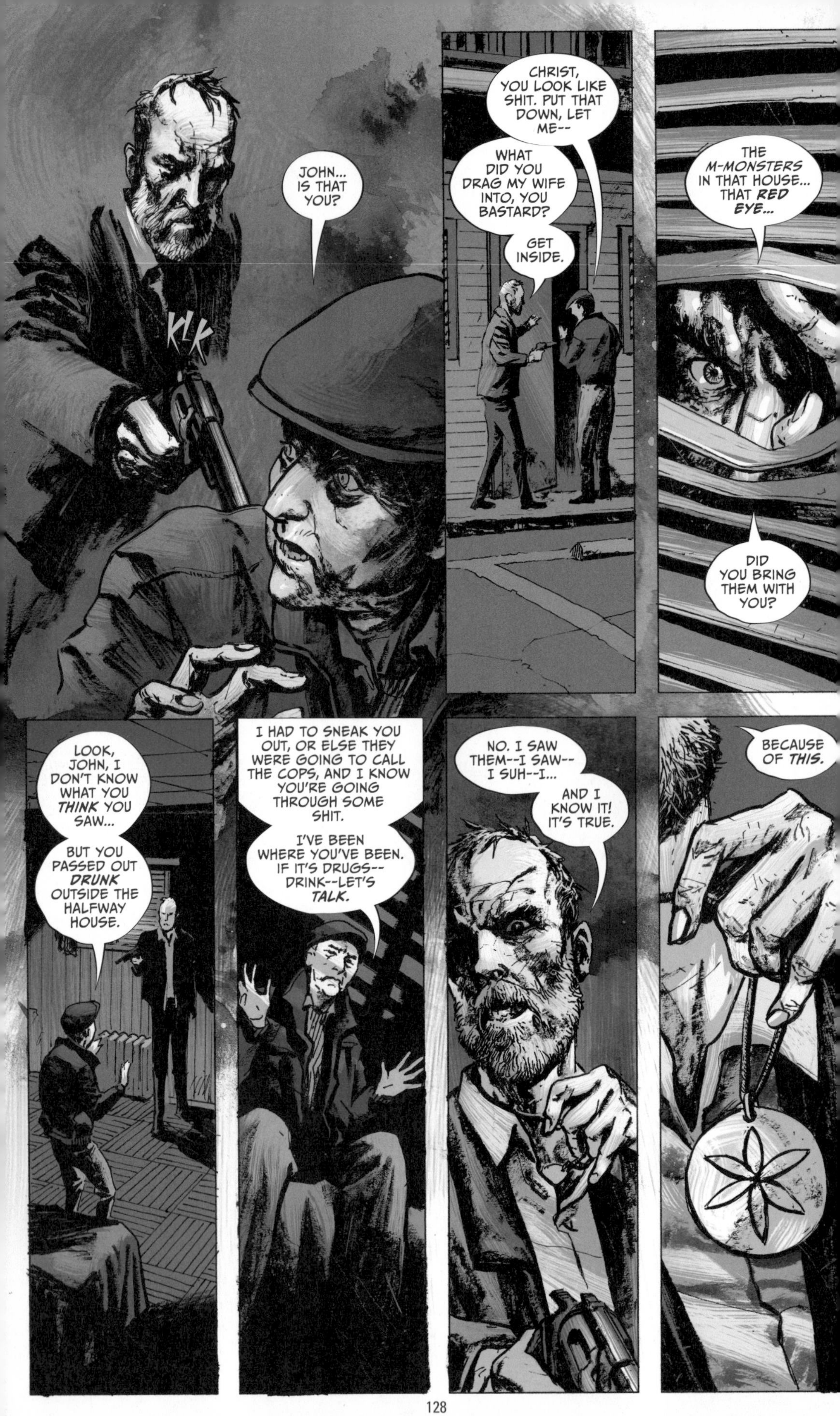
KLIK
JOHN... IS THAT YOU?
CHRIST, YOU LOOK LIKE SHIT. PUT THAT DOWN, LET ME--
WHAT DID YOU DRAG MY WIFE INTO, YOU BASTARD?
GET INSIDE.
THE M-MONSTERS IN THAT HOUSE... THAT RED EYE...
DID YOU BRING THEM WITH YOU?
LOOK, JOHN, I DON'T KNOW WHAT YOU THINK YOU SAW...
BUT YOU PASSED OUT DRUNK OUTSIDE THE HALFWAY HOUSE.
I HAD TO SNEAK YOU OUT, OR ELSE THEY WERE GOING TO CALL THE COPS, AND I KNOW YOU'RE GOING THROUGH SOME SHIT.
I'VE BEEN WHERE YOU'VE BEEN. IF IT'S DRUGS--DRINK--LET'S TALK.
NO. I SAW THEM--I SAW--I SUH--I...
AND I KNOW IT! IT'S TRUE.
BECAUSE OF THIS.

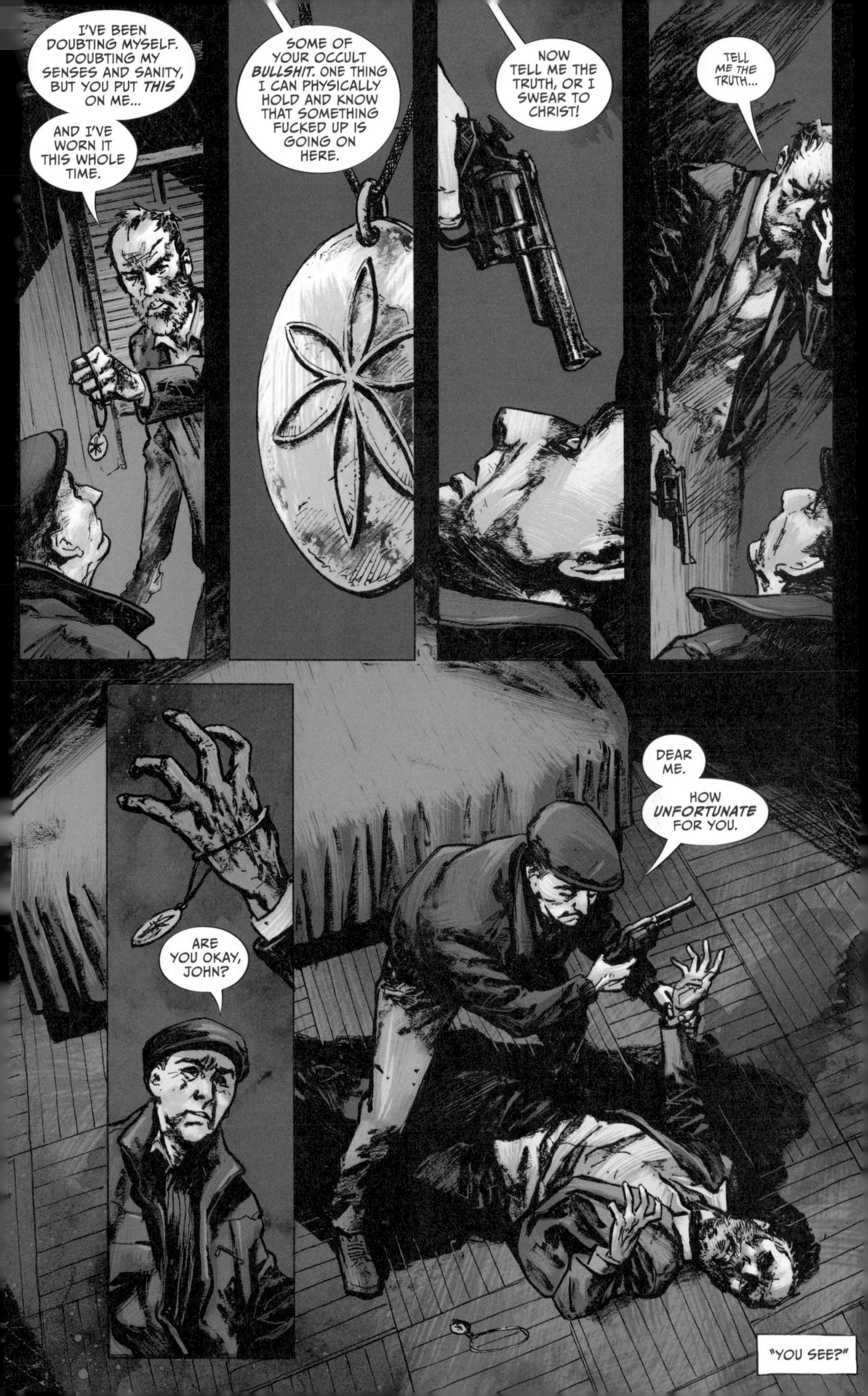
I'VE BEEN DOUBTING MYSELF. DOUBTING MY SENSES AND SANITY, BUT YOU PUT *THIS* ON ME...
AND I'VE WORN IT THIS WHOLE TIME.
SOME OF YOUR OCCULT ***BULLSHIT.*** ONE THING I CAN PHYSICALLY HOLD AND KNOW THAT SOMETHING FUCKED UP IS GOING ON HERE.
NOW TELL ME THE TRUTH, OR I SWEAR TO CHRIST!
TELL ME THE TRUTH...
ARE YOU OKAY, JOHN?
DEAR ME.
HOW ***UNFORTUNATE*** FOR YOU.
"YOU SEE?"

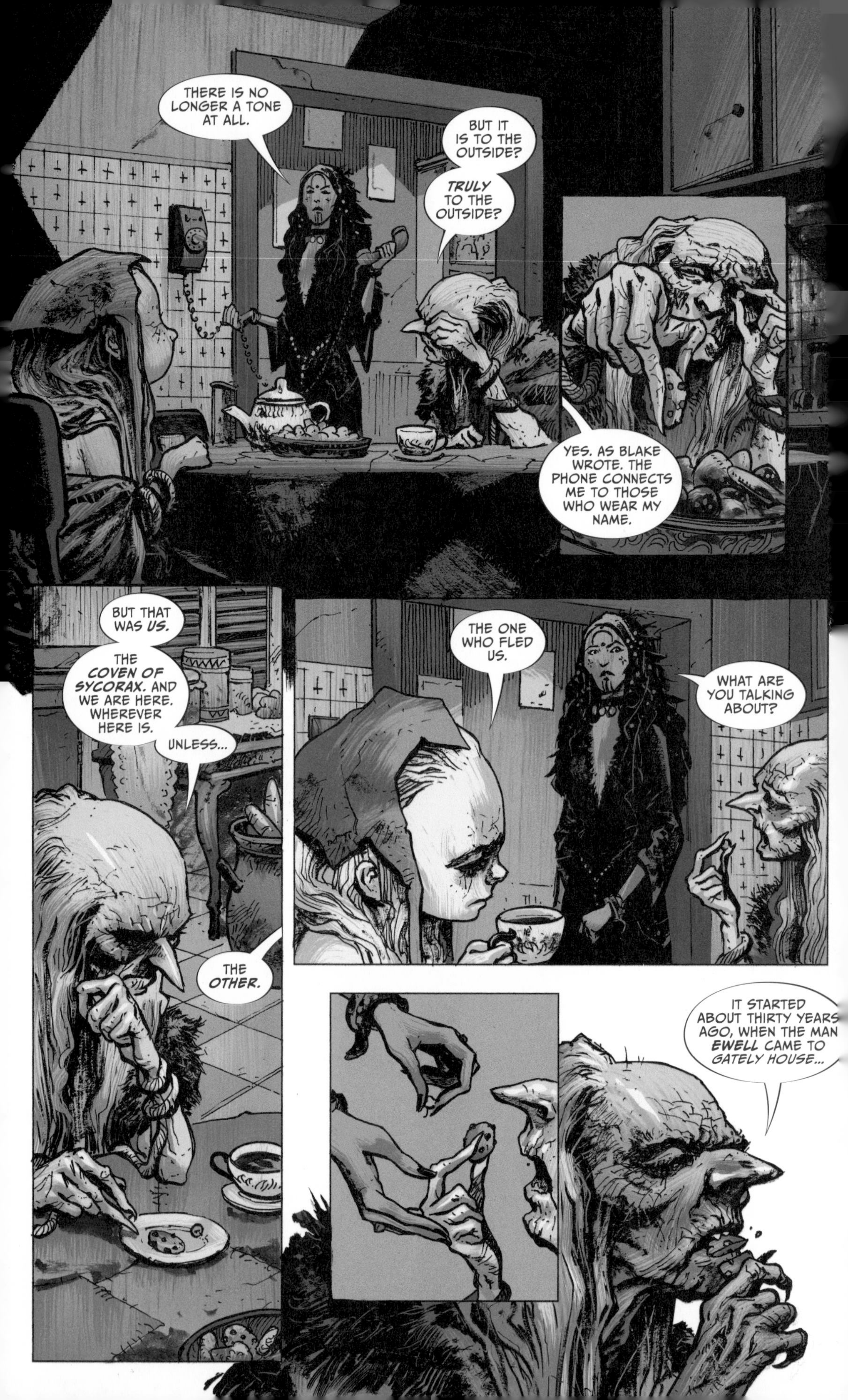
THERE IS NO LONGER A TONE AT ALL.
BUT IT IS TO THE OUTSIDE?
TRULY TO THE OUTSIDE?
YES. AS BLAKE WROTE. THE PHONE CONNECTS ME TO THOSE WHO WEAR MY NAME.
BUT THAT WAS US.
THE COVEN OF SYCORAX. AND WE ARE HERE. WHEREVER HERE IS.
UNLESS...
THE OTHER.
THE ONE WHO FLED US.
WHAT ARE YOU TALKING ABOUT?
IT STARTED ABOUT THIRTY YEARS AGO, WHEN THE MAN EWELL CAME TO GATELY HOUSE...

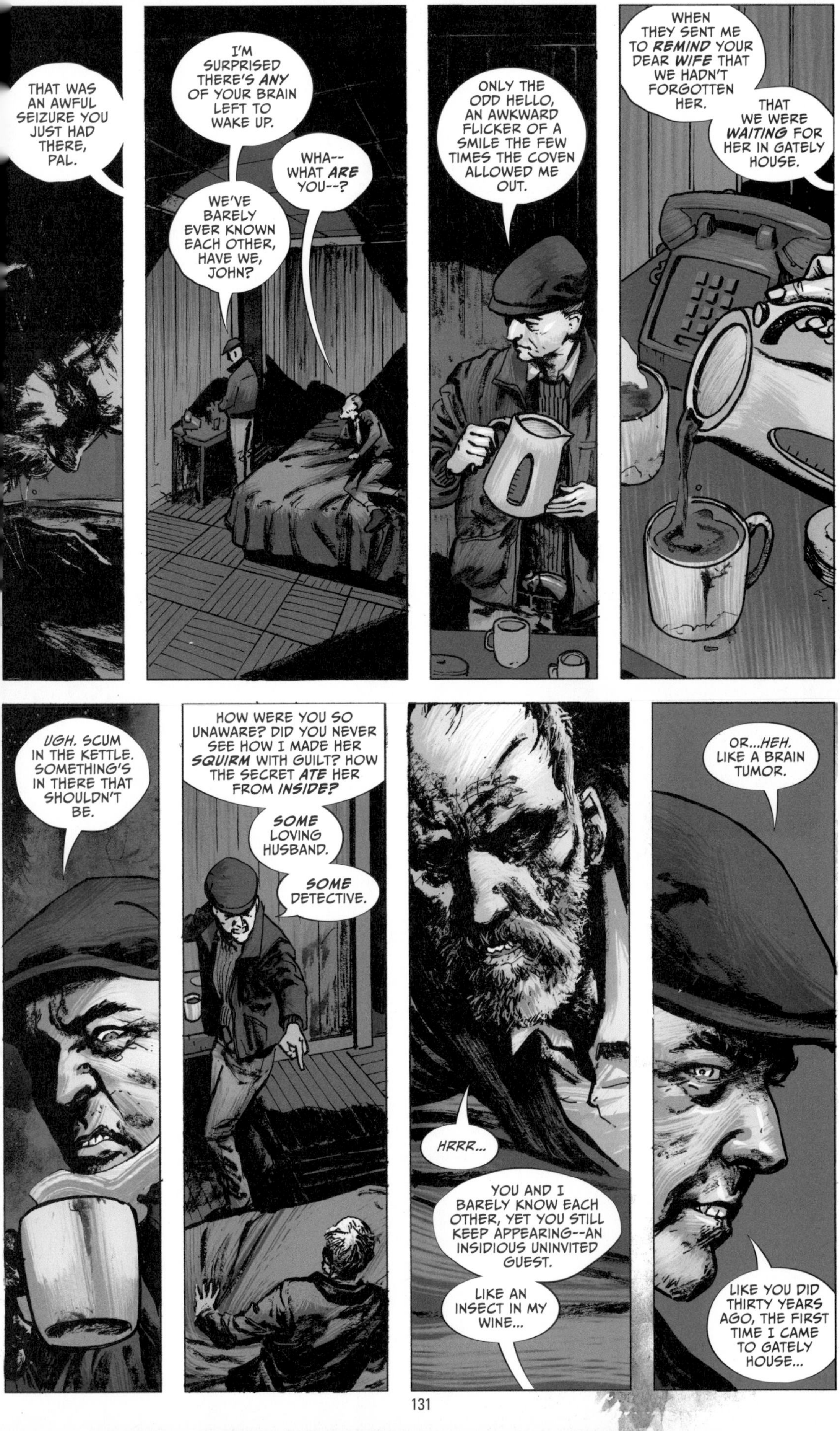
THAT WAS AN AWFUL SEIZURE YOU JUST HAD THERE, PAL.
I'M SURPRISED THERE'S ANY OF YOUR BRAIN LEFT TO WAKE UP.
WE'VE BARELY EVER KNOWN EACH OTHER, HAVE WE, JOHN?
WHA-- WHAT ARE YOU--?
ONLY THE ODD HELLO, AN AWKWARD FLICKER OF A SMILE THE FEW TIMES THE COVEN ALLOWED ME OUT.
WHEN THEY SENT ME TO REMIND YOUR DEAR WIFE THAT WE HADN'T FORGOTTEN HER.
THAT WE WERE WAITING FOR HER IN GATELY HOUSE.
UGH. SCUM IN THE KETTLE. SOMETHING'S IN THERE THAT SHOULDN'T BE.
HOW WERE YOU SO UNAWARE? DID YOU NEVER SEE HOW I MADE HER SQUIRM WITH GUILT? HOW THE SECRET ATE HER FROM INSIDE?
SOME LOVING HUSBAND.
SOME DETECTIVE.
HRRR...
YOU AND I BARELY KNOW EACH OTHER, YET YOU STILL KEEP APPEARING--AN INSIDIOUS UNINVITED GUEST.
LIKE AN INSECT IN MY WINE...
OR...HEH. LIKE A BRAIN TUMOR.
LIKE YOU DID THIRTY YEARS AGO, THE FIRST TIME I CAME TO GATELY HOUSE...

"HE WAS AN ADDICT AND A *THIEF*."

"I WAS A WARRIOR AGAINST THE FORCES OF DARKNESS."

"BUT HIS *ADDICTION* WAS TO *MAGIC*. HIS FAMILY'S BLOOD CONTAINED A RICH VEIN OF IT, OF WHICH HE'D RECEIVED A BARE CAPILLARY."

"I WAS BORN WITH THE CAPACITY TO BE A GREAT MAGICIAN. TO KEEP AT BAY HORRORS THAT THE WAKING WORLD DENIES EXIST. I NEEDED ONLY THE RIGHT TOOLS TO DO THIS WORK."

"HE THOUGHT MAGIC THE PATH TO AN EASY LIFE, AND SO WOULD STEAL IT--*LEECH* IT--WHEREVER HE COULD TRACK IT DOWN."

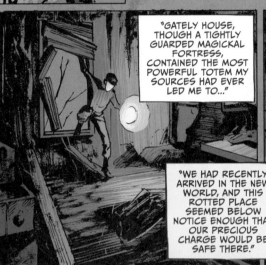

"GATELY HOUSE, THOUGH A TIGHTLY GUARDED MAGICKAL FORTRESS, CONTAINED THE MOST POWERFUL TOTEM MY SOURCES HAD EVER LED ME TO..."

"WE HAD RECENTLY ARRIVED IN THE NEW WORLD, AND THIS ROTTED PLACE SEEMED BELOW NOTICE ENOUGH THAT OUR PRECIOUS CHARGE WOULD BE SAFE THERE."

"BUT IT TURNED OUT TO BE TOO TIGHTLY GUARDED, EVEN FOR MY SKILLS."

"WE WOULD NOT HAVE THOUGHT A LEECH LIKE HIM FOOLHARDY ENOUGH TO TRY AND STEAL FROM US."

OH GOD, PLEASE-- DON'T HURT ME, *PLEASE*.

WHAT DO WE DO, *CRONE?*

IF WE LET HIM GO, WE'LL HAVE TO MOVE.

I DON'T WANT TO MOVE, I'M *TIRED* OF MOVING. I WANT TO STAY HERE A FEW DECADES. IT'S WARM.

AND WHAT IF HE PURSUES?

I WON'T-- CHRIST, I WON'T, I SWEAR!

PROBABLY EASIER JUST TO *KILL* HIM.

BESIDES, IMAGINE IF LUCIFER HEARD SOMEONE HAD EVEN GOTTEN THEIR HANDS ON *HER* BONES...

OH, IMAGINE INDEED.

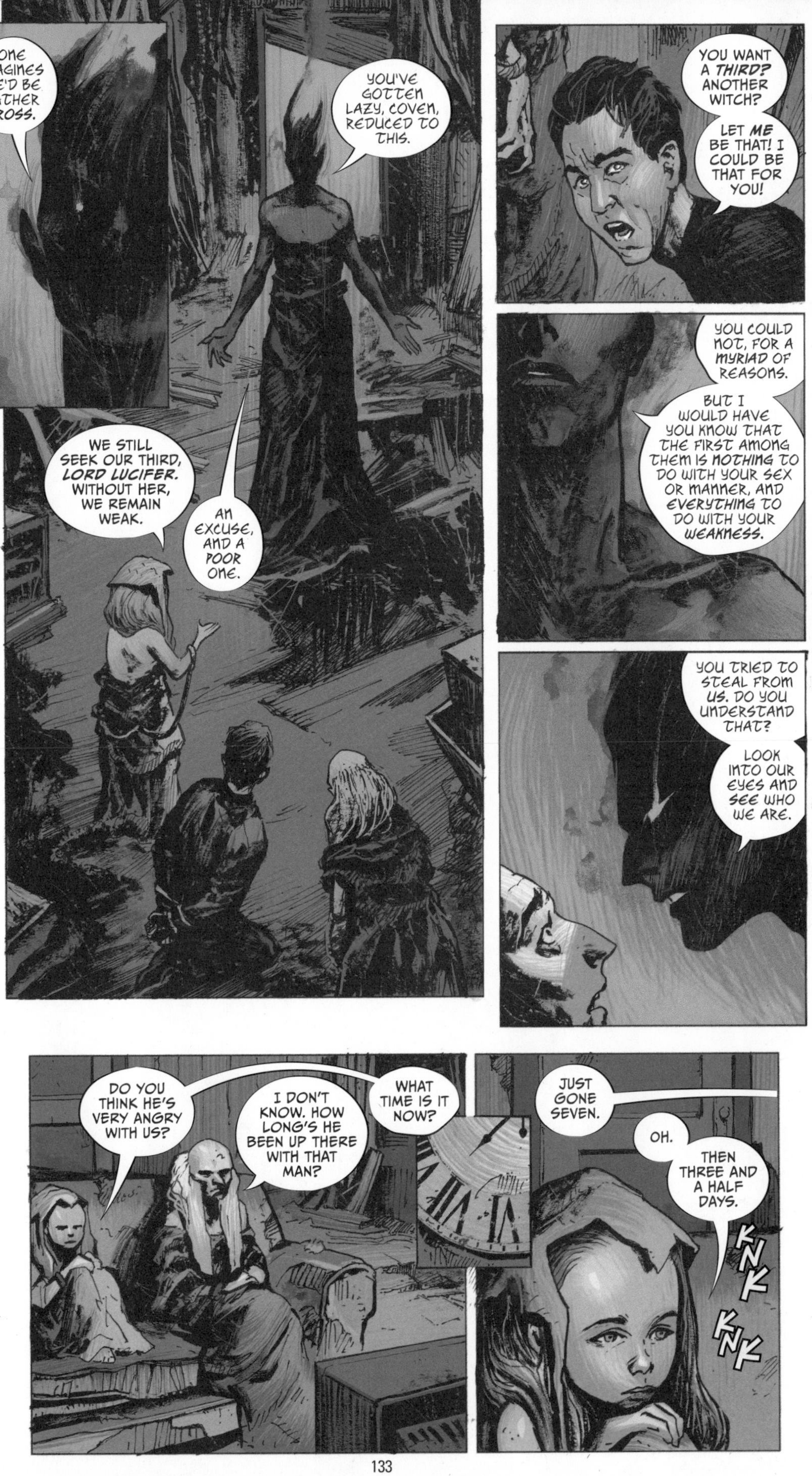
ONE IMAGINES WE'D BE RATHER CROSS.
YOU'VE GOTTEN LAZY, COVEN, REDUCED TO THIS.
WE STILL SEEK OUR THIRD, LORD LUCIFER. WITHOUT HER, WE REMAIN WEAK.
AN EXCUSE, AND A POOR ONE.
YOU WANT A THIRD? ANOTHER WITCH?
LET ME BE THAT! I COULD BE THAT FOR YOU!
YOU COULD NOT, FOR A MYRIAD OF REASONS.
BUT I WOULD HAVE YOU KNOW THAT THE FIRST AMONG THEM IS NOTHING TO DO WITH YOUR SEX OR MANNER, AND EVERYTHING TO DO WITH YOUR WEAKNESS.
YOU TRIED TO STEAL FROM US. DO YOU UNDERSTAND THAT?
LOOK INTO OUR EYES AND SEE WHO WE ARE.
DO YOU THINK HE'S VERY ANGRY WITH US?
I DON'T KNOW. HOW LONG'S HE BEEN UP THERE WITH THAT MAN?
WHAT TIME IS IT NOW?
JUST GONE SEVEN.
OH.
THEN THREE AND A HALF DAYS.
KNK
KNK

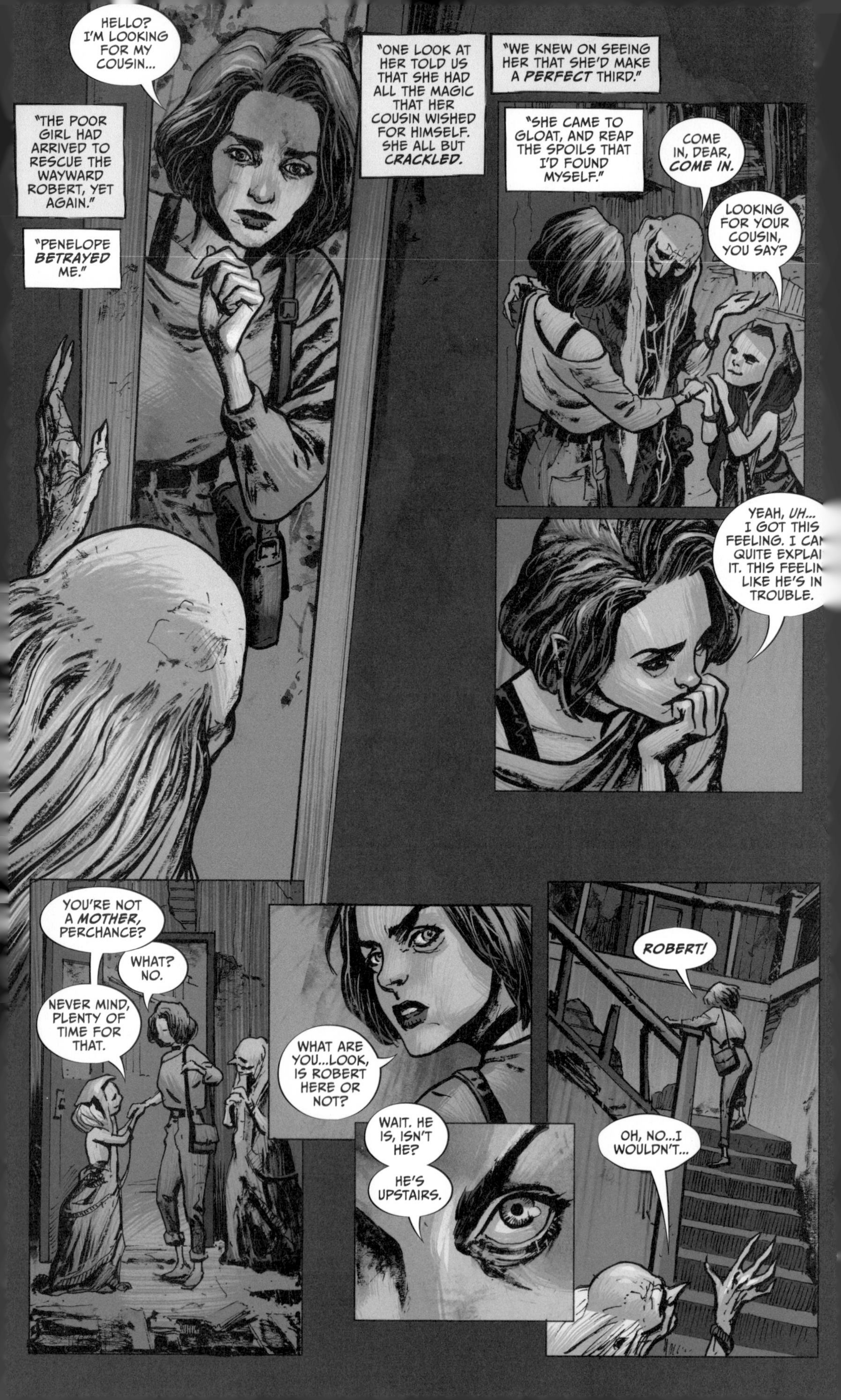
HELLO? I'M LOOKING FOR MY COUSIN...
"THE POOR GIRL HAD ARRIVED TO RESCUE THE WAYWARD ROBERT, YET AGAIN."
"PENELOPE BETRAYED ME."
"ONE LOOK AT HER TOLD US THAT SHE HAD ALL THE MAGIC THAT HER COUSIN WISHED FOR HIMSELF. SHE ALL BUT CRACKLED.
"WE KNEW ON SEEING HER THAT SHE'D MAKE A PERFECT THIRD."
"SHE CAME TO GLOAT, AND REAP THE SPOILS THAT I'D FOUND MYSELF."
COME IN, DEAR, COME IN.
LOOKING FOR YOUR COUSIN, YOU SAY?
YEAH, UH... I GOT THIS FEELING. I CAN QUITE EXPLAI IT. THIS FEELIN LIKE HE'S IN TROUBLE.
YOU'RE NOT A MOTHER, PERCHANCE?
WHAT? NO.
NEVER MIND, PLENTY OF TIME FOR THAT.
WHAT ARE YOU...LOOK, IS ROBERT HERE OR NOT?
WAIT. HE IS, ISN'T HE?
HE'S UPSTAIRS.
ROBERT!
OH, NO...I WOULDN'T...

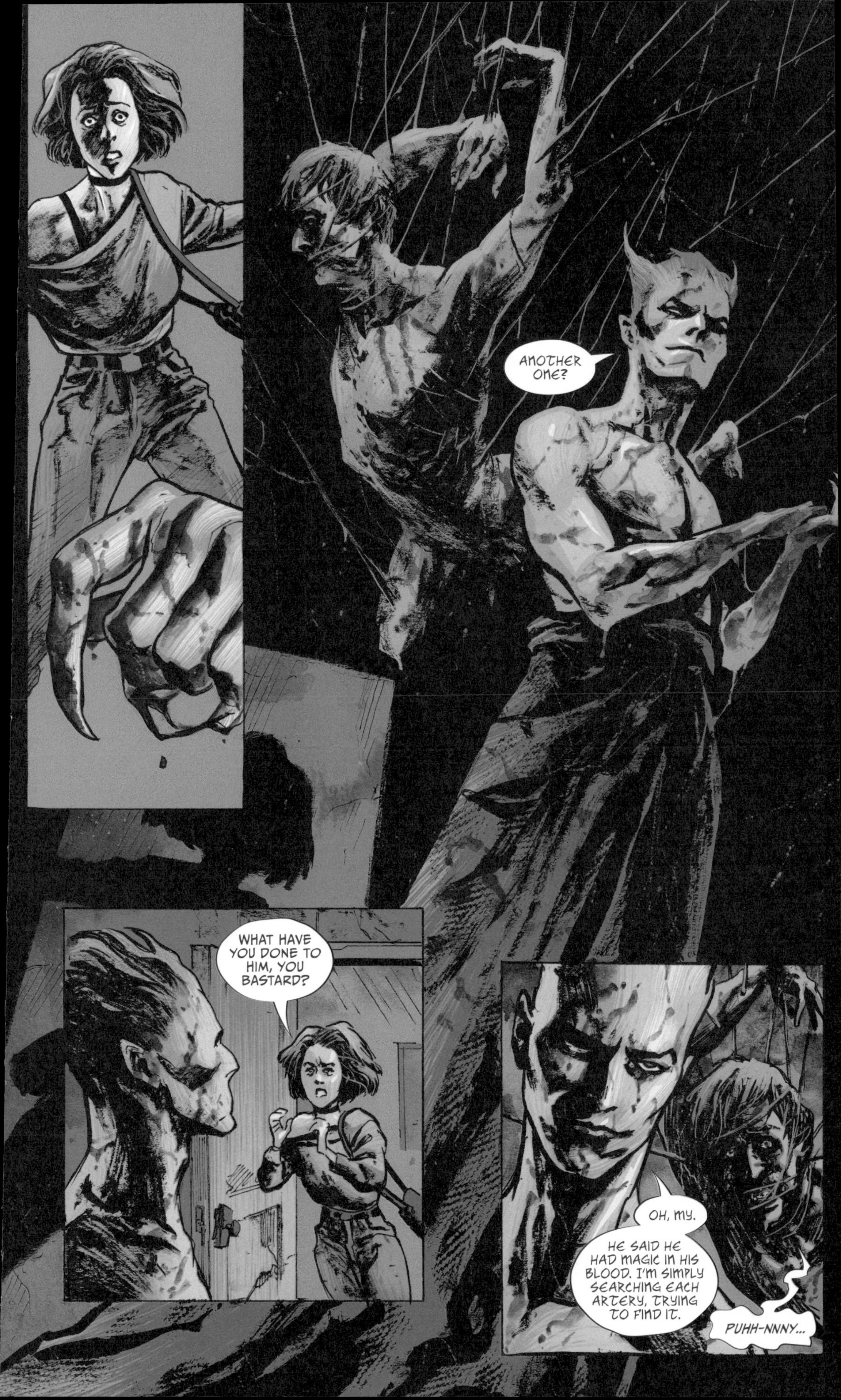
ANOTHER ONE?
WHAT HAVE YOU DONE TO HIM, YOU BASTARD?
OH, MY.
HE SAID HE HAD MAGIC IN HIS BLOOD. I'M SIMPLY SEARCHING EACH ARTERY, TRYING TO FIND IT.
PUHH-NNNY...

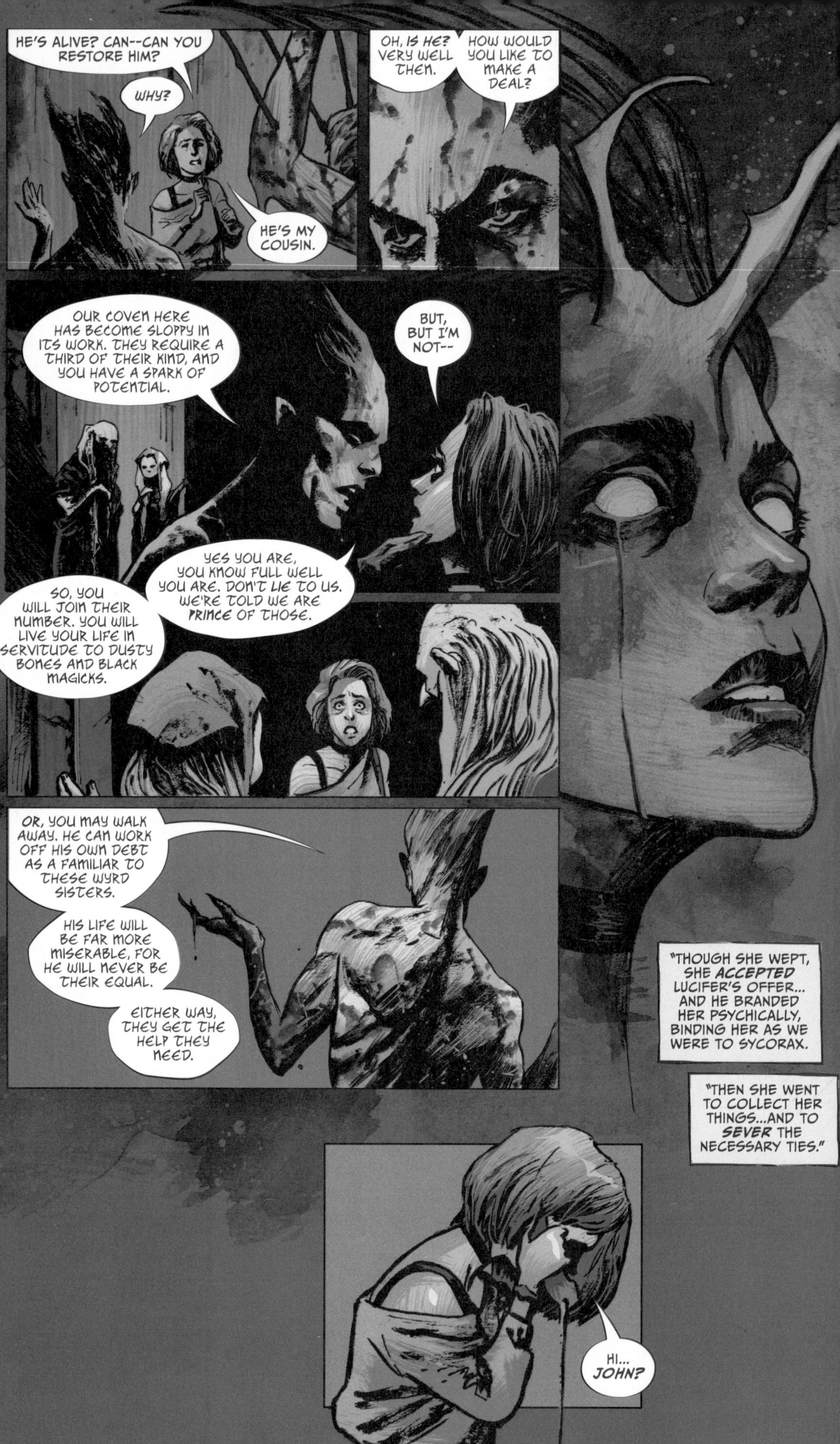
HE'S ALIVE? CAN--CAN YOU RESTORE HIM?
WHY?
HE'S MY COUSIN.
OH, IS HE? VERY WELL THEN.
HOW WOULD YOU LIKE TO MAKE A DEAL?
OUR COVEN HERE HAS BECOME SLOPPY IN ITS WORK. THEY REQUIRE A THIRD OF THEIR KIND, AND YOU HAVE A SPARK OF POTENTIAL.
BUT, BUT I'M NOT--
YES YOU ARE, YOU KNOW FULL WELL YOU ARE. DON'T LIE TO US. WE'RE TOLD WE ARE PRINCE OF THOSE.
SO, YOU WILL JOIN THEIR NUMBER. YOU WILL LIVE YOUR LIFE IN SERVITUDE TO DUSTY BONES AND BLACK MAGICKS.
OR, YOU MAY WALK AWAY. HE CAN WORK OFF HIS OWN DEBT AS A FAMILIAR TO THESE WYRD SISTERS.
HIS LIFE WILL BE FAR MORE MISERABLE, FOR HE WILL NEVER BE THEIR EQUAL.
EITHER WAY, THEY GET THE HELP THEY NEED.
"THOUGH SHE WEPT, SHE ACCEPTED LUCIFER'S OFFER... AND HE BRANDED HER PSYCHICALLY, BINDING HER AS WE WERE TO SYCORAX.
"THEN SHE WENT TO COLLECT HER THINGS...AND TO SEVER THE NECESSARY TIES."
HI... JOHN?

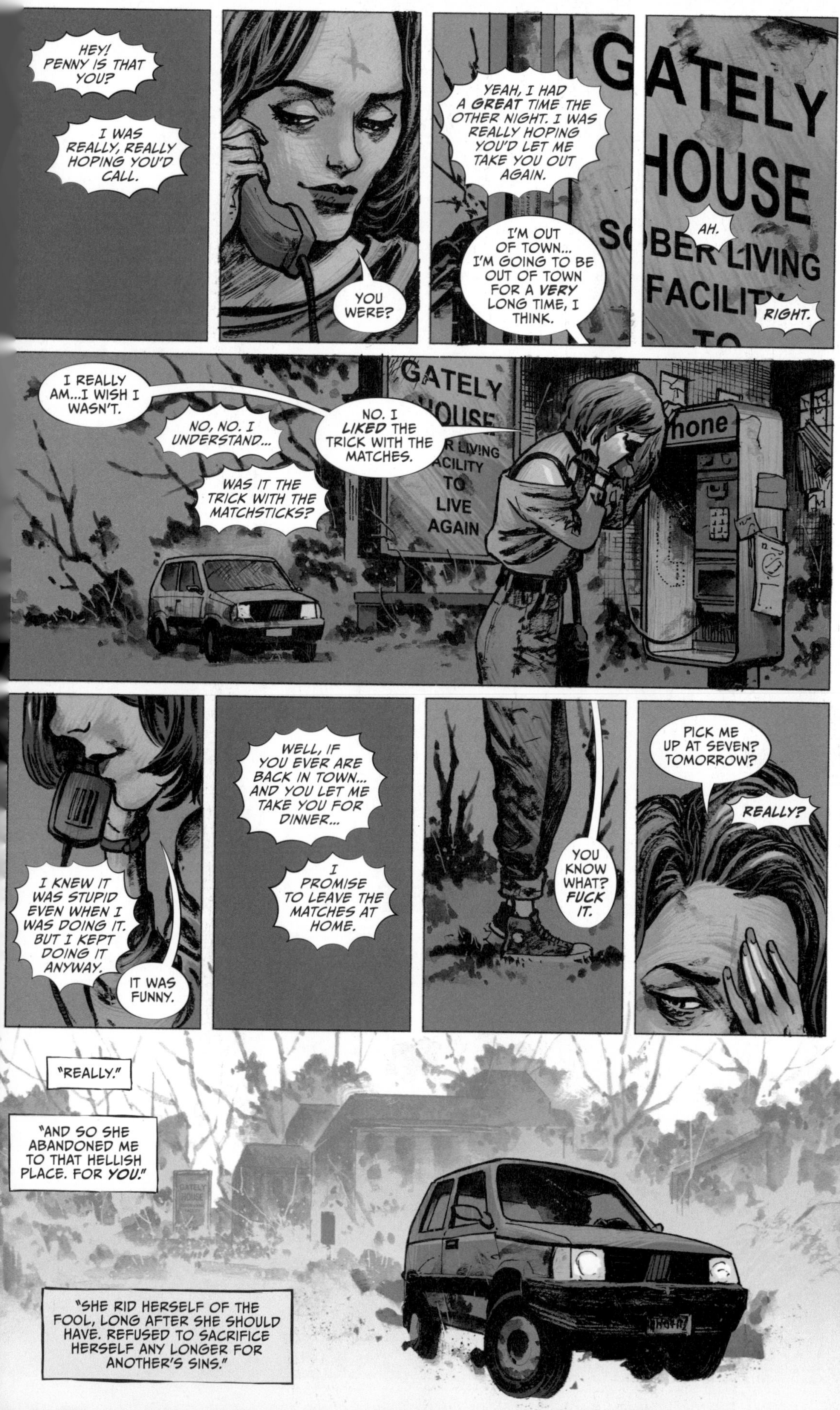
HEY! PENNY IS THAT YOU?
I WAS REALLY, REALLY HOPING YOU'D CALL.
YOU WERE?
YEAH, I HAD A GREAT TIME THE OTHER NIGHT. I WAS REALLY HOPING YOU'D LET ME TAKE YOU OUT AGAIN.
I'M OUT OF TOWN... I'M GOING TO BE OUT OF TOWN FOR A VERY LONG TIME, I THINK.
GATELY HOUSE SOBER LIVING FACILITY TO
AH.
RIGHT.
I REALLY AM...I WISH I WASN'T.
NO, NO. I UNDERSTAND...
WAS IT THE TRICK WITH THE MATCHSTICKS?
NO. I LIKED THE TRICK WITH THE MATCHES.
GATELY HOUSE SOBER LIVING FACILITY TO LIVE AGAIN
Phone
I KNEW IT WAS STUPID EVEN WHEN I WAS DOING IT. BUT I KEPT DOING IT ANYWAY.
IT WAS FUNNY.
WELL, IF YOU EVER ARE BACK IN TOWN... AND YOU LET ME TAKE YOU FOR DINNER...
I PROMISE TO LEAVE THE MATCHES AT HOME.
YOU KNOW WHAT? FUCK IT.
PICK ME UP AT SEVEN? TOMORROW?
REALLY?
"REALLY."
"AND SO SHE ABANDONED ME TO THAT HELLISH PLACE. FOR YOU."
GATELY HOUSE
"SHE RID HERSELF OF THE FOOL, LONG AFTER SHE SHOULD HAVE. REFUSED TO SACRIFICE HERSELF ANY LONGER FOR ANOTHER'S SINS."

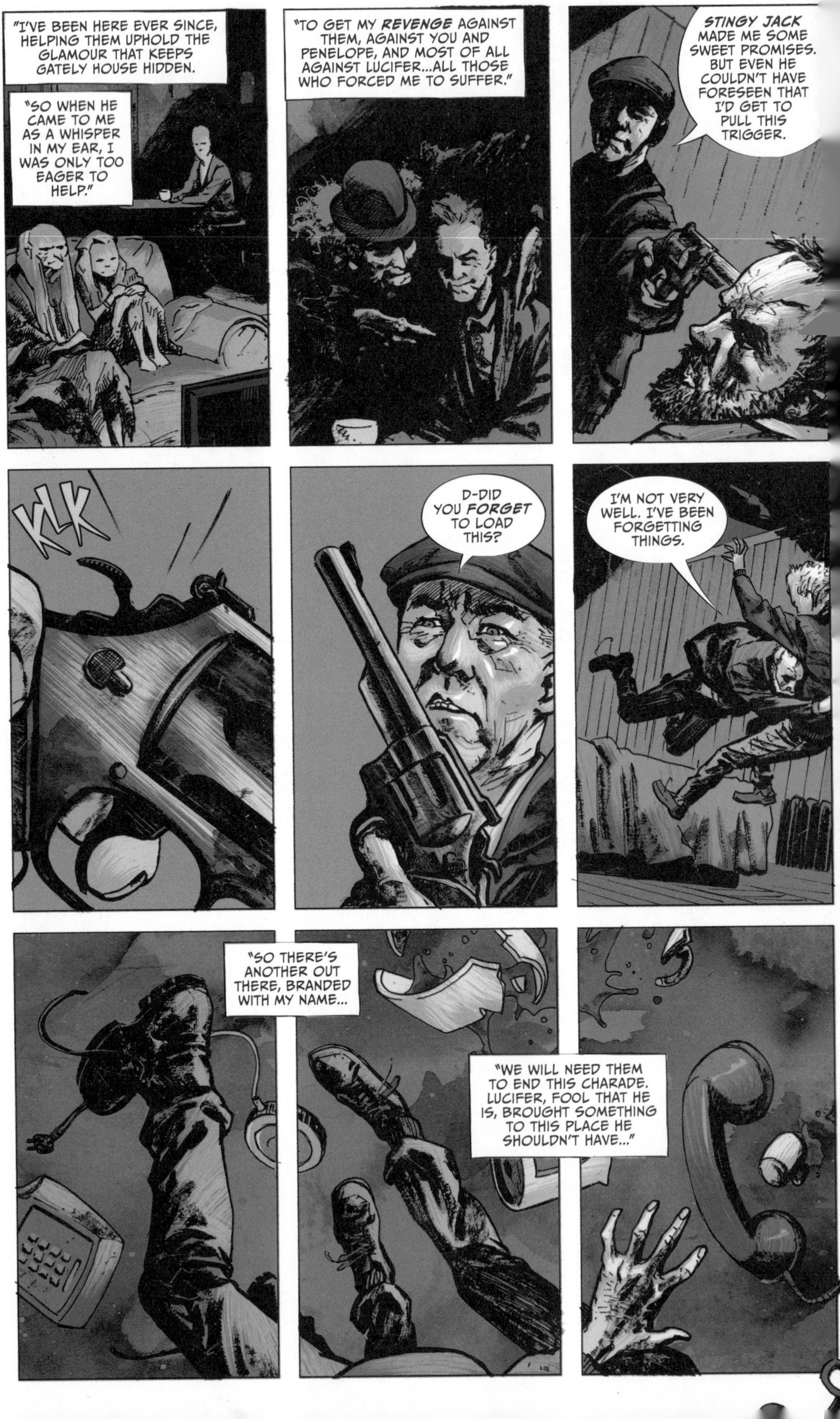
"I'VE BEEN HERE EVER SINCE, HELPING THEM UPHOLD THE GLAMOUR THAT KEEPS GATELY HOUSE HIDDEN.
"SO WHEN HE CAME TO ME AS A WHISPER IN MY EAR, I WAS ONLY TOO EAGER TO HELP."
"TO GET MY REVENGE AGAINST THEM, AGAINST YOU AND PENELOPE, AND MOST OF ALL AGAINST LUCIFER...ALL THOSE WHO FORCED ME TO SUFFER."
STINGY JACK MADE ME SOME SWEET PROMISES. BUT EVEN HE COULDN'T HAVE FORESEEN THAT I'D GET TO PULL THIS TRIGGER.
KLK
D-DID YOU FORGET TO LOAD THIS?
I'M NOT VERY WELL. I'VE BEEN FORGETTING THINGS.
"SO THERE'S ANOTHER OUT THERE, BRANDED WITH MY NAME...
"WE WILL NEED THEM TO END THIS CHARADE. LUCIFER, FOOL THAT HE IS, BROUGHT SOMETHING TO THIS PLACE HE SHOULDN'T HAVE..."

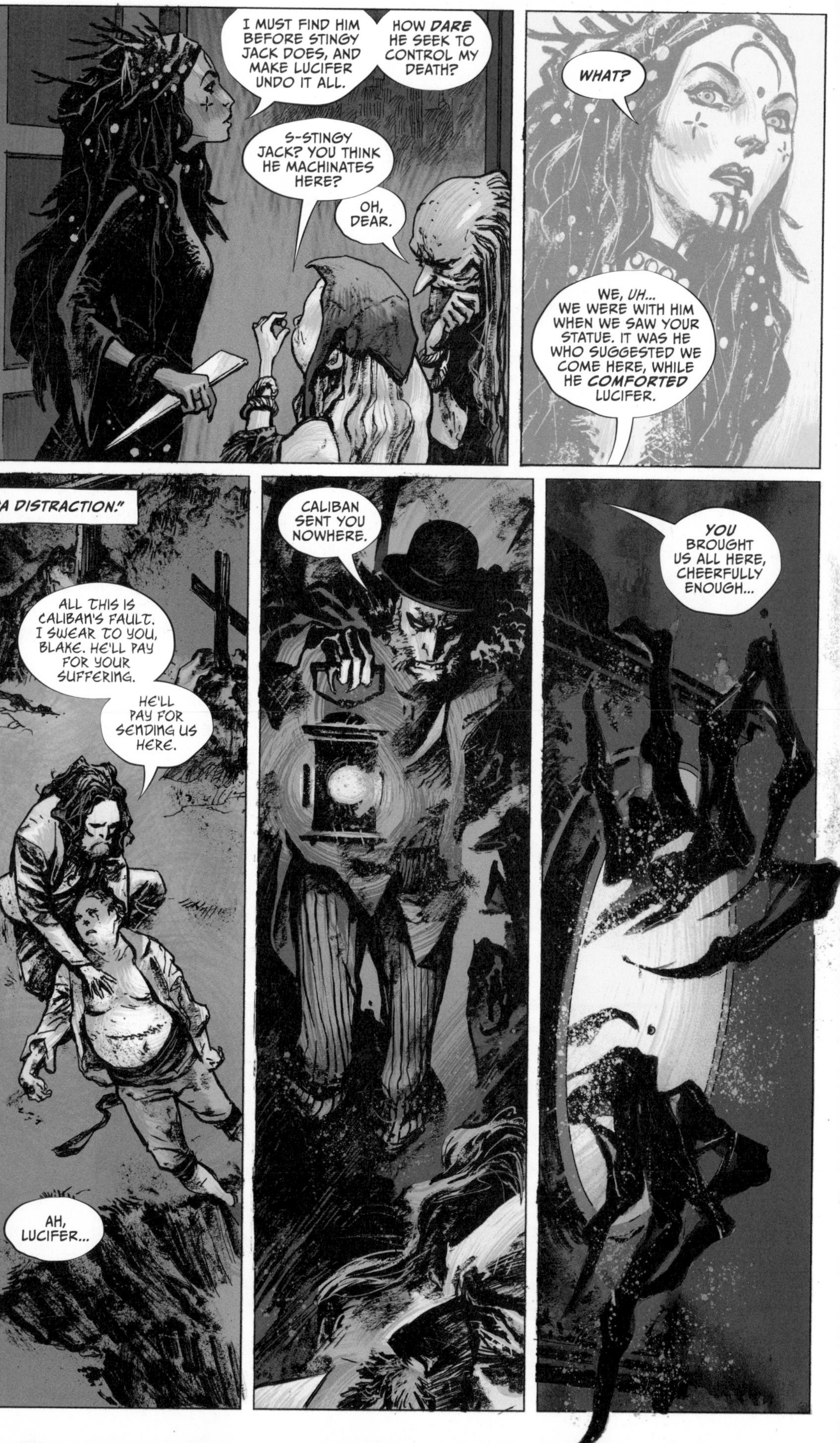
I MUST FIND HIM BEFORE STINGY JACK DOES, AND MAKE LUCIFER UNDO IT ALL.
HOW DARE HE SEEK TO CONTROL MY DEATH?
S-STINGY JACK? YOU THINK HE MACHINATES HERE?
OH, DEAR.
WHAT?
WE, UH... WE WERE WITH HIM WHEN WE SAW YOUR STATUE. IT WAS HE WHO SUGGESTED WE COME HERE, WHILE HE COMFORTED LUCIFER.
"A DISTRACTION."
ALL THIS IS CALIBAN'S FAULT. I SWEAR TO YOU, BLAKE. HE'LL PAY FOR YOUR SUFFERING.
HE'LL PAY FOR SENDING US HERE.
AH, LUCIFER...
CALIBAN SENT YOU NOWHERE.
YOU BROUGHT US ALL HERE, CHEERFULLY ENOUGH...

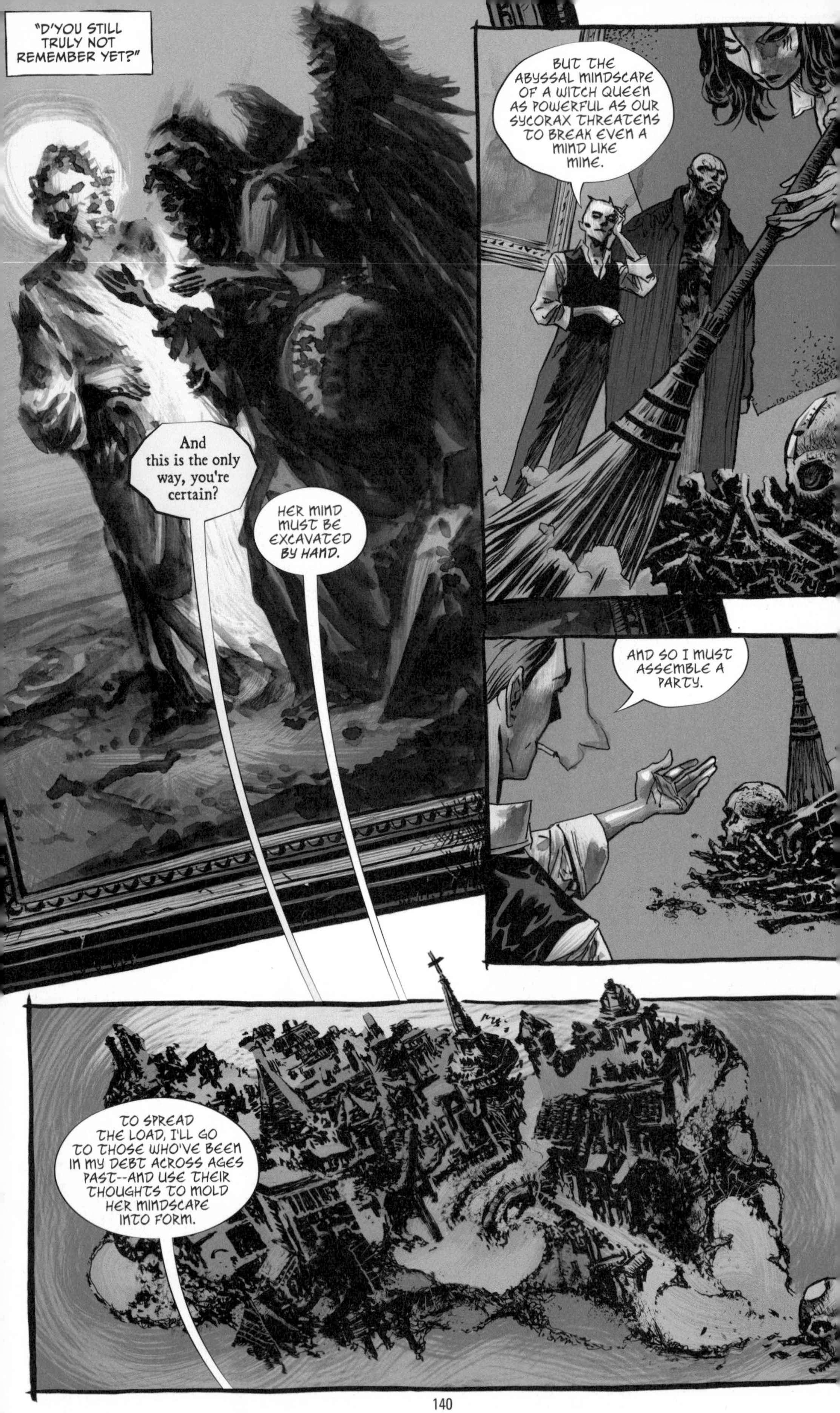
"D'YOU STILL TRULY NOT REMEMBER YET?"
And this is the only way, you're certain?
HER MIND MUST BE EXCAVATED BY HAND.
BUT THE ABYSSAL MINDSCAPE OF A WITCH QUEEN AS POWERFUL AS OUR SYCORAX THREATENS TO BREAK EVEN A MIND LIKE MINE.
AND SO I MUST ASSEMBLE A PARTY.
TO SPREAD THE LOAD, I'LL GO TO THOSE WHO'VE BEEN IN MY DEBT ACROSS AGES PAST--AND USE THEIR THOUGHTS TO MOLD HER MINDSCAPE INTO FORM.

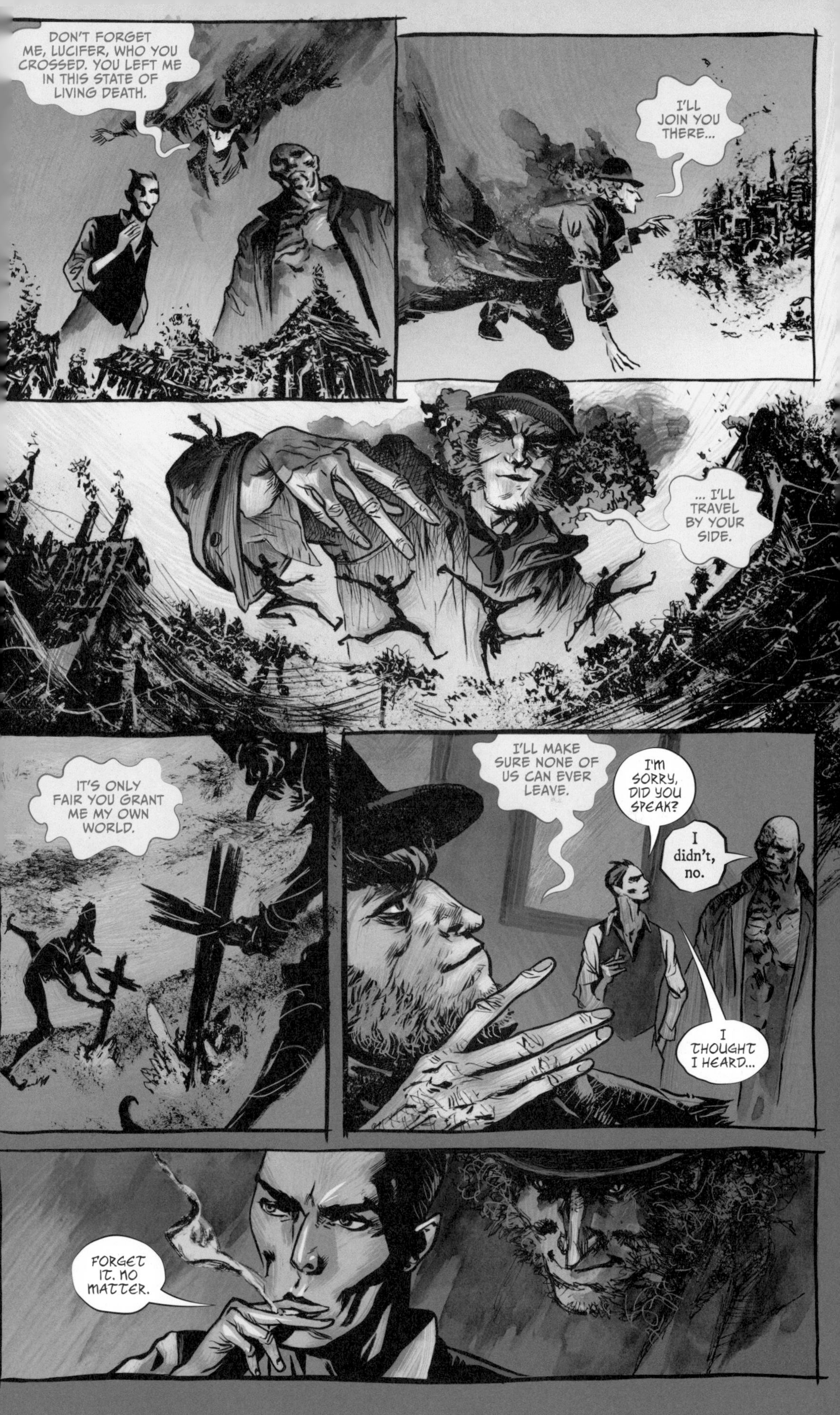
DON'T FORGET ME, LUCIFER, WHO YOU CROSSED. YOU LEFT ME IN THIS STATE OF LIVING DEATH.
I'LL JOIN YOU THERE...
... I'LL TRAVEL BY YOUR SIDE.
IT'S ONLY FAIR YOU GRANT ME MY OWN WORLD.
I'LL MAKE SURE NONE OF US CAN EVER LEAVE.
I'M SORRY, DID YOU SPEAK?
I didn't, no.
I THOUGHT I HEARD...
FORGET IT. NO MATTER.

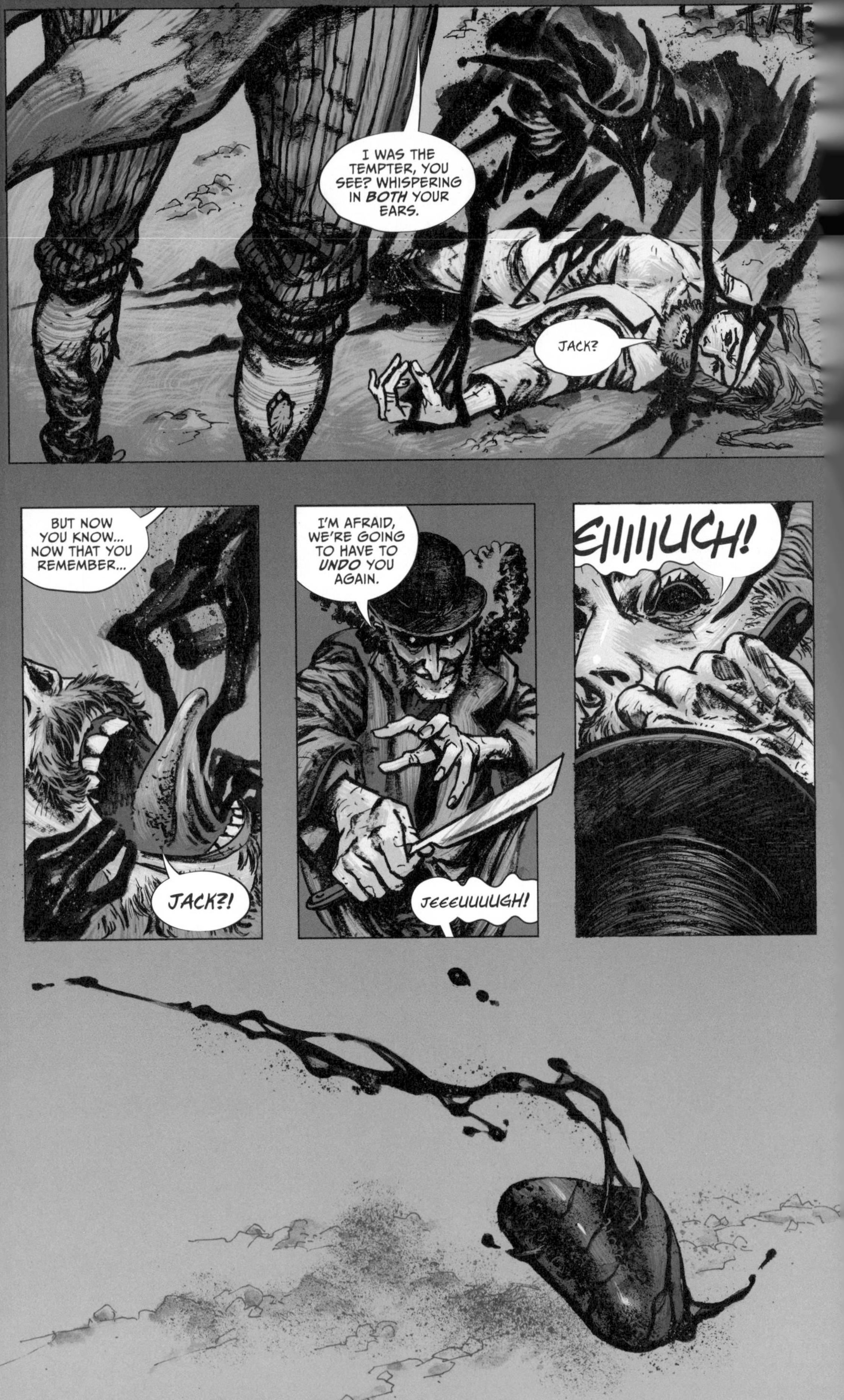
I WAS THE TEMPTER, YOU SEE? WHISPERING IN BOTH YOUR EARS.
JACK?
BUT NOW YOU KNOW... NOW THAT YOU REMEMBER...
JACK?!
I'M AFRAID, WE'RE GOING TO HAVE TO UNDO YOU AGAIN.
JEEEUUUUGH!
EIIIIUCH!

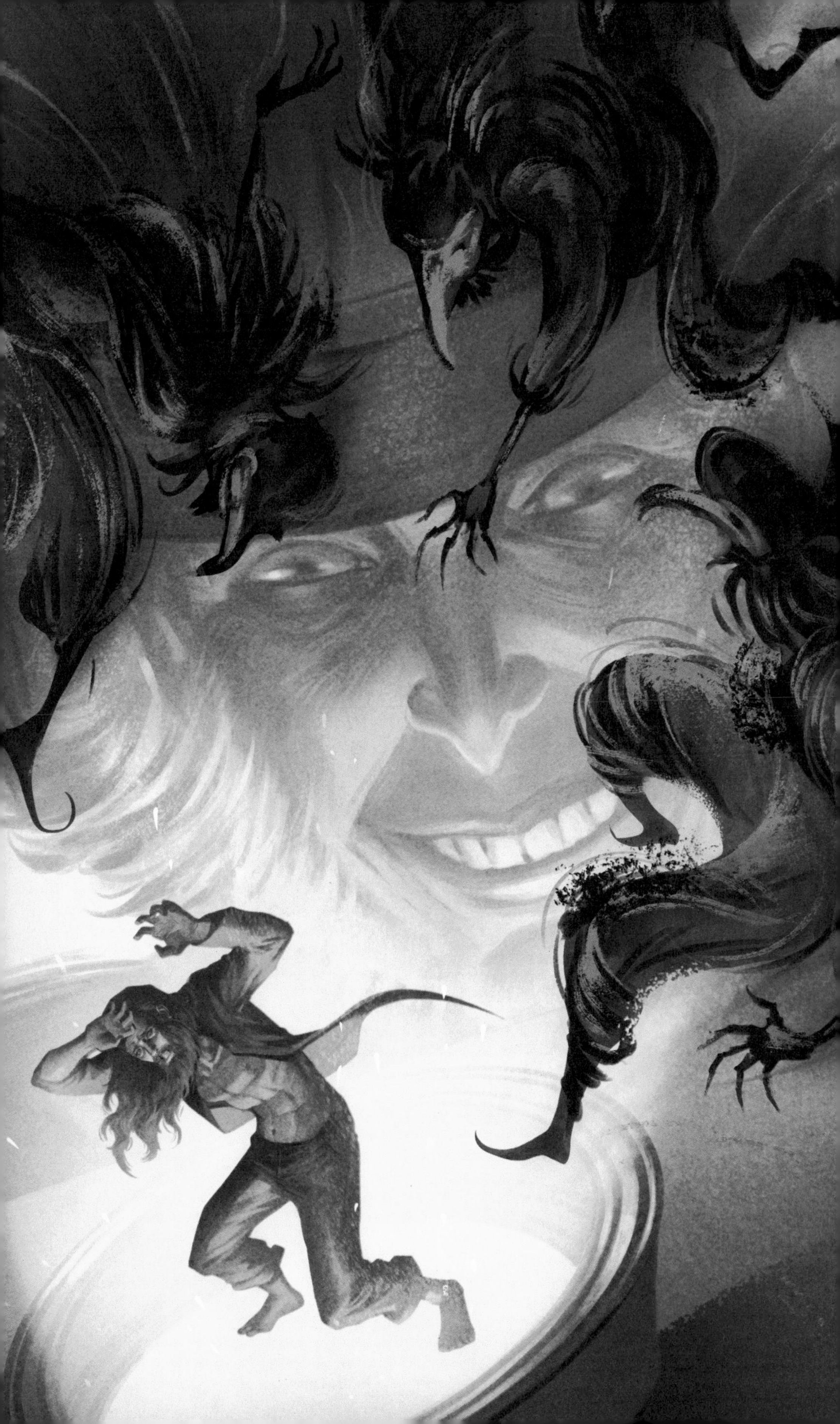

LUCIFER

The Man Who Bested the Devil, Not Once But Twice

WRITTEN BY
Dan Watters

ILLUSTRATED BY
Max Fiumara
Sebastian Fiumara

COLORS BY
Dave McCaig

LETTERS BY
Steve Wands

COVER ART BY
Reiko Murakami

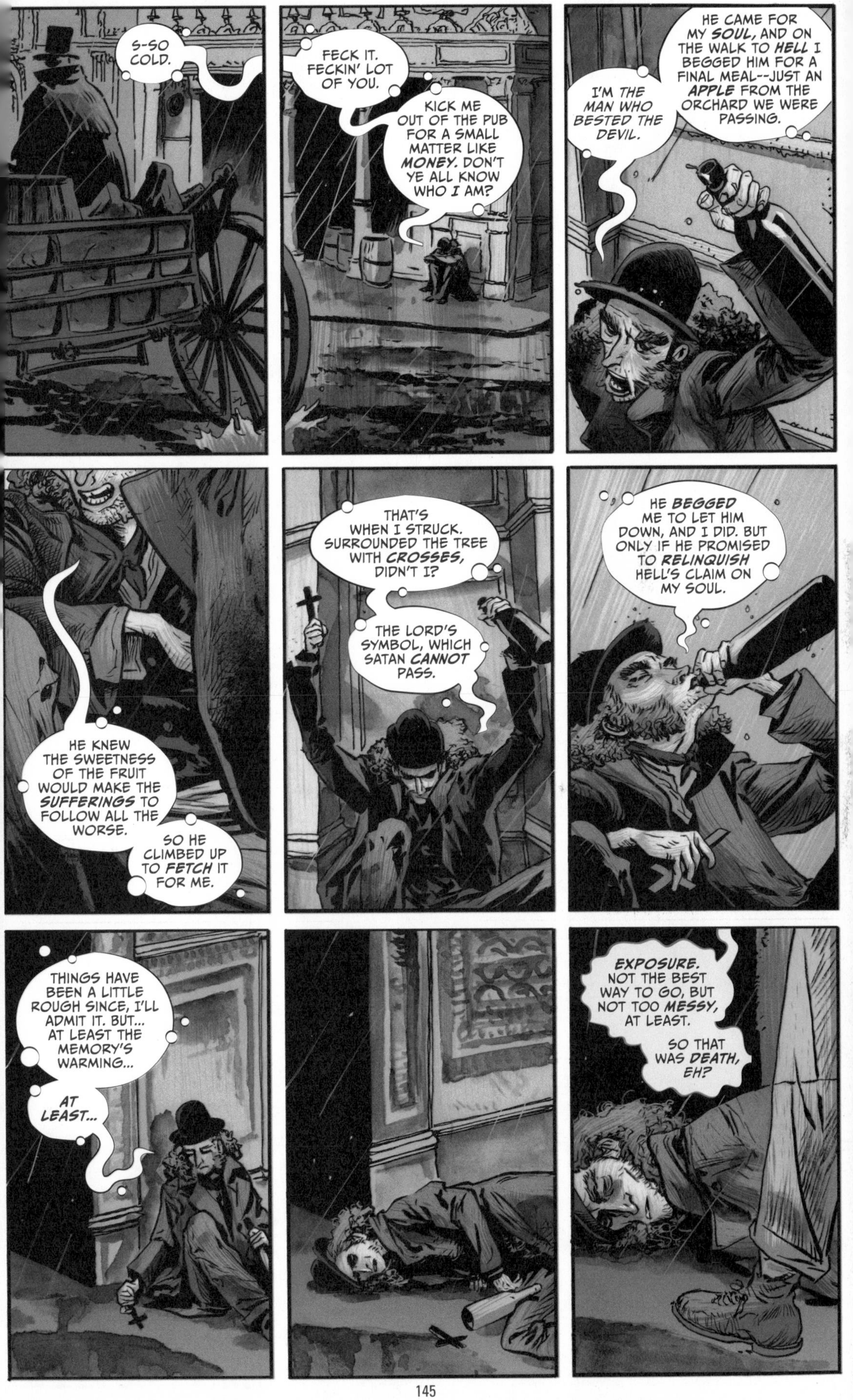
S-SO COLD.
FECK IT. FECKIN' LOT OF YOU.
KICK ME OUT OF THE PUB FOR A SMALL MATTER LIKE MONEY. DON'T YE ALL KNOW WHO I AM?
I'M THE MAN WHO BESTED THE DEVIL.
HE CAME FOR MY SOUL, AND ON THE WALK TO HELL I BEGGED HIM FOR A FINAL MEAL--JUST AN APPLE FROM THE ORCHARD WE WERE PASSING.
HE KNEW THE SWEETNESS OF THE FRUIT WOULD MAKE THE SUFFERINGS TO FOLLOW ALL THE WORSE.
SO HE CLIMBED UP TO FETCH IT FOR ME.
THAT'S WHEN I STRUCK. SURROUNDED THE TREE WITH CROSSES, DIDN'T I?
THE LORD'S SYMBOL, WHICH SATAN CANNOT PASS.
HE BEGGED ME TO LET HIM DOWN, AND I DID. BUT ONLY IF HE PROMISED TO RELINQUISH HELL'S CLAIM ON MY SOUL.
THINGS HAVE BEEN A LITTLE ROUGH SINCE, I'LL ADMIT IT. BUT... AT LEAST THE MEMORY'S WARMING...
AT LEAST...
EXPOSURE. NOT THE BEST WAY TO GO, BUT NOT TOO MESSY, AT LEAST.
SO THAT WAS DEATH, EH?

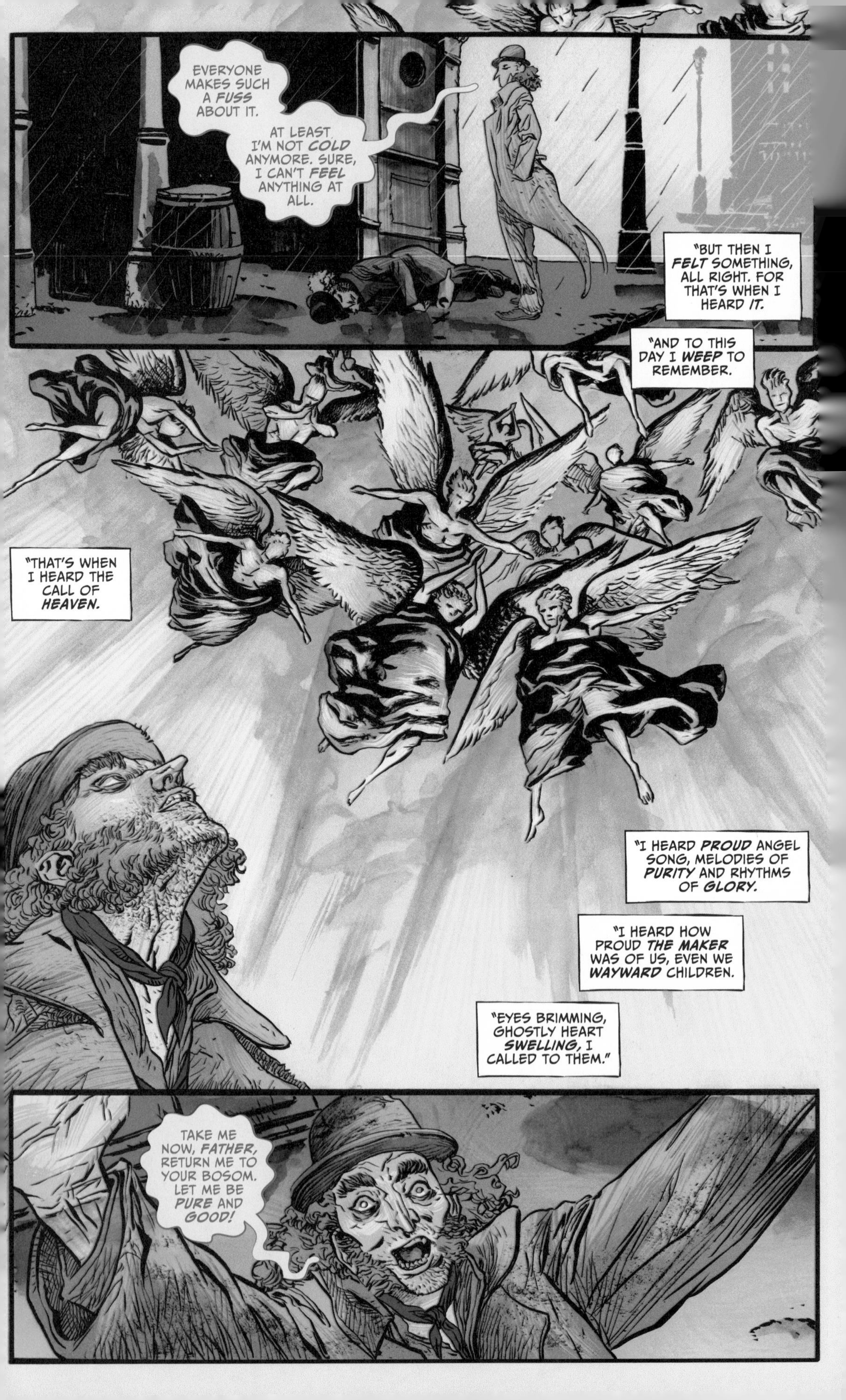
EVERYONE MAKES SUCH A FUSS ABOUT IT.
AT LEAST, I'M NOT COLD ANYMORE. SURE, I CAN'T FEEL ANYTHING AT ALL.
"BUT THEN I FELT SOMETHING, ALL RIGHT. FOR THAT'S WHEN I HEARD IT.
"AND TO THIS DAY I WEEP TO REMEMBER.
"THAT'S WHEN I HEARD THE CALL OF HEAVEN.
"I HEARD PROUD ANGEL SONG, MELODIES OF PURITY AND RHYTHMS OF GLORY.
"I HEARD HOW PROUD THE MAKER WAS OF US, EVEN WE WAYWARD CHILDREN.
"EYES BRIMMING, GHOSTLY HEART SWELLING, I CALLED TO THEM."
TAKE ME NOW, FATHER, RETURN ME TO YOUR BOSOM. LET ME BE PURE AND GOOD!

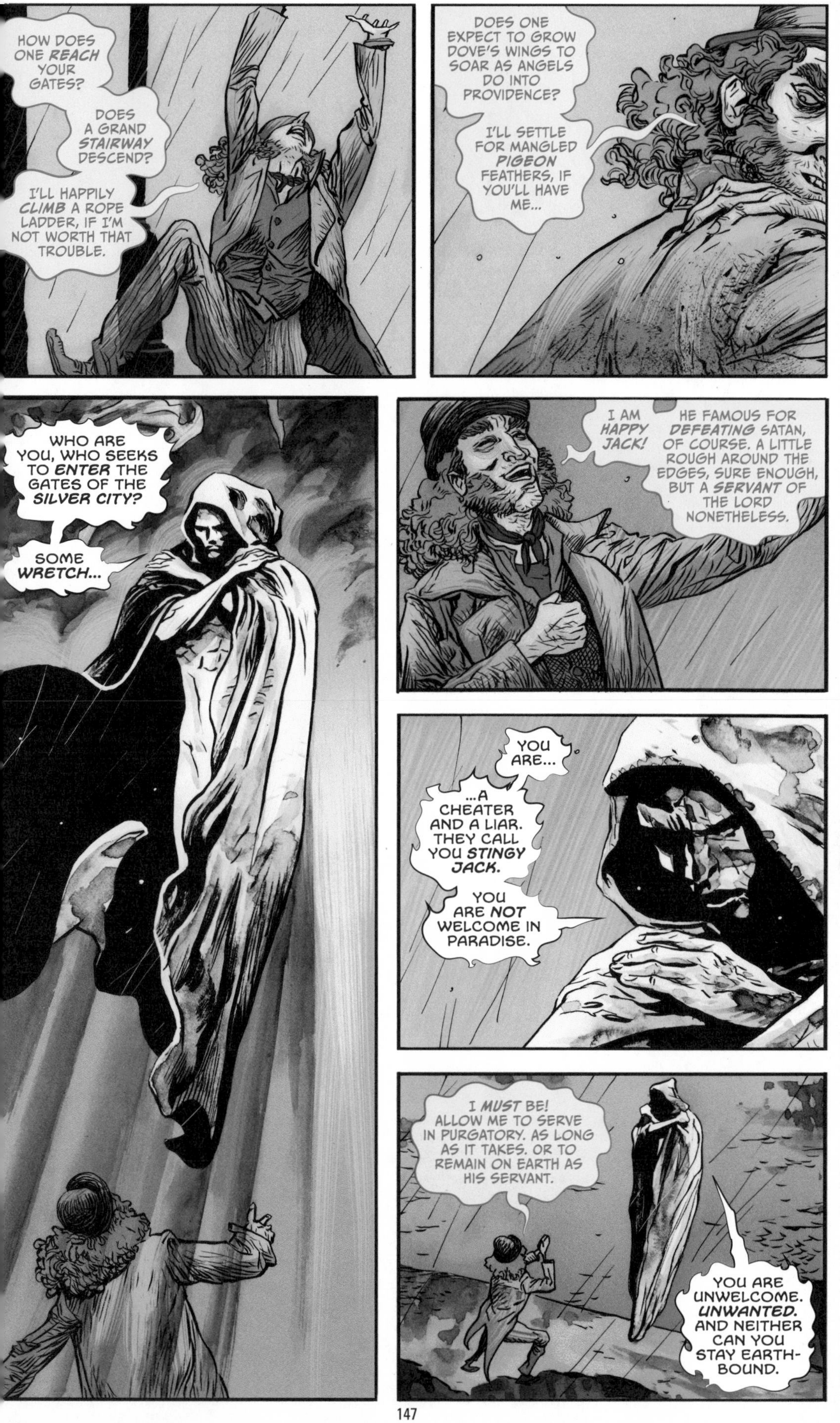
HOW DOES ONE REACH YOUR GATES?
DOES A GRAND STAIRWAY DESCEND?
I'LL HAPPILY CLIMB A ROPE LADDER, IF I'M NOT WORTH THAT TROUBLE.
DOES ONE EXPECT TO GROW DOVE'S WINGS TO SOAR AS ANGELS DO INTO PROVIDENCE?
I'LL SETTLE FOR MANGLED PIGEON FEATHERS, IF YOU'LL HAVE ME...
WHO ARE YOU, WHO SEEKS TO ENTER THE GATES OF THE SILVER CITY?
SOME WRETCH...
I AM HAPPY JACK!
HE FAMOUS FOR DEFEATING SATAN, OF COURSE. A LITTLE ROUGH AROUND THE EDGES, SURE ENOUGH, BUT A SERVANT OF THE LORD NONETHELESS.
YOU ARE...
...A CHEATER AND A LIAR. THEY CALL YOU STINGY JACK.
YOU ARE NOT WELCOME IN PARADISE.
I MUST BE! ALLOW ME TO SERVE IN PURGATORY. AS LONG AS IT TAKES. OR TO REMAIN ON EARTH AS HIS SERVANT.
YOU ARE UNWELCOME. UNWANTED. AND NEITHER CAN YOU STAY EARTH-BOUND.

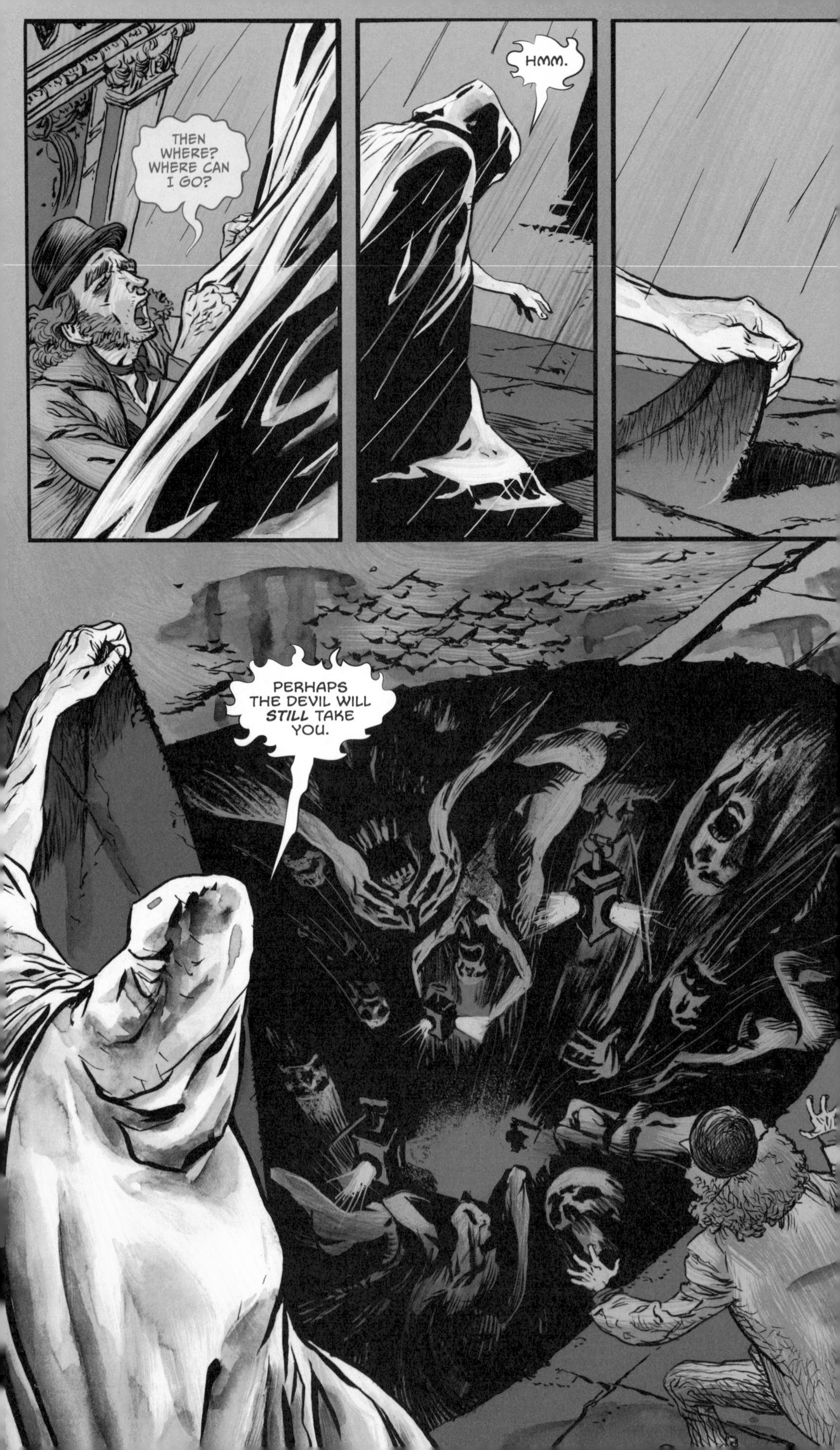
THEN WHERE? WHERE CAN I GO?
HMM.
PERHAPS THE DEVIL WILL STILL TAKE YOU.

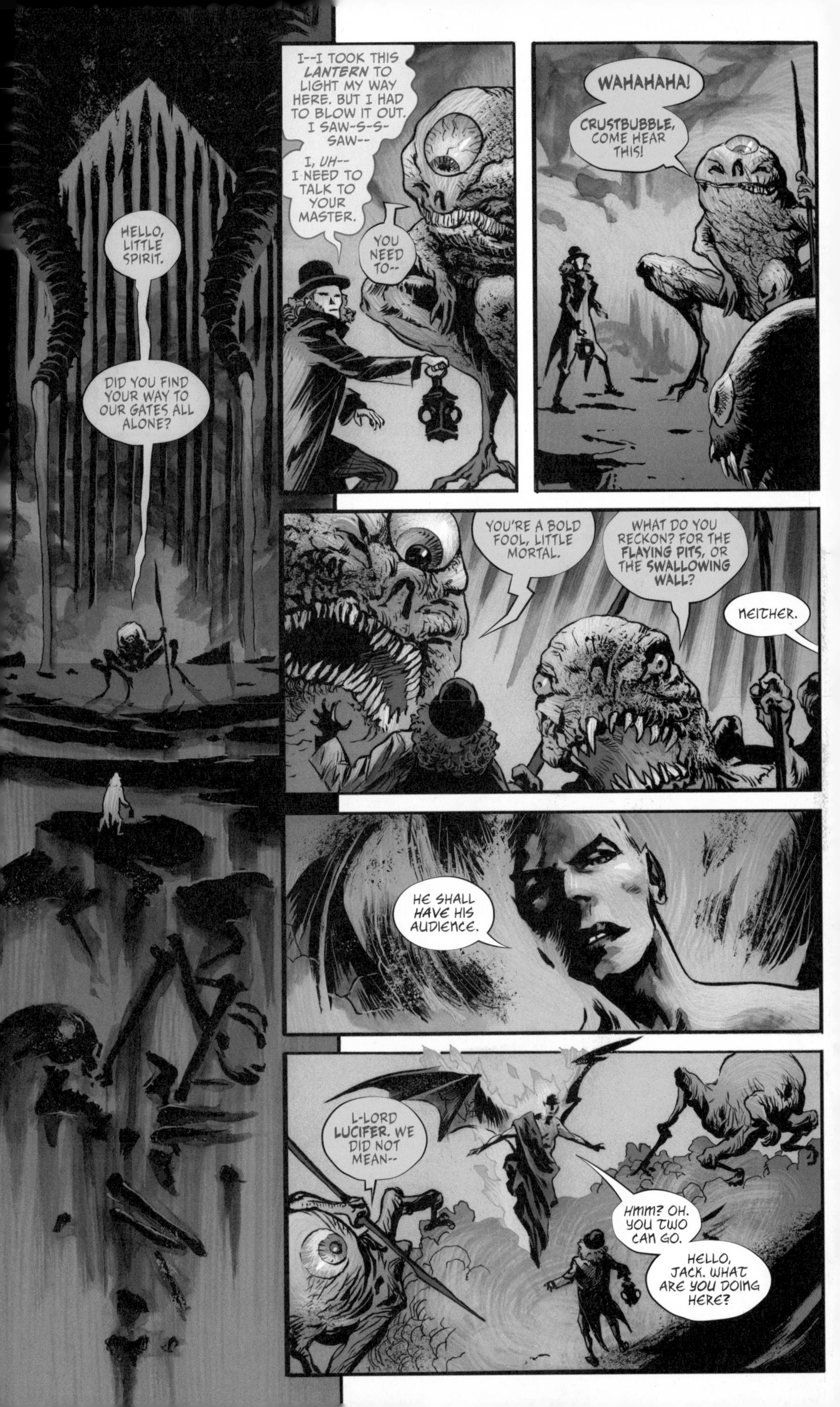
HELLO, LITTLE SPIRIT.
DID YOU FIND YOUR WAY TO OUR GATES ALL ALONE?
I--I TOOK THIS LANTERN TO LIGHT MY WAY HERE. BUT I HAD TO BLOW IT OUT. I SAW-S-S-SAW--
I, UH-- I NEED TO TALK TO YOUR MASTER.
YOU NEED TO--
WAHAHAHA!
CRUSTBUBBLE, COME HEAR THIS!
YOU'RE A BOLD FOOL, LITTLE MORTAL.
WHAT DO YOU RECKON? FOR THE FLAYING PITS, OR THE SWALLOWING WALL?
NEITHER.
HE SHALL HAVE HIS AUDIENCE.
L-LORD LUCIFER. WE DID NOT MEAN--
HMM? OH. YOU TWO CAN GO.
HELLO, JACK. WHAT ARE YOU DOING HERE?

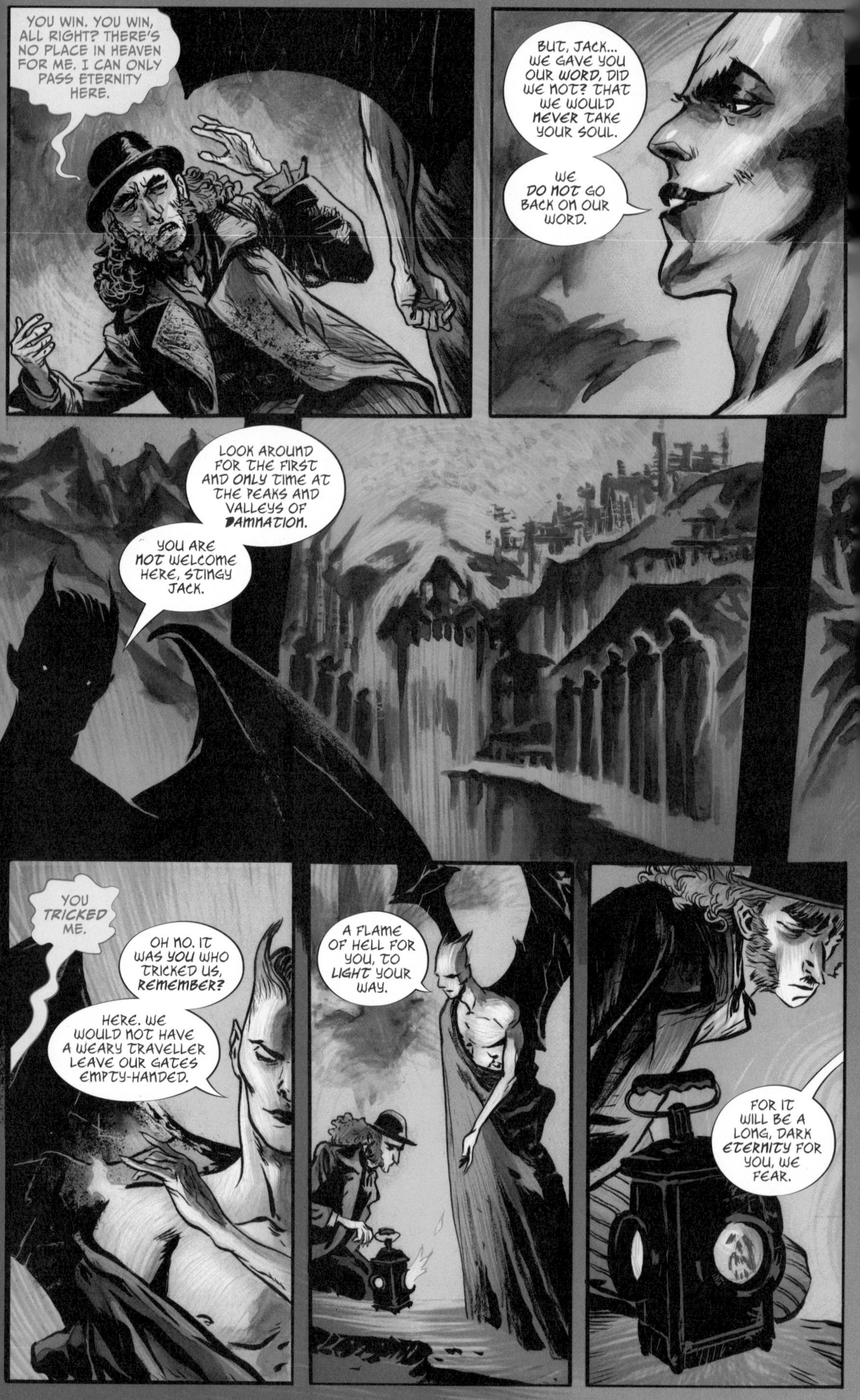
YOU WIN. YOU WIN, ALL RIGHT? THERE'S NO PLACE IN HEAVEN FOR ME. I CAN ONLY PASS ETERNITY HERE.
BUT, JACK... WE GAVE YOU OUR WORD, DID WE NOT? THAT WE WOULD NEVER TAKE YOUR SOUL.
WE DO NOT GO BACK ON OUR WORD.
LOOK AROUND FOR THE FIRST AND ONLY TIME AT THE PEAKS AND VALLEYS OF DAMNATION.
YOU ARE NOT WELCOME HERE, STINGY JACK.
YOU TRICKED ME.
OH NO. IT WAS YOU WHO TRICKED US, REMEMBER?
HERE. WE WOULD NOT HAVE A WEARY TRAVELLER LEAVE OUR GATES EMPTY-HANDED.
A FLAME OF HELL FOR YOU, TO LIGHT YOUR WAY.
FOR IT WILL BE A LONG, DARK ETERNITY FOR YOU, WE FEAR.

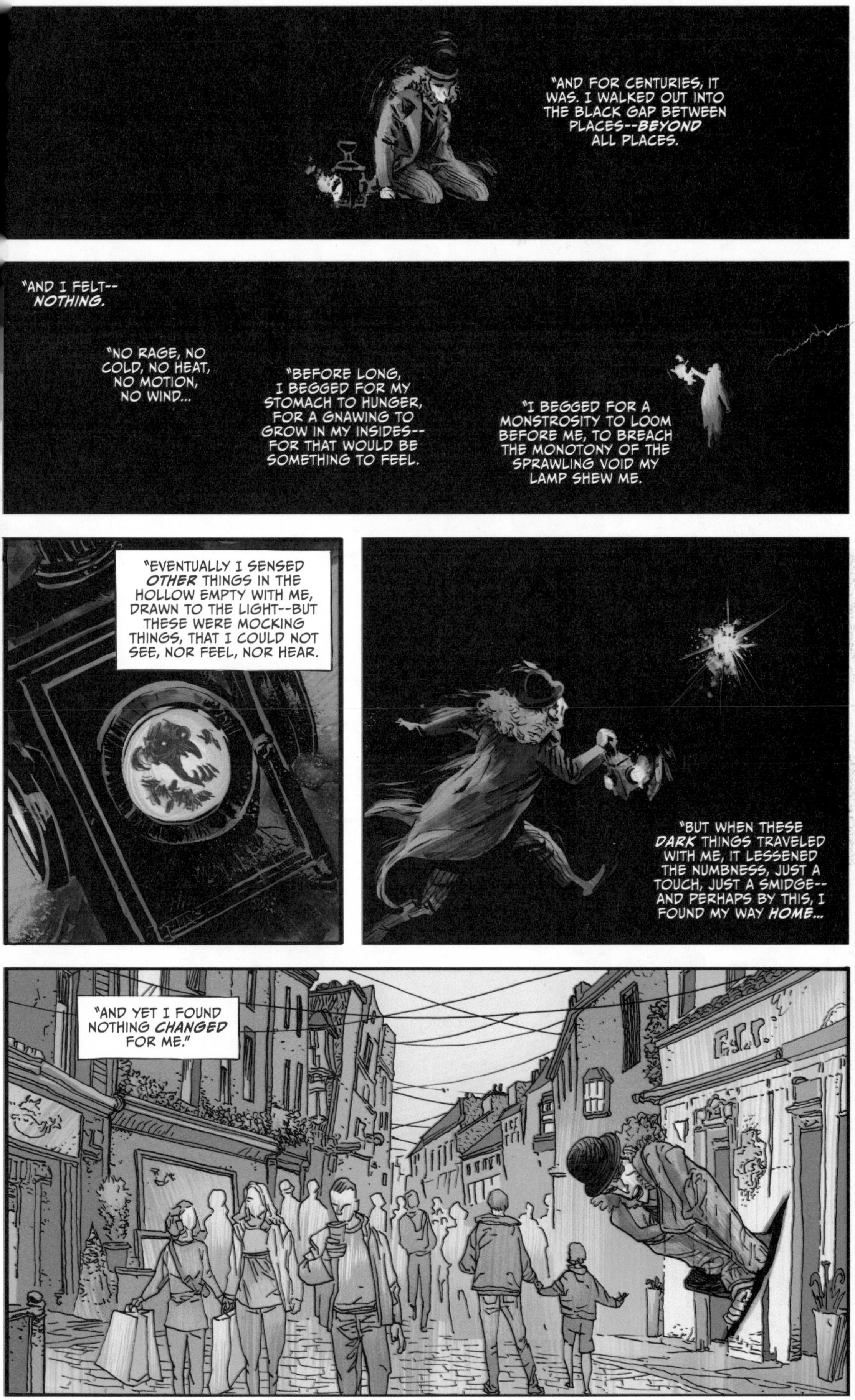
"AND FOR CENTURIES, IT WAS. I WALKED OUT INTO THE BLACK GAP BETWEEN PLACES--*BEYOND* ALL PLACES.
"AND I FELT-- *NOTHING.*
"NO RAGE, NO COLD, NO HEAT, NO MOTION, NO WIND...
"BEFORE LONG, I BEGGED FOR MY STOMACH TO HUNGER, FOR A GNAWING TO GROW IN MY INSIDES-- FOR THAT WOULD BE SOMETHING TO FEEL.
"I BEGGED FOR A MONSTROSITY TO LOOM BEFORE ME, TO BREACH THE MONOTONY OF THE SPRAWLING VOID MY LAMP SHEW ME.
"EVENTUALLY I SENSED *OTHER* THINGS IN THE HOLLOW EMPTY WITH ME, DRAWN TO THE LIGHT--BUT THESE WERE MOCKING THINGS, THAT I COULD NOT SEE, NOR FEEL, NOR HEAR.
"BUT WHEN THESE *DARK* THINGS TRAVELED WITH ME, IT LESSENED THE NUMBNESS, JUST A TOUCH, JUST A SMIDGE-- AND PERHAPS BY THIS, I FOUND MY WAY *HOME...*
"AND YET I FOUND NOTHING *CHANGED* FOR ME."

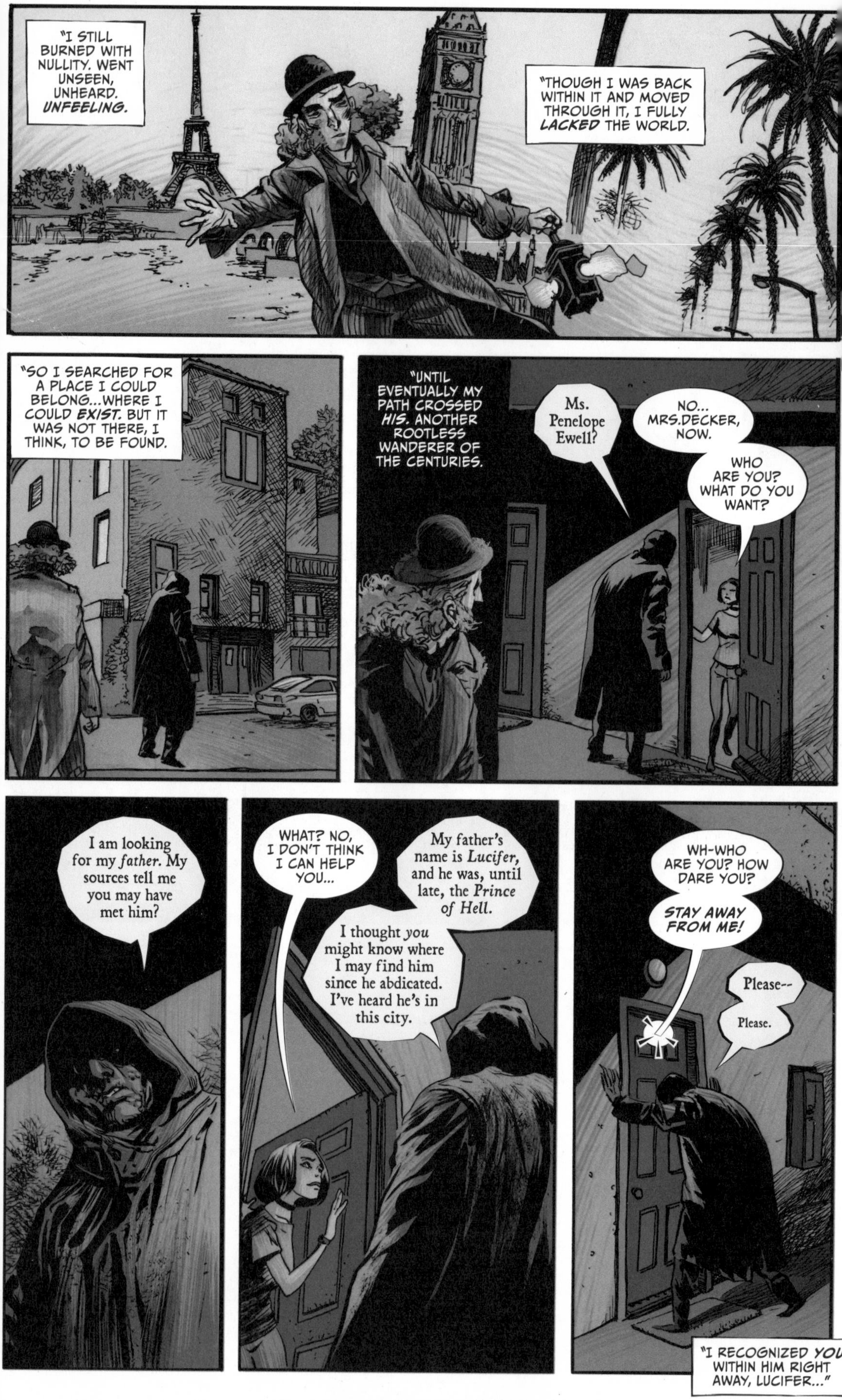
"I STILL BURNED WITH NULLITY. WENT UNSEEN, UNHEARD. UNFEELING.
"THOUGH I WAS BACK WITHIN IT AND MOVED THROUGH IT, I FULLY LACKED THE WORLD.
"SO I SEARCHED FOR A PLACE I COULD BELONG...WHERE I COULD EXIST. BUT IT WAS NOT THERE, I THINK, TO BE FOUND.
"UNTIL EVENTUALLY MY PATH CROSSED HIS. ANOTHER ROOTLESS WANDERER OF THE CENTURIES.
Ms. Penelope Ewell?
NO... MRS.DECKER, NOW.
WHO ARE YOU? WHAT DO YOU WANT?
I am looking for my father. My sources tell me you may have met him?
WHAT? NO, I DON'T THINK I CAN HELP YOU...
My father's name is Lucifer, and he was, until late, the Prince of Hell.
I thought you might know where I may find him since he abdicated. I've heard he's in this city.
WH-WHO ARE YOU? HOW DARE YOU?
STAY AWAY FROM ME!
Please--
Please.
"I RECOGNIZED YOU WITHIN HIM RIGHT AWAY, LUCIFER..."

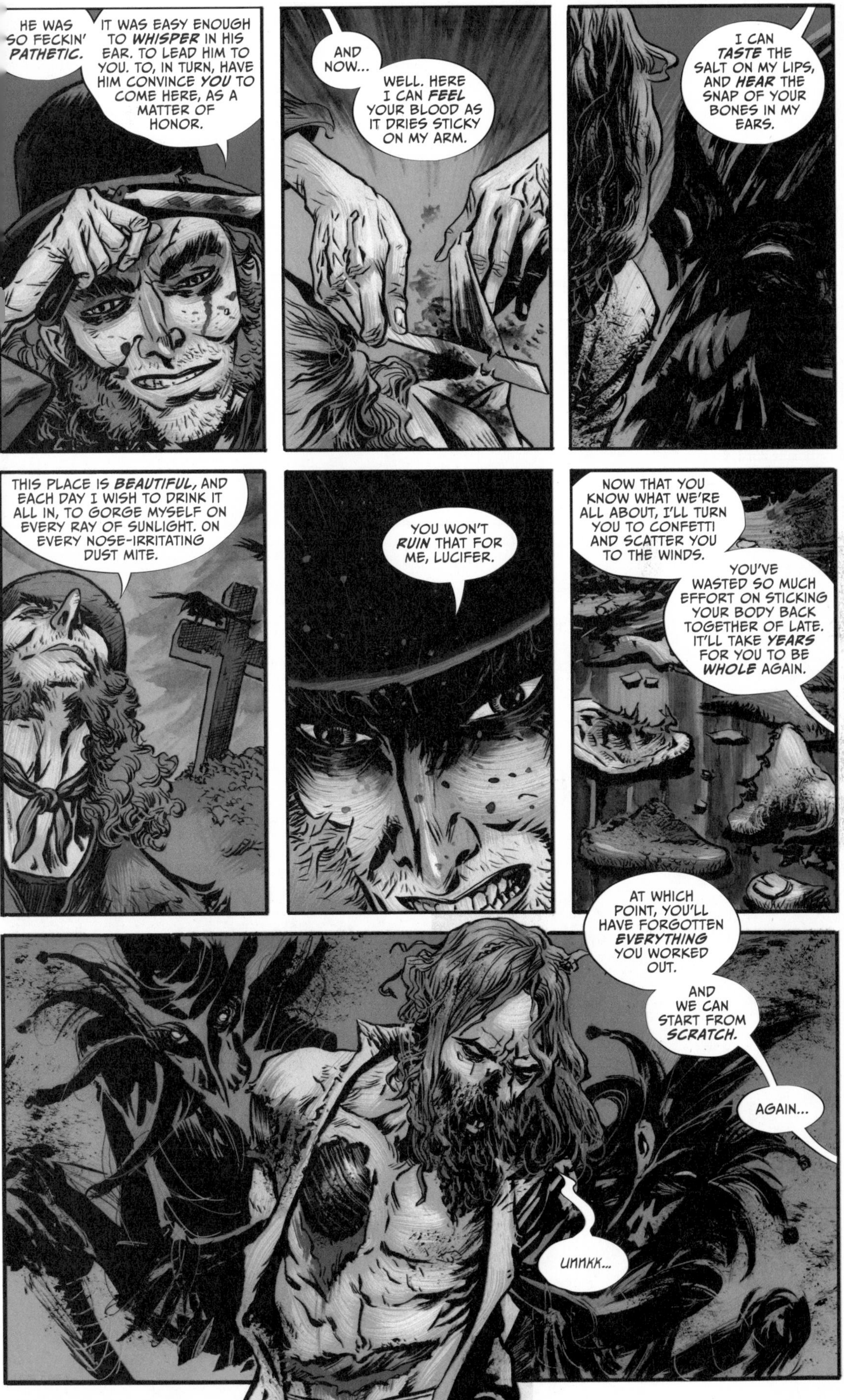

HE WAS SO FECKIN' PATHETIC.
IT WAS EASY ENOUGH TO WHISPER IN HIS EAR. TO LEAD HIM TO YOU. TO, IN TURN, HAVE HIM CONVINCE YOU TO COME HERE, AS A MATTER OF HONOR.
AND NOW...
WELL. HERE I CAN FEEL YOUR BLOOD AS IT DRIES STICKY ON MY ARM.
I CAN TASTE THE SALT ON MY LIPS, AND HEAR THE SNAP OF YOUR BONES IN MY EARS.
THIS PLACE IS BEAUTIFUL, AND EACH DAY I WISH TO DRINK IT ALL IN, TO GORGE MYSELF ON EVERY RAY OF SUNLIGHT. ON EVERY NOSE-IRRITATING DUST MITE.
YOU WON'T RUIN THAT FOR ME, LUCIFER.
NOW THAT YOU KNOW WHAT WE'RE ALL ABOUT, I'LL TURN YOU TO CONFETTI AND SCATTER YOU TO THE WINDS.
YOU'VE WASTED SO MUCH EFFORT ON STICKING YOUR BODY BACK TOGETHER OF LATE. IT'LL TAKE YEARS FOR YOU TO BE WHOLE AGAIN.
AT WHICH POINT, YOU'LL HAVE FORGOTTEN EVERYTHING YOU WORKED OUT.
AND WE CAN START FROM SCRATCH.
AGAIN...
UNNKK...

"AND
AGAIN...

"AND
AGAIN...

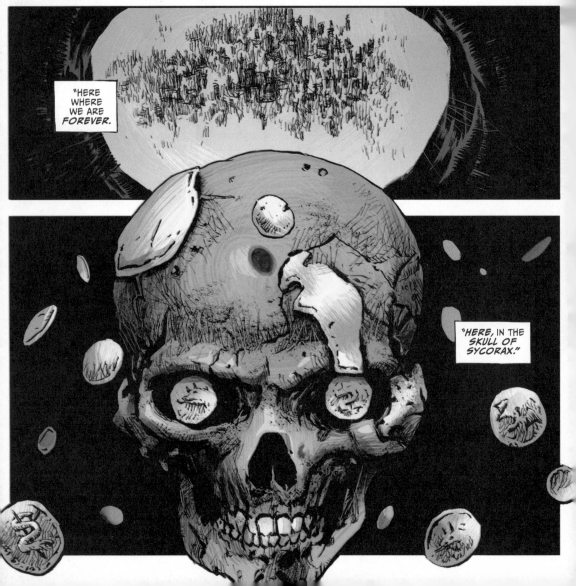

"HERE
WHERE
WE ARE
FOREVER.

"HERE, IN THE
SKULL OF
SYCORAX."

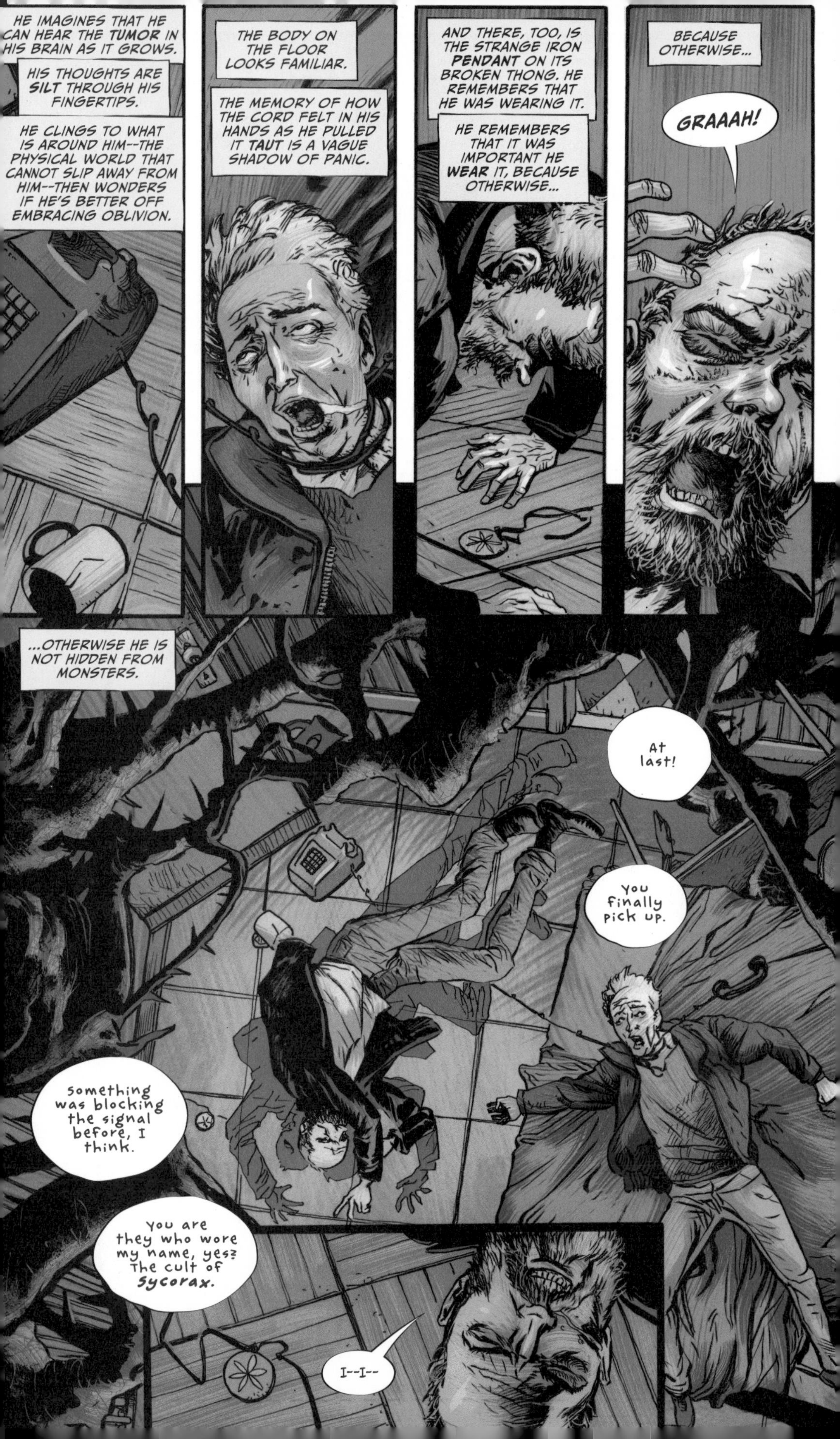

HE IMAGINES THAT HE CAN HEAR THE TUMOR IN HIS BRAIN AS IT GROWS.
HIS THOUGHTS ARE SILT THROUGH HIS FINGERTIPS.
HE CLINGS TO WHAT IS AROUND HIM--THE PHYSICAL WORLD THAT CANNOT SLIP AWAY FROM HIM--THEN WONDERS IF HE'S BETTER OFF EMBRACING OBLIVION.
THE BODY ON THE FLOOR LOOKS FAMILIAR.
THE MEMORY OF HOW THE CORD FELT IN HIS HANDS AS HE PULLED IT TAUT IS A VAGUE SHADOW OF PANIC.
AND THERE, TOO, IS THE STRANGE IRON PENDANT ON ITS BROKEN THONG. HE REMEMBERS THAT HE WAS WEARING IT.
HE REMEMBERS THAT IT WAS IMPORTANT HE WEAR IT, BECAUSE OTHERWISE...
BECAUSE OTHERWISE...
GRAAAH!
...OTHERWISE HE IS NOT HIDDEN FROM MONSTERS.
At last!
You finally pick up.
Something was blocking the signal before, I think.
You are they who wore my name, yes? The cult of Sycorax.
I--I--

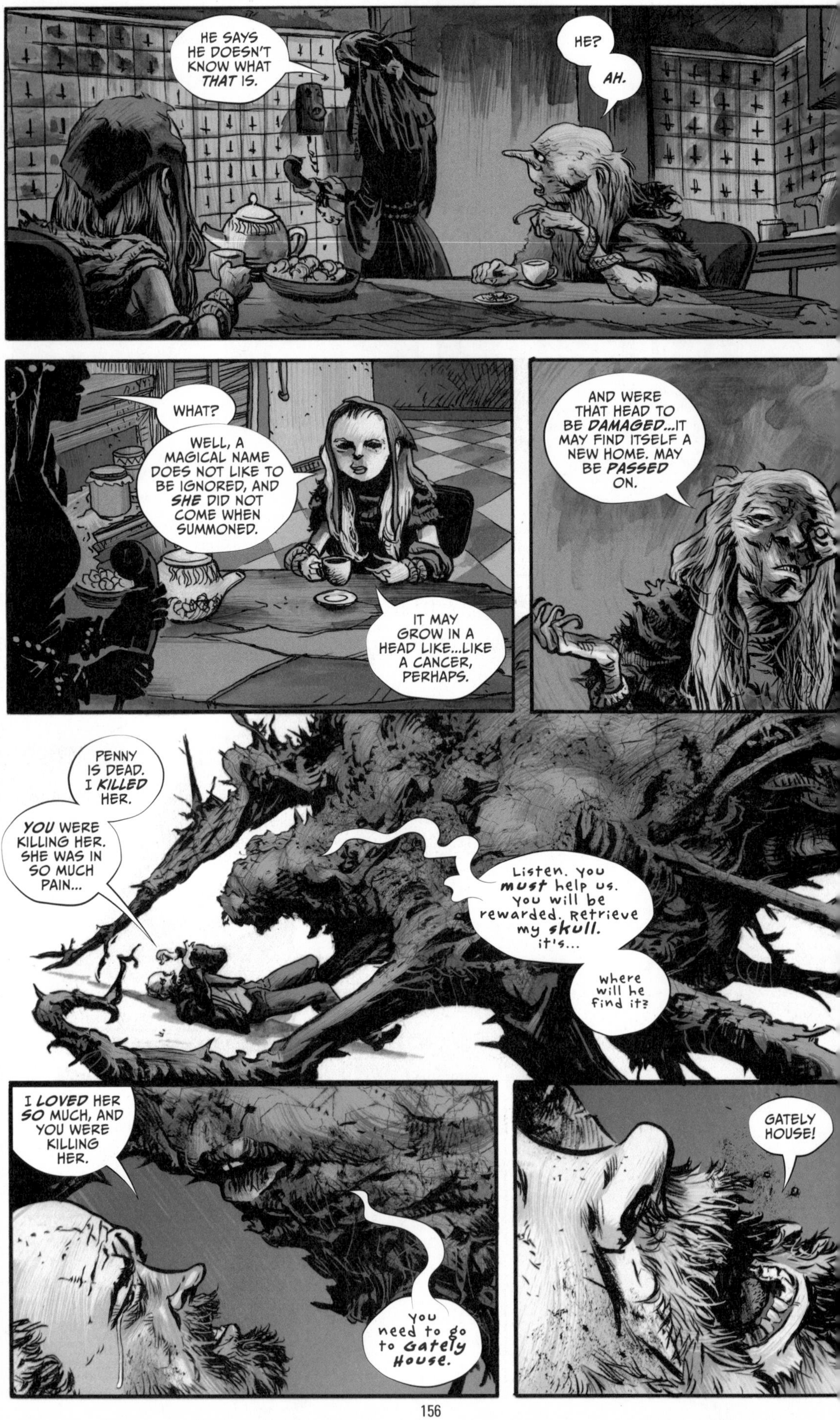

HE SAYS HE DOESN'T KNOW WHAT THAT IS.
HE? AH.
WHAT?
WELL, A MAGICAL NAME DOES NOT LIKE TO BE IGNORED, AND SHE DID NOT COME WHEN SUMMONED.
IT MAY GROW IN A HEAD LIKE...LIKE A CANCER, PERHAPS.
AND WERE THAT HEAD TO BE DAMAGED...IT MAY FIND ITSELF A NEW HOME. MAY BE PASSED ON.
PENNY IS DEAD. I KILLED HER.
YOU WERE KILLING HER. SHE WAS IN SO MUCH PAIN...
Listen. You must help us. You will be rewarded. Retrieve my skull. it's...
where will he find it?
I LOVED HER SO MUCH, AND YOU WERE KILLING HER.
You need to go to Gately House.
GATELY HOUSE!

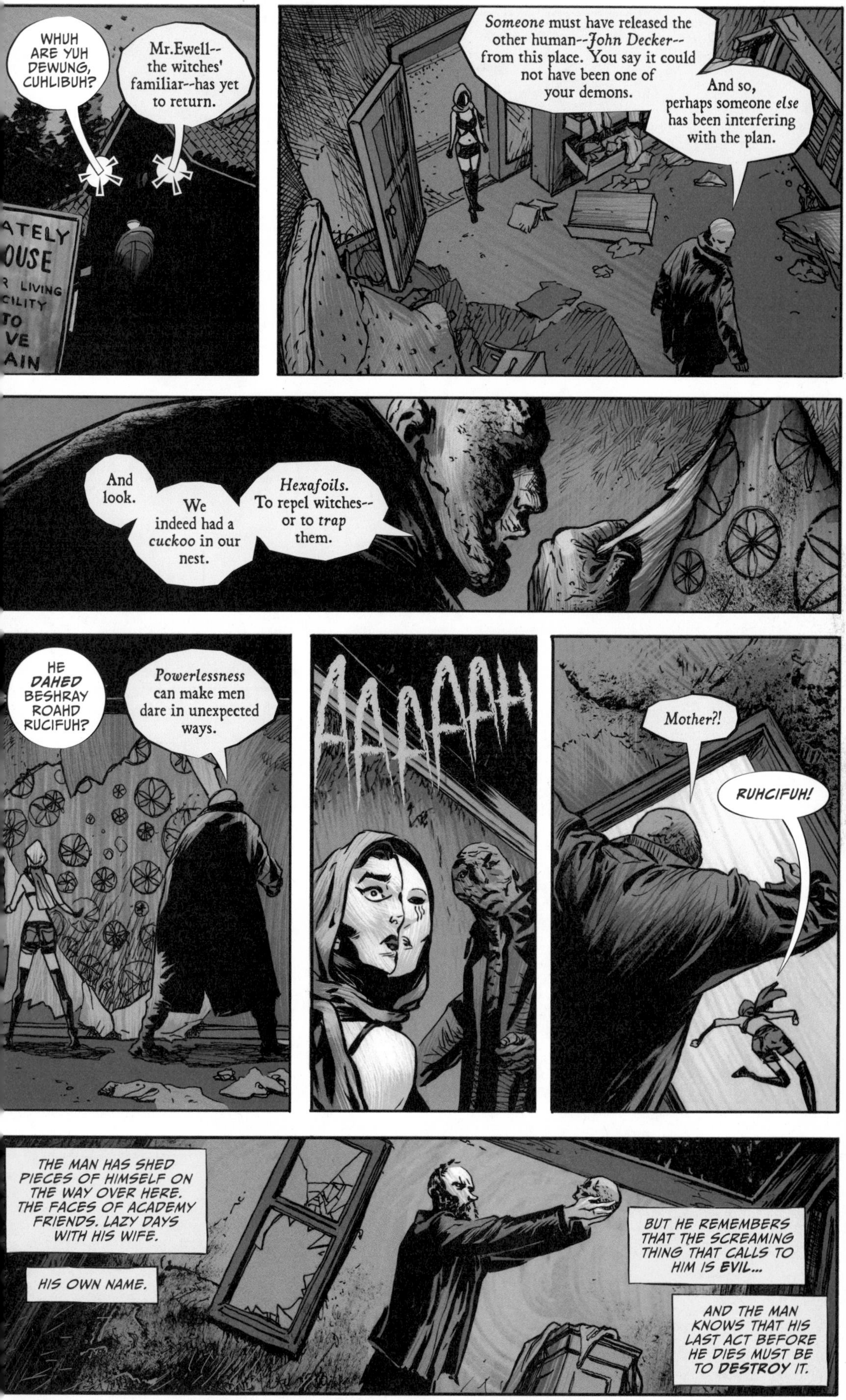

WHUH ARE YUH DEWUNG, CUHLIBUH?
Mr.Ewell-- the witches' familiar--has yet to return.
ATELY OUSE R LIVING CILITY TO VE AIN
Someone must have released the other human--John Decker--from this place. You say it could not have been one of your demons.
And so, perhaps someone else has been interfering with the plan.
And look.
We indeed had a cuckoo in our nest.
Hexafoils. To repel witches--or to trap them.
HE DAHED BESHRAY ROAHD RUCIFUH?
Powerlessness can make men dare in unexpected ways.
AAAAAH
Mother?!
RUHCIFUH!
THE MAN HAS SHED PIECES OF HIMSELF ON THE WAY OVER HERE. THE FACES OF ACADEMY FRIENDS. LAZY DAYS WITH HIS WIFE.
HIS OWN NAME.
BUT HE REMEMBERS THAT THE SCREAMING THING THAT CALLS TO HIM IS EVIL...
AND THE MAN KNOWS THAT HIS LAST ACT BEFORE HE DIES MUST BE TO DESTROY IT.

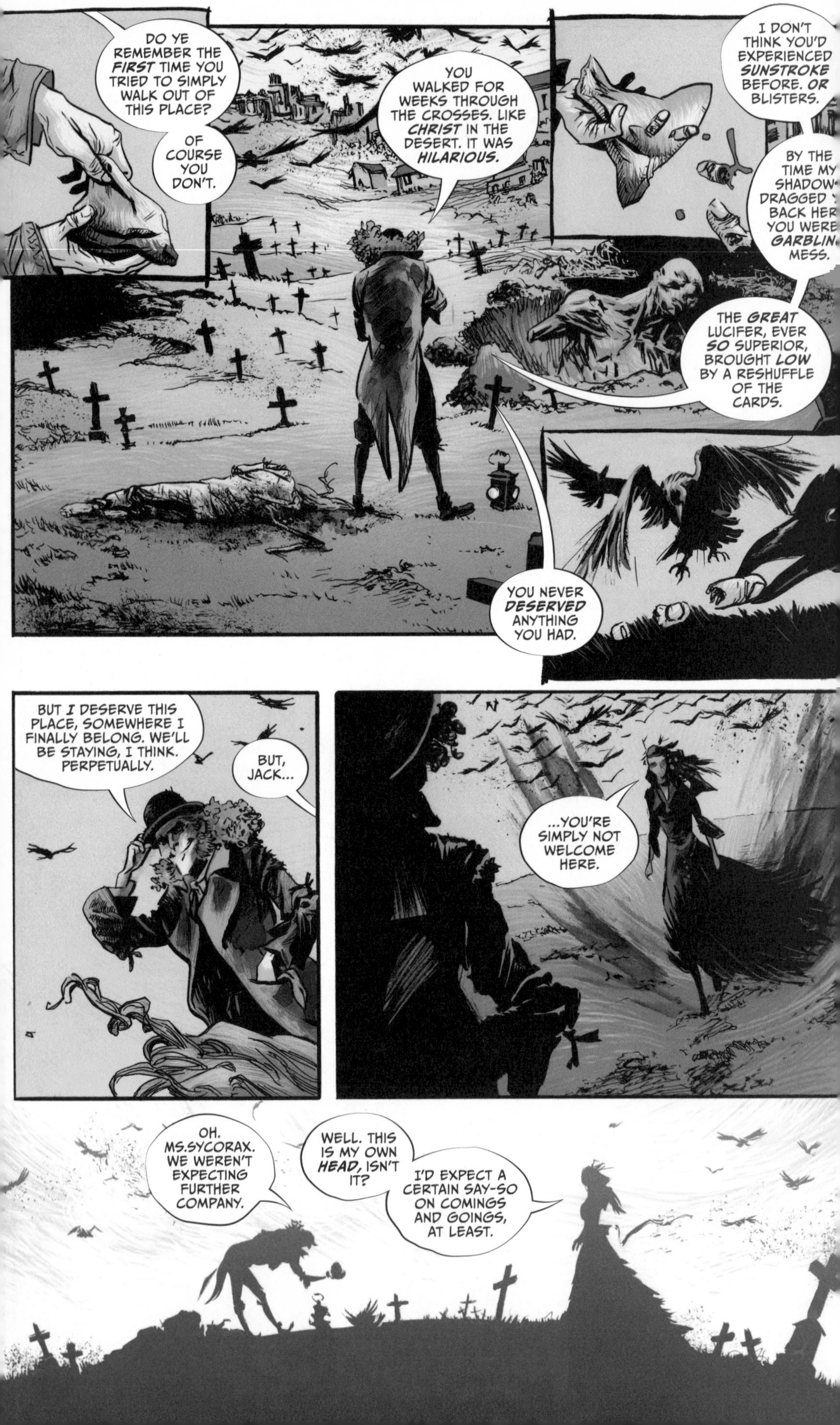
DO YE REMEMBER THE FIRST TIME YOU TRIED TO SIMPLY WALK OUT OF THIS PLACE?
OF COURSE YOU DON'T.
YOU WALKED FOR WEEKS THROUGH THE CROSSES. LIKE CHRIST IN THE DESERT. IT WAS HILARIOUS.
I DON'T THINK YOU'D EXPERIENCED SUNSTROKE BEFORE. OR BLISTERS.
BY THE TIME MY SHADOW DRAGGED Y BACK HER YOU WERE GARBLIN MESS.
THE GREAT LUCIFER, EVER SO SUPERIOR, BROUGHT LOW BY A RESHUFFLE OF THE CARDS.
YOU NEVER DESERVED ANYTHING YOU HAD.
BUT I DESERVE THIS PLACE, SOMEWHERE I FINALLY BELONG. WE'LL BE STAYING, I THINK. PERPETUALLY.
BUT, JACK...
...YOU'RE SIMPLY NOT WELCOME HERE.
OH. MS.SYCORAX. WE WEREN'T EXPECTING FURTHER COMPANY.
WELL. THIS IS MY OWN HEAD, ISN'T IT?
I'D EXPECT A CERTAIN SAY-SO ON COMINGS AND GOINGS, AT LEAST.

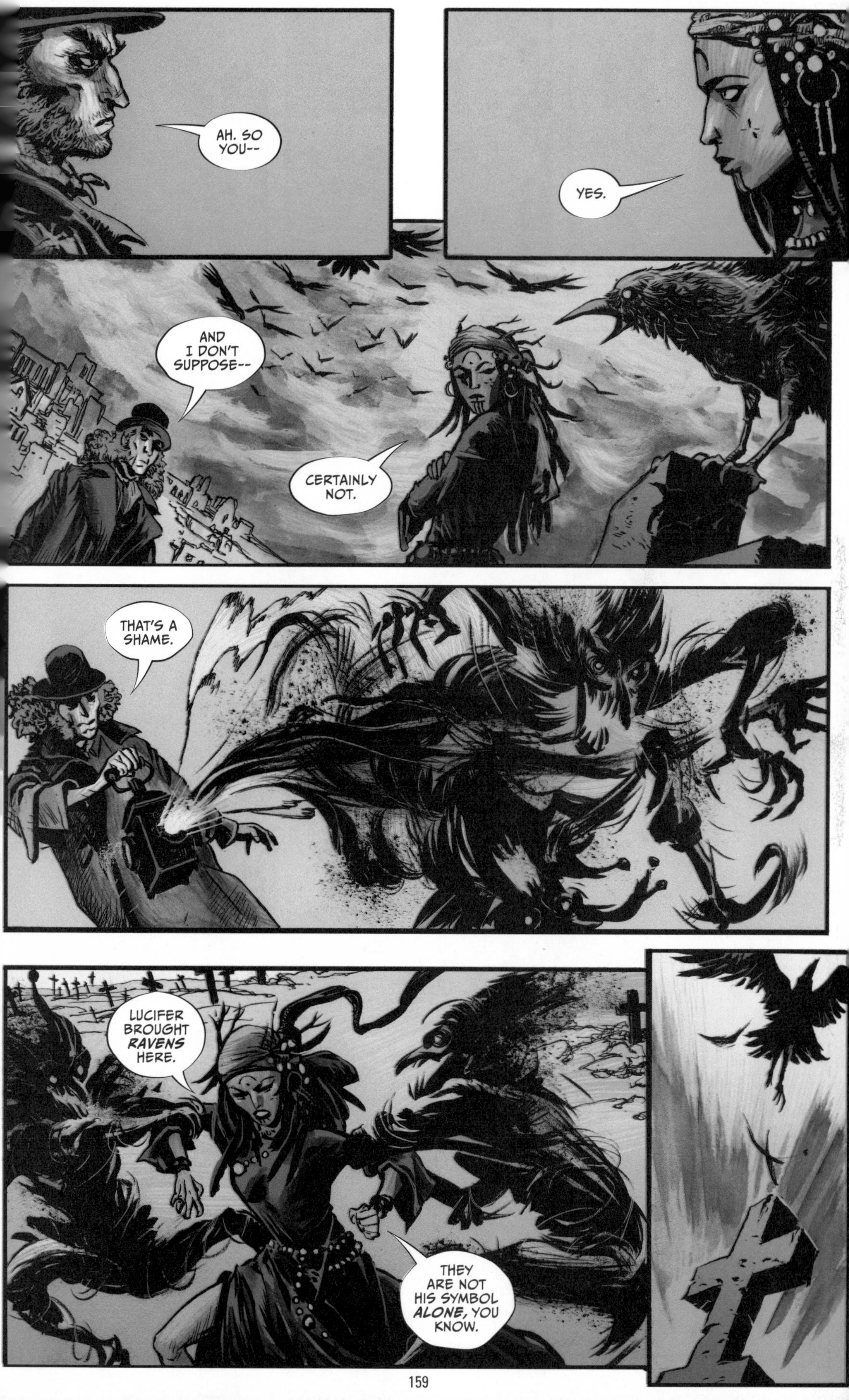
AH. SO YOU--
YES.
AND I DON'T SUPPOSE--
CERTAINLY NOT.
THAT'S A SHAME.
LUCIFER BROUGHT *RAVENS* HERE.
THEY ARE NOT HIS SYMBOL *ALONE*, YOU KNOW.

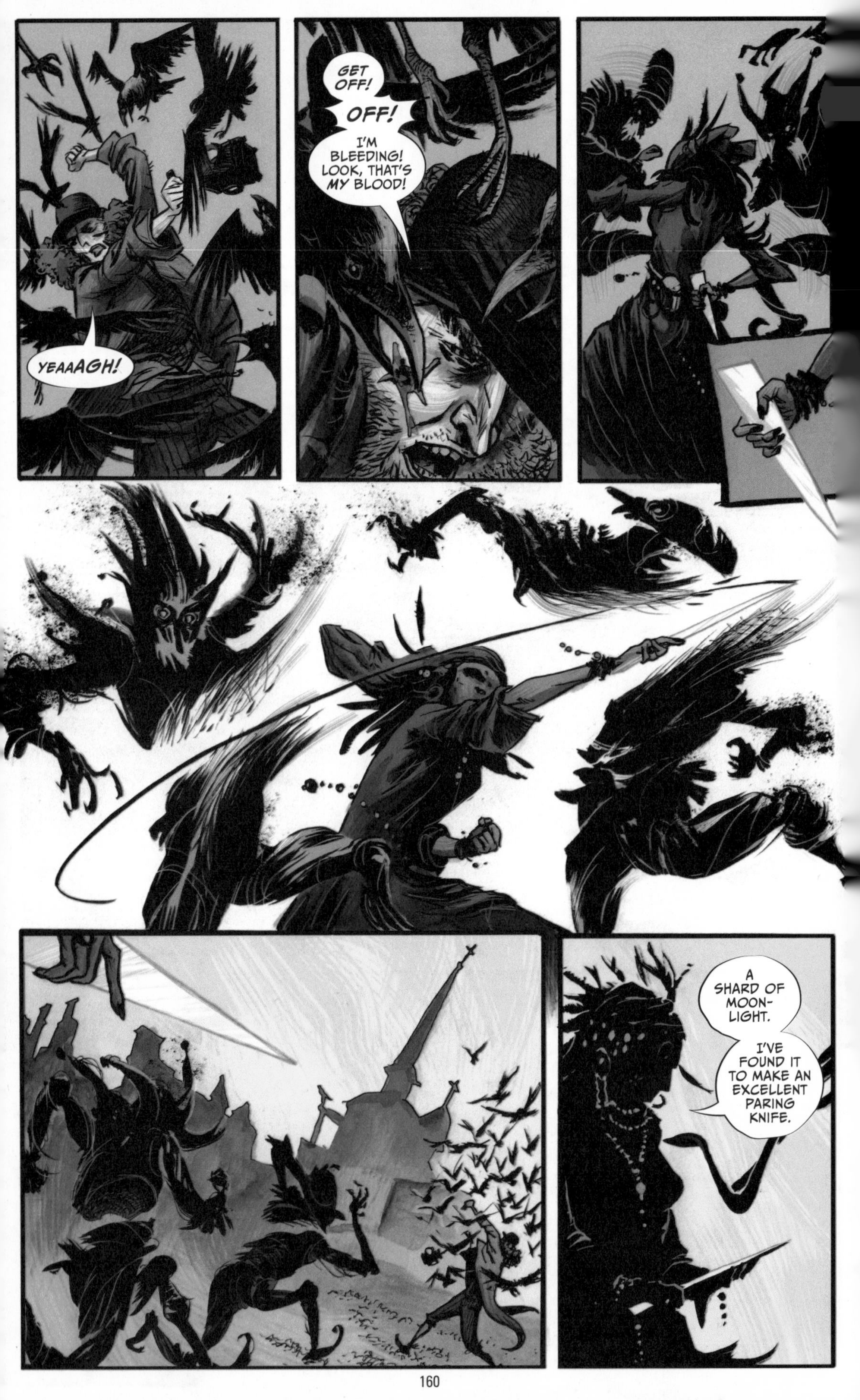
YEAAAGH!
GET OFF!
OFF!
I'M BLEEDING! LOOK, THAT'S MY BLOOD!
A SHARD OF MOON-LIGHT.
I'VE FOUND IT TO MAKE AN EXCELLENT PARING KNIFE.

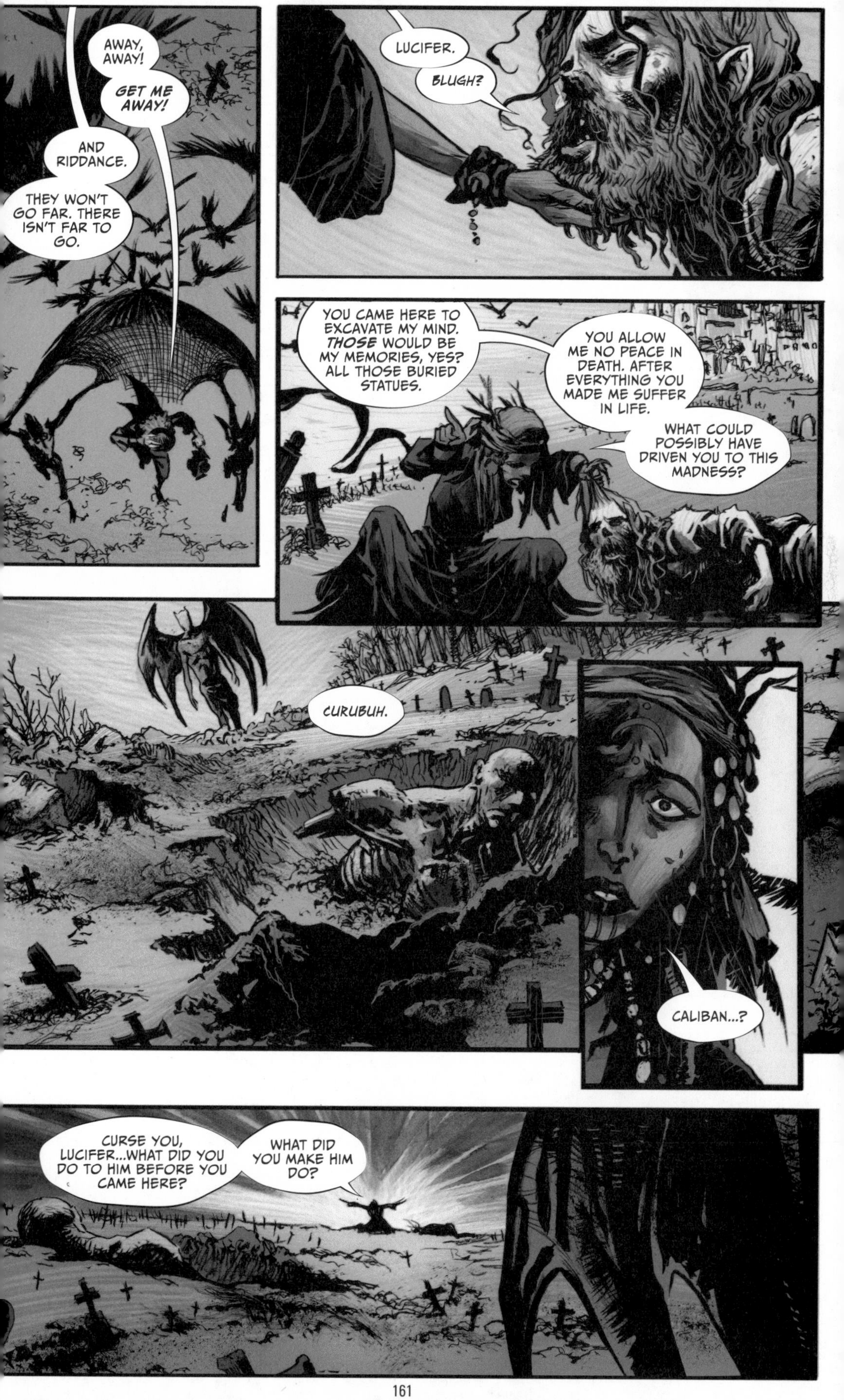
AWAY, AWAY!
GET ME AWAY!
AND RIDDANCE.
THEY WON'T GO FAR. THERE ISN'T FAR TO GO.
LUCIFER.
BLUGH?
YOU CAME HERE TO EXCAVATE MY MIND. THOSE WOULD BE MY MEMORIES, YES? ALL THOSE BURIED STATUES.
YOU ALLOW ME NO PEACE IN DEATH. AFTER EVERYTHING YOU MADE ME SUFFER IN LIFE.
WHAT COULD POSSIBLY HAVE DRIVEN YOU TO THIS MADNESS?
CURUBUH.
CALIBAN...?
CURSE YOU, LUCIFER...WHAT DID YOU DO TO HIM BEFORE YOU CAME HERE?
WHAT DID YOU MAKE HIM DO?

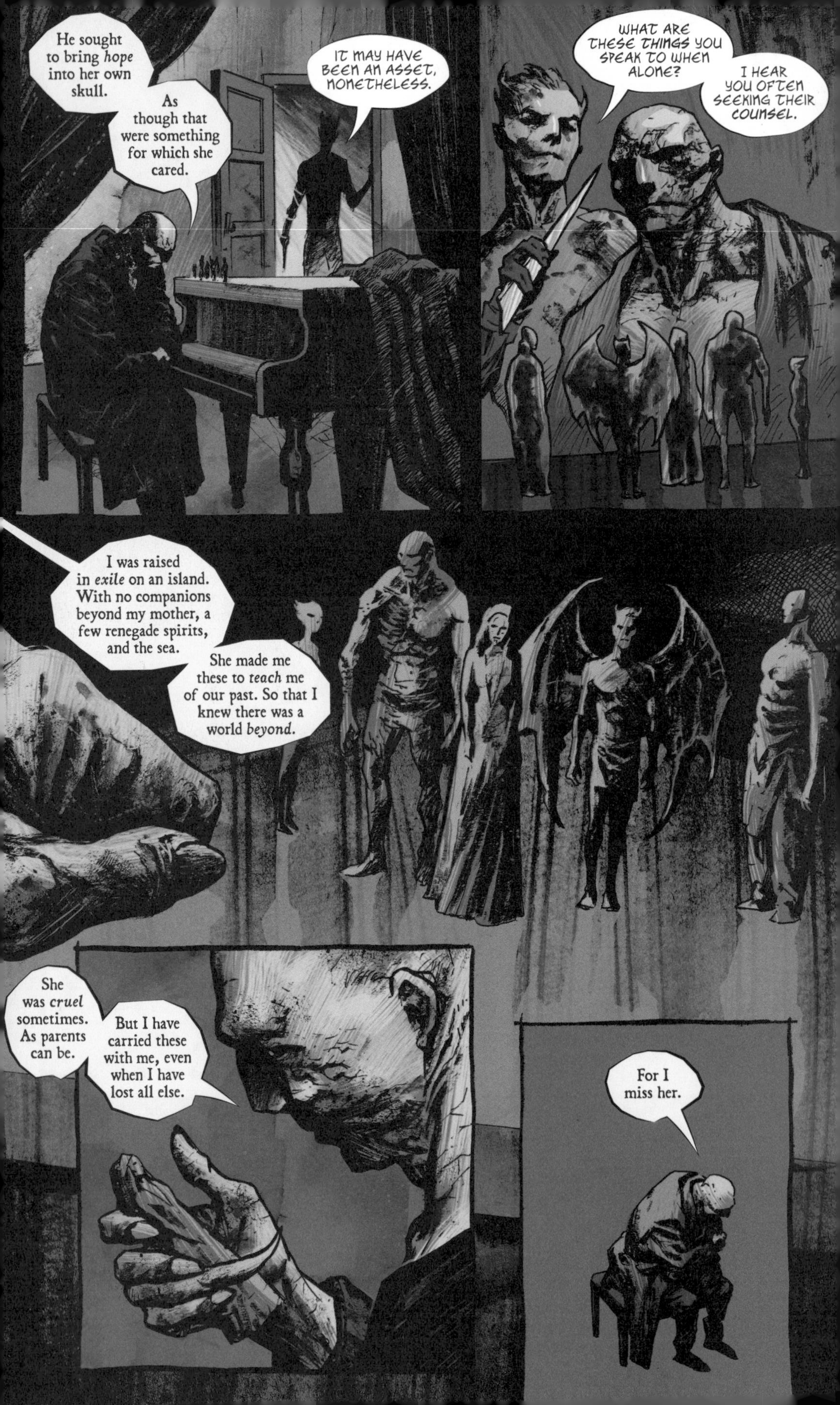
He sought to bring *hope* into her own skull.
As though that were something for which she cared.
IT MAY HAVE BEEN AN ASSET, NONETHELESS.
WHAT ARE THESE THINGS YOU SPEAK TO WHEN ALONE?
I HEAR YOU OFTEN SEEKING THEIR COUNSEL.
I was raised in *exile* on an island. With no companions beyond my mother, a few renegade spirits, and the sea.
She made me these to *teach* me of our past. So that I knew there was a world *beyond*.
She was *cruel* sometimes. As parents can be.
But I have carried these with me, even when I have lost all else.
For I miss her.

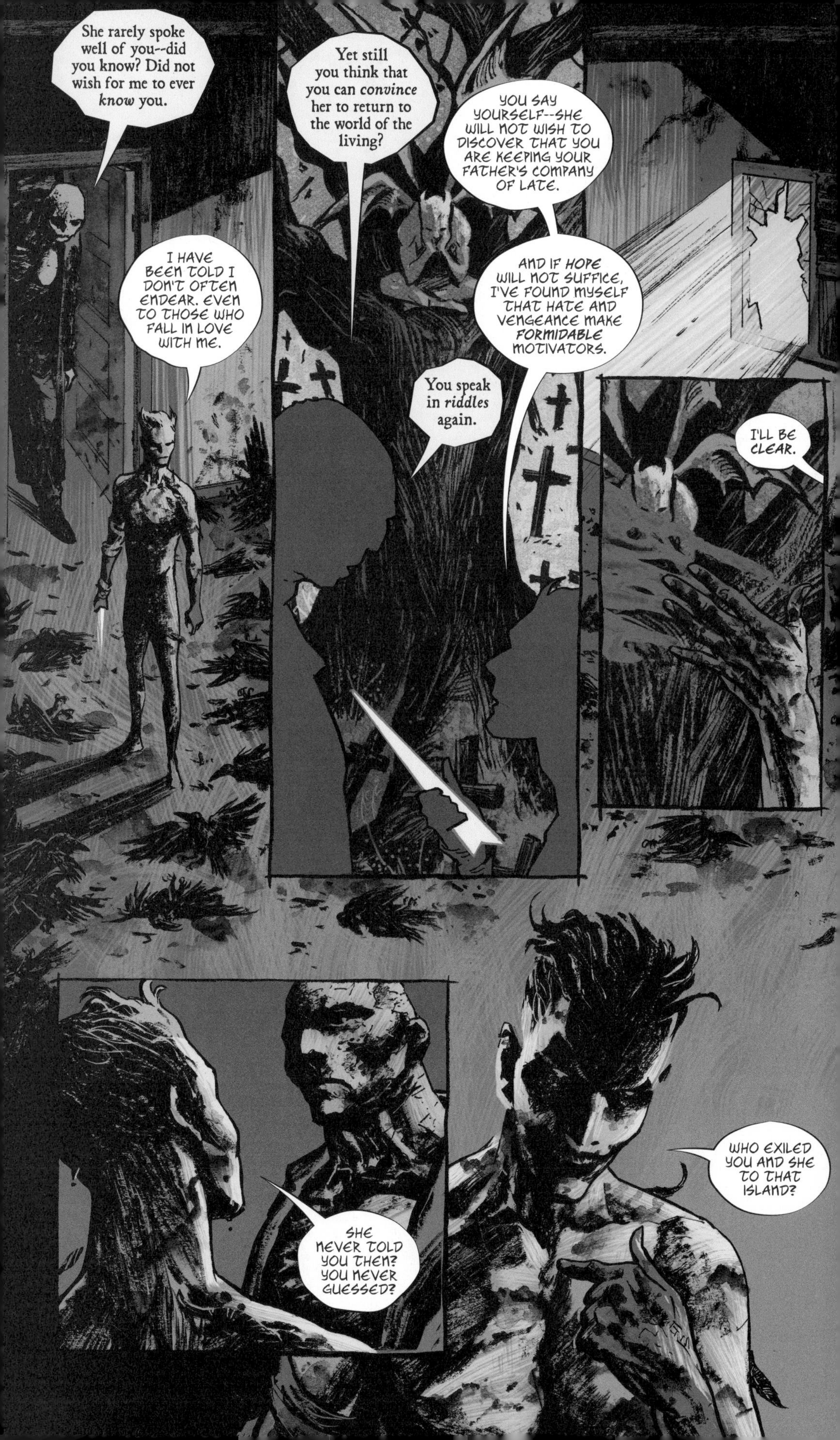
She rarely spoke well of you--did you know? Did not wish for me to ever *know* you.
I HAVE BEEN TOLD I DON'T OFTEN ENDEAR. EVEN TO THOSE WHO FALL IN LOVE WITH ME.
Yet still you think that you can *convince* her to return to the world of the living?
YOU SAY YOURSELF--SHE WILL NOT WISH TO DISCOVER THAT YOU ARE KEEPING YOUR FATHER'S COMPANY OF LATE.
AND IF *HOPE* WILL NOT SUFFICE, I'VE FOUND MYSELF THAT HATE AND VENGEANCE MAKE *FORMIDABLE* MOTIVATORS.
You speak in *riddles* again.
I'LL BE *CLEAR.*
WHO EXILED YOU AND SHE TO THAT ISLAND?
SHE NEVER TOLD YOU THEN? YOU NEVER GUESSED?

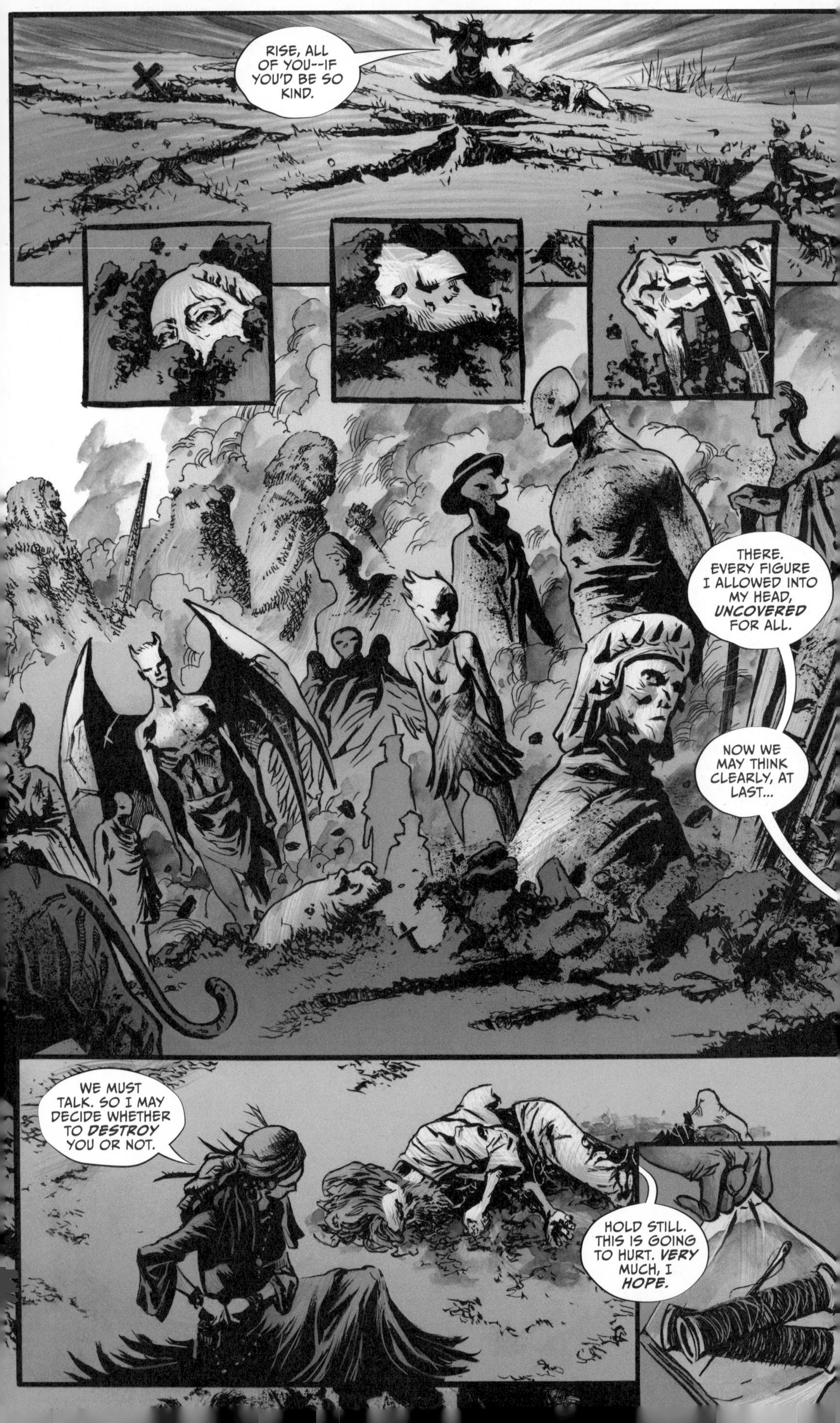

RISE, ALL OF YOU--IF YOU'D BE SO KIND.
THERE. EVERY FIGURE I ALLOWED INTO MY HEAD, *UNCOVERED* FOR ALL.
NOW WE MAY THINK CLEARLY, AT LAST...
WE MUST TALK. SO I MAY DECIDE WHETHER TO *DESTROY* YOU OR NOT.
HOLD STILL. THIS IS GOING TO HURT. *VERY* MUCH, I *HOPE.*

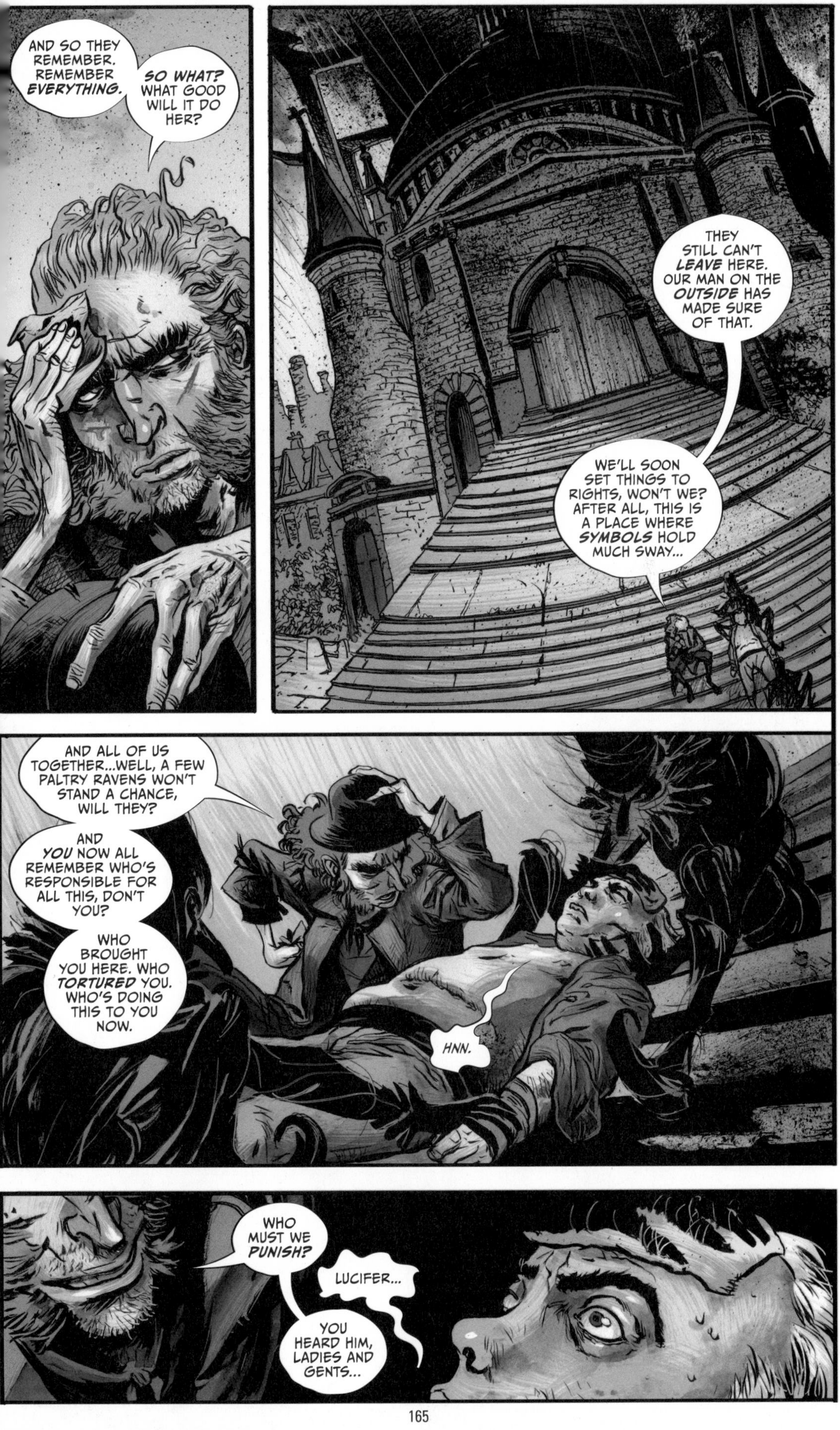
AND SO THEY REMEMBER. REMEMBER EVERYTHING.
SO WHAT? WHAT GOOD WILL IT DO HER?
THEY STILL CAN'T LEAVE HERE. OUR MAN ON THE OUTSIDE HAS MADE SURE OF THAT.
WE'LL SOON SET THINGS TO RIGHTS, WON'T WE? AFTER ALL, THIS IS A PLACE WHERE SYMBOLS HOLD MUCH SWAY...
AND ALL OF US TOGETHER...WELL, A FEW PALTRY RAVENS WON'T STAND A CHANCE, WILL THEY?
AND YOU NOW ALL REMEMBER WHO'S RESPONSIBLE FOR ALL THIS, DON'T YOU?
WHO BROUGHT YOU HERE. WHO TORTURED YOU. WHO'S DOING THIS TO YOU NOW.
HNN.
WHO MUST WE PUNISH?
LUCIFER...
YOU HEARD HIM, LADIES AND GENTS...

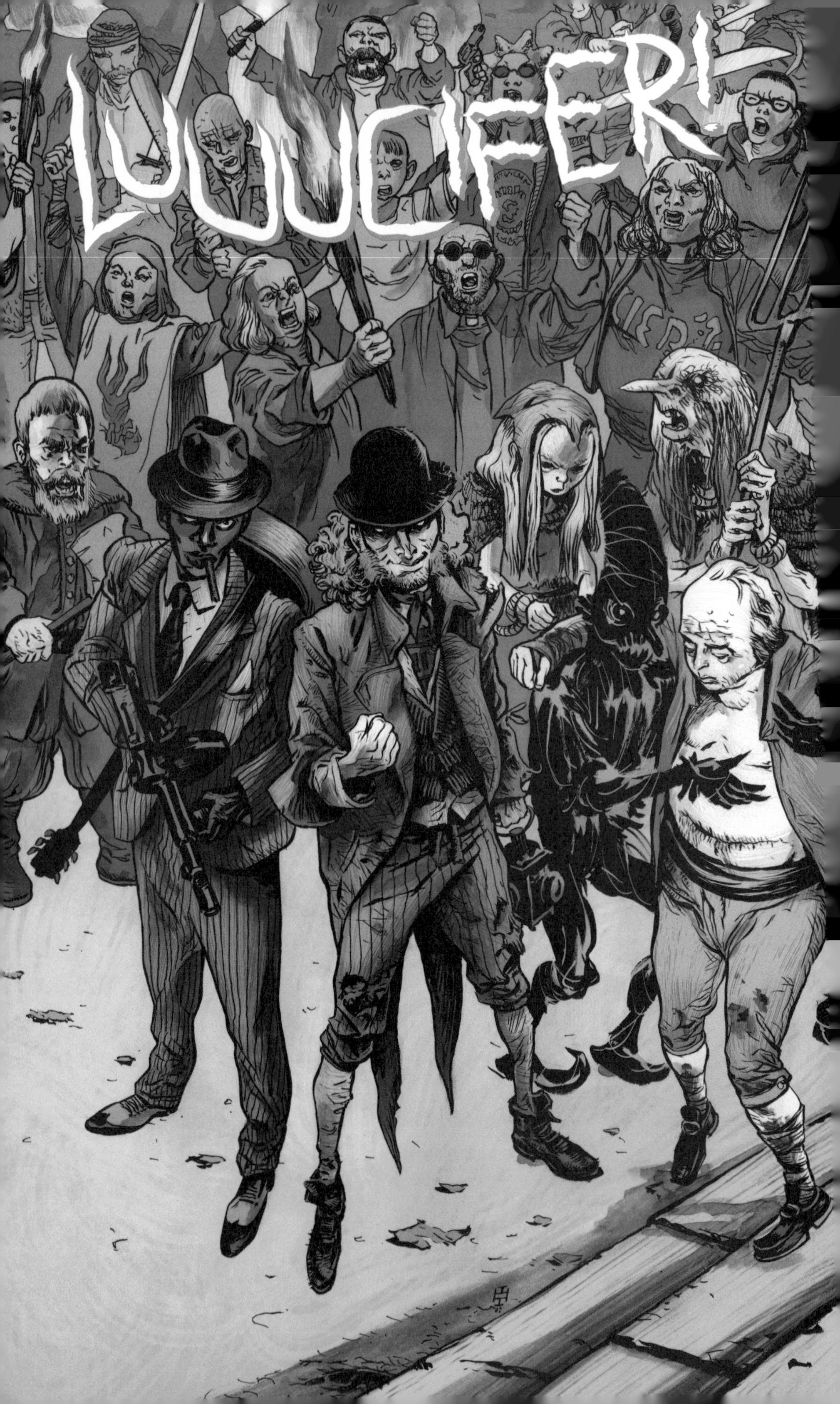
LUUUCIFER!

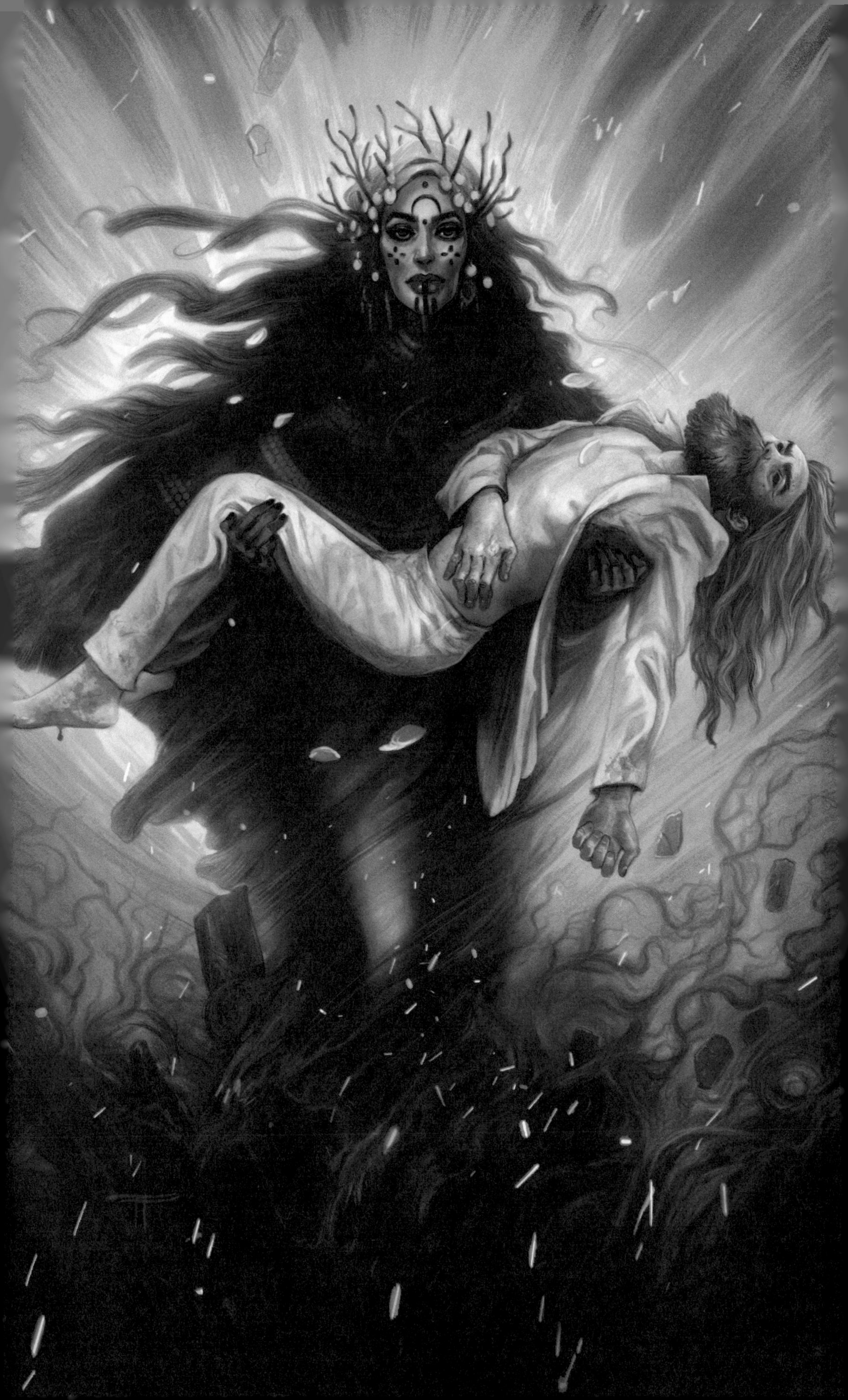

LUCIFER

A Long-Awaited Comeuppance

WRITTEN BY
Dan Watters

ILLUSTRATED BY
Max Fiumara
Sebastian Fiumara

COLORS BY
Dave McCaig

LETTERS BY
Steve Wands

COVER ART BY
Tiffany Turrill

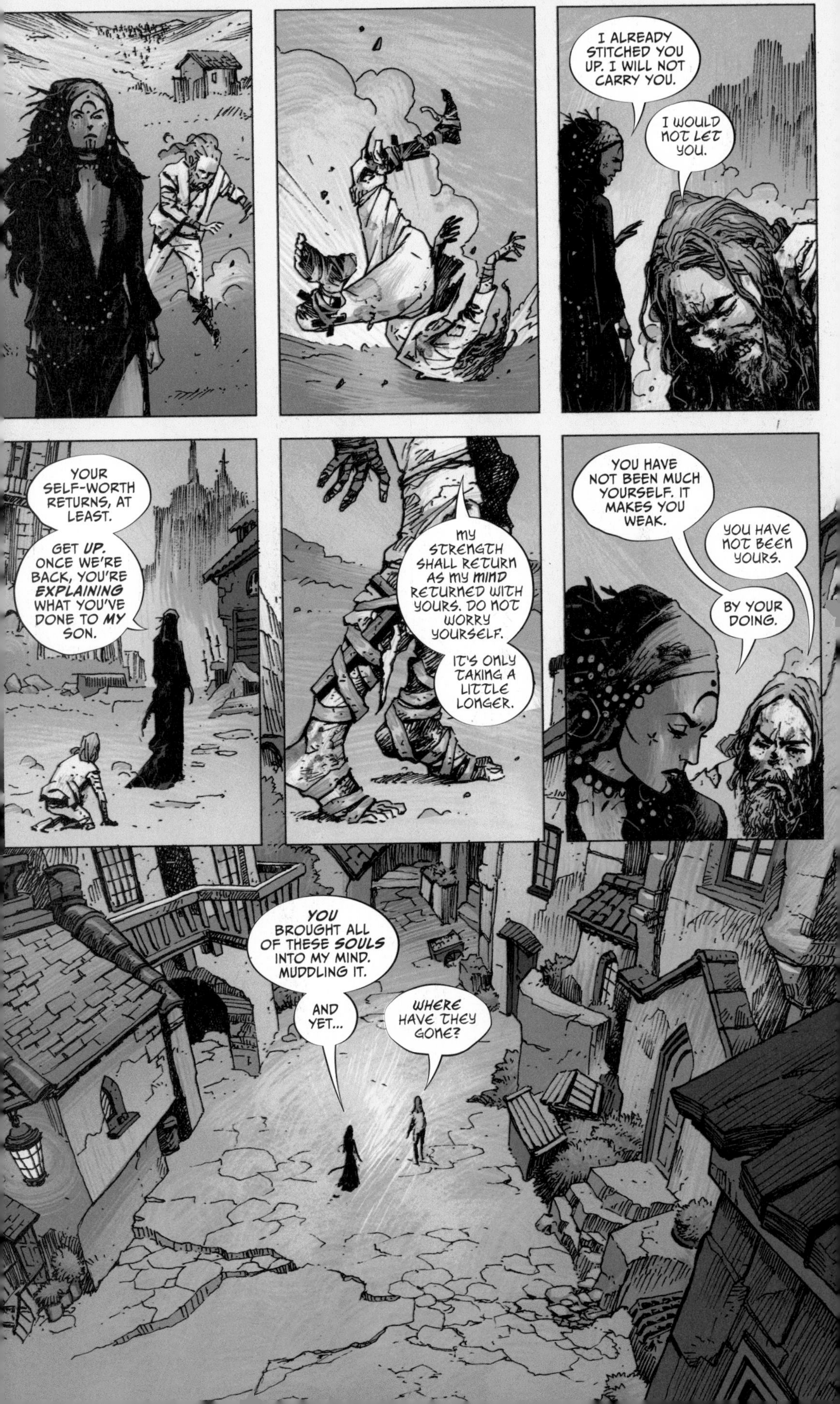
I ALREADY STITCHED YOU UP. I WILL NOT CARRY YOU.
I WOULD NOT LET YOU.
YOUR SELF-WORTH RETURNS, AT LEAST.
GET *UP*. ONCE WE'RE BACK, YOU'RE *EXPLAINING* WHAT YOU'VE DONE TO *MY* SON.
MY STRENGTH SHALL RETURN AS MY *MIND* RETURNED WITH YOURS. DO NOT WORRY YOURSELF.
IT'S ONLY TAKING A LITTLE LONGER.
YOU HAVE NOT BEEN MUCH YOURSELF. IT MAKES YOU WEAK.
YOU HAVE NOT BEEN YOURS.
BY YOUR DOING.
YOU BROUGHT ALL OF THESE *SOULS* INTO MY MIND. MUDDLING IT.
AND YET...
WHERE HAVE THEY GONE?

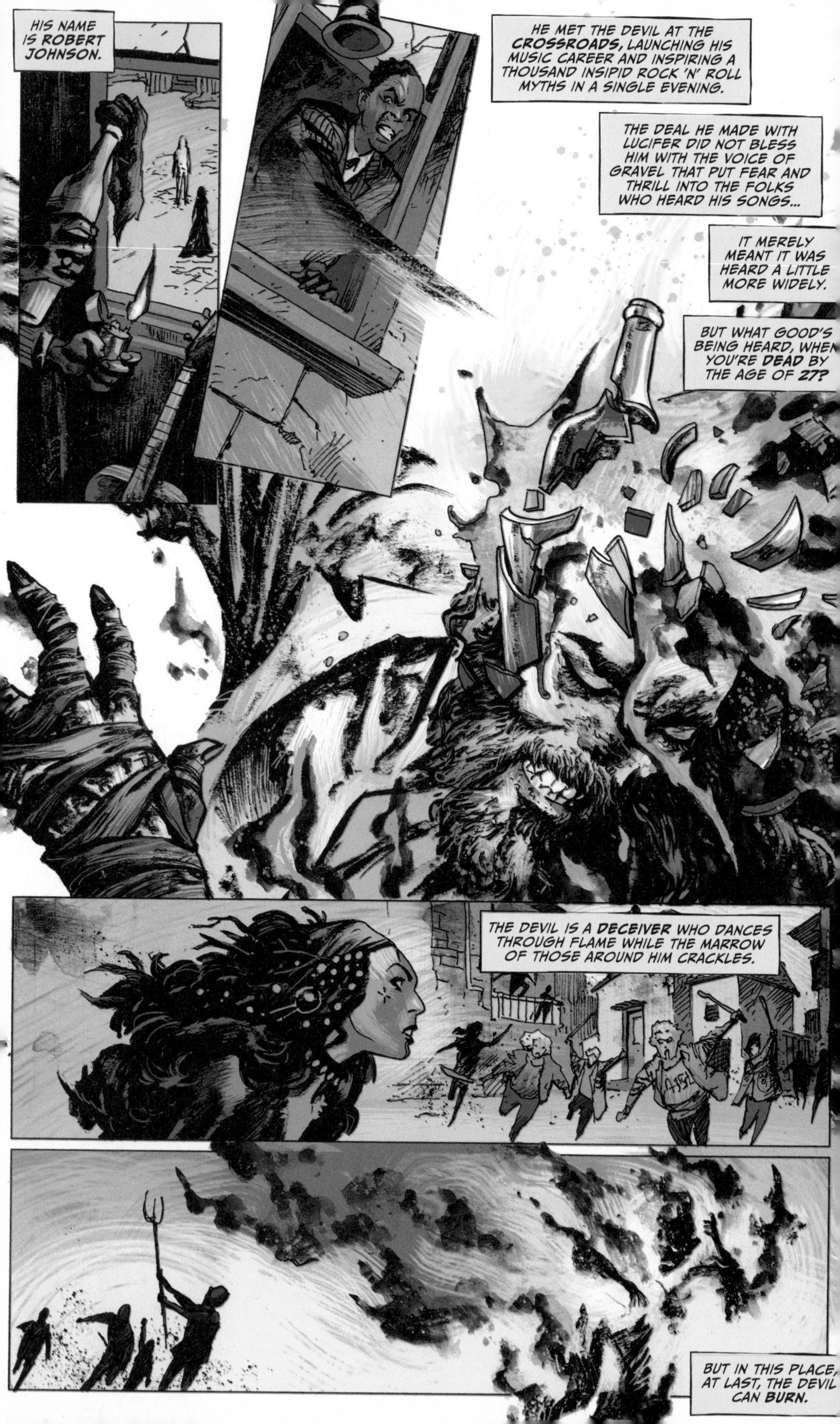
HIS NAME IS ROBERT JOHNSON.
HE MET THE DEVIL AT THE CROSSROADS, LAUNCHING HIS MUSIC CAREER AND INSPIRING A THOUSAND INSIPID ROCK 'N' ROLL MYTHS IN A SINGLE EVENING.
THE DEAL HE MADE WITH LUCIFER DID NOT BLESS HIM WITH THE VOICE OF GRAVEL THAT PUT FEAR AND THRILL INTO THE FOLKS WHO HEARD HIS SONGS...
IT MERELY MEANT IT WAS HEARD A LITTLE MORE WIDELY.
BUT WHAT GOOD'S BEING HEARD, WHEN YOU'RE DEAD BY THE AGE OF 27?
THE DEVIL IS A DECEIVER WHO DANCES THROUGH FLAME WHILE THE MARROW OF THOSE AROUND HIM CRACKLES.
BUT IN THIS PLACE, AT LAST, THE DEVIL CAN BURN.

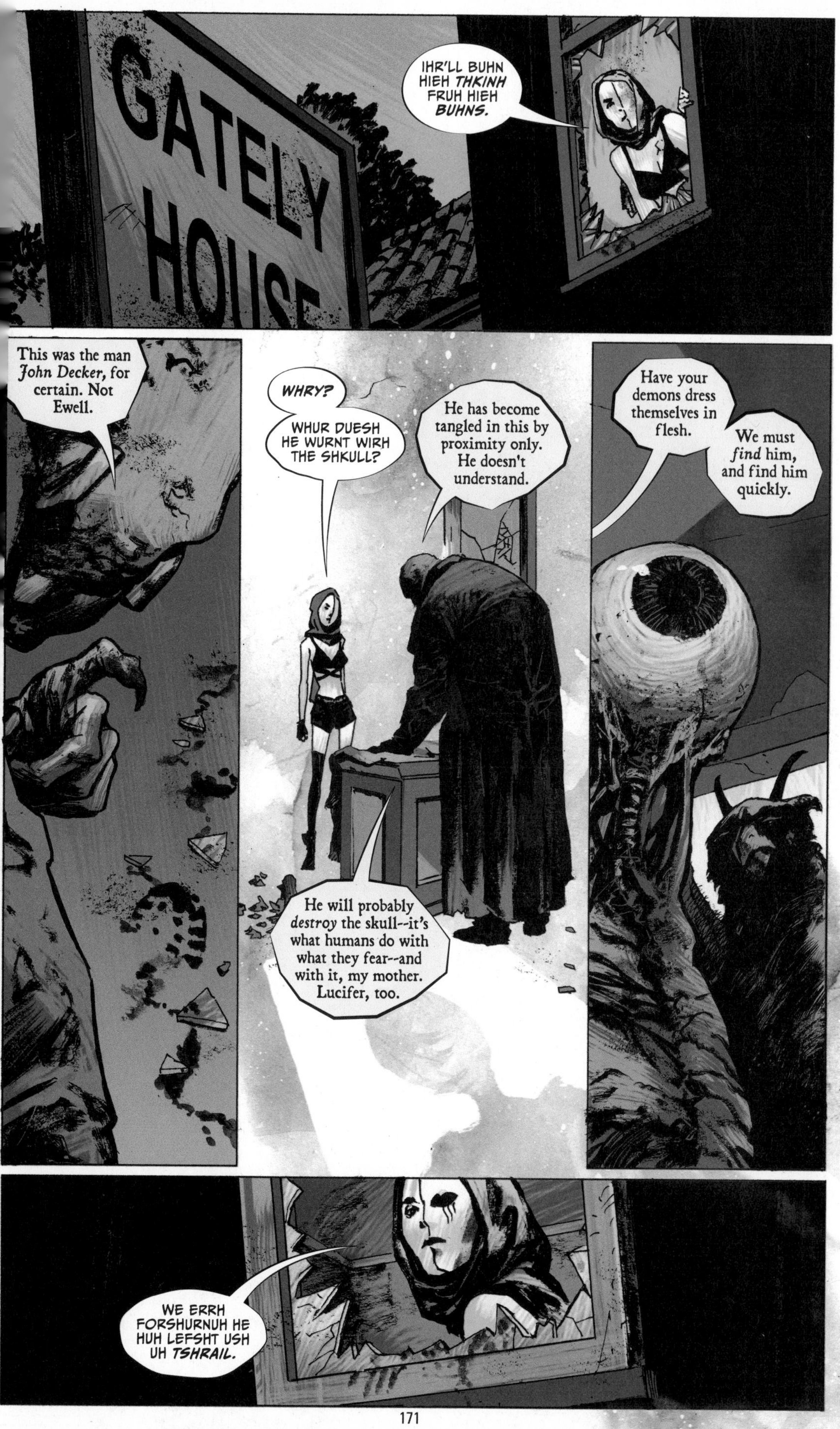

GATELY HOUSE
IHR'LL BUHN HIEH *THKINH* FRUH HIEH *BUHNS.*
This was the man *John Decker,* for certain. Not Ewell.
WHRY?
WHUR DUESH HE WURNT WIRH THE SHKULL?
He has become tangled in this by proximity only. He doesn't understand.
He will probably *destroy* the skull--it's what humans do with what they fear--and with it, my mother. Lucifer, too.
Have your demons dress themselves in flesh.
We must *find* him, and find him quickly.
WE ERRH FORSHURNUH HE HUH LEFSHT USH UH *TSHRAIL.*

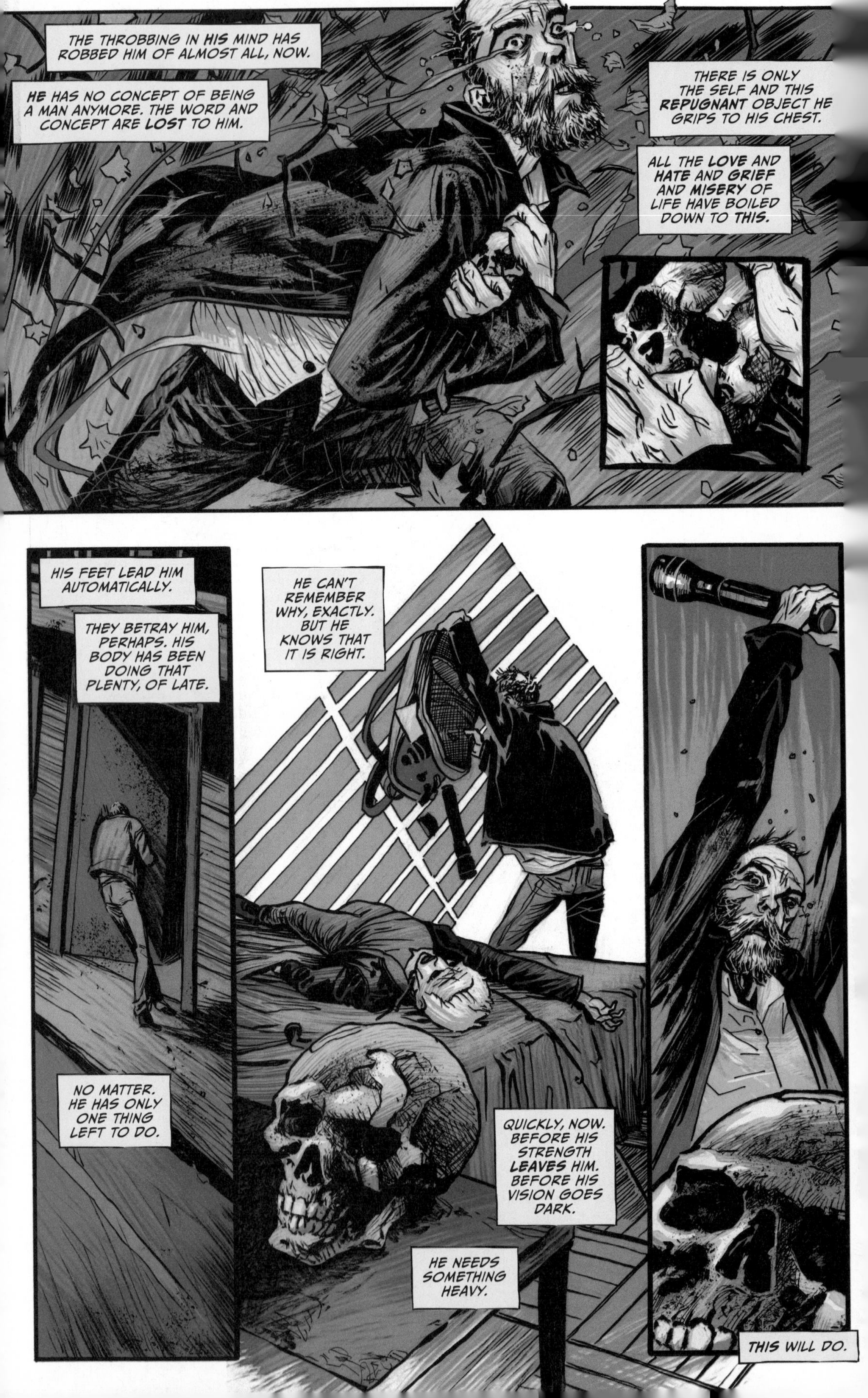

THE THROBBING IN HIS MIND HAS ROBBED HIM OF ALMOST ALL, NOW.
HE HAS NO CONCEPT OF BEING A MAN ANYMORE. THE WORD AND CONCEPT ARE LOST TO HIM.
THERE IS ONLY THE SELF AND THIS REPUGNANT OBJECT HE GRIPS TO HIS CHEST.
ALL THE LOVE AND HATE AND GRIEF AND MISERY OF LIFE HAVE BOILED DOWN TO THIS.
HIS FEET LEAD HIM AUTOMATICALLY.
THEY BETRAY HIM, PERHAPS. HIS BODY HAS BEEN DOING THAT PLENTY, OF LATE.
NO MATTER. HE HAS ONLY ONE THING LEFT TO DO.
HE CAN'T REMEMBER WHY, EXACTLY. BUT HE KNOWS THAT IT IS RIGHT.
QUICKLY, NOW. BEFORE HIS STRENGTH LEAVES HIM. BEFORE HIS VISION GOES DARK.
HE NEEDS SOMETHING HEAVY.
THIS WILL DO.

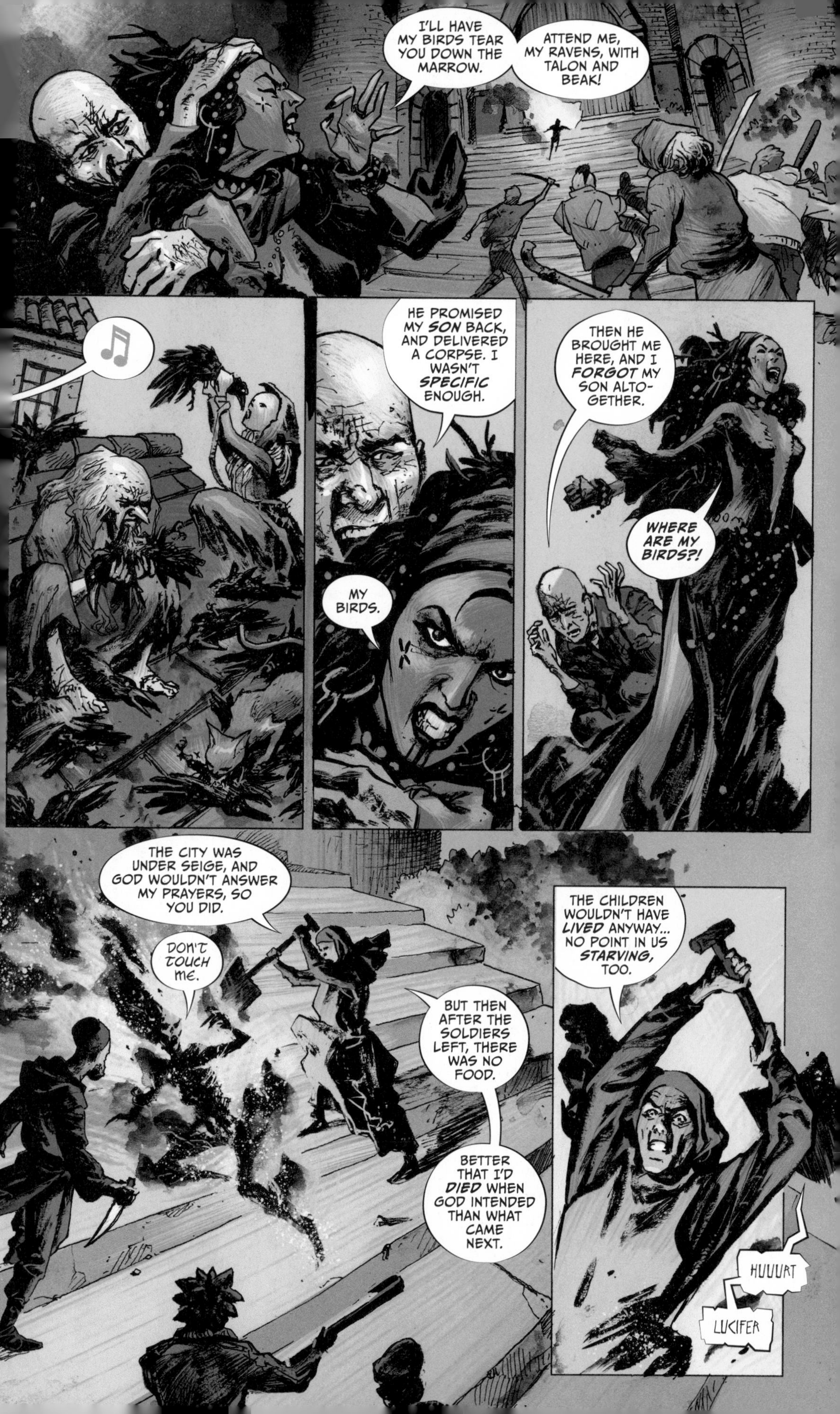
I'LL HAVE MY BIRDS TEAR YOU DOWN THE MARROW.
ATTEND ME, MY RAVENS, WITH TALON AND BEAK!
♫
HE PROMISED MY SON BACK, AND DELIVERED A CORPSE. I WASN'T SPECIFIC ENOUGH.
MY BIRDS.
THEN HE BROUGHT ME HERE, AND I FORGOT MY SON ALTOGETHER.
WHERE ARE MY BIRDS?!
THE CITY WAS UNDER SEIGE, AND GOD WOULDN'T ANSWER MY PRAYERS, SO YOU DID.
DON'T TOUCH ME.
BUT THEN AFTER THE SOLDIERS LEFT, THERE WAS NO FOOD.
BETTER THAT I'D DIED WHEN GOD INTENDED THAN WHAT CAME NEXT.
THE CHILDREN WOULDN'T HAVE LIVED ANYWAY... NO POINT IN US STARVING, TOO.
HUUURT
LUCIFER

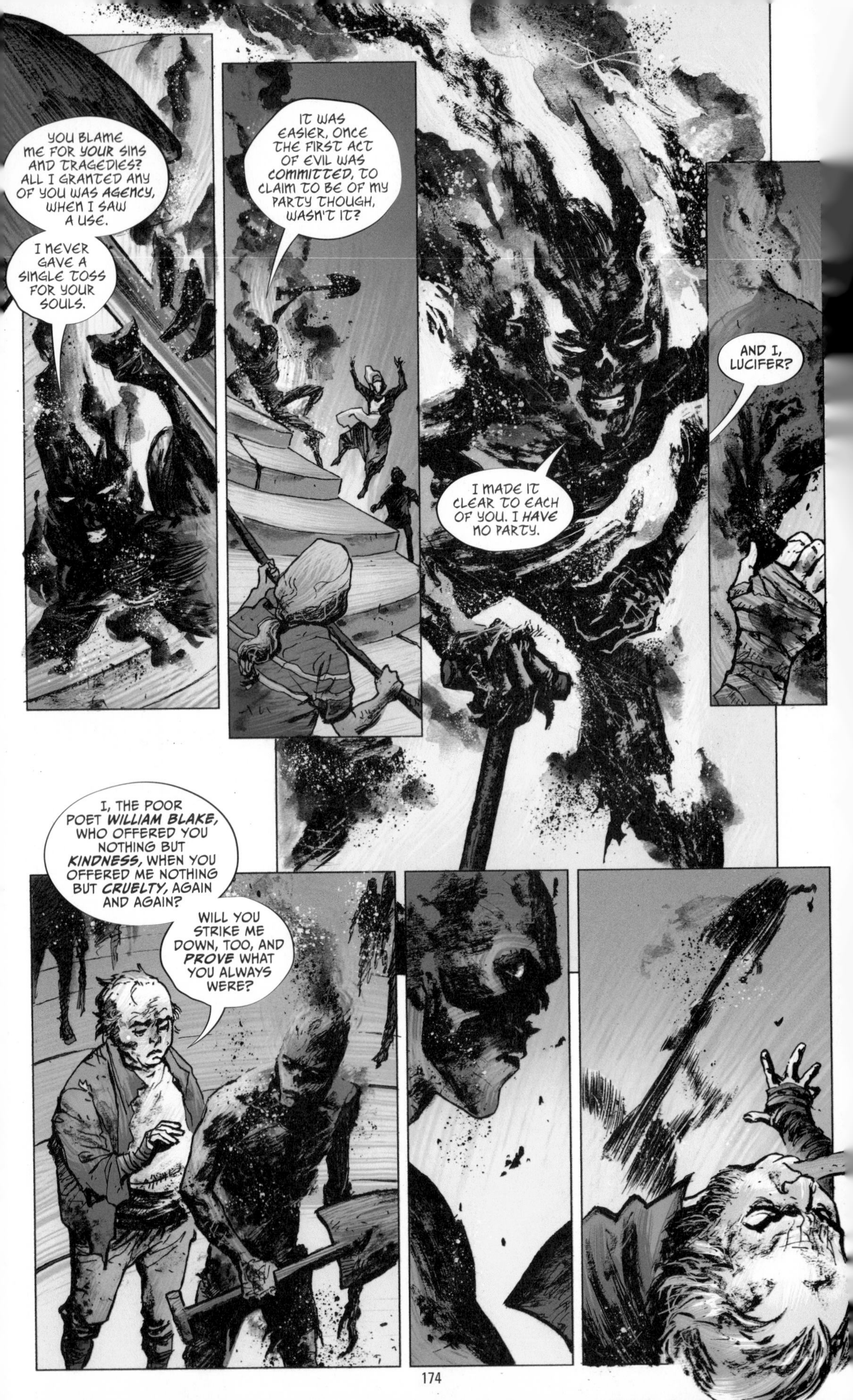
YOU BLAME ME FOR YOUR SINS AND TRAGEDIES? ALL I GRANTED ANY OF YOU WAS AGENCY, WHEN I SAW A USE.
I NEVER GAVE A SINGLE TOSS FOR YOUR SOULS.
IT WAS EASIER, ONCE THE FIRST ACT OF EVIL WAS COMMITTED, TO CLAIM TO BE OF MY PARTY THOUGH, WASN'T IT?
I MADE IT CLEAR TO EACH OF YOU. I HAVE NO PARTY.
AND I, LUCIFER?
I, THE POOR POET WILLIAM BLAKE, WHO OFFERED YOU NOTHING BUT KINDNESS, WHEN YOU OFFERED ME NOTHING BUT CRUELTY, AGAIN AND AGAIN?
WILL YOU STRIKE ME DOWN, TOO, AND PROVE WHAT YOU ALWAYS WERE?

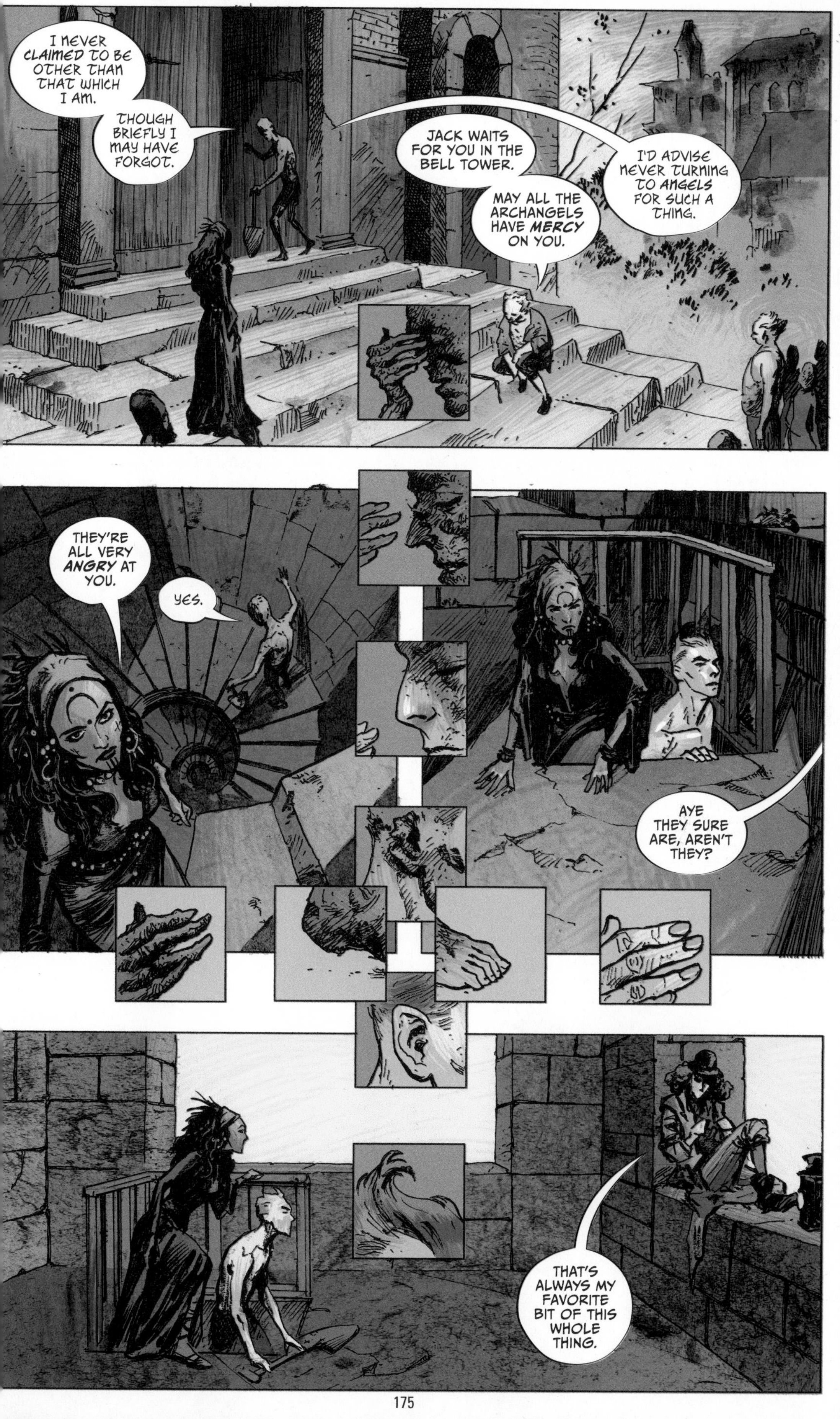
I NEVER CLAIMED TO BE OTHER THAN THAT WHICH I AM.
THOUGH BRIEFLY I MAY HAVE FORGOT.
JACK WAITS FOR YOU IN THE BELL TOWER.
I'D ADVISE NEVER TURNING TO ANGELS FOR SUCH A THING.
MAY ALL THE ARCHANGELS HAVE MERCY ON YOU.
THEY'RE ALL VERY ANGRY AT YOU.
YES.
AYE THEY SURE ARE, AREN'T THEY?
THAT'S ALWAYS MY FAVORITE BIT OF THIS WHOLE THING.

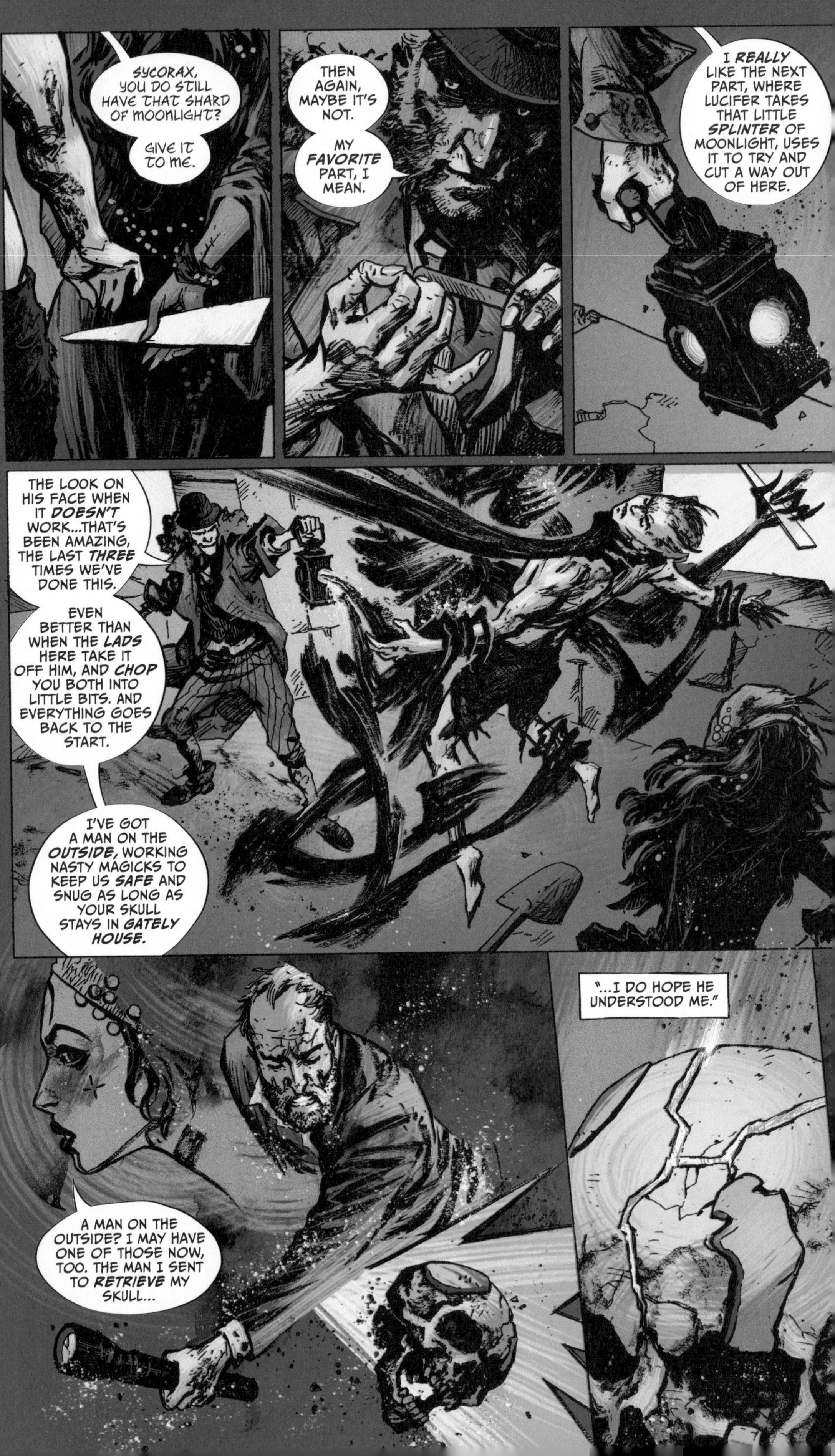
SYCORAX, YOU DO STILL HAVE THAT SHARD OF MOONLIGHT?
GIVE IT TO ME.
THEN AGAIN, MAYBE IT'S NOT.
MY FAVORITE PART, I MEAN.
I REALLY LIKE THE NEXT PART, WHERE LUCIFER TAKES THAT LITTLE SPLINTER OF MOONLIGHT, USES IT TO TRY AND CUT A WAY OUT OF HERE.
THE LOOK ON HIS FACE WHEN IT DOESN'T WORK...THAT'S BEEN AMAZING, THE LAST THREE TIMES WE'VE DONE THIS.
EVEN BETTER THAN WHEN THE LADS HERE TAKE IT OFF HIM, AND CHOP YOU BOTH INTO LITTLE BITS. AND EVERYTHING GOES BACK TO THE START.
I'VE GOT A MAN ON THE OUTSIDE, WORKING NASTY MAGICKS TO KEEP US SAFE AND SNUG AS LONG AS YOUR SKULL STAYS IN GATELY HOUSE.
A MAN ON THE OUTSIDE? I MAY HAVE ONE OF THOSE NOW, TOO. THE MAN I SENT TO RETRIEVE MY SKULL...
"...I DO HOPE HE UNDERSTOOD ME."

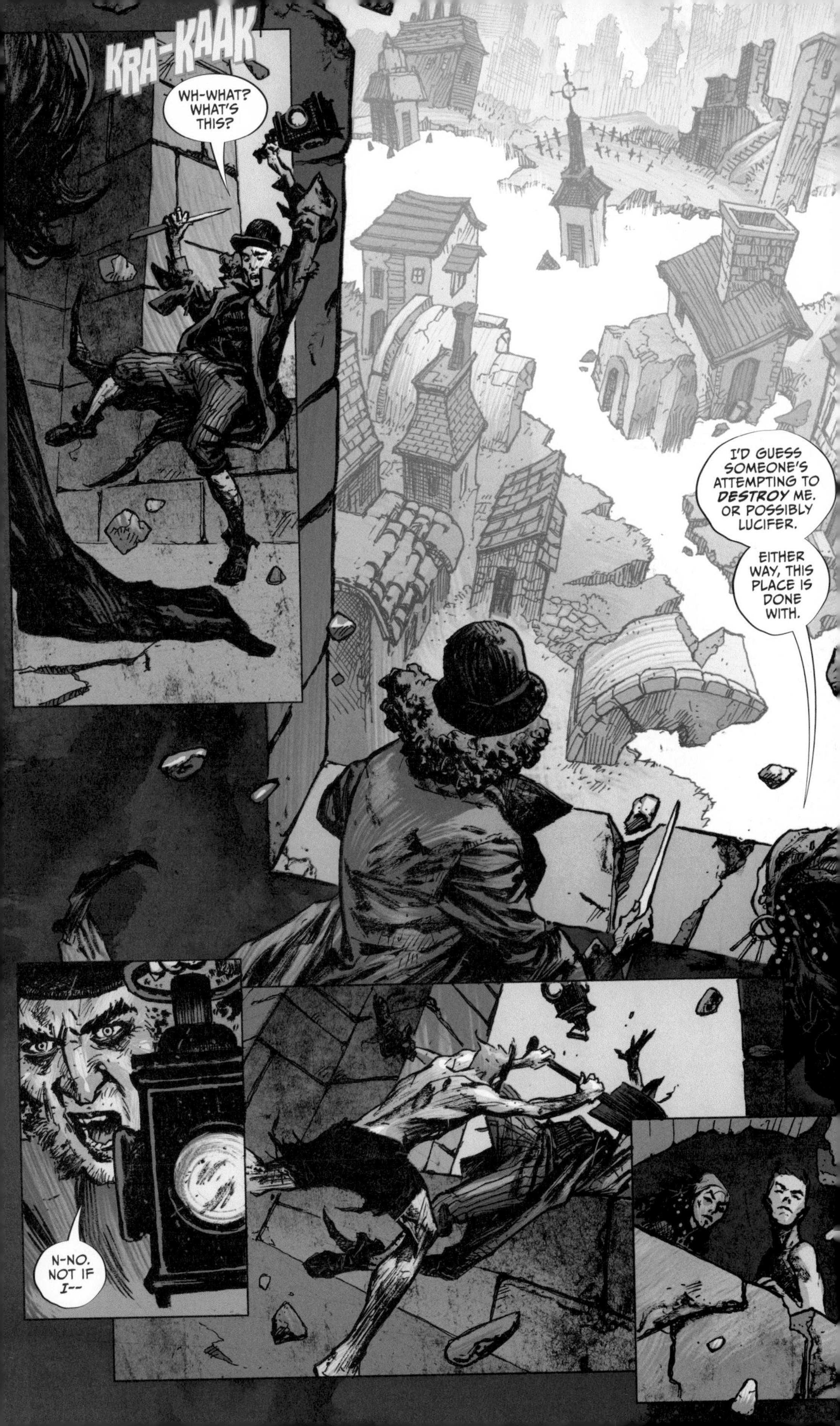
KRA-KAAK
WH-WHAT? WHAT'S THIS?
I'D GUESS SOMEONE'S ATTEMPTING TO *DESTROY* ME. OR POSSIBLY LUCIFER.
EITHER WAY, THIS PLACE IS DONE WITH.
N-NO. NOT IF *I*--

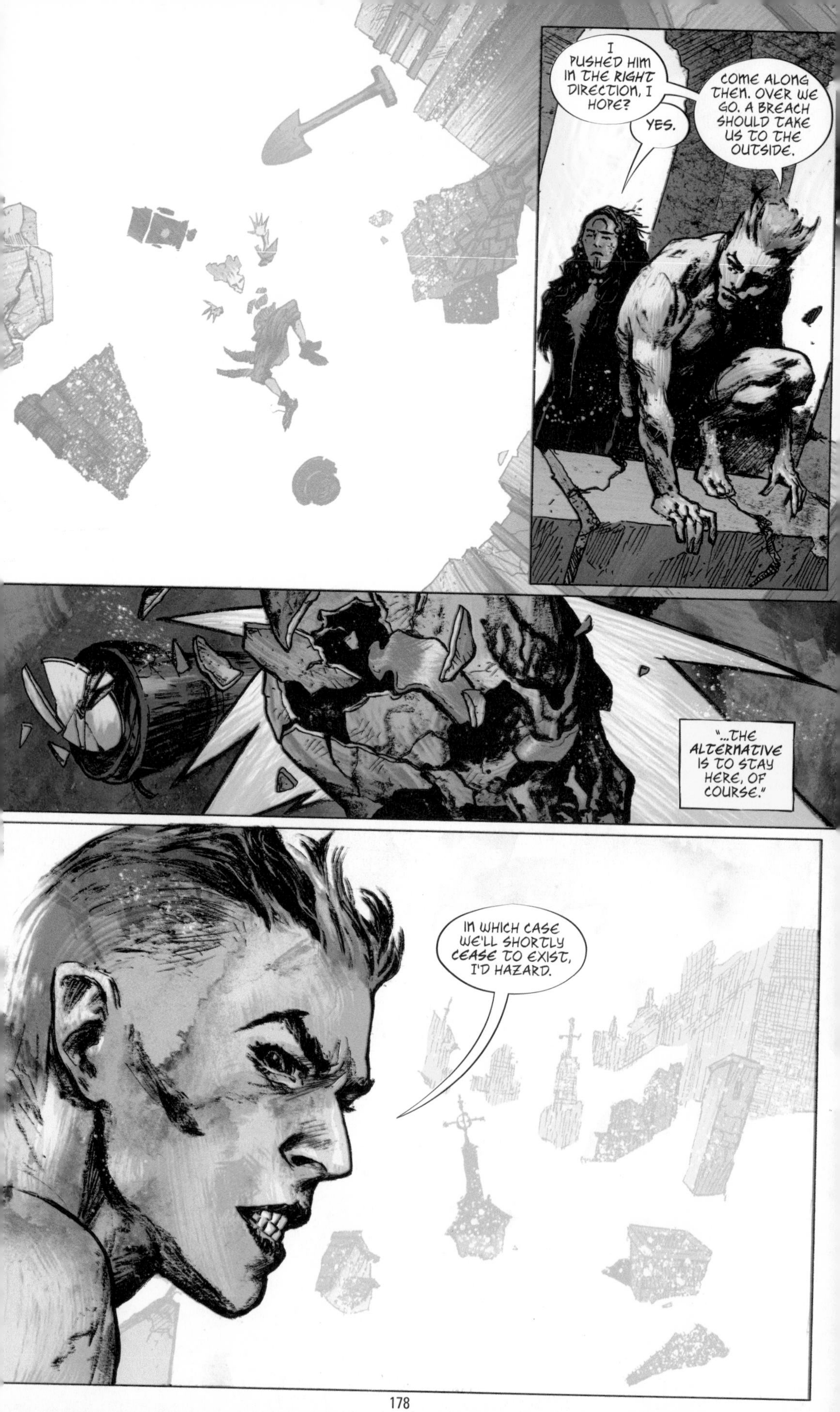
I PUSHED HIM IN THE RIGHT DIRECTION, I HOPE?
YES.
COME ALONG THEN. OVER WE GO. A BREACH SHOULD TAKE US TO THE OUTSIDE.
"...THE ALTERNATIVE IS TO STAY HERE, OF COURSE."
IN WHICH CASE WE'LL SHORTLY CEASE TO EXIST, I'D HAZARD.

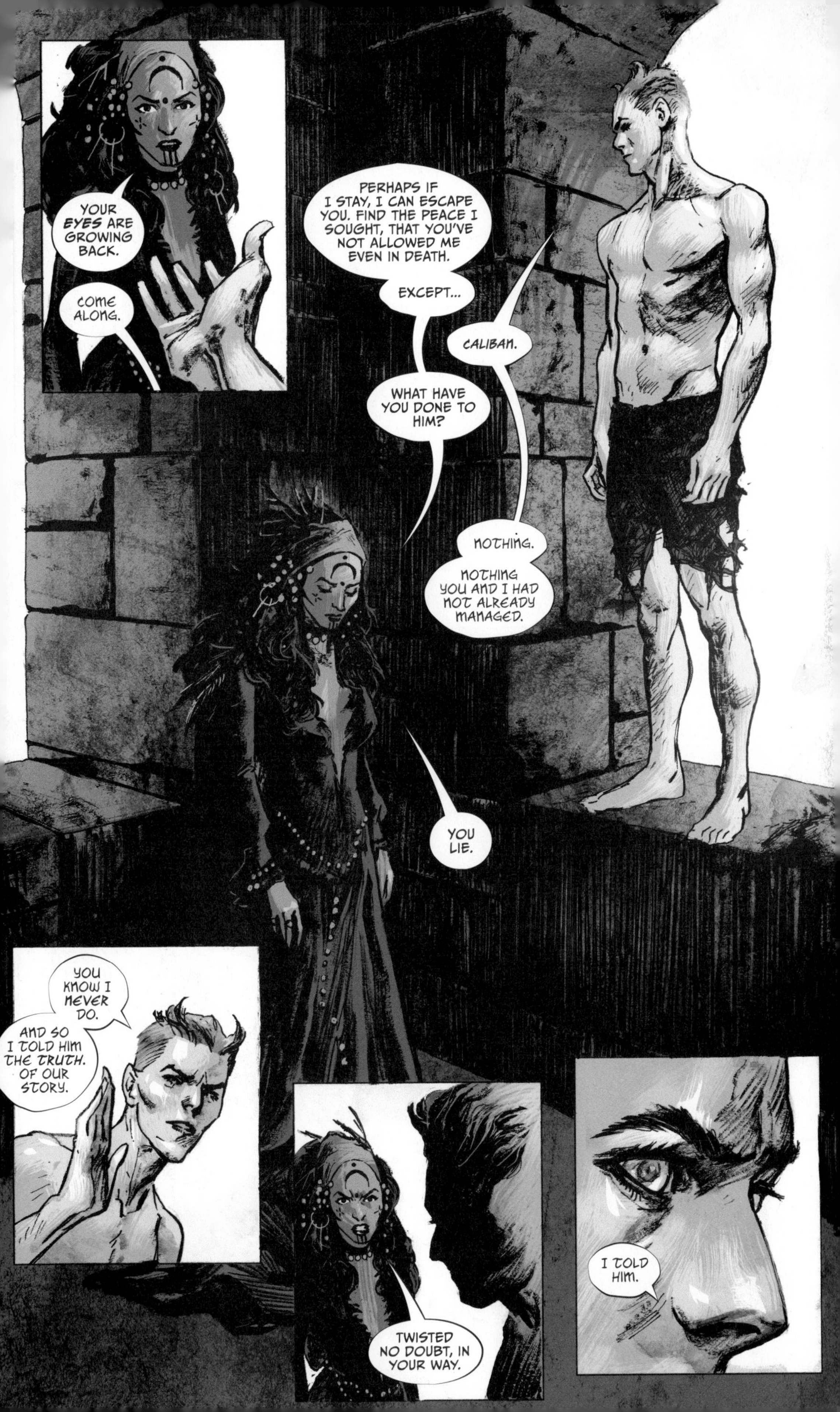

YOUR EYES ARE GROWING BACK.
COME ALONG.
PERHAPS IF I STAY, I CAN ESCAPE YOU. FIND THE PEACE I SOUGHT, THAT YOU'VE NOT ALLOWED ME EVEN IN DEATH.
EXCEPT...
CALIBAN.
WHAT HAVE YOU DONE TO HIM?
NOTHING.
NOTHING YOU AND I HAD NOT ALREADY MANAGED.
YOU LIE.
YOU KNOW I NEVER DO.
AND SO I TOLD HIM THE TRUTH. OF OUR STORY.
TWISTED NO DOUBT, IN YOUR WAY.
I TOLD HIM.

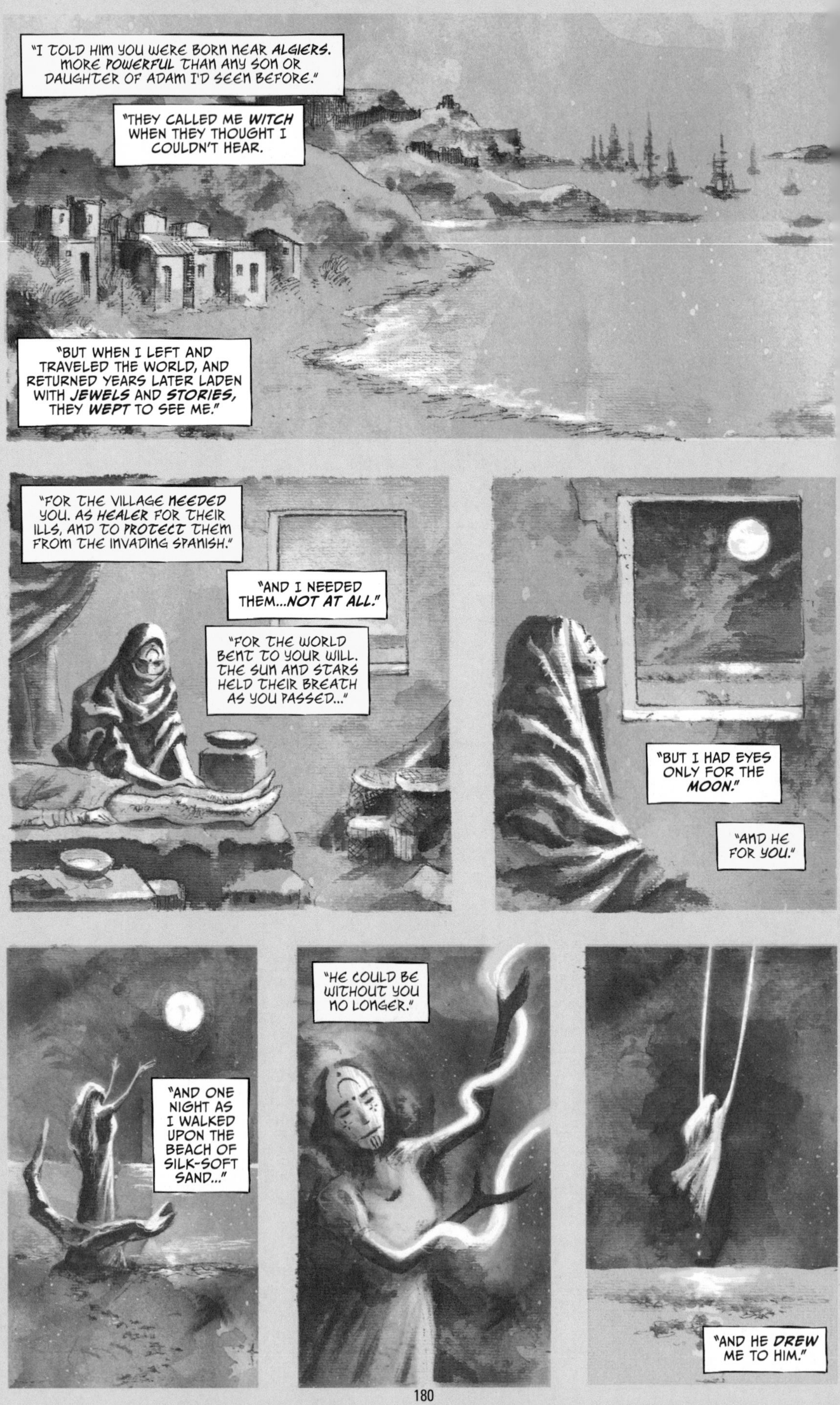
"I TOLD HIM YOU WERE BORN NEAR ALGIERS. MORE POWERFUL THAN ANY SON OR DAUGHTER OF ADAM I'D SEEN BEFORE."
"THEY CALLED ME WITCH WHEN THEY THOUGHT I COULDN'T HEAR.
"BUT WHEN I LEFT AND TRAVELED THE WORLD, AND RETURNED YEARS LATER LADEN WITH JEWELS AND STORIES, THEY WEPT TO SEE ME."
"FOR THE VILLAGE NEEDED YOU. AS HEALER FOR THEIR ILLS, AND TO PROTECT THEM FROM THE INVADING SPANISH."
"AND I NEEDED THEM...NOT AT ALL."
"FOR THE WORLD BENT TO YOUR WILL. THE SUN AND STARS HELD THEIR BREATH AS YOU PASSED..."
"BUT I HAD EYES ONLY FOR THE MOON."
"AND HE FOR YOU."
"AND ONE NIGHT AS I WALKED UPON THE BEACH OF SILK-SOFT SAND..."
"HE COULD BE WITHOUT YOU NO LONGER."
"AND HE DREW ME TO HIM."

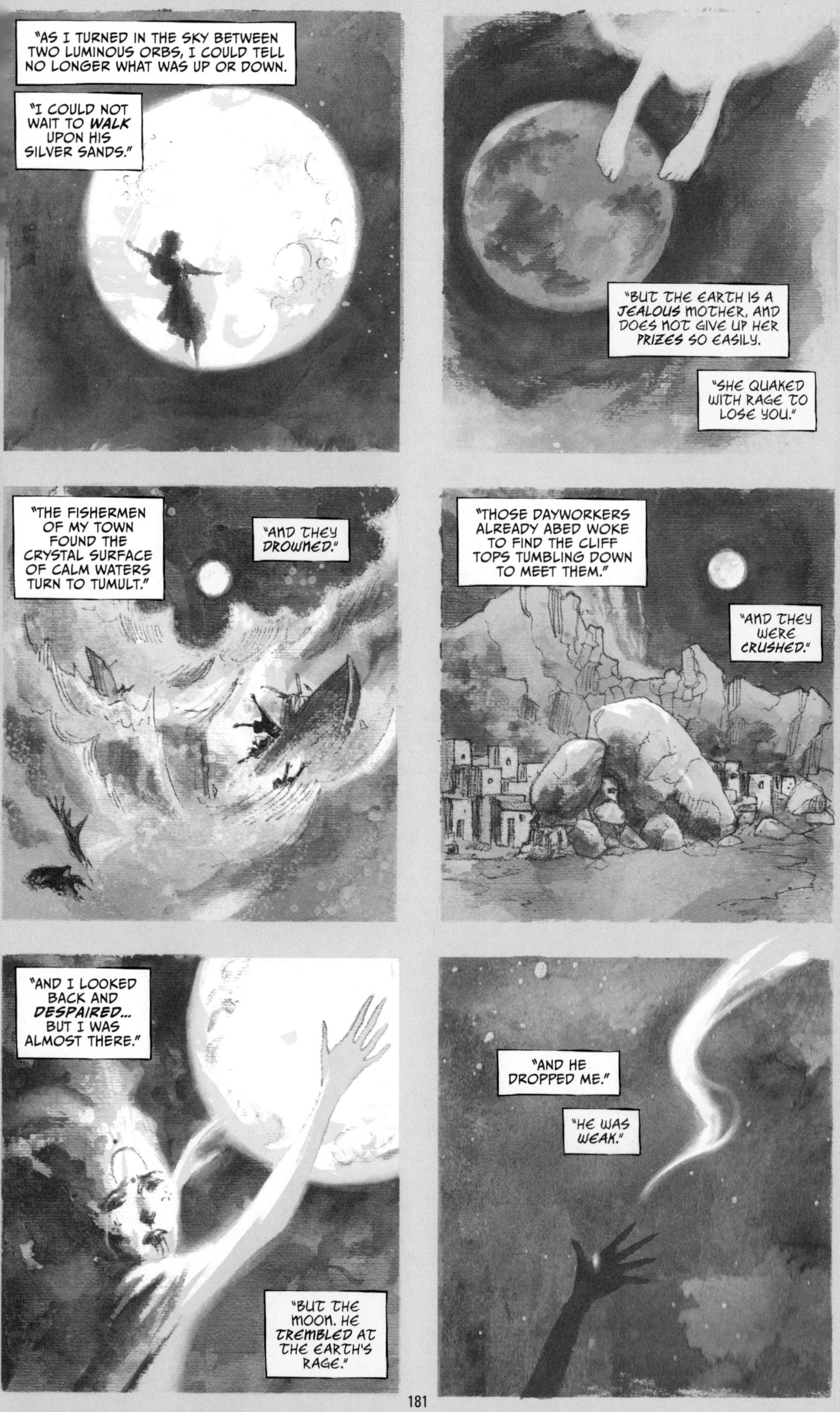
"AS I TURNED IN THE SKY BETWEEN TWO LUMINOUS ORBS, I COULD TELL NO LONGER WHAT WAS UP OR DOWN.
"I COULD NOT WAIT TO WALK UPON HIS SILVER SANDS."
"BUT THE EARTH IS A JEALOUS MOTHER, AND DOES NOT GIVE UP HER PRIZES SO EASILY.
"SHE QUAKED WITH RAGE TO LOSE YOU."
"THE FISHERMEN OF MY TOWN FOUND THE CRYSTAL SURFACE OF CALM WATERS TURN TO TUMULT."
"AND THEY DROWNED."
"THOSE DAYWORKERS ALREADY ABED WOKE TO FIND THE CLIFF TOPS TUMBLING DOWN TO MEET THEM."
"AND THEY WERE CRUSHED."
"AND I LOOKED BACK AND DESPAIRED... BUT I WAS ALMOST THERE."
"BUT THE MOON. HE TREMBLED AT THE EARTH'S RAGE."
"AND HE DROPPED ME."
"HE WAS WEAK."

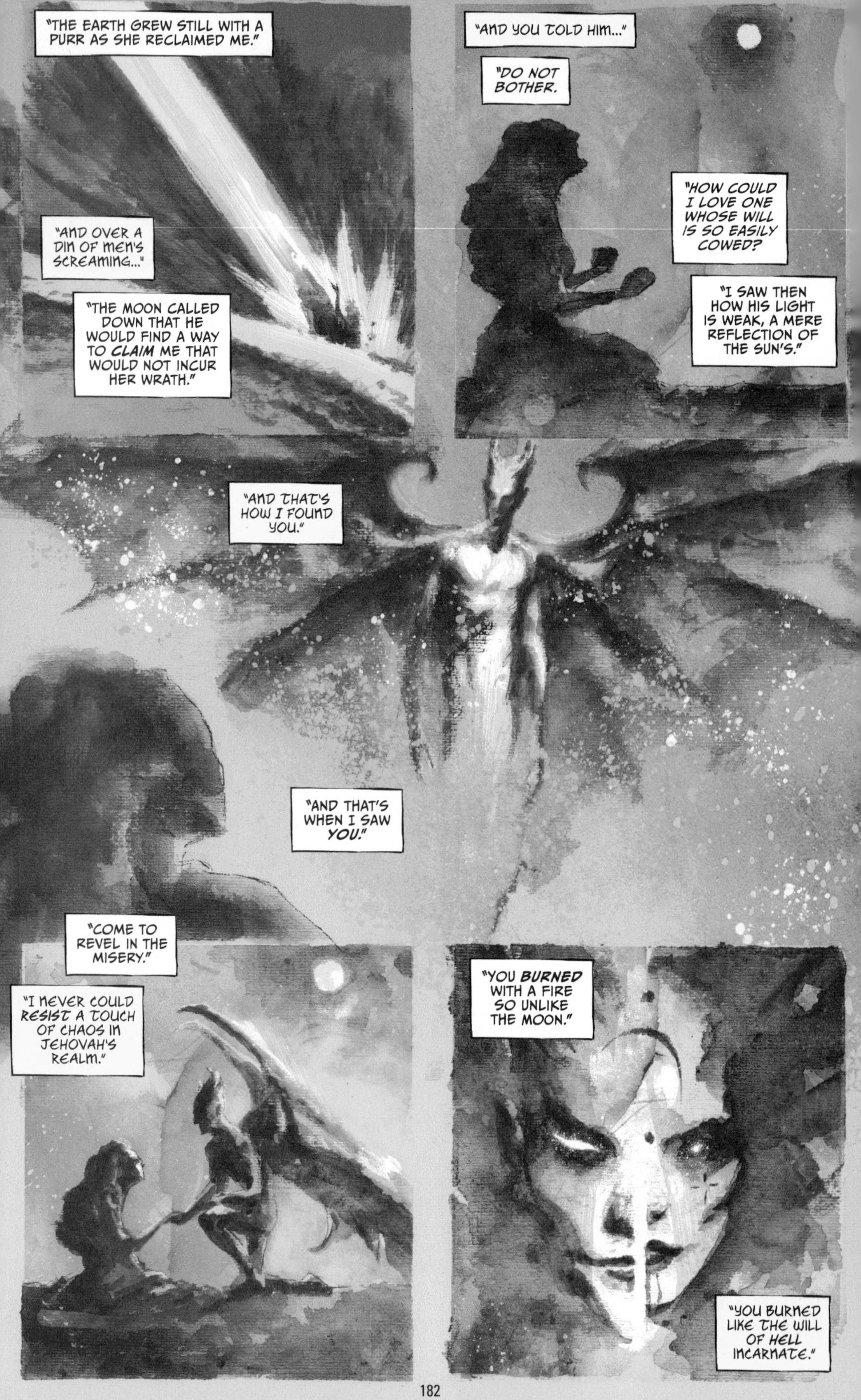
"THE EARTH GREW STILL WITH A PURR AS SHE RECLAIMED ME."
"AND OVER A DIN OF MEN'S SCREAMING..."
"THE MOON CALLED DOWN THAT HE WOULD FIND A WAY TO CLAIM ME THAT WOULD NOT INCUR HER WRATH."
"AND YOU TOLD HIM..."
"DO NOT BOTHER.
"HOW COULD I LOVE ONE WHOSE WILL IS SO EASILY COWED?
"I SAW THEN HOW HIS LIGHT IS WEAK, A MERE REFLECTION OF THE SUN'S."
"AND THAT'S HOW I FOUND YOU."
"AND THAT'S WHEN I SAW YOU."
"COME TO REVEL IN THE MISERY."
"I NEVER COULD RESIST A TOUCH OF CHAOS IN JEHOVAH'S REALM."
"YOU BURNED WITH A FIRE SO UNLIKE THE MOON."
"YOU BURNED LIKE THE WILL OF HELL INCARNATE."

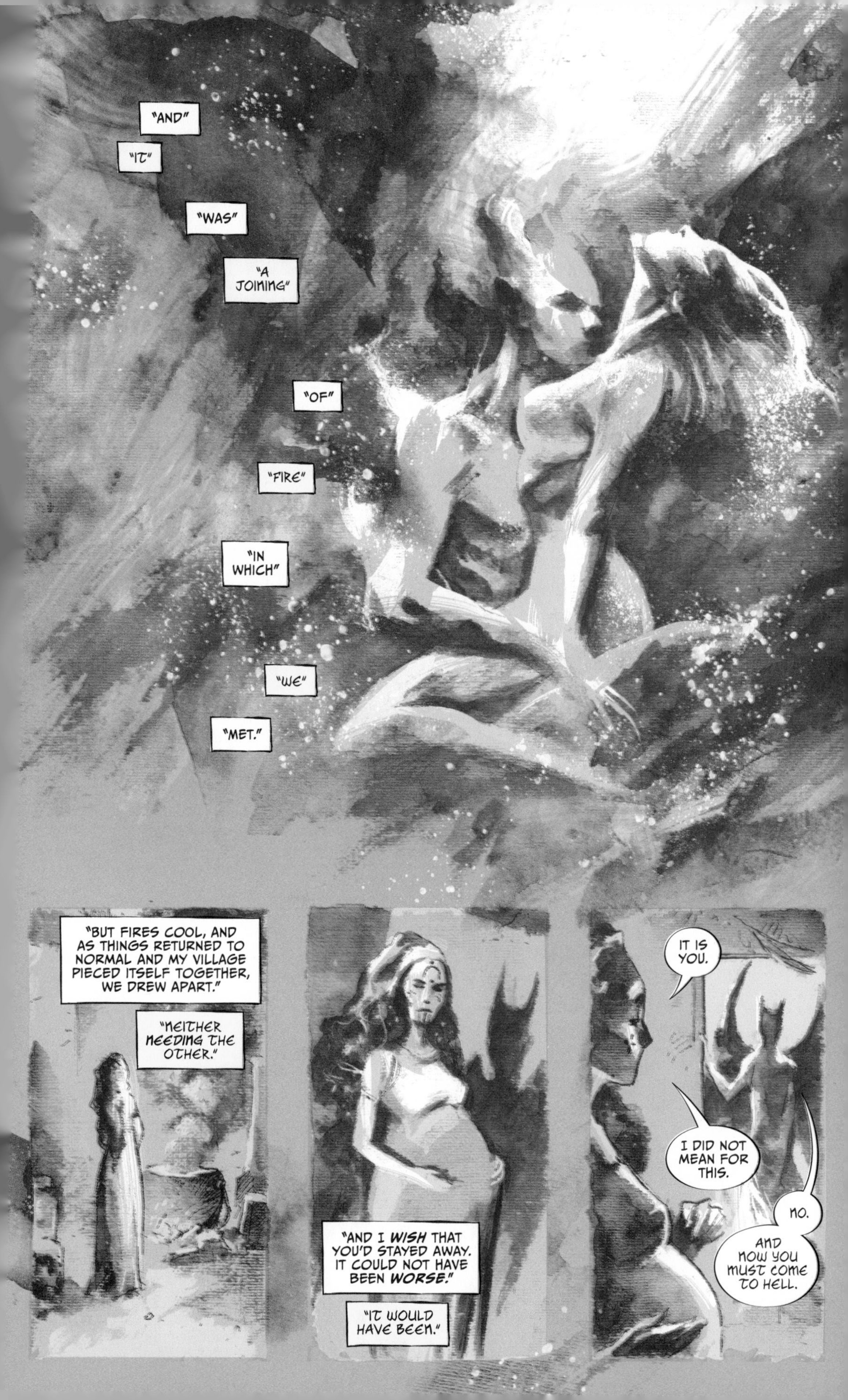
"AND"
"IT"
"WAS"
"A JOINING"
"OF"
"FIRE"
"IN WHICH"
"WE"
"MET."
"BUT FIRES COOL, AND AS THINGS RETURNED TO NORMAL AND MY VILLAGE PIECED ITSELF TOGETHER, WE DREW APART."
"NEITHER NEEDING THE OTHER."
"AND I WISH THAT YOU'D STAYED AWAY. IT COULD NOT HAVE BEEN WORSE."
"IT WOULD HAVE BEEN."
IT IS YOU.
I DID NOT MEAN FOR THIS.
NO.
AND NOW YOU MUST COME TO HELL.

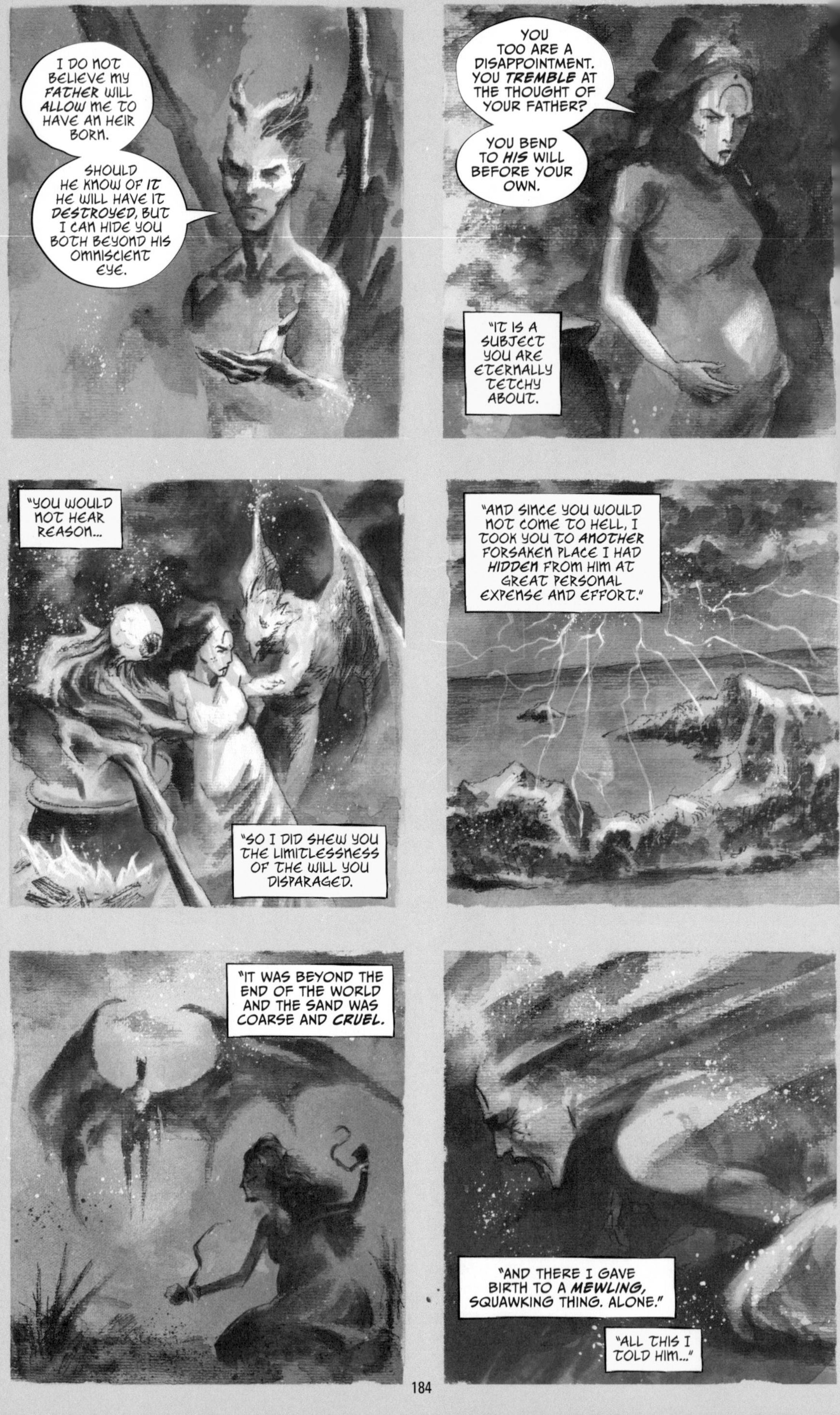
I DO NOT BELIEVE MY FATHER WILL ALLOW ME TO HAVE AN HEIR BORN.
SHOULD HE KNOW OF IT HE WILL HAVE IT DESTROYED, BUT I CAN HIDE YOU BOTH BEYOND HIS OMNISCIENT EYE.
YOU TOO ARE A DISAPPOINTMENT. YOU TREMBLE AT THE THOUGHT OF YOUR FATHER?
YOU BEND TO HIS WILL BEFORE YOUR OWN.
"IT IS A SUBJECT YOU ARE ETERNALLY TETCHY ABOUT.
"YOU WOULD NOT HEAR REASON...
"SO I DID SHEW YOU THE LIMITLESSNESS OF THE WILL YOU DISPARAGED.
"AND SINCE YOU WOULD NOT COME TO HELL, I TOOK YOU TO ANOTHER FORSAKEN PLACE I HAD HIDDEN FROM HIM AT GREAT PERSONAL EXPENSE AND EFFORT."
"IT WAS BEYOND THE END OF THE WORLD AND THE SAND WAS COARSE AND CRUEL.
"AND THERE I GAVE BIRTH TO A MEWLING, SQUAWKING THING. ALONE."
"ALL THIS I TOLD HIM..."

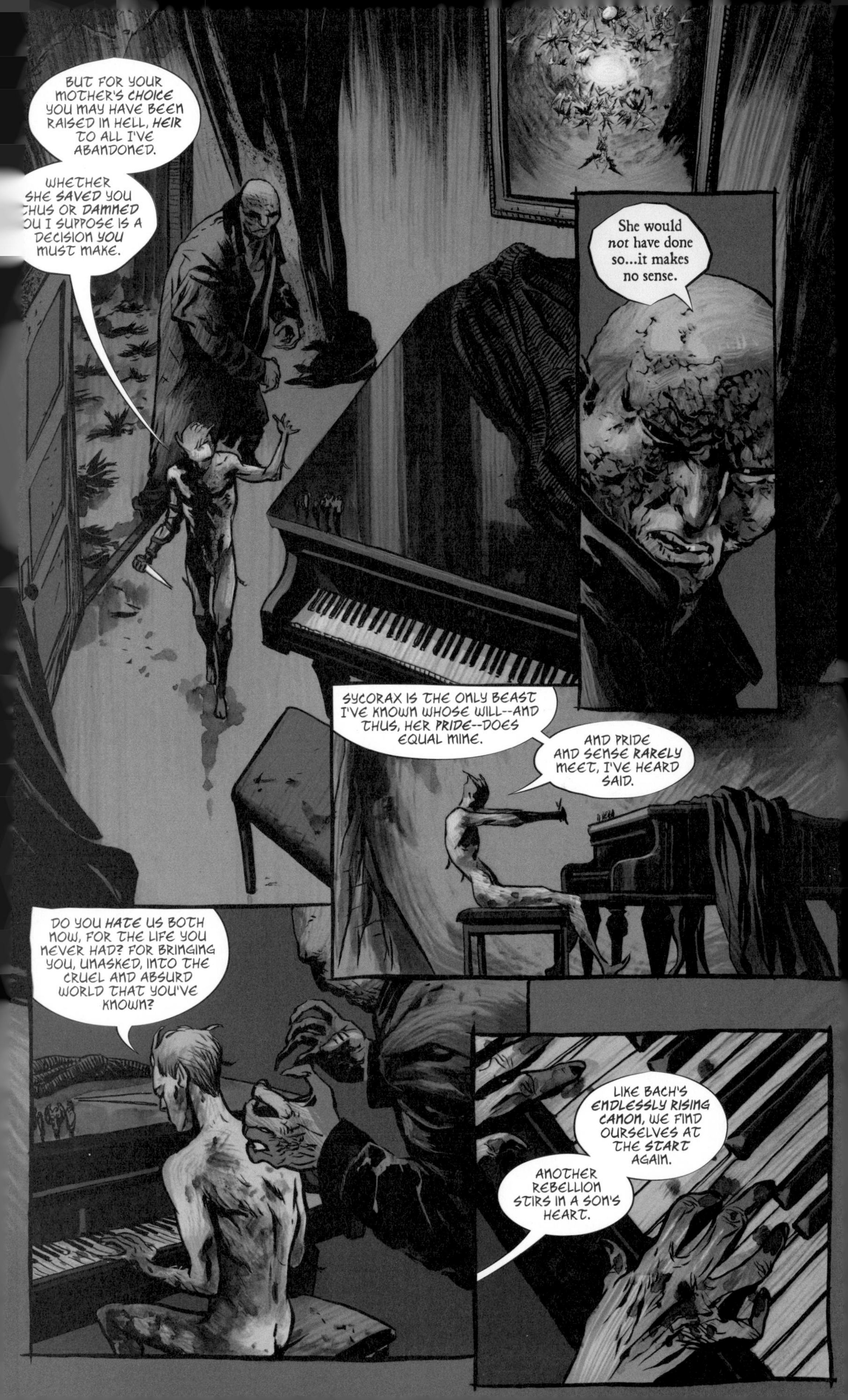
BUT FOR YOUR MOTHER'S CHOICE YOU MAY HAVE BEEN RAISED IN HELL, HEIR TO ALL I'VE ABANDONED.
WHETHER SHE SAVED YOU THUS OR DAMNED YOU I SUPPOSE IS A DECISION YOU MUST MAKE.
She would not have done so...it makes no sense.
SYCORAX IS THE ONLY BEAST I'VE KNOWN WHOSE WILL--AND THUS, HER PRIDE--DOES EQUAL MINE.
AND PRIDE AND SENSE RARELY MEET, I'VE HEARD SAID.
DO YOU HATE US BOTH NOW, FOR THE LIFE YOU NEVER HAD? FOR BRINGING YOU, UNASKED, INTO THE CRUEL AND ABSURD WORLD THAT YOU'VE KNOWN?
LIKE BACH'S ENDLESSLY RISING CANON, WE FIND OURSELVES AT THE START AGAIN.
ANOTHER REBELLION STIRS IN A SON'S HEART.

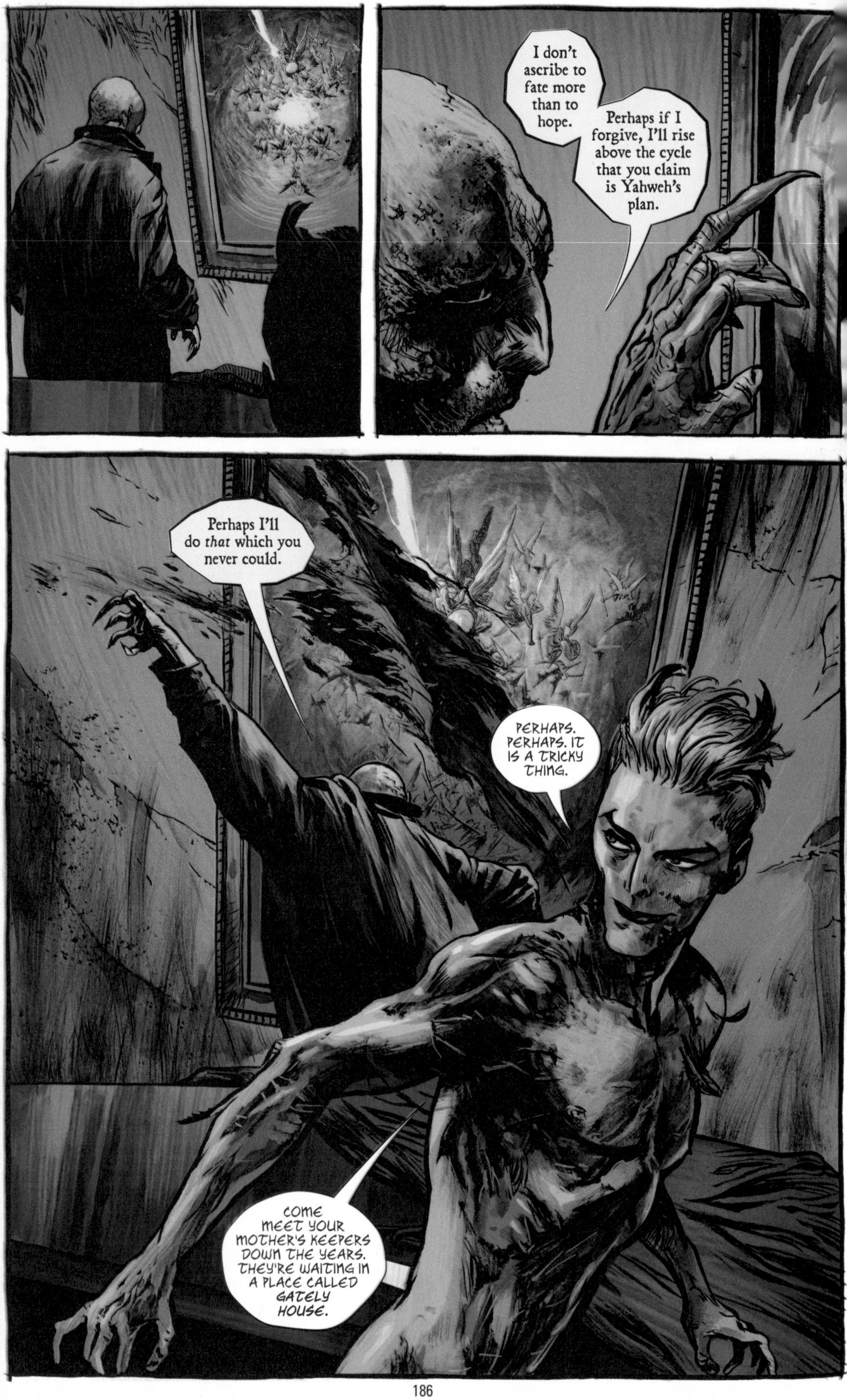
I don't ascribe to fate more than to hope.
Perhaps if I forgive, I'll rise above the cycle that you claim is Yahweh's plan.
Perhaps I'll do *that* which you never could.
PERHAPS. PERHAPS. IT IS A TRICKY THING.
COME MEET YOUR MOTHER'S KEEPERS DOWN THE YEARS. THEY'RE WAITING IN A PLACE CALLED GATELY HOUSE.

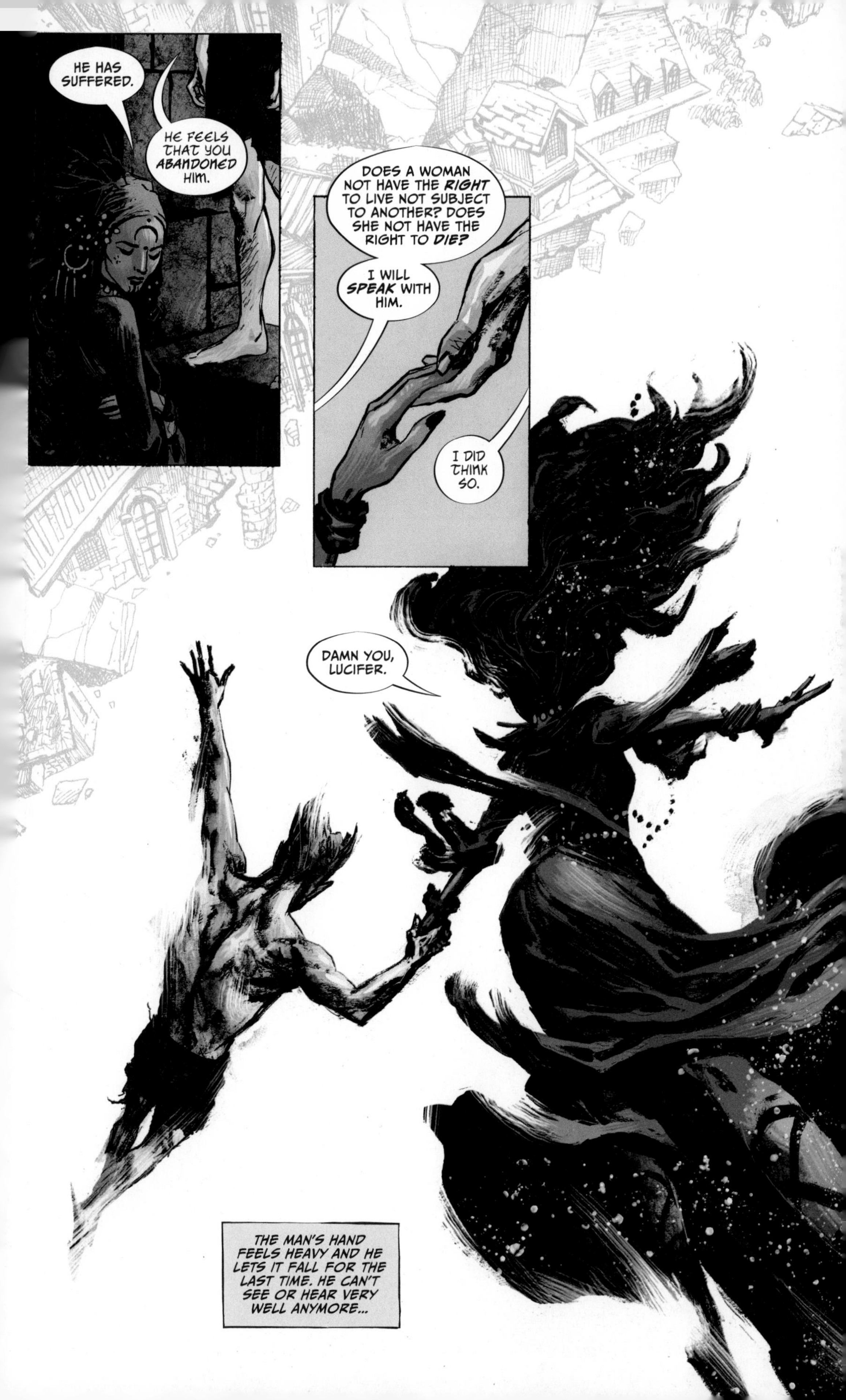
HE HAS SUFFERED.
HE FEELS THAT YOU ABANDONED HIM.
DOES A WOMAN NOT HAVE THE RIGHT TO LIVE NOT SUBJECT TO ANOTHER? DOES SHE NOT HAVE THE RIGHT TO DIE?
I WILL SPEAK WITH HIM.
I DID THINK SO.
DAMN YOU, LUCIFER.
THE MAN'S HAND FEELS HEAVY AND HE LETS IT FALL FOR THE LAST TIME. HE CAN'T SEE OR HEAR VERY WELL ANYMORE...

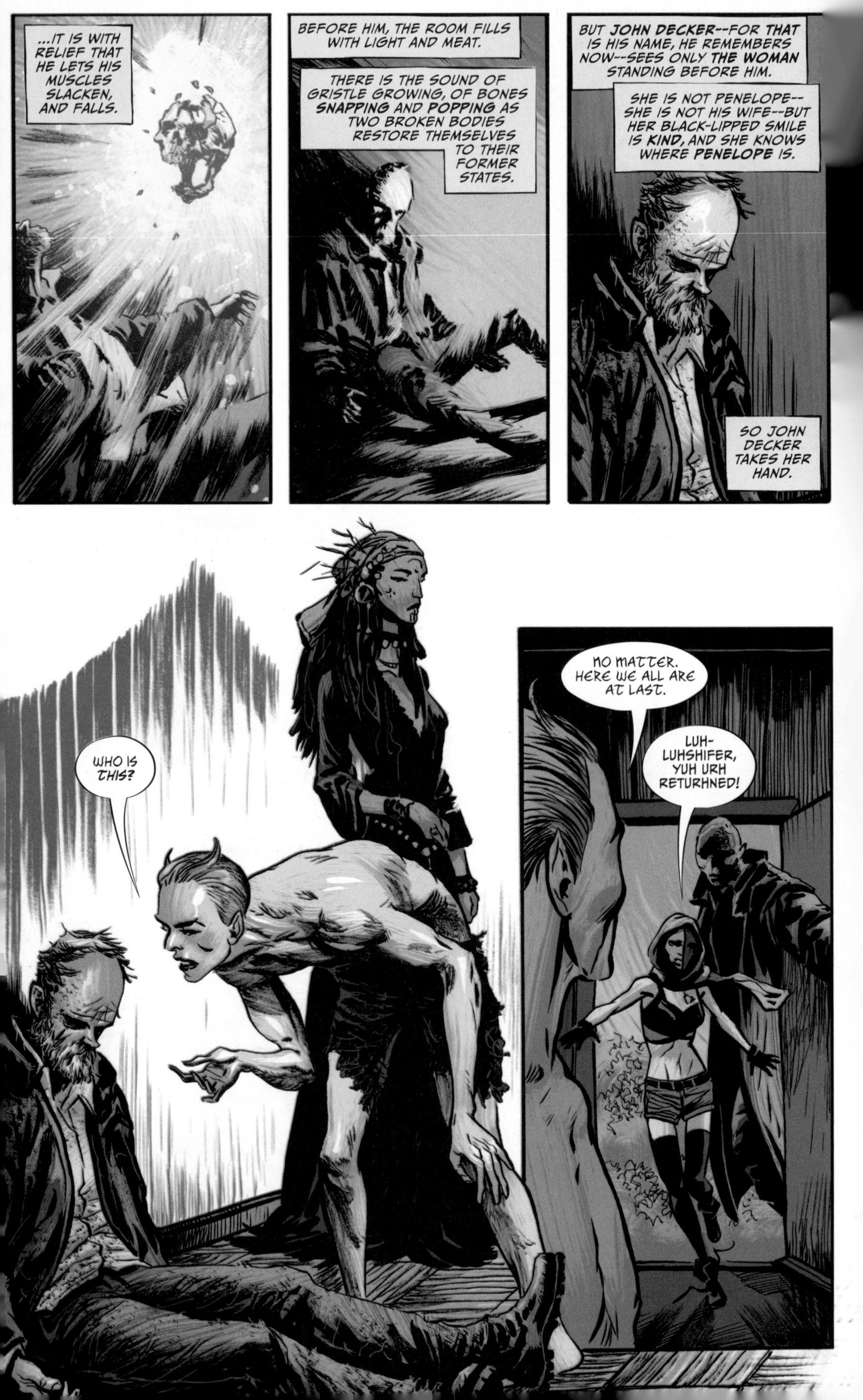
...IT IS WITH RELIEF THAT HE LETS HIS MUSCLES SLACKEN, AND FALLS.
BEFORE HIM, THE ROOM FILLS WITH LIGHT AND MEAT.
THERE IS THE SOUND OF GRISTLE GROWING, OF BONES SNAPPING AND POPPING AS TWO BROKEN BODIES RESTORE THEMSELVES TO THEIR FORMER STATES.
BUT JOHN DECKER--FOR THAT IS HIS NAME, HE REMEMBERS NOW--SEES ONLY THE WOMAN STANDING BEFORE HIM.
SHE IS NOT PENELOPE-- SHE IS NOT HIS WIFE--BUT HER BLACK-LIPPED SMILE IS KIND, AND SHE KNOWS WHERE PENELOPE IS.
SO JOHN DECKER TAKES HER HAND.
WHO IS THIS?
NO MATTER. HERE WE ALL ARE AT LAST.
LUH-LUHSHIFER, YUH URH RETURHNED!

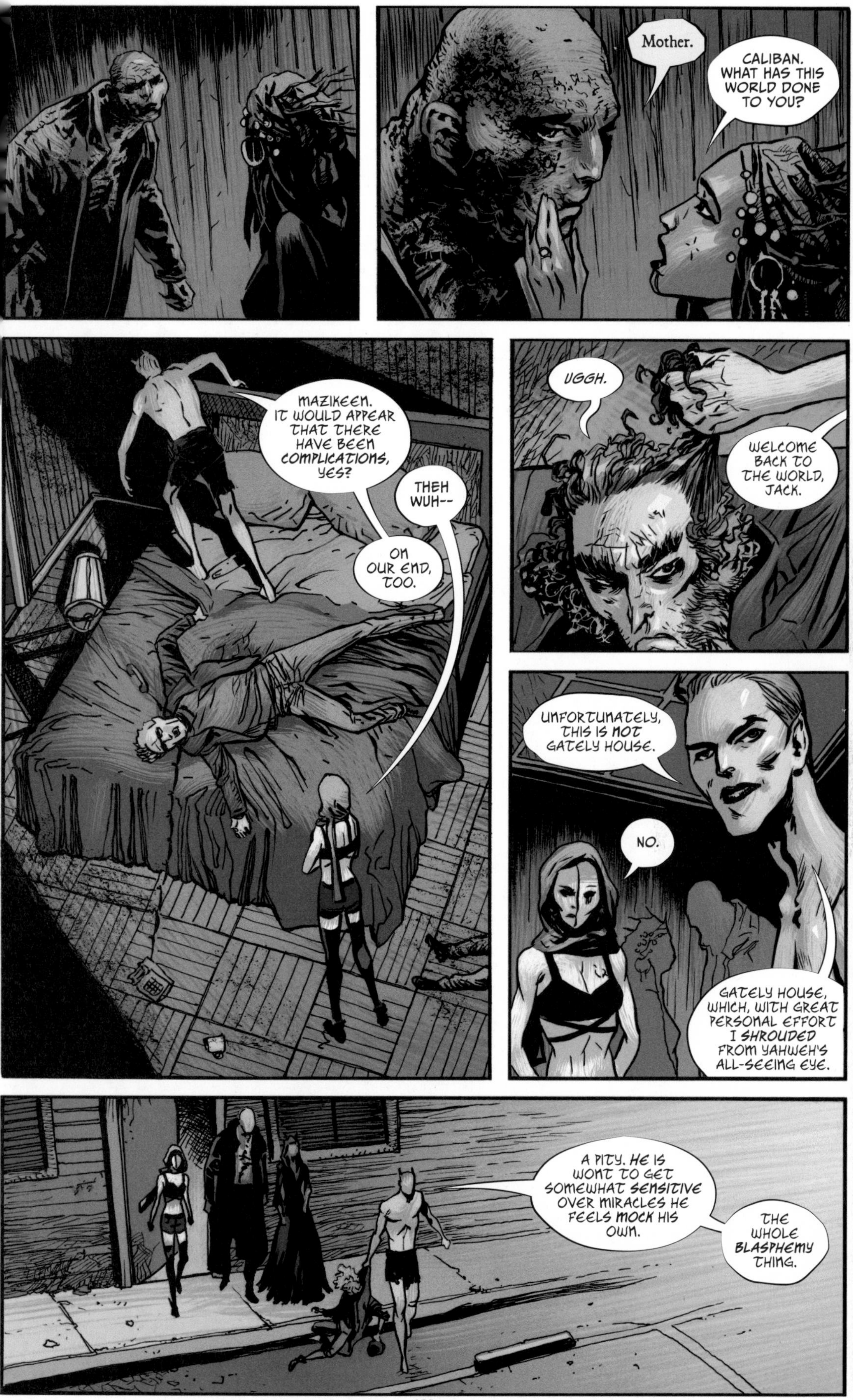
Mother.
CALIBAN. WHAT HAS THIS WORLD DONE TO YOU?
MAZIKEEN. IT WOULD APPEAR THAT THERE HAVE BEEN COMPLICATIONS, YES?
THEN WUH--
ON OUR END, TOO.
UGGH.
WELCOME BACK TO THE WORLD, JACK.
UNFORTUNATELY, THIS IS NOT GATELY HOUSE.
NO.
GATELY HOUSE, WHICH, WITH GREAT PERSONAL EFFORT I SHROUDED FROM YAHWEH'S ALL-SEEING EYE.
A PITY. HE IS WONT TO GET SOMEWHAT SENSITIVE OVER MIRACLES HE FEELS MOCK HIS OWN.
THE WHOLE BLASPHEMY THING.

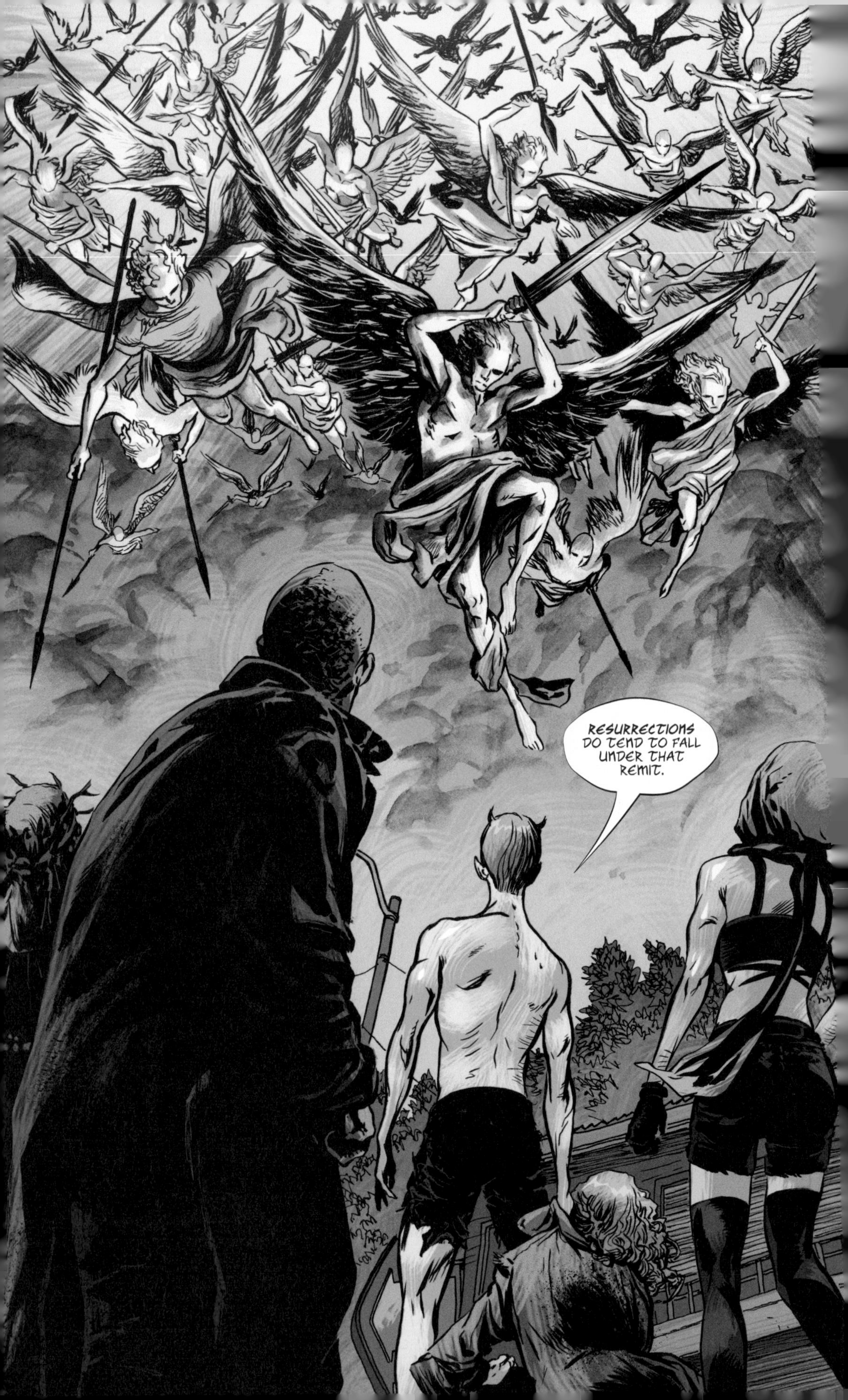
RESURRECTIONS DO TEND TO FALL UNDER THAT REMIT.

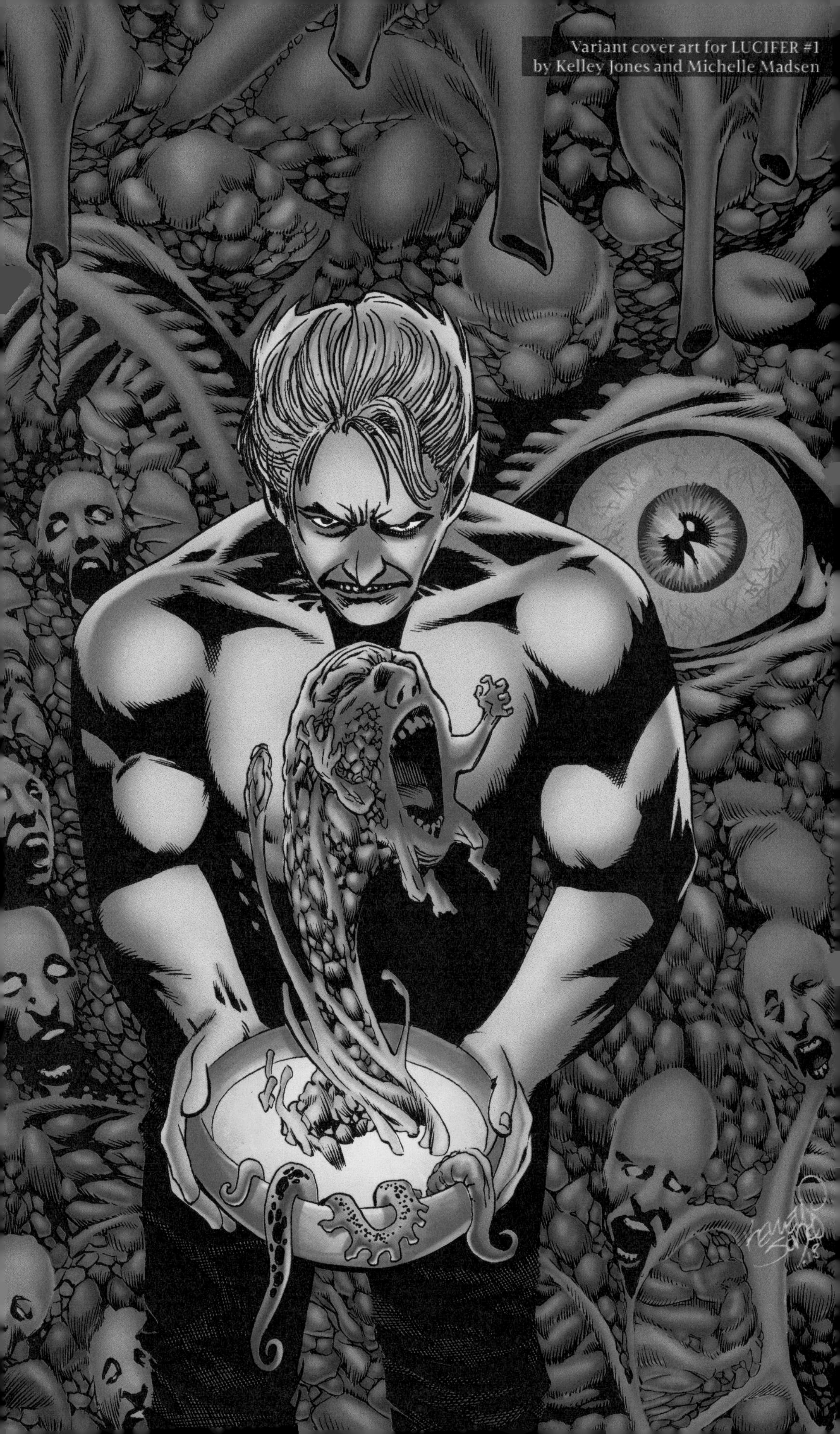
Variant cover art for LUCIFER #1
by Kelley Jones and Michelle Madsen

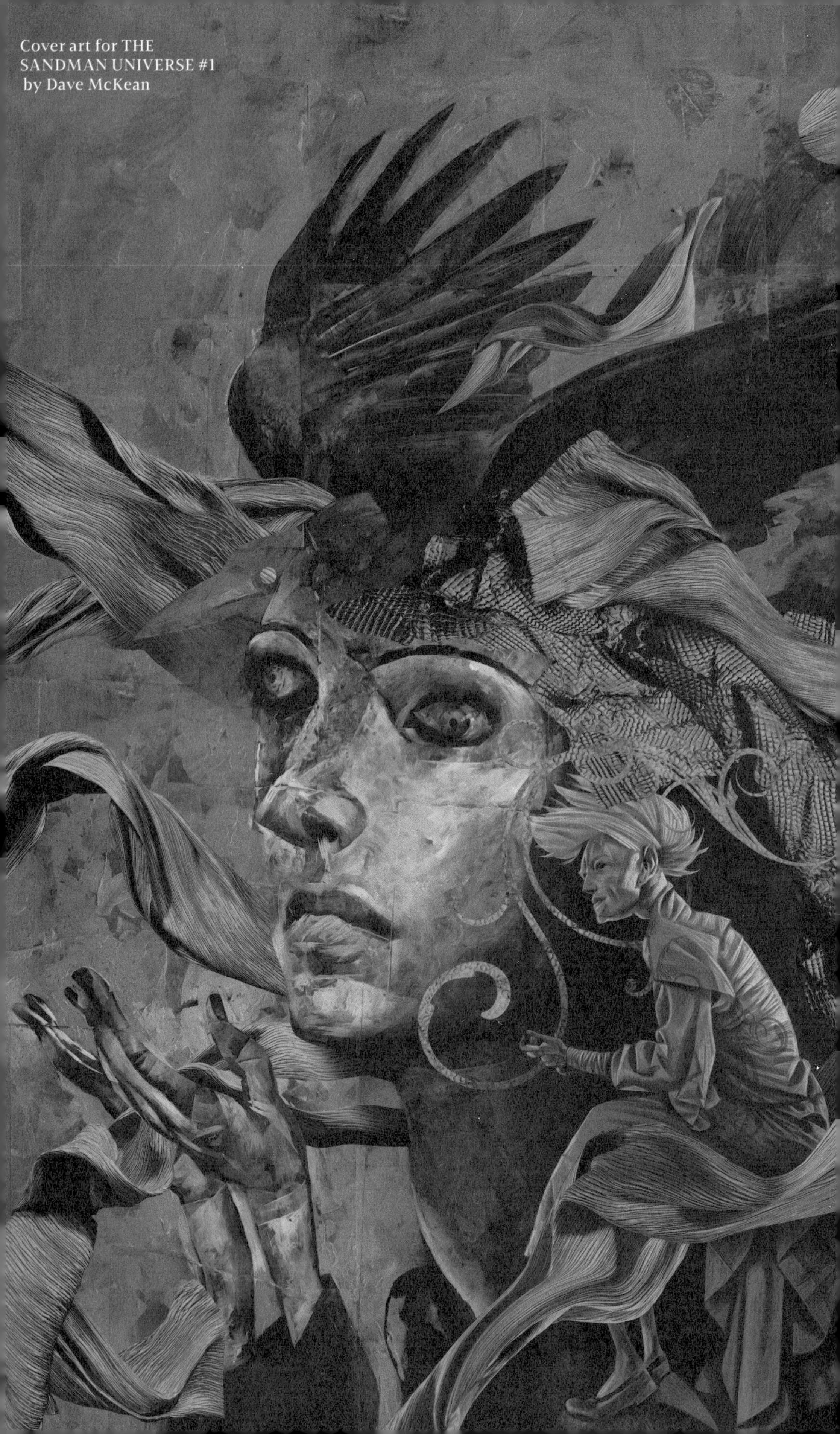

Cover art for THE SANDMAN UNIVERSE #1 by Dave McKean

MAX AND SEBASTIAN FIUMARA SKETCHBOOK

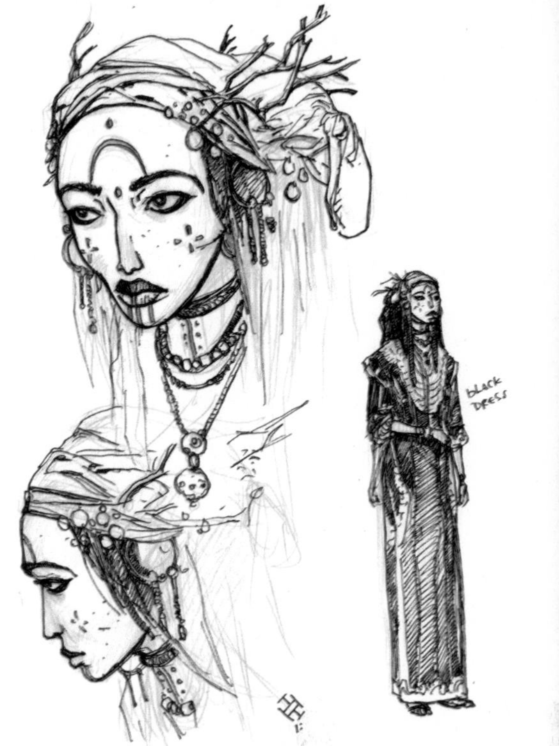
black dress

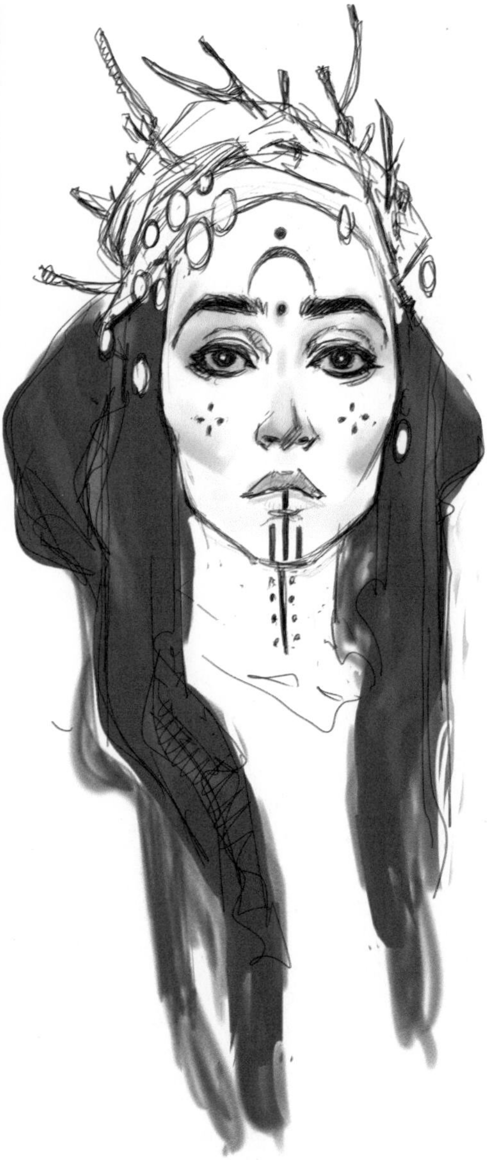

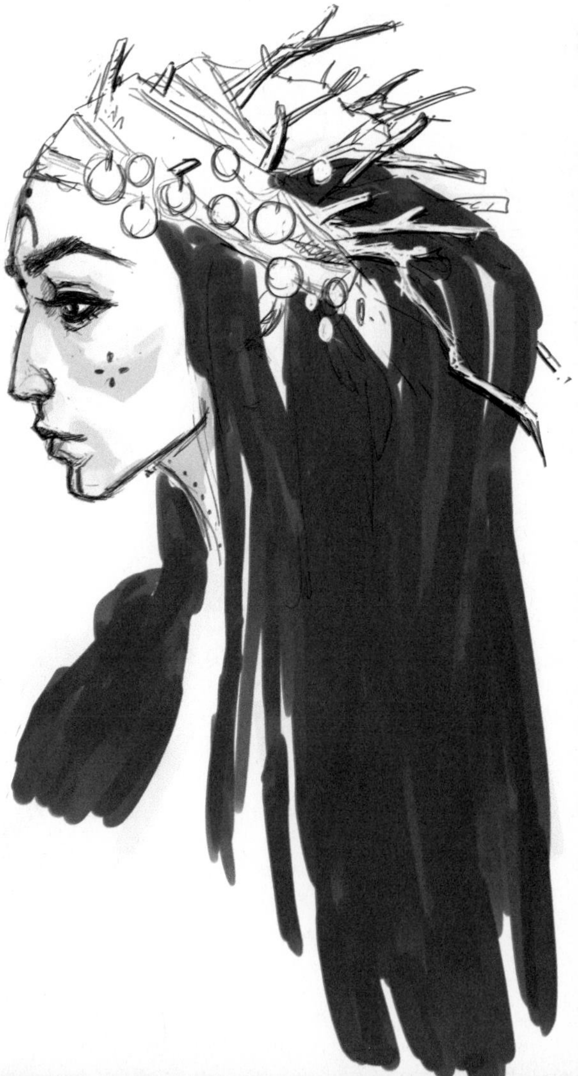

Sycorax

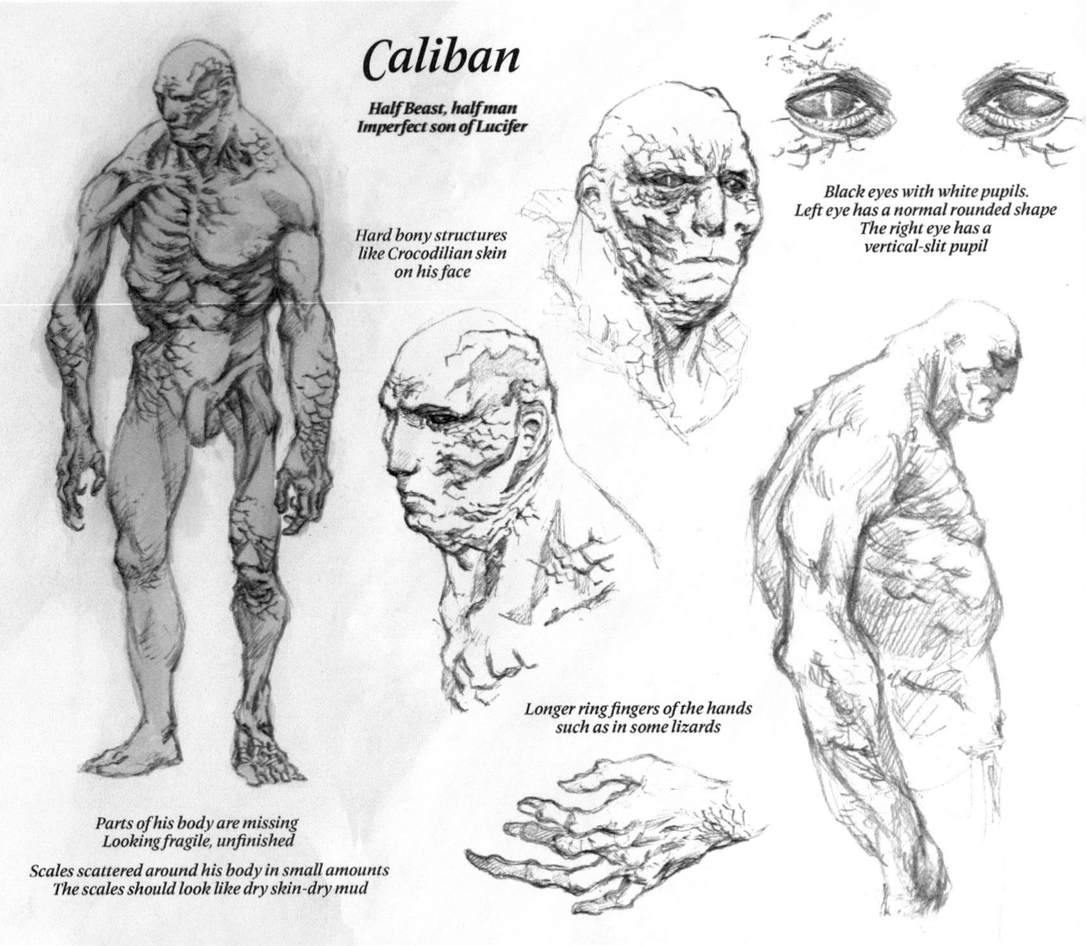
Caliban
Half Beast, half man
Imperfect son of Lucifer
Hard bony structures
like Crocodilian skin
on his face
Black eyes with white pupils.
Left eye has a normal rounded shape
The right eye has a
vertical-slit pupil
Longer ring fingers of the hands
such as in some lizards
Parts of his body are missing
Looking fragile, unfinished
Scales scattered around his body in small amounts
The scales should look like dry skin-dry mud

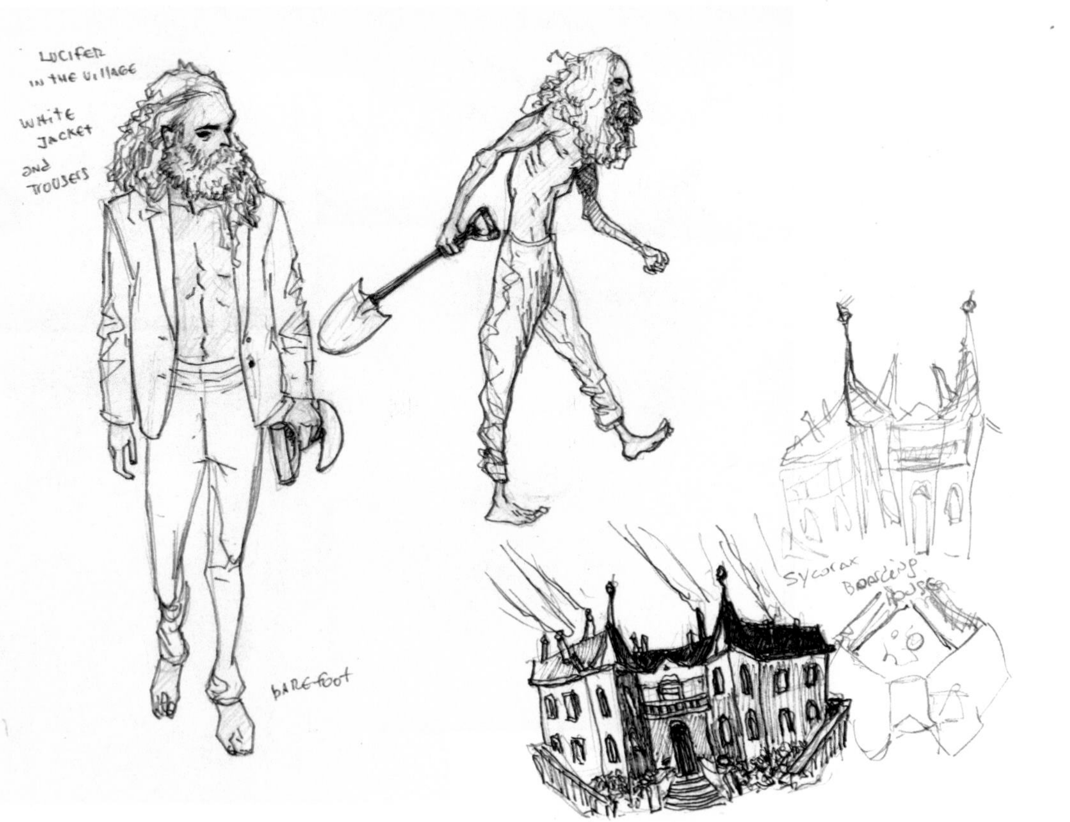
LUCIFER
IN THE VILLAGE
WHITE
JACKET
and
TROUSERS
BAREFOOT
SYCORAX
BOARDING
HOUSE

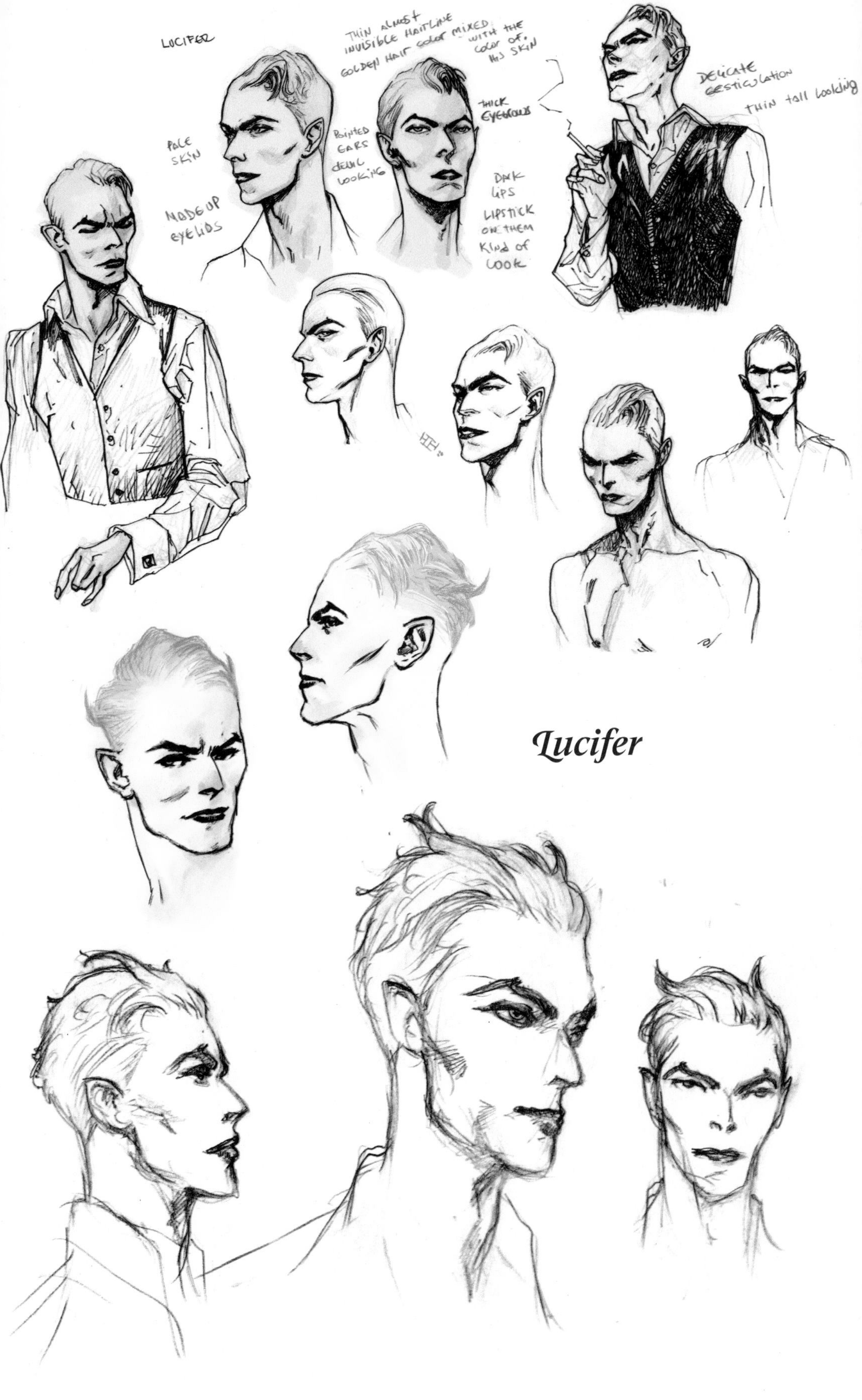
LUCIFER
THIN ALMOST INVISIBLE HAIRLINE
GOLDEN HAIR COLOR MIXED WITH THE COLOR OF HIS SKIN
PALE SKIN
MADE UP EYELIDS
POINTED EARS DEVIL LOOKING
THICK EYEBROWS
DARK LIPS
LIPSTICK ON THEM KIND OF LOOK
DELICATE GESTICULATION
THIN TALL LOOKING

Lucifer

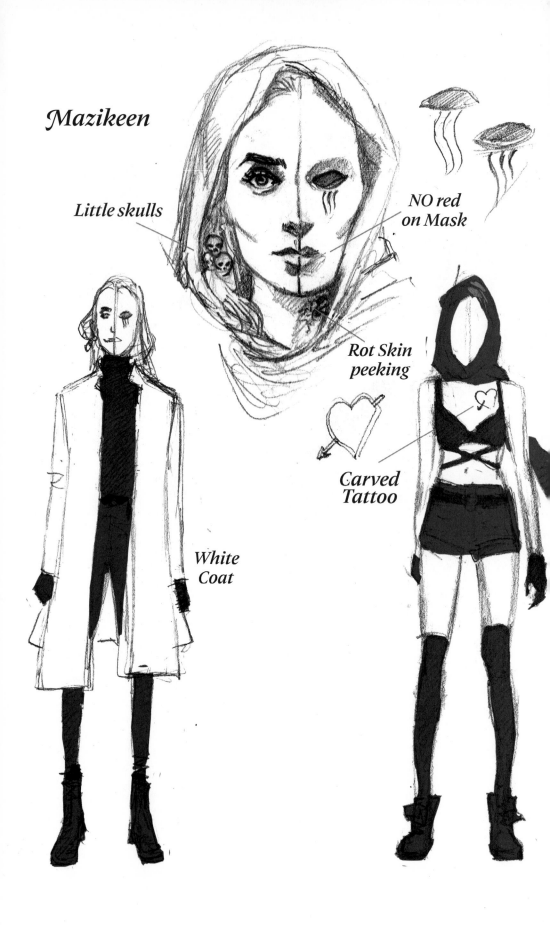

Mazikeen

Little skulls

NO red
on Mask

Rot Skin
peeking

Carved
Tattoo

White
Coat

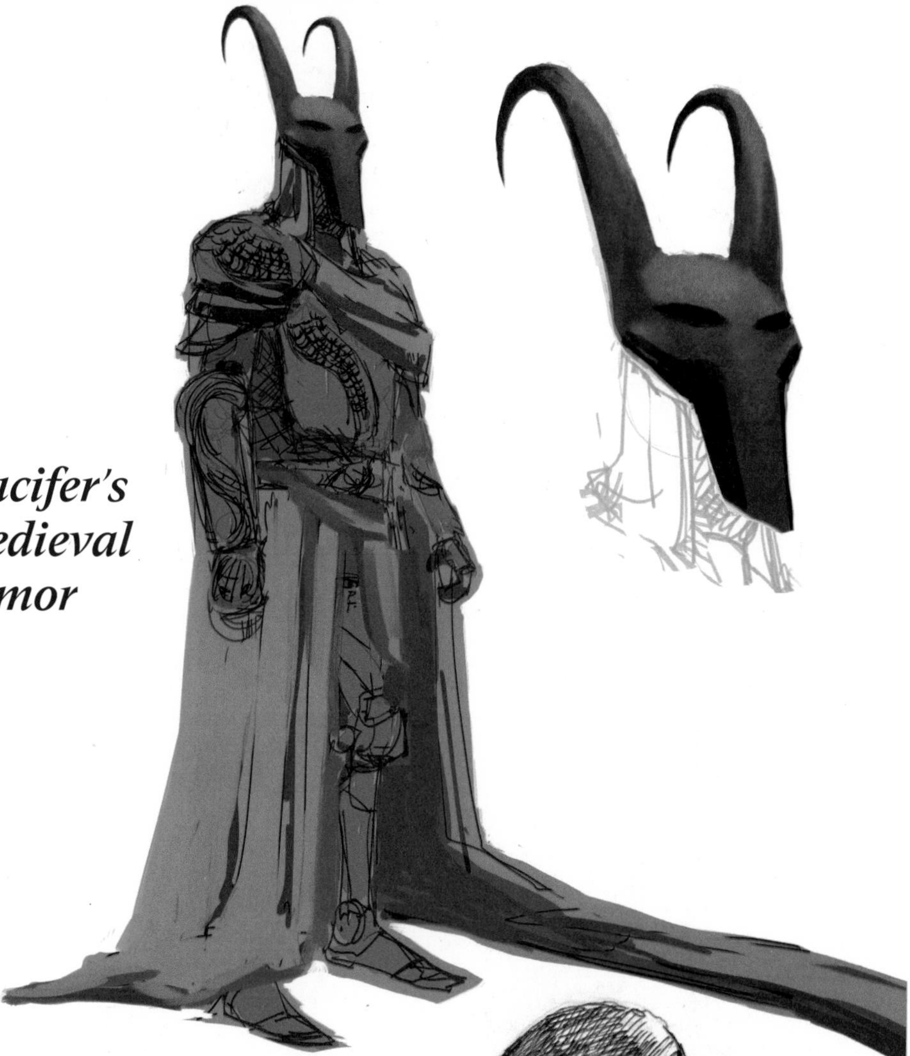

Lucifer's Medieval Armor

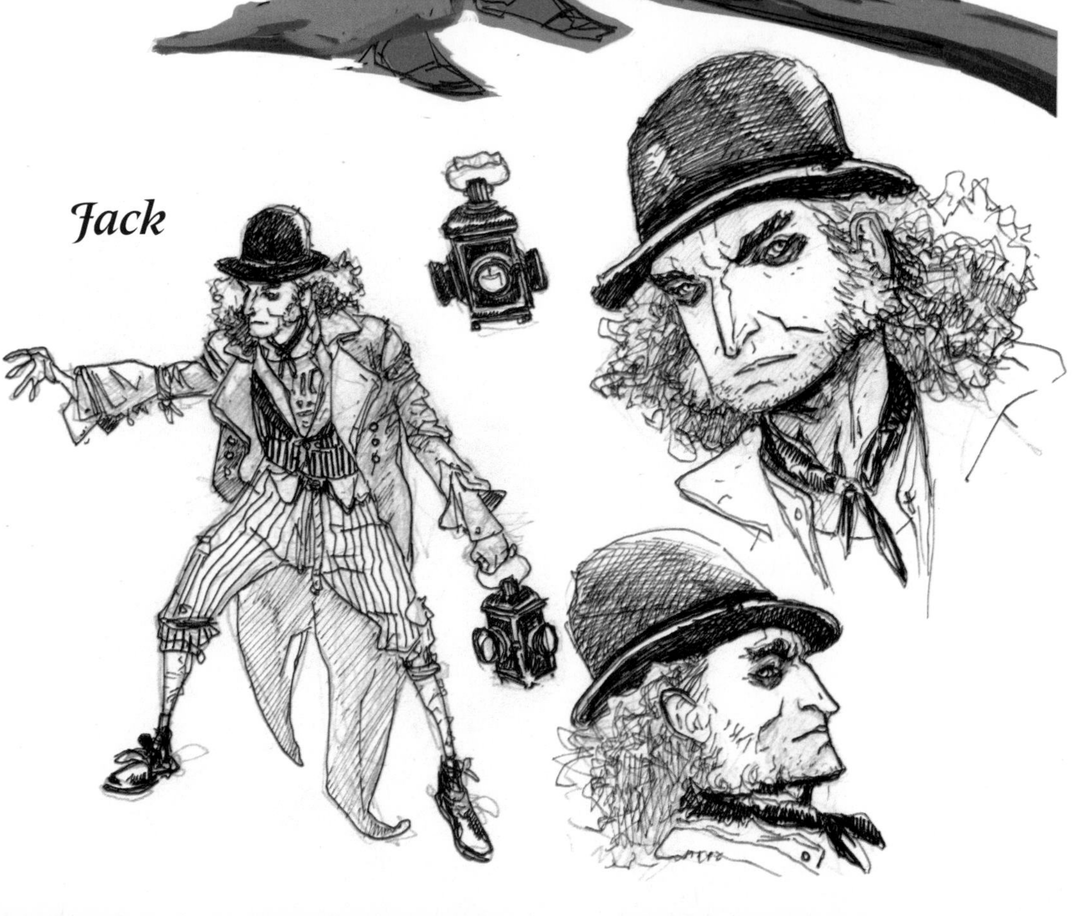

Jack

John Decker

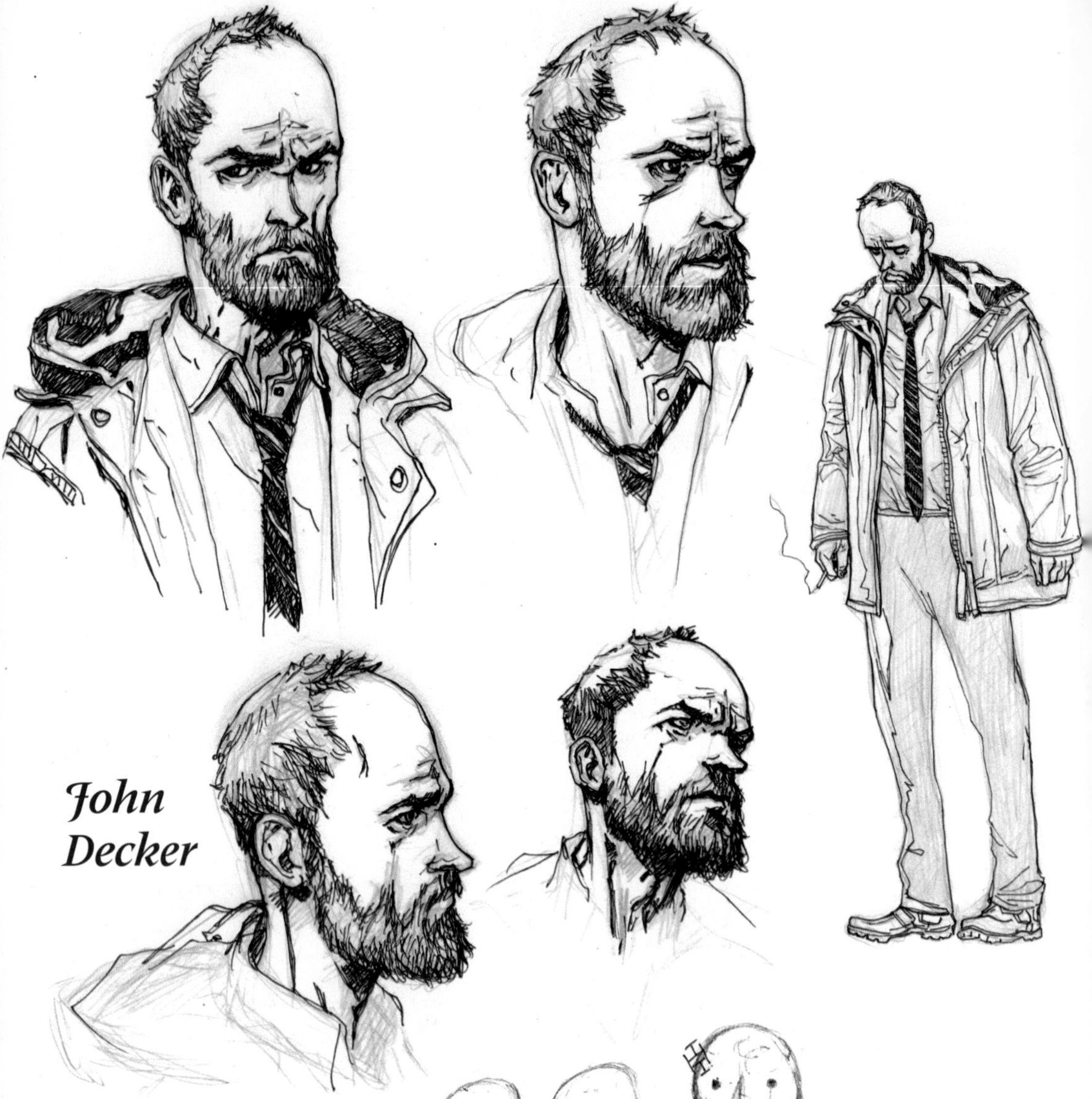

Setebos

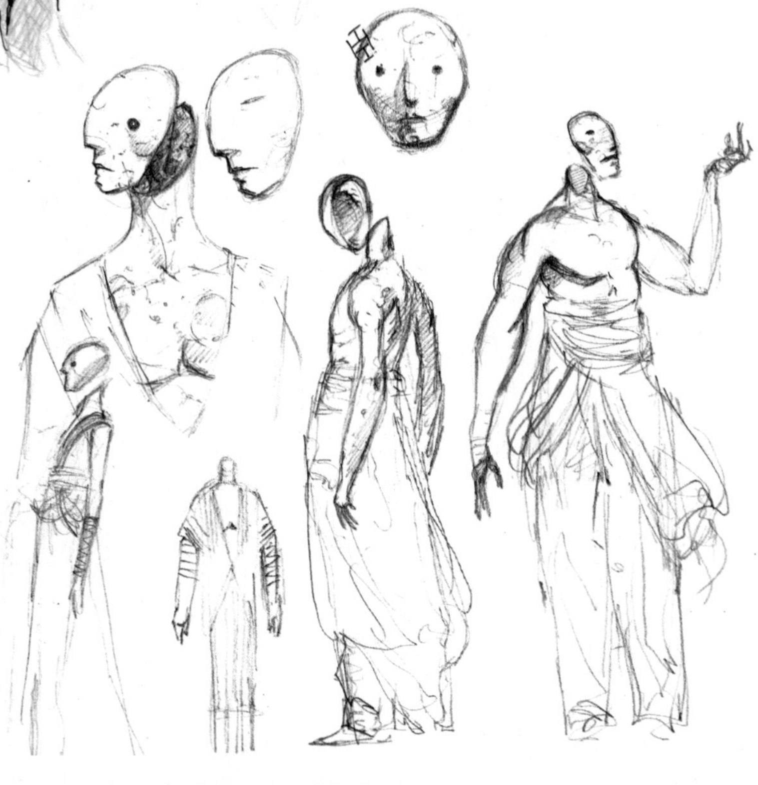

Witches

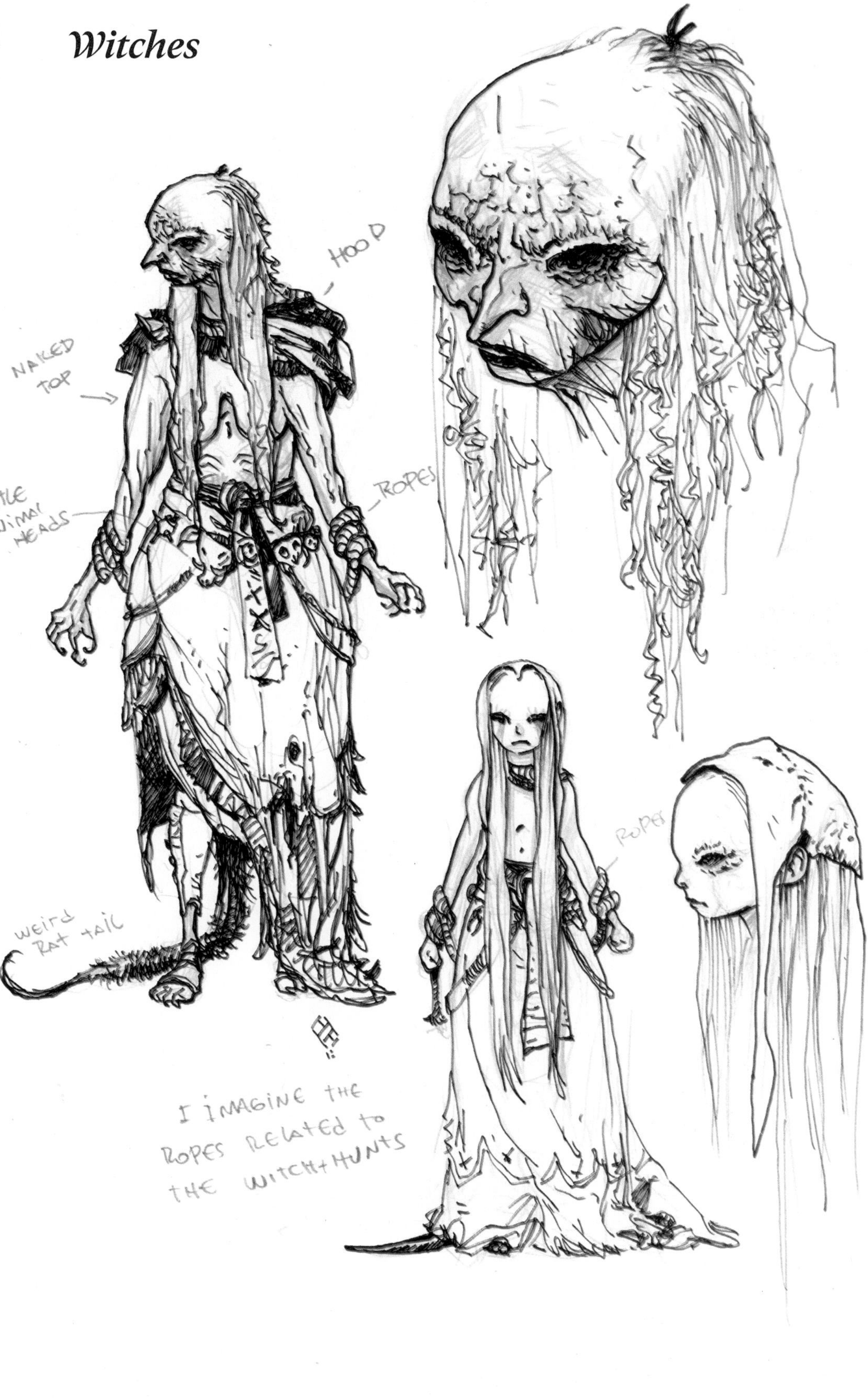
HOOD
NAKED TOP
ROPES
weird Rat tail
ROPES
I IMAGINE THE ROPES RELATED TO THE WITCH-HUNTS

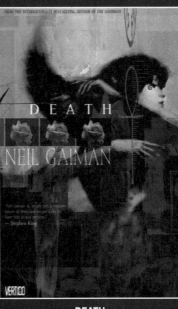